Instructor's Manual to Accompany

Understanding
Health
Insurance

A Guide to Billing and Reimbursement

Ninth Edition

D1548723

Instructor's Manual to Accompany

Understanding Health Insurance

A Guide to Billing and Reimbursement

Ninth Edition

Michelle A. Green, MPS, RHIA, CMA, CPC

Distinguished Teaching Professor
SUNY Alfred State College, Alfred, NY

JoAnn C. Rowell

Founder and Former Chairperson
Medical Assisting Department Anne Arundel
Community College, Arnold, MD

Additional Content Contributed by

Lynette M. Williamson, MBA, RHIA, CCS, CPC

Program Coordinator, Health Information Technology Department
Camden Community College, Blackwood, NJ

Ruth M. Burke

Medical Billing and Coding Program Specialist
The Community College of Baltimore County, MD
Adjunct Faculty, The Community College of Baltimore County, MD
Adjunct Faculty, Harford Community College, MD
Consultant on Administrative Procedures to Health Care Practices in Maryland and Virginia
President of the Independent Medical Billers Alliance (IMBA)
Member of the Maryland Medical Group Management Association (MGMA)

DELMAR
CENGAGE Learning

Australia • Brazil • Japan • Korea • Mexico • Singapore • Spain • United Kingdom • United States

DELMAR
CENGAGE Learning

Instructor's Manual to Accompany Understanding Health Insurance: A Guide to Billing and Reimbursement, Ninth Edition
Michelle A. Green and JoAnn C. Rowell

Vice President, Health Care Business Unit: **William Brottmiller**

Director of Learning Solutions: **Matthew Kane**

Managing Editor: **Marah Bellegarde**

Senior Acquisitions Editor: **Rhonda Dearborn**

Product Manager: **Jadin Babin-Kavanaugh**

Marketing Director: **Jennifer McAvey**

Senior Marketing Manager: **Lynn Henn**

Marketing Manager: **Michele McTighe**

Marketing Coordinator: **Andrea Eobstel**

Technology Project Manager: **Erin Pollay**

Production Director: **Carolyn Miller**

Content Project Manager: **Jessica McNavich**

Senior Art Director: **Jack Pendleton**

For product information and technology assistance, contact us at
Professional & Career Group Customer Support, 1-800-648-7450
For permission to use material from this text or product, submit all requests online at **www.cengage.com/permissions**
Further permissions questions can be emailed to
permissionrequest@cengage.com

ExamView® and ExamView Pro® are registered trademarks of FSCreations, Inc. Windows is a registered trademark of the Microsoft Corporation used herein under license. Macintosh and Power Macintosh are registered trademarks of Apple Computer, Inc. Used herein under license.

© 2008 Cengage Learning. All Rights Reserved. Cengage Learning WebTutor™ is a trademark of Cengage Learning.

ISBN-1-4180-6708-3

Delmar Cengage Learning
5 Maxwell Drive
Clifton Park, NY 12065-2919
USA

Cengage Learning products are represented in Canada by Nelson Education, Ltd.

For your lifelong learning solutions, visit **delmar.cengage.com**

Visit our corporate website at **www.cengage.com**

CPT copyright 2007 American Medical Association. All rights reserved. CPT is a registered trademark of the American Medical Association. Applicable FARS/DFARS Restrictions Apply to Government Use. Fee schedules, relative value units, conversion factors and/or related components are not assigned by the AMA, are not part of CPT, and the AMA is not recommending their use. The AMA does not directly or indirectly practice medicine or dispense medical services. The AMA assumes no liability for data contained or not contained herein.

Notice to the Reader
Publisher does not warrant or guarantee any of the products described herein or perform any independent analysis in connection with any of the product information contained herein. Publisher does not assume, and expressly disclaims, any obligation to obtain and include information other than that provided to it by the manufacturer. The reader is expressly warned to consider and adopt all safety precautions that might be indicated by the activities described herein and to avoid all potential hazards. By following the instructions contained herein, the reader willingly assumes all risks in connection with such instructions. The publisher makes no representations or warranties of any kind, including but not limited to, the warranties of fitness for particular purpose or merchantability, nor are any such representations implied with respect to the material set forth herein, and the publisher takes no responsibility with respect to such material. The publisher shall not be liable for any special, consequential, or exemplary damages resulting, in whole or part, from the readers' use of, or reliance upon, this material.

Printed in Canada
2 3 4 5 6 7 11 10 09 08

CONTENTS

SECTION II ANSWER KEYS TO TEXTBOOK CHAPTER EXERCISES AND REVIEWS

SECTION III CHAPTER EXAMS AND ANSWER KEYS TO CHAPTER EXAMS

SECTION IV ANSWER KEYS TO TEXTBOOK APPENDIX CASE STUDIES

SECTION V INSTRUCTOR'S MATERIALS

PART 2: Instructor's Manual to Accompany the WORKBOOK

SECTION VI ANSWER KEYS TO WORKBOOK CHAPTER ASSIGNMENTS

SECTION VII ANSWER KEY TO WORKBOOK APPENDIX A: MOCK CMRS EXAM

SECTION VIII ANSWER KEY TO WORKBOOK APPENDIX B: MOCK CPC-P EXAM

PREFACE

This Instructor's Manual is organized into eight sections:

- Section I: Preparing Your Course
- Section II: Answer Keys to Textbook Chapter Exercises and Reviews
- Section III: Chapter Exams and Answer Keys to Chapter Exams
- Section IV: Answer Keys to Textbook Appendix Case Studies
- Section V: Instructor's Materials
- Section VI: Answer Keys to Workbook Chapter Assignments
- Section VII: Answer Key to Mock CMRS Exam
- Section VIII: Answer Key to Mock CPC-P Exam

Section I (Preparing Your Course) assists instructors in the organization of their course. Sample semester plans are provided along with policies for administering exams and grading assignments and exams. The purpose of creating lesson plans is discussed, and chapter lesson plans that can be modified for individual use are included.

Section II (Answer Keys to Textbook Chapter Exercises and Reviews) and Section III (Chapter Exams and Answer Keys to Chapter Exams) are organized according to chapter.

Section IV (Answer Keys to Textbook Appendix Case Studies), and Section VI (Answer Keys to Workbook Chapter Assignments) are organized according to chapter.

Section V (Instructor's Materials) contains final examination case studies, answer keys to final examination case studies, a blank CMS-1500 claim, and blank case study forms for creating customized tests.

Section VII (Answer Key to Mock CMRS Exam) and Section VIII (Answer Key to Mock CPC-P Exam) contain answers to the mock exams.

NOTE: Chapter exams (and answers) in this Instructor's Manual contain different questions from those found in the computerized test bank in the electronic classroom manager. The chapter exams are the same as those included in the WebTutor, which provides detailed feedback for the answers.

TEACHING TIP:

For ease of reference in locating the sections in the Instructor's Manual, consider placing a sticky note as a tab at the beginning of each section.

StudyWare

The StudyWare CD-ROM located inside the back cover of the textbook allows students to review concepts learned in each chapter.

> **TEACHING TIP:**
>
> StudyWare is an automated study guide for students. Instead of publishing (and selling!) a separate study guide of questions for students to complete, Delmar Learning bundles StudyWare with the textbook. Your students will notice that all types of questions are included in StudyWare (e.g., multiple choice, matching, true/false, and fill-in-the-blank). The software organizes the questions in a game format (e.g., fill-in-the-blank as hangman and crossword puzzles), which makes it fun for students to use.

Online Companion

Additional resources can be found online at **www.delmarlearning.com/companions**. Student Resources are not password-protected, but Instructor Resources are password-protected. To access the protected instructor's content in the online companion (OLC), use the following information:

Username: greenolc
Password: enter

> **TEACHING TIP:**
>
> The online companion (OLC) also includes files that contain updates to the textbook and its supplements, which were changes made to the textbook, Workbook, Instructor's Manual, StudyWare, WebTutor, and/or computerized test bank after publication (e.g., revised codes due to coding updates). You are welcome to e-mail the authors at **delmarauthor@yahoo.com** with questions or comments. The authors will respond to your e-mails, and appropriate updates will be posted to the OLC to provide clarification about textbook and Workbook content.

Electronic Classroom Manager

The electronic classroom manager (ECM) contains an electronic version of this Instructor's Manual in Adobe PDF format, a computerized test bank (CTB), Microsoft PowerPoint presentations, and an insurance, billing and coding curriculum guide. Go to **www.delmarlearning.com** or contact your Delmar Learning sales representative to order the ECM.

> **TEACHING TIP:**
>
> The CTB contains true/false, short answer, completion, multiple choice, and matching questions. ExamView software is also included on the ECM CD-ROM to allow you to generate exams quickly, which can be printed or Web-enabled. This means that you can create different versions of the same exam for large classes of students (when students can't be separated from each other by an empty desk).
>
> For online courses, PowerPoint presentations can be Web-enabled. Just use Microsoft's PowerPoint software to open a presentation; click "File," then "Save as

(continues)

TEACHING TIP (continued):

Web Page." Upload the *.mht file you created to your online course or to the Web. Students do not need Microsoft PowerPoint software installed on their computer to view the presentation. (If your students have Microsoft PowerPoint software installed on their computers, you can just upload the *.ppt files from the ECM CD-ROM to your online course or the Web.)

An Insurance, Billing, and Coding Curriculum Guide is also located on the ECM CD-ROM to assist you in developing new academic programs and in modifying existing programs. The guide contains information about the job outlook and salaries for coders, available professional certification examinations, and curriculum coordination (e.g., marketing, student advising, teaching, professional practice experiences (internships), program approval, and program assessment). Content taught in a coding curriculum is linked to AAPC, AHIMA, and AMBA educational standards. Content is also linked to Delmar Learning products to assist you in selecting textbooks for instruction. Course outlines and course syllabi are included as samples, and they can be modified for your program. (In Adobe Reader, click on "File," then "Save as Text" to convert the guide to a document that can be opened in word processing software. All of the formatting will be lost, but you can scroll through the document to locate the content you want to cut/paste and modify to reformat. You might find it easier to print pages from the guide, edit them, and then keyboard new documents for your use.)

WebTutor

WebTutor is available as a downloadable course cartridge or e-Pack for schools that use Blackboard, eCollege, WebCT, or another platform (e.g., Angel, Desire2Learn, Educator) as an online learning management system. Go to **webtutor.thomsonlearning.com** to order WebTutor.

TEACHING TIP:

WebTutor can be used to teach a course entirely online or to Web-enhance an on-campus course. (Your textbook author teaches entirely online; but if she ever has an opportunity to teach a face-to-face course again, she will use WebTutor to administer all quizzes and exams outside of class time in her college's testing center because that will add five hours or more of teaching time to her courses.)

Chapter exams in this Instructor's Manual contain the same questions as those included in WebTutor. Detailed feedback is provided for incorrect answers when students take exams using WebTutor. (Administering quizzes and exams outside of class time is possible because students are provided with detailed feedback once they submit their quiz or exam. The instructor can delay viewing of detailed feedback until all students have submitted the quiz or exam. For a face-to-face course, the instructor can devote part of a class to discussing the exam results and questions about difficult exam items. For an online course, students can e-mail the instructor or post discussion comments about exam issues.

PART 1: Instructor's Manual to Accompany the TEXTBOOK

SECTION I Preparing Your Course

Understanding Health Insurance is a comprehensive textbook that covers billing and reimbursement, insurance claims processing, and the ICD-9-CM, CPT, and HCPCS level II coding systems. It is organized so that content can be taught in a one-semester course.

SEMESTER PLAN

The one-semester plan assumes 45 hours of classroom lecture (or 3 hours per week for 15 weeks). Your course may also include an additional 45 hours of laboratory during the semester, for which corresponding workbook chapters can be assigned. The final examination is not included in the 45-hour plan.

Week	Chapter
1	Chapter 1 - Health Insurance Specialist Career
2	Chapter 2 - Introduction to Health Insurance
	Chapter 3 - Managed Health Care
3	Chapter 4 - Development of an Insurance Claim
4	Chapter 5 - Legal and Regulatory Issues
	Exam 1
5	Chapter 6 - ICD-9-CM Coding
6	Chapter 7 - CPT Coding
7	Chapter 8 - HCPCS Level II Coding
	Exam 2
8	Chapter 9 - CMS Reimbursement Methodologies
	Chapter 10 - Coding for Medical Necessity
9	Chapter 11 - Essential CMS-1500 Claim Instructions
10	Chapter 12 - Commercial Insurance
	Exam 3
11	Chapter 13 - Blue Cross Blue Shield
12	Chapter 14 - Medicare
13	Chapter 15 - Medicaid
	Exam 4
14	Chapter 16 - TRICARE
15	Chapter 17 - Workers' Compensation
Finals Week	**Final Examination**

NOTE: There is no Exam 5. Instead, content from Chapters 16 and 17 are included on the final examination.

TEACHING TIP:

Consider using WebTutor to administer quizzes and exams, whether your course is offered entirely online or face-to-face. The detailed feedback for incorrect answers in WebTutor will prove helpful to students. If you teach face-to-face, you can administer the online exams in a classroom setting or use your college's testing center. Then, devote part of a class to answering students' questions about the exam so they have a good understanding about the concepts they hadn't mastered.

The textbook author enjoys this discussion with students, and she encourages students to challenge the authenticity of questions and answers as a critical thinking activity. When students convince her that a question was badly written or there could have been more than one answer, she rewards them by adding appropriate points to their exam grade. Then, of course, she revises that exam item for future use! This turns what can be an intimidating process, especially for a new instructor, into a fun learning activity for all. Students learn to think critically, new instructors don't dread discussing exam results, and everyone benefits because exam items are revised and perfected each time the course is taught. (As an aside, it can take up to five years for a new instructor to feel totally comfortable discussing exam results. Embracing students' questions and criticisms is a way to jump-start the "road to comfort.")

ADMINISTERING EXAMS

Administer short quizzes that cover definitions, coding conventions, and so on, to ensure that students keep up with reading assignments. Unit exams include theory and coding practice. If time permits, you may want to include content from the chapter(s) covered in the last unit on the final examination (instead of administering a separate unit exam).

GRADING CODING ASSIGNMENTS AND EXAMS

It is important to communicate your grading policy for coding assignments and exams. Refer to the suggested grading policies for ICD-9-CM and HCPCS level II/CPT coding assignments and exams below.

ICD-9-CM Coding

Assign one point for each correct code, including required fourth and fifth digits for diagnosis codes (and required third and fourth digits for procedure codes). Deduct one-half point for each additional code listed that is not required by ICD-9-CM coding principles (e.g., student assigns a code to a qualified diagnosis as well as its signs and symptoms).

HCPCS Level II and CPT Coding

Assign one point for each correct code, plus one point for each required modifier. Deduct one-half point for each additional code or modifier that is not required according to CPT/HCPCS level II guidelines and notes.

GRADING COMPLETED CMS-1500 CLAIMS

Students who are required to use the textbook CD-ROM to complete claims are encouraged to save their work to a disk. The software requires students to enter their name in the "Name" for each computer session. The name then appears at the top of all printed case study claims. Security of each student's work is maintained because a student's name that is attached to a stored file cannot be changed. Students who obtain another student's disk or stored case file will not be able to submit printed claims and summary sheets as their own work. For Case Studies: Set Two, students can use the Justification Note option to explain why they believe a particular block was graded as incorrect by the computer.

Completed CMS-1500 claims can be graded according to the following sample scale.

- Three points are assigned for a clean claim with no errors.
- Two points are assigned for a clean claim with noncritical typographical errors, causing no underpayment or delay in payment of the claim.
- One point is assigned when there are errors that would cause slight delay or small underpayment of the claim, such as wrong place of service, wrong type of service, or wrong number of units.
- Zero points are assigned for a claim containing any critical error that would result in denial of the claim as unprocessable. Critical errors include information that is excluded or misplaced on the claim, incorrect destination of a secondary claim, nonspecific diagnosis number used when specific diagnostic information is available in the chart entry, diagnosis code does not justify the procedure, the procedure code is wrong, and so on.

> **NOTE:** Do not penalize a student who has completed blocks not required by the payer if the information supplied is correctly entered.

An alternate system for grading claims on the final exam is to assign one point for each required block on a claim. Treat Block 21 as one entry, and each horizontal line in Block 24 as an individual entry.

LESSON PLANS

Lesson plans assist instructors in preparing for class so that specific activities and objectives are accomplished. Lesson plans for each textbook chapter have been created to assist you in organizing your course. Just complete the information in the Time row for each chapter; then enter the class and lab numbers to set up your course. (The lesson plans can be used for a one- or two-semester course.

CHAPTER 1 Health Insurance Specialist Career

LESSON PLAN

Time:
- 2 hours instructor preparation
- 1 hour introduction to course
- 2 hours in-class lecture
- 3 hours in-class lab (if laboratory component is included as part of the course)

Topics:
- Health insurance overview
- Education and training
- Job responsibilities
- Professional credentials

Overview: This chapter presents an overview of the health insurance specialist career, background necessary for education and training, responsibilities the student can expect to perform on the job, and professional credentialing opportunities.

Objectives:
- Define key terms.
- Identify career opportunities available in health insurance.
- Discuss the education and training requirements of a health insurance specialist.
- Describe the job responsibilities of a health insurance specialist.
- Differentiate among the three professional organizations that support health insurance specialists, and identify professional credentials offered by each.

	Task	Resource
Prior to class:	• Read textbook prepare lecture notes	• *Understanding Health Insurance (UHI)*, Chapter 1
	• Review answers to chapter review	• *Instructor's Manual to Accompany UHI*, Chapter 1
	• Select workbook assignments for homework	• *Workbook to Accompany UHI*, Chapter 1
	• Prepare course syllabus	• *Instructor's Manual, UHI*, Chapter 1
	• Prepare chapter quiz	• *Instructor's Manual, UHI*, Chapter 1
Class 1:	• Distribute and explain course syllabus	• Prepared course syllabus
	• Point out major features of the textbook	• *UHI*, Preface
	• Review WebTutor features (if applicable)	• *UHI*, Preface
	• Assign Chapter 1 as reading assignment	• *UHI*, Chapter 1
Class 2:	• Lecture on Chapter 1 content	• Lecture notes prepared, *UHI*, Chapter 1
	• Encourage students to create flash cards	• *UHI*, Chapter 1
	• Assign chapter review as homework	• *UHI*, Chapter 1
Class 3:	• Review previous class lecture and answer student questions about chapter content	• Ask students to identify key topics and issues from previous class lecture
	• Continue lecture on Chapter 1 content	• *UHI*, Chapter 1
	• Collect homework (and grade)	• *Instructor's Manual, UHI*, Chapter 1
	• Administer chapter quiz	• *UHI*, Chapter 1
	• Assign Chapter 2 as reading assignment	• *UHI*, Chapter 2

Lab 1:	• Point out major features of workbook • Communicate assignments to be accomplished during lab, and explain how each is to be completed • Rotate among students as they complete lab assignments, to provide individual assistance • Consider reviewing rough draft work during lab and allowing students to submit final draft at the beginning of the next lab class • Assign additional workbook assignments for homework

• *Workbook to Accompany UHI*, Preface
• *Workbook to Accompany UHI*, Chapter 1

Assessment:
• Homework assignments
• Chapter quiz
• In-class participation
• Lab assignments

CHAPTER 2 Introduction to Health Insurance

LESSON PLAN

Time:	• 6 hours instructor preparation • 2 hours in-class lecture • 3 hours in-class lab (if laboratory component is included as part of the course)
Topics:	• What is health insurance? • Automobile, disability, and liability insurance • Major developments in health insurance • Health insurance coverage statistics
Overview:	This chapter presents an overview of types of health insurance coverage, as well as disability, liability, malpractice, property, life, and health insurance. Insurance terms and concepts are also explained.
Objectives:	• Define key terms. • State the difference between medical care and health care. • Differentiate among automobile, disability, and liability insurance. • Discuss the history of health care reimbursement from 1860 to the present. • Identify and explain the impact of significant events in the history of health care reimbursement. • Interpret health insurance coverage statistics.

	Task	**Resource**
Prior to class:	• Read textbook and prepare lecture notes • Review answers to chapter review • Select workbook assignments for homework • Prepare chapter quiz	• *Understanding Health Insurance (UHI)*, Chapter 2 • *Instructor's Manual to Accompany UHI*, Chapter 2 • *Workbook to Accompany UHI*, Chapter 2 • *Instructor's Manual, UHI*, Chapter 2
Class 4:	• Lecture on Chapter 2 content • Encourage students to create flash cards • Assign chapter review as homework	• Lecture notes prepared, *UHI*, Chapter 2 • *UHI*, Chapter 2 • *UHI*, Chapter 2
Class 5:	• Review previous class lecture and answer student questions about chapter content • Collect homework (and grade) • Continue lecture on Chapter 2 content • Administer chapter quiz • Assign Chapter 3 as reading assignment	• Ask students to identify key topics and issues from previous class lecture • *Instructor's Manual, UHI*, Chapter 2 • *Instructor's Manual, UHI*, Chapter 2 • *UHI*, Chapter 2 • *UHI*, Chapter 3
Lab 2:	• Communicate assignments to be accomplished during lab, and explain how each is to be completed • Rotate among students as they complete lab assignments, to provide individual assistance • Consider reviewing rough draft work during lab and allowing students to submit final draft at the beginning of the next lab class • Assign additional workbook assignments for homework	• *Workbook to Accompany UHI*, Chapter 2
Assessment:	• Homework assignments • Chapter quiz • In-class participation • Lab assignments	

CHAPTER 3 Managed Health Care

LESSON PLAN

Time:
- 6 hours instructor preparation
- 2 hours in-class lecture
- 1½ hours in-class lab (if laboratory component is included as part of course)

Topics:
- History of managed care
- Managed care organizations
- Managed care models
- Consumer-directed health plans
- Accreditation of managed health care organizations
- Effects of managed care on a physician's practice

Overview: This chapter presents an overview of managed health care.

Objectives:
- Define key terms.
- Compare managed care with traditional health insurance.
- Discuss the history of managed care in the United States.
- Explain the role of a managed care organization.
- Apply the concept of managed care capitation.
- Explain the role of a gatekeeper in managed care.
- Describe six managed care models, and provide details about each.
- Differentiate between the two organizations that accredit managed care organizations.
- Implement administrative procedures so that the physician's practice appropriately responds to managed care organization program activities.

	Task	Resource
Prior to class:	• Read textbook and prepare lecture notes • Review answers to chapter review • Select workbook assignments for homework • Prepare chapter quiz	• *Understanding Health Insurance (UHI),* Chapter 3 • *Instructor's Manual to Accompany UHI,* Chapter 3 • *Workbook to Accompany UHI,* Chapter 3 • *Instructor's Manual, UHI,* Chapter 3
Class 6:	• Lecture on Chapter 3 content • Encourage students to create flash cards • Assign chapter review as homework	• Lecture notes prepared, *UHI,* Chapter 3 • *UHI,* Chapter 3 • *UHI,* Chapter 3
Class 7:	• Review previous class lecture and answer student questions about chapter content • Collect homework (and grade) • Continue lecture on Chapter 3 content • Administer chapter quiz • Assign Chapter 4 as reading assignment	• Ask students to identify key topics and issues from previous class lecture • *Instructor's Manual, UHI,* Chapter 3 • *Instructor's Manual, UHI,* Chapter 3 • *UHI,* Chapter 3 • *UHI,* Chapter 4
Lab 3: **(Part I)**	• Communicate assignments to be accomplished during lab, and explain how each is to be completed • Rotate among students as they complete lab assignments, to provide individual assistance • Consider reviewing rough draft work during lab and allowing students to submit final draft at the beginning of the next lab class • Assign additional workbook assignments for homework	• *Workbook to Accompany UHI,* Chapter 3

Assessment:
- Homework assignments
- Chapter quiz
- In-class participation
- Lab assignments

> **NOTE:** The first half of Lab 3 covers *UHI*, Chapter 3 assignments.

CHAPTER 4 Development of an Insurance Claim

LESSON PLAN

Time:
- 6 hours instructor preparation
- 2 hours in-class lecture
- 1½ hours in-class lab (if laboratory component is included as part of course)

Topics:
- Development of an insurance claim
- Managing new patients
- Managing established patients
- Insurance claim life cycle
- Maintaining insurance claim files
- Credit and collections

Overview: This chapter provides an overview of the development of a health insurance claim in the health care provider's office and the major steps taken to process that claim by the insurance company.

Objectives:
- Define key terms.
- Facilitate the registration and insurance claims process for a new or established patient.
- Discuss the life cycle of an insurance claim.
- Determine insurance coverage when a patient has more than one policy or a child is covered by both parents.
- Differentiate between manual and electronic claims processing procedures.
- Detail the processing of a claim by an insurance company.
- Interpret information on a remittance advice.
- Maintain a medical practice's insurance claim files.
- Identify problems that result in delinquent claims, and resolve those problems.

	Task	Resource
Prior to class:	• Read textbook and prepare lecture notes	• *Understanding Health Insurance (UHI)*, Chapter 4
	• Review answers to chapter review	• *Instructor's Manual to Accompany UHI*, Chapter 4
	• Select workbook assignments for homework	• *Workbook to Accompany UHI*, Chapter 4
	• Prepare chapter quiz	• *Instructor's Manual, UHI*, Chapter 4
Class 8:	• Lecture on Chapter 4 content	• Lecture notes prepared, *UHI*, Chapter 4
	• Encourage students to create flash cards	• *UHI*, Chapter 4
	• Assign chapter review as homework	• *UHI*, Chapter 4
Class 9:	• Review previous class lecture and answer student questions about chapter content	• Ask students to identify key topics and issues from previous class lecture
	• Continue lecture on Chapter 4 content	• *Instructor's Manual, UHI*, Chapter 4
	• Collect homework (and grade)	• *Instructor's Manual, UHI*, Chapter 4
	• Administer chapter quiz	• *Instructor's Manual, UHI*, Chapter 4
	• Assign Chapter 5 reading assignment	• *UHI*, Chapter 5
Lab 3:	• Communicate assignments to be	• *Workbook to Accompany UHI*, Chapter 4

(Part II)
accomplished during lab, and explain how each is to be completed
- Rotate among students as they complete lab assignments, to provide individual assistance
- Consider reviewing rough draft work during lab and allowing students to submit final draft at the beginning of the next lab class
- Assign additional workbook assignments for homework

Assessment:
- Homework assignments
- Chapter quiz
- In-class participation
- Lab assignments

> **NOTE:** The second half of Lab 3 covers *UHI*, Chapter 4 assignments.

CHAPTER 5 Legal and Regulatory Issues

LESSON PLAN

Time:
- 6 hours instructor preparation
- 2 hours in-class lecture
- 1 hour unit exam, which covers Chapters 1–5
- 3 hours in-class lab (if laboratory component is included as part of course)

Topics:
- Introduction to legal and regulatory considerations
- Federal laws and events that affect health care
- Retention of records
- Medical necessity
- Health Insurance Portability and Accountability Act

Overview: This chapter presents an overview of legal and regulatory terminology and summarizes laws and regulations that affect health insurance processing.

Objectives:
- Define key terms.
- Provide examples of a statute, regulation, and case law, and explain the use of the *Federal Register.*
- Summarize federal legislation and regulations that affect health care.
- Explain the concept of medical necessity.
- List and explain HIPAA's provisions.

	Task	**Resource**
Prior to class:	• Read textbook and prepare lecture notes • Review answers to chapter review • Select workbook assignments for homework • Prepare chapter quiz	• *Understanding Health Insurance (UHI)*, Chapter 5 • *Instructor's Manual to Accompany UHI*, Chapter 5 • *Workbook to Accompany UHI*, Chapter 5 • *Instructor's Manual, UHI*, Chapter 5
Class 10:	• Lecture on Chapter 5 content • Encourage students to create flash cards • Assign chapter review as homework	• Lecture notes prepared, *UHI*, Chapter 5 • *UHI*, Chapter 5 • *UHI*, Chapter 5
Class 11:	• Review previous class lecture and answer student questions about chapter content • Continue lecture on Chapter 5 content • Collect homework (and grade) • Administer chapter quiz • Review unit exam (Chapters 1–5)	• Ask students to identify key topics and issues from previous class lecture • *Instructor's Manual, UHI*, Chapter 5 • *Instructor's Manual, UHI*, Chapter 5 • *Instructor's Manual, UHI*, Chapter 5 • *UHI*, Chapters 1–5
Class 12:	• Unit exam on Chapters 1–5 • Assign Chapter 6 reading assignment	• *Electronic Classroom Manager*, Chapters 1–5 • *UHI*, Chapter 6

Lab 4:
- Communicate assignments to be accomplished during lab, and explain how each is to be completed
- Rotate among students as they complete lab assignments, to provide individual assistance
- Consider reviewing rough draft work during lab and allowing students to submit final draft at the beginning of the next lab class
- Assign additional workbook assignments for homework

- *Workbook to Accompany UHI*, Chapter 5

Assessment:
- Homework assignments
- Chapter quiz
- In-class participation
- Lab assignments
- Unit exam

> **RECOMMENDED READING:** McWay, D.C. (2003). *Legal aspects of health information management.* 2nd ed. Clifton Park, NY: Delmar Learning.

CHAPTER 6 ICD-9-CM Coding

LESSON PLAN

Time:
- 6 hours instructor preparation
- 3 hours in-class lecture
- 3 hours in-class lab (if laboratory component is included as part of course)

Topics:
- Overview of ICD-9-CM
- Outpatient coding guidelines
- ICD-9-CM coding system
- ICD-9-CM Index to Diseases
- ICD-9-CM Tabular List of Diseases
- ICD-9-CM Index to Procedures and Tabular List of procedures
- ICD-9-CM Index to Diseases tables
- ICD-9-CM Supplementary classifications
- Coding special disorders according to ICD-9-CM
- Reminders to ensure accurate ICD-9-CM coding
- ICD-10-CM: diagnostic coding for the future

Overview: This chapter presents an overview of ICD-9-CM coding guidelines and conventions, and it includes assignments to allow students to practice assigning ICD-9-CM codes to diagnoses, conditions, signs, and symptoms.

Objectives:
- Define key terms.
- Explain the purpose of reporting diagnosis codes on insurance claims.
- List and apply CMS outpatient guidelines in coding diagnoses.
- Identify and properly use ICD-9-CM's coding conventions.
- Accurately code diagnoses according to ICD-9-CM.

	Task	**Resource**
Prior to class:	• Read textbook and prepare lecture notes • Review answers to chapter review • Select workbook assignments for homework • Prepare chapter quiz	• *Understanding Health Insurance (UHI)*, Chapter 6 • *Instructor's Manual to Accompany UHI*, Chapter 6 • *Workbook to Accompany UHI*, Chapter 6 • *Instructor's Manual, UHI*, Chapter 6
Class 13:	• Lecture on Chapter 6 content • Encourage students to create flash cards • Assign chapter review as homework	• Lecture notes prepared, *UHI*, Chapter 6 • *UHI*, Chapter 6 • *UHI*, Chapter 6
Class 14:	• Review previous class lecture and answer student questions about chapter content • Continue lecture on Chapter 6 content • Collect homework (and grade)	• Ask students to identify key topics and issues from previous class lecture • *Instructor's Manual, UHI*, Chapter 6 • *Instructor's Manual, UHI*, Chapter 6
Class 15:	• Review previous class lecture and answer student questions about chapter content • Continue lecture on Chapter 6 content • Administer chapter quiz • Assign Chapter 7 as reading assignment	• Ask students to identify key topics and issues from previous class lecture • *UHI*, Chapter 6 • *Instructor's Manual, UHI*, Chapter 6 • *UHI*, Chapter 7

Lab 5:

- Communicate assignments to be accomplished during lab, and explain how each is to be completed
- Rotate among students as they complete lab assignments, to provide individual assistance
- Consider reviewing rough draft work during lab and allowing students to submit final draft at the beginning of the next lab class
- Assign additional workbook assignments for homework

- *Workbook to Accompany UHI*, Chapter 6

Assessment:

- Homework assignments
- Chapter quiz
- In-class participation
- Lab assignments

> **RECOMMENDED READING:** *Journal of the American Health Information Management Association; Coding Edge,* American Academy of Professional Coders; *Advance for Health Information Professionals,* Merion Publications

CHAPTER 7 CPT Coding

LESSON PLAN

Time:	• 6 hours instructor preparation
	• 3 hours in-class lecture
	• 3 hours in-class lab (if laboratory component is included as part of course)
Topics:	• Overview of CPT
	• CPT categories, subcategories, and headings
	• CPT index
	• CPT modifiers
	• Coding procedures and services
	• Evaluation and management section
	• Anesthesia section
	• Surgery section
	• Radiology section
	• Pathology and laboratory section
	• Medicine section
Overview:	This chapter presents an overview of CPT coding guidelines and conventions, and it includes assignments to allow students to practice assigning CPT codes to procedures and services.
Objectives:	• Define key terms.
	• Explain the format used in CPT.
	• Locate main terms and subterms in the CPT index.
	• Select appropriate modifiers to add to CPT codes.
	• Assign CPT codes to procedures and services.

	Task	**Resource**
Prior to class:	• Read textbook and prepare lecture notes	• *Understanding Health Insurance (UHI),* Chapter 7
	• Review answers to chapter review	• *Instructor's Manual to Accompany UHI*, Chapter 7
	• Select workbook assignments for homework	• *Workbook to Accompany UHI*, Chapter 7
	• Prepare chapter quiz	• *Instructor's Manual, UHI*, Chapter 7
Class 16:	• Lecture on Chapter 7 content	• Lecture notes prepared, *UHI*, Chapter 7
	• Encourage students to create flash cards	• *UHI*, Chapter 7
	• Assign chapter review as homework	• *UHI*, Chapter 7
Class 17:	• Review previous class lecture and answer student questions about chapter content	• Ask students to identify key topics and issues from previous class lecture
	• Continue lecture on Chapter 7 content	• *Instructor's Manual, UHI*, Chapter 7
	• Collect homework (and grade)	• *Instructor's Manual, UHI*, Chapter 7
Class 18:	• Review previous class lecture and answer student questions about chapter content	• Ask students to identify key topics and issues from previous class lecture
	• Continue lecture on Chapter 7 content	• *UHI*, Chapter 7
	• Administer chapter quiz	• *Instructor's Manual, UHI*, Chapter 7
	• Assign Chapter 8 as reading assignment	• *UHI*, Chapter 8

Lab 6:
- Communicate assignments to be accomplished during lab, and explain how each is to be completed
- Rotate among students as they complete lab assignments, to provide individual assistance
- Consider reviewing rough draft work during lab and allowing students to submit final draft at the beginning of the next lab class
- Assign additional workbook assignments for homework

- *Workbook to Accompany UHI*, Chapter 7

Assessment:
- Homework assignments
- Chapter quiz
- In-class participation
- Lab assignments

CHAPTER 8 HCPCS Level II Coding

LESSON PLAN

Time:
- 3 hours instructor preparation
- 2 hours in-class lecture
- 3 hours in-class lab (if laboratory component is included as part of course)

Topics:
- Overview of HCPCS
- HCPCS level II national codes
- Determining payer responsibility
- Assigning HCPCS level II codes

Overview: This chapter presents an overview of HCPCS coding, and it includes assignments to allow students to practice assigning HCPCS codes to procedures and services.

Objectives:
- Define key terms.
- Describe the HCPCS levels.
- Assign HCPCS level II codes and modifiers.
- Identify claims to be submitted to regional MAC, Medicare administrative contractors, or both, according to HCPCS level II code number.
- List situations in which both HCPCS level I and II codes are assigned.

	Task	**Resource**
Prior to class:	• Read textbook and prepare lecture notes • Review answers to chapter review • Select workbook assignments for homework • Prepare chapter quiz	• *Understanding Health Insurance (UHI)*, Chapter 8 • *Instructor's Manual to Accompany UHI*, Chapter 8 • *Workbook to Accompany UHI*, Chapter 8 • *Instructor's Manual, UHI*, Chapter 8
Class 19:	• Lecture on Chapter 8 content • Encourage students to create flash cards • Assign chapter review as homework	• Lecture notes prepared, *UHI*, Chapter 8 • *UHI*, Chapter 8 • *UHI*, Chapter 8
Class 20:	• Review previous class lecture and answer student questions about chapter content • Continue lecture on Chapter 8 content • Collect homework (and grade) • Administer chapter quiz • Assign Chapter 9 as reading assignment	• Ask students to identify key topics and issues from previous class lecture • *Instructor's Manual, UHI*, Chapter 8 • *Instructor's Manual, UHI*, Chapter 8 • *Instructor's Manual, UHI*, Chapter 8 • *UHI*, Chapter 9
Lab 7:	• Communicate assignments to be accomplished during lab, and explain how each is to be completed • Rotate among students as they complete lab assignments, to provide individual assistance • Consider reviewing rough draft work during lab and allowing students to submit final draft at the beginning of the next lab class • Assign additional workbook assignments for homework	• *Workbook to Accompany UHI*, Chapter 8

Assessment:
- Homework assignments
- Chapter quiz
- In-class participation
- Lab assignments

CHAPTER 9 CMS Reimbursement Methodologies

LESSON PLAN

Time:	• 3 hours instructor preparation • 2 hours in-class lecture • 3 hours in-class lab (if laboratory component is included as part of course)
Topics:	• Historical perspective of CMS reimbursement systems • CMS payment systems • Ambulance fee schedule • Ambulatory surgery center rates • Clinical laboratory fee schedule • Durable medical equipment, prosthetics/orthotics, and supplies fee schedule • End-stage renal disease (ESRD) composite rate payment system • Home health prospective payment system • Hospital inpatient prospective payment system • Hospital outpatient prospective payment system • Inpatient psychiatric facility prospective payment system • Inpatient rehabilitation facility prospective payment system • Long-term (acute) care hospital prospective payment system • Skilled nursing facility prospective payment system • Medicare physician fee schedule • Chargemaster • Revenue cycle management • UB-04 claim
Overview:	This chapter presents an overview of CMS reimbursement methodologies, and it includes assignments to allow students to calculate the Medicare PFS, patient coinsurance amounts, Medicare payments, and Medicare write-offs.
Objectives:	• Define key terms. • Explain the historical development of CMS reimbursement systems. • List and define each CMS payment system. • Apply special rules for the Medicare physician fee schedule payment system. • Interpret a chargemaster. • Explain hospital revenue cycle management. • Complete a UB-04 claim.

	Task	**Resource**
Prior to class:	• Read textbook and prepare lecture notes • Review answers to chapter review • Select workbook assignments for homework • Prepare chapter quiz	• *Understanding Health Insurance (UHI),* Chapter 9 • *Instructor's Manual to Accompany UHI,* Chapter 9 • *Workbook to Accompany UHI,* Chapter 9 • *Instructor's Manual, UHI,* Chapter 9
Class 21:	• Lecture on Chapter 9 content • Encourage students to create flash cards • Assign chapter review as homework	• Lecture notes prepared, *UHI,* Chapter 9 • *UHI,* Chapter 9 • *UHI,* Chapter 9

Class 22:
- Review previous class lecture and answer student questions about chapter content
- Continue lecture on Chapter 9 content
- Collect homework (and grade)
- Administer chapter quiz
- Assign Chapter 10 as reading assignment

- Ask students to identify key topics and issues from previous class lecture
- *Instructor's Manual, UHI*, Chapter 9
- *Instructor's Manual, UHI*, Chapter 9
- *Instructor's Manual, UHI*, Chapter 9
- *UHI*, Chapter 10

Lab 8:
- Communicate assignments to be accomplished during lab, and explain how each is to be completed

- Rotate among students as they complete lab assignments, to provide individual assistance
- Consider reviewing rough draft work during lab and allowing students to submit final draft at the beginning of the next lab class
- Assign additional workbook assignments for homework

- *Workbook to Accompany UHI*, Chapter 9

Assessment:
- Homework assignments
- Chapter quiz
- In-class participation
- Lab assignments

CHAPTER 10 Coding for Medical Necessity

LESSON PLAN

Time:
- 3 hours instructor preparation
- 2 hours in-class lecture
- 3 hours in-class lab (if laboratory component is included as part of course)

Topics:
- Coding and billing considerations
- Applying coding guidelines
- Coding from case scenarios
- Coding from patient records

Overview: This chapter presents an overview of coding for medical necessity as it relates to the completion and submission of CMS-1500 claims, and it includes assignments to allow students to practice coding for medical necessity.

Objectives:
- Define key terms.
- Select and code diagnoses and procedures from case studies and sample records.
- Research local coverage determinations.

	Task	**Resource**
Prior to class:	• Read textbook and prepare lecture notes	• *Understanding Health Insurance (UHI)*, Chapter 10
	• Review answers to chapter review	• *Instructor's Manual to Accompany UHI*, Chapter 10
	• Select workbook assignments for homework	• *Workbook to Accompany UHI*, Chapter 10
	• Prepare chapter quiz	• *Instructor's Manual, UHI*, Chapter 10
Class 23:	• Lecture on Chapter 10 content	• Lecture notes prepared, *UHI*, Chapter 10
	• Encourage students to create flash cards	• *UHI*, Chapter 10
	• Assign chapter exercises and review as homework	• *UHI*, Chapter 10
	• Review Chapters 6–10 for unit exam	• *UHI*, Chapters 6–10
Class 24:	• Unit exam (Chapters 6–10)	• *Electronic Classroom Manager*, Chapters 6–10
	• Assign Chapter 11 reading assignment	• *UHI*, Chapter 11
Lab 9:	• Communicate assignments to be accomplished during lab, and explain how each is to be completed	• *UHI* textbook and *Workbook to Accompany*
		• *UHI*, Chapter 10
	• Rotate among students as they complete lab assignments, to provide individual assistance	
	• Consider reviewing rough draft work during lab and allowing students to submit final draft at the beginning of the next lab class	
	• Assign additional workbook assignments for homework	

Assessment:
- Homework assignments
- Chapter quiz
- In-class participation
- Lab assignments
- Unit exam

> **NOTE:** Because Chapter 10 contains application-based exercises, students complete them outside of class or during lab, with discussion of answers during lab.

CHAPTER 11 Essential CMS-1500 Claim Instructions

LESSON PLAN

Time:
- 3 hours instructor preparation
- 2 hours in-class lecture
- 1½ hours in-class lab (if laboratory component is included as part of course)

Topics:
- Insurance billing guidelines
- Optical scanning guidelines
- Entering patient and policyholder names
- Entering provider names
- Entering mailing addresses and telephone numbers
- Recovery of funds from responsible payers
- National provider identifier (NPI)
- Assignment of benefits versus accept assignment
- Reporting diagnosis: ICD-9-CM codes
- Reporting procedures and services: HCPCS/CPT
- National standard employer identifier codes
- Signature of physician or supplier
- Reporting the billing entity
- Processing secondary claims
- Common errors that delay processing
- Final steps in processing claims
- Maintaining insurance claim files for the practice

Overview: This chapter presents information about completing commonly used blocks on the CMS-1500 claim and alerts students to common errors that delay claims processing.

Objectives:
- Define key terms.
- List and define general insurance billing guidelines.
- Apply optical scanning guidelines when completing claims.
- Enter patient and policyholder names, provider names, mailing addresses, and telephone numbers according to claims completion guidelines.
- Describe how funds are recovered from responsible payers.
- Explain the use of the national provider identifier (NPI).
- Differentiate between assignment of benefits and accept assignment.
- Report ICD-9-CM, HCPCS level II, and CPT codes according to claims completion guidelines.
- Explain the use of the national standard employer identifier.
- Explain when the signature of a physician or supplier is required on a claim.
- Enter the billing entity according to claims completion guidelines.
- Explain how secondary claims are processed.
- List and describe common errors that delay claims processing.
- State the final steps required in claims processing.
- Establish insurance claim files for a physician's practice.

	Task	Resource
Prior to class:	• Read textbook and prepare lecture notes	• *Understanding Health Insurance (UHI)*, Chapter 11
	• Review answers to chapter review	• *Instructor's Manual to Accompany UHI*, Chapter 11
	• Select workbook assignments for homework	• *Workbook to Accompany UHI*, Chapter 11
	• Prepare chapter quiz	• *Instructor's Manual, UHI*, Chapter 11

Class 25:
- Lecture on Chapter 11 content
- Encourage students to create flash cards
- Assign chapter exercises and review as homework

- Lecture notes prepared, *UHI*, Chapter 11
- *UHI*, Chapter 11
- *UHI*, Chapter 11

Task

Resource

Class 26:
- Review previous lecture and answer student questions about content
- Continue lecturing on Chapter 11 content
- Administer chapter quiz
- Collect homework (and grade)
- Assign Chapter 12 reading assignment

- *UHI*, Chapter 11

- *UHI*, Chapter 11
- *Instructor's Manual, UHI*, Chapter 11
- *Instructor's Manual, UHI*, Chapter 11
- *UHI*, Chapter 12

Lab 10:
- Communicate assignments to be accomplished during lab, and explain how each is to be completed
- Rotate among students as they complete lab assignments, to provide individual assistance
- Consider reviewing rough draft work during lab and allowing students to submit final draft at the beginning of the next lab class
- Assign additional workbook assignments for homework

- *UHI* textbook and *Workbook to Accompany UHI*, Chapter 11

Assessment:
- Homework assignments
- Chapter quiz
- In-class participation
- Lab assignments

> **NOTE:** The first half of Lab 10 covers *UHI*, Chapter 11 assignments.

CHAPTER 12 Commercial Insurance

LESSON PLAN

Time:
- 3 hours instructor preparation
- 2 hours in-class lecture
- 3 hours in-class lab (if laboratory component is included as part of course)

Topics:
- Commercial claims
- Claims instructions
- Commercial secondary coverage

Overview: This chapter presents information about completing claims for submission to commercial insurance companies.

Objectives:
- Differentiate between primary and secondary commercial claims.
- Complete commercial primary fee-for-service claims.
- Complete commercial secondary fee-for-service claims.

	Task	**Resource**
Prior to class:	• Read textbook and prepare lecture notes	• *Understanding Health Insurance (UHI)*, Chapter 12
	• Review answers to chapter review	• *Instructor's Manual to Accompany UHI*, Chapter 12
	• Select workbook assignments for homework	• *Workbook to Accompany UHI*, Chapter 12
	• Prepare chapter quiz	• *Instructor's Manual, UHI*, Chapter 12
Class 27:	• Lecture on Chapter 12 content	• Lecture notes prepared, *UHI*, Chapter 12
	• Encourage students to create flash cards	• *UHI*, Chapter 12
	• Assign chapter exercises and review as homework	• *UHI*, Chapter 12
Class 28:	• Review previous lecture and answer student questions about content	• *UHI*, Chapter 12
	• Continue lecturing on Chapter 12 content	• *UHI*, Chapter 12
	• Administer chapter quiz	• *Instructor's Manual, UHI*, Chapter 12
	• Collect homework (and grade)	• *Instructor's Manual, UHI*, Chapter 12
	• Review for unit exam	• *UHI*, Chapters 9–12
Class 29:	• Unit exam, Chapters 9–12	• *Electronic Classroom Manager*, Chapters 9–12
	• Assign Chapter 13 reading assignment	• *UHI*, Chapter 13
Lab 10:	• Communicate assignments to be accomplished during lab, and explain how each is to be completed	• *UHI* textbook and *Workbook to Accompany UHI*, Chapter 12
	• Rotate among students as they complete lab assignments, to provide individual assistance	
	• Consider reviewing rough draft work during lab and allowing students to submit final draft at the beginning of the next lab class	
	• Assign additional workbook assignments for homework	

Assessment:
- Homework assignments
- Chapter quiz
- In-class participation
- Lab assignments
- Unit exam

> **NOTE:** The second half of Lab 10 covers *UHI*, Chapter 12 assignments.

CHAPTER 13 Blue Cross Blue Shield

LESSON PLAN

Time:
- 3 hours instructor preparation
- 3 hours in-class lecture
- 3 hours in-class lab (if laboratory component is included as part of course)

Topics:
- History of Blue Cross and Blue Shield
- Blue Cross Blue Shield plans
- Billing notes
- Claims instructions
- BCBS secondary coverage

Overview: This chapter presents information about completing claims for submission to Blue Cross and Blue Shield plans.

Objectives:
- Define key terms.
- Explain the history of Blue Cross and Blue Shield.
- Differentiate among Blue Cross/Blue Shield plans.
- Apply Blue Cross Blue Shield billing notes when completing CMS-1500 claims.
- Complete Blue Cross Blue Shield primary and secondary claims.

	Task	Resource
Prior to class:	• Read textbook and prepare lecture notes • Review answers to chapter review • Select workbook assignments for homework • Prepare chapter quiz	• *Understanding Health Insurance (UHI)*, Chapter 13 • *Instructor's Manual to Accompany UHI*, Chapter 13 • *Workbook to Accompany UHI*, Chapter 13 • *Instructor's Manual, UHI*, Chapter 13
Class 30:	• Lecture on Chapter 13 content • Encourage students to create flash cards • Assign chapter exercises and review as homework	• Lecture notes prepared, *UHI*, Chapter 13 • *UHI*, Chapter 13 • *UHI*, Chapter 13
Class 31:	• Review previous lecture and answer student questions about content • Continue lecturing on Chapter 13 content • Collect homework (and grade)	• *UHI*, Chapter 13 • *UHI*, Chapter 13 • *Instructor's Manual, UHI*, Chapter 13
Class 32:	• Review previous lecture and answer student questions about content • Continue lecturing on Chapter 13 content • Administer chapter quiz • Assign Chapter 14 reading assignment	• *UHI*, Chapter 13 • *UHI*, Chapter 13 • *Instructor's Manual, UHI*, Chapter 13 • *UHI*, Chapter 14
Lab 11:	• Communicate assignments to be accomplished during lab, and explain how each is to be completed • Rotate among students as they complete lab assignments, to provide individual assistance	• *UHI* textbook and *Workbook to Accompany UHI*, Chapter 13

- Consider reviewing rough draft work during lab and allowing students to submit final draft at the beginning of the next lab class
- Assign additional workbook assignments for homework

Assessment:
- Homework assignments
- Chapter quiz
- In-class participation
- Lab assignments

CHAPTER 14 Medicare

LESSON PLAN

Time:
- 3 hours instructor preparation
- 3 hours in-class lecture
- 3 hours in-class lab (if laboratory component is included as part of course)

Topics:
- Medicare eligibility
- Medicare enrollment
- Medicare Part A
- Medicare Part B
- Medicare Part C
- Medicare Part D
- Other Medicare health plans
- Employer and union health plans
- Medigap
- Participating providers
- Nonparticipating providers
- Surgical disclosure notice
- Mandatory claims submission
- Private contracting
- Advance beneficiary notice
- Experimental and investigational procedures
- Medicare as primary payer
- Medicare as secondary payer
- Medicare summary notice
- Billing notes
- Claims instructions
- Medicare and Medigap claims
- Medicare-Medicaid crossover claims
- Medicare as Secondary Payer Claims
- Roster billing for mass vaccination programs

Overview: This chapter presents information about completing claims for submission to Medicare administrative contractors.

Objectives:
- Define key terms.
- Describe the Medicare enrollment process.
- Differentiate among Medicare Part A, Part B, Part C, and Part D coverage.
- Define other Medicare health plans, employer and union health plans, Medigap, and private contracting.
- Calculate Medicare reimbursement amounts for participating and nonparticipating providers.
- Determine when a Medicare surgical disclosure notice and an advance beneficiary notice are required.

- Explain the Medicare mandatory claims submission process.
- List and explain Medicare's experimental and investigational procedures.
- Differentiate between Medicare as primary payer and Medicare as secondary payer.
- Interpret a Medicare Summary Notice.
- Apply Medicare billing notes when completing CMS-1500 claims.
- Complete Medicare primary, Medigap, Medicare/Medicaid crossover, secondary, and roster billing claims.

	Task	**Resource**
Prior to class:	• Read textbook and prepare lecture notes • Review answers to chapter review • Select workbook assignments for homework • Prepare chapter quiz	• *Understanding Health Insurance (UHI)*, Chapter 14 • *Instructor's Manual to Accompany UHI*, Chapter 14 • *Workbook to Accompany UHI*, Chapter 14 • *Instructor's Manual, UHI*, Chapter 14
Class 33:	• Lecture on Chapter 14 content • Encourage students to create flash cards • Assign chapter exercises and review as homework	• Lecture notes prepared, *UHI*, Chapter 14 • *UHI*, Chapter 14 • *UHI*, Chapter 14
Class 34:	• Review previous lecture and answer student questions about content • Continue lecturing on Chapter 14 content • Administer chapter quiz • Collect homework (and grade)	• *UHI*, Chapter 14 • *UHI*, Chapter 14 • *Instructor's Manual, UHI*, Chapter 14 • *Instructor's Manual, UHI*, Chapter 14
Class 35:	• Review previous lecture and answer student questions about content • Continue lecturing on Chapter 14 content • Assign Chapter 15 reading assignment	• *UHI*, Chapter 14 • *UHI*, Chapter 14 • *UHI*, Chapter 15
Lab 12:	• Communicate assignments to be accomplished during lab, and explain how each is to be completed • Rotate among students as they complete lab assignments, to provide individual assistance • Consider reviewing rough draft work during lab and allowing students to submit final draft at the beginning of the next lab class • Assign additional workbook assignments for homework	• *UHI* textbook and *Workbook to Accompany UHI*, Chapter 14
Assessment:	• Homework assignments • Chapter quiz • In-class participation • Lab assignments	

CHAPTER 15 Medicaid

LESSON PLAN

Time:
- 3 hours instructor preparation
- 3 hours in-class lecture
- 3 hours in-class lab (if laboratory component is included as part of course)

Topics:
- Medicaid eligibility
- Medicaid covered services
- Payment for Medicaid services
- Billing notes
- Claims instructions
- Medicaid as secondary payer claims
- Mother/baby claims

Overview: This chapter presents information about completing claims for submission to Medicaid administrative contractors.

Objectives:
- Define key terms.
- Explain Medicaid eligibility guidelines.
- List Medicaid covered services required by the federal government.
- Describe how payments for Medicaid services are processed.
- Apply Medicaid billing notes when completing CMS-1500 claims.
- Complete Medicaid primary, secondary, and mother/baby claims.

	Task	**Resource**
Prior to class:	• Read textbook and prepare lecture notes • Review answers to chapter review • Select workbook assignments for homework • Prepare chapter quiz	• *Understanding Health Insurance (UHI)*, Chapter 15 • *Instructor's Manual to Accompany UHI*, Chapter 15 • *Workbook to Accompany UHI*, Chapter 15 • *Instructor's Manual, UHI*, Chapter 15
Class 36:	• Lecture on Chapter 15 content • Encourage students to create flash cards • Assign chapter exercises and review as homework	• Lecture notes prepared, *UHI*, Chapter 15 • *UHI*, Chapter 15 • *UHI*, Chapter 15
Class 37:	• Review previous lecture and answer student questions about content • Continue lecturing on Chapter 15 content • Administer chapter quiz • Collect homework (and grade) • Review for unit exam	• *UHI*, Chapter 15 • *UHI*, Chapter 15 • *Instructor's Manual, UHI*, Chapter 15 • *Instructor's Manual, UHI*, Chapter 15 • *UHI*, Chapters 13–15
Class 38:	• Unit exam • Assign Chapter 16 reading assignment	• *Electronic Classroom Manager*, Chapters 13–15 • *UHI*, Chapter 16
Lab 13:	• Communicate assignments to be accomplished during lab, and explain how each is to be completed	• *UHI* textbook and *Workbook to Accompany UHI*, Chapter 15

- Rotate among students as they complete lab assignments, to provide individual assistance
- Consider reviewing rough draft work during lab and allowing students to submit final draft at the beginning of the next lab class
- Assign additional workbook assignments for homework

Assessment:
- Homework assignments
- Chapter quiz
- In-class participation
- Lab assignments
- Unit exam

CHAPTER 16 TRICARE

LESSON PLAN

Time:
- 3 hours instructor preparation
- 3 hours in-class lecture
- 3 hours in-class lab (if laboratory component is included as part of course)

Topics:
- TRICARE background
- TRICARE administration
- CHAMPVA
- TRICARE options
- TRICARE programs and demonstration projects
- TRICARE supplemental plans
- Billing notes
- Claims instructions
- Primary TRICARE with a supplemental policy
- TRICARE as secondary payer

Overview:
- This chapter presents information about completing claims for submission to TRICARE payers.

Objectives:
- Define key terms.
- Explain the historical background of TRICARE.
- Describe how TRICARE is administered.
- Define CHAMPVA.
- List and explain the TRICARE options, programs and demonstration projects, and supplemental plans.
- Apply TRICARE billing notes when completing CMS-1500 claims.
- Complete TRICARE claims properly.

	Task	Resource
Prior to class:	• Read textbook and prepare lecture notes	• *Understanding Health Insurance (UHI)*, Chapter 16
	• Review answers to chapter review	• *Instructor's Manual to Accompany UHI*, Chapter 16
	• Select workbook assignments for homework	• *Workbook to Accompany UHI*, Chapter 16
	• Prepare chapter quiz	• *Instructor's Manual, UHI*, Chapter 16
Class 39:	• Lecture on Chapter 16 content	• Lecture notes prepared, *UHI*, Chapter 16
	• Encourage students to create flash cards	• *UHI*, Chapter 16
	• Assign chapter exercises and review as homework	• *UHI*, Chapter 16
Class 40:	• Review previous lecture and answer student questions about content	• *UHI*, Chapter 16
	• Continue lecturing on Chapter 16 content	• *UHI*, Chapter 16
	• Administer chapter quiz	• *Instructor's Manual, UHI*, Chapter 16
	• Collect homework (and grade)	• *Instructor's Manual, UHI*, Chapter 16
Class 41:	• Review previous lecture and answer student questions about content	• *UHI*, Chapter 16
	• Continue lecturing on Chapter 16 content	• *UHI*, Chapter 16
	• Administer chapter quiz	• *Instructor's Manual, UHI*, Chapter 16
	• Assign Chapter 17 reading assignment	• *UHI*, Chapter 17

Lab 14:

- Communicate assignments to be *UHI*, accomplished during lab, and explain how each is to be completed
- Rotate among students as they complete lab assignments, to provide individual assistance
- Consider reviewing rough draft work during lab and allowing students to submit final draft at the beginning of the next lab class
- Assign additional workbook assignments for homework

- *UHI* textbook and *Workbook to Accompany*

  Chapter 16

Assessment:

- Homework assignments
- Chapter quiz
- In-class participation
- Lab assignments

CHAPTER 17 Workers' Compensation

LESSON PLAN

Time:
- 3 hours instructor preparation
- 3 hours in-class lecture
- 3 hours in-class lab (if laboratory component is included as part of course)

Topics:
- Federal workers' compensation programs
- State workers' compensation programs
- Eligibility for workers' compensation coverage
- Classification of workers' compensation cases
- Special handling of workers' compensation cases
- Workers' compensation and managed care
- First report of injury
- Progress reports
- Appeals and adjudication
- Fraud and abuse
- Billing notes
- Claims instructions

Overview: This chapter presents information about completing claims for submission to workers' compensation payers.

Objectives:
- Define key terms.
- Describe federal and state workers' compensation programs.
- List eligibility requirements for workers' compensation coverage.
- Classify workers' compensation cases.
- Describe special handling practices for workers' compensation cases.
- Explain how managed care applies to workers' compensation coverage.
- Submit first report of injury and progress reports.
- Describe workers' compensation appeals and adjudication processes.
- State examples of workers' compensation fraud and abuse.
- Apply workers' compensation billing notes when completing CMS-1500 claims.
- Complete workers' compensation claims properly.

	Task	**Resource**
Prior to class:	• Read textbook and prepare lecture notes	• *Understanding Health Insurance (UHI)*, Chapter 17
	• Review answers to chapter review	• *Instructor's Manual to Accompany UHI*, Chapter 17
	• Select workbook assignments for homework	• *Workbook to Accompany UHI*, Chapter 17
	• Prepare chapter quiz	• *Instructor's Manual, UHI*, Chapter 17
Class 42:	• Lecture on Chapter 17 content	• Lecture notes prepared, *UHI*, Chapter 17
	• Encourage students to create flash cards	• *UHI*, Chapter 17
	• Assign chapter exercises and review as homework	• *UHI*, Chapter 17
Class 43:	• Review previous lecture and answer student questions about content	• *UHI*, Chapter 17
	• Continue lecturing on Chapter 17 content	• *UHI*, Chapter 17
	• Administer chapter quiz	• *Instructor's Manual, UHI*, Chapter 17
	• Collect homework (and grade)	• *Instructor's Manual, UHI*, Chapter 17

Class 44:	• Review previous lecture and answer student questions about content	• *UHI*, Chapter 17
	• Continue lecturing on Chapter 17 content	• *UHI*, Chapter 17
Class 45:	• Review for comprehesive final exam	• *UHI*, Chapters 1–17
Lab 15:	• Communicate assignments to be accomplished during lab, and explain how each is to be completed	• *UHI* textbook and *Workbook to Accompany UHI*, Chapter 17
	• Rotate among students as they complete lab assignments, to provide individual assistance	
	• Consider reviewing rough draft work during lab and allowing students to submit final draft at the beginning of the next lab class	
	• Assign additional workbook assignments for homework	
Assessment:	• Homework assignments	
	• Chapter quiz	
	• In-class participation	
	• Lab assignments	

SECTION II Answer Keys to Textbook Chapter Exercises and Reviews

CHAPTER 1 Health Insurance Specialist Career

ANSWERS TO REVIEW

1.	b	9.	c
2.	c	10.	a
3.	b	11.	a
4.	b	12.	a
5.	a	13.	b
6.	c	14.	a
7.	c	15.	b
8.	c		

CHAPTER 2 Introduction to Health Insurance

ANSWERS TO REVIEW

1.	c	9.	a
2.	a	10.	a
3.	b	11.	a
4.	c	12.	b
5.	d	13.	a
6.	a	14.	b
7.	c	15.	a
8.	b		

CHAPTER 3 Managed Health Care

ANSWERS TO REVIEW

1.	c	6.	c
2.	b	7.	b
3.	a	8.	a
4.	b	9.	b
5.	a	10.	d

CHAPTER 4 Development of an Insurance Claim

ANSWERS TO REVIEW

1.	b	14.	b
2.	d	15.	a
3.	d	16.	b
4.	a	17.	a
5.	a	18.	c
6.	b	19.	a
7.	d	20.	a
8.	b	21.	d
9.	b	22.	d
10.	c	23.	b
11.	c	24.	d
12.	d	25.	b
13.	a		

CHAPTER 5 Legal and Regulatory Issues

RECOMMENDED READING: McWay, D.C. (2003). *Legal aspects of health information management.* 2nd ed. Clifton Park, NY: Delmar Learning.

ANSWERS TO REVIEW

1.	d	**6.**	b
2.	c	**7.**	a
3.	a	**8.**	b
4.	c	**9.**	c
5.	a	**10.**	b

CHAPTER 6 ICD-9-CM Coding

ANSWERS TO ICD-9-CM CODING EXERCISES

(The underlined word is the condition found in the Index to Diseases.)

EXERCISE 6-1 Finding the Condition in the Index to Diseases

1.	Bronchiole <u>spasm</u>	519.11
2.	Congenital <u>candidiasis</u> (age 3)	771.7

NOTE: Code 771.7 is assigned during the first 28 days of the patient's life, and code 112.9 is assigned if the patient is older than 28 days. (This exercise does not indicate the patient's age. Therefore, either code is acceptable. In practice, review the medical record to determine the patient's age to assign the correct code.)

3.	<u>Irritable</u> bladder	596.8
4.	Earthquake <u>injury</u> (No site mentioned. *See* Injury in Index to External Causes)	E909.0
5.	<u>Exposure</u> to AIDS	V01.79
6.	Ground <u>itch</u>	126.9
7.	<u>Nun's</u> knees	727.2
8.	<u>Mice</u> in right knee joint	717.6
9.	Contact <u>dermatitis</u>	692.9
10.	Ascending <u>neuritis</u>	355.2

EXERCISE 6-2 Working with Coding Conventions (Index to Diseases)

1.	Acute purulent <u>sinusitis</u>	461.9 - (purulent) is a nonessential modifier
2.	<u>Fracture</u>, mandible	802.20 - (closed) is a nonessential modifier
3.	Actinomycotic <u>meningitis</u>	039.8, 320.7 - sequence bracketed code second
4.	Psychomotor akinetic <u>epilepsy</u>	345.40 - requires fifth digit
5.	3 cm <u>laceration</u>, right forearm	881.00 - *See also* wound, open
6.	<u>Contusion</u>, abdomen	868.00 - NEC
7.	<u>Pneumonia due</u> to *H. influenzae*	482.2 - Subcategory
8.	Delayed healing, open <u>wound</u>, abdomen	879.3 - Boxed Note describes "delayed healing" as "complicated"
9.	Bile duct <u>cicatrix</u>	576.8 "Trust the Index."
10.	Uncontrolled type II <u>diabetes</u> mellitus with osteomyelitis	250.82, 731.8 - Bracketed code

EXERCISE 6-3 Confirming Codes in the Tabular List of Diseases

1.	515	Postinflammatory pulmonary <u>fibrosis</u>	C
2.	250.1	Type II <u>diabetes</u>	250.10
3.	727.67	Nontraumatic <u>rupture</u> of Achilles tendon	C
4.	422.0	Acute <u>myocarditis</u> due to Coxsackie virus	E (074.23)
5.	813.22	<u>Malunion</u>, closed right radial fracture	E (733.81)
6.	483.0	Mycoplasmic <u>pneumonia</u>	C
7.	795.71	Positive <u>HIV</u> test, asymptomatic	E (V08)
8.	796.2	<u>Elevated</u> blood pressure	C
9.	718.06	Old <u>tear</u> of right knee meniscus	E (717.5)
10.	383.1	Tuberculous <u>mastoiditis</u>	E (015.60)

EXERCISE 6-4 Working with Tabular List of Diseases Coding Conventions

1.	<u>Pregnancy</u> complicated by chronic gonorrhea; chronic gonococcal <u>endometritis</u>	647.10 - fifth digit required 098.36 - use additional code
2.	Benign <u>neoplasm</u>, ear cartilage	215.0 - ear cartilage is not excluded
3.	<u>Cervicitis</u>, tuberculous	016.70 - *Includes*
4.	Uncontrolled type II <u>diabetes</u> with polyneuropathy	250.62 357.2 - Use additional code
5.	Congenital <u>hemangioma</u> on face	228.01 - Site is skin. *Includes*
6.	<u>Hiss-Russell</u> shigellosis	004.1 - "Trust the Index."
7.	Closed <u>fracture</u>, right leg	827.0 - NOS
8.	Diabetic <u>cataract</u>	250.50, 366.41 - Use additional code
9.	Muscular <u>atrophy</u>, left leg	728.2 - NEC
10.	Chronic smoker's bronchitis with acute <u>bronchitis</u>	466.0 (the acute disorder) and 491.0 - Includes (the underlying chronic condition)

EXERCISE 6-5 Hypertension/Hypertensive Coding

1.	Essential <u>hypertension</u>	401.9
2.	Transient <u>hypertension</u> due to pregnancy	642.30 (episode of care is not stated)
3.	Malignant <u>hypertensive</u> crisis	401.0
4.	Heart disease with <u>hypertension</u>	402.90
5.	Orthostatic <u>hypertension</u>, benign	401.1

EXERCISE 6-6 Neoplasm Coding I

1.	<u>Kaposi's</u> sarcoma	176.9
2.	<u>Lipoma</u>, skin, upper back	214.1
3.	<u>Carcinoma</u> *in situ*, skin, left cheek	232.3
4.	Scrotum <u>mass</u>	608.89
5.	<u>Neurofibroma</u>	215.9
6.	<u>Cyst</u> on left ovary	620.2
7.	<u>Ganglion</u> right wrist	727.41
8.	<u>Yaws</u>, frambeside	102.2
9.	Breast, chronic <u>cystic</u> disease	610.1
10.	Hürthle cell <u>tumor</u>	226

EXERCISE 6-7 Neoplasm Coding II

1. Ca (<u>carcinoma</u>) of the lung
   162.9

2. Metastasis from the lung (Neoplasms table)
   162.9 (lung is primary), 199.1 (unknown secondary site)

3. Abdominal <u>mass</u>
   789.30

4. <u>Carcinoma</u> of the breast (female) with metastasis to the axillary lymph nodes
   174.9, 196.3

5. <u>Carcinoma</u> of axillary lymph nodes and lungs, metastatic from the breast (female)
   174.9 (breast is primary) 196.3, 197.0 (secondary sites)

EXERCISE 6-8 Using the Table of Drugs and Chemicals

1. Adverse <u>reaction</u> to pertussis vaccine (<u>Table of Drugs and Chemicals, Therapeutic</u>)
   995.29 (unspecified adverse effect) E948.6 (therapeutic use)

2. Cardiac arrhythmia caused by interaction between prescribed ephedrine and unprescribed alcohol (<u>Table of Drugs and Chemicals, Poisoning</u>)
   971.2 (poisoning, ephedrine), 980.0 (poisoning, alcohol), 427.9 (arrhythmia), E980.4, E980.9 (undetermined external cause)

3. <u>Stupor</u>, due to overdose on Nytol (suicide attempt) (<u>Table of Drugs and Chemicals, Poisoning, Suicide</u>)
   963.0 (poisoning, Nytol), 780.09 (stupor), E950.4 (suicide attempt)

4. High blood pressure due to prescribed Albuterol
   401.9 (hypertension) E945.7 (therapeutic use)

5. Rash due to combining prescribed Amoxicillin with nonprescribed Benadryl
   960.0 (poisoning, Amoxicillin) 963.0 (poisoning, Benadryl) E980.4 (undetermined external cause) 693.0 (rash)

EXERCISE 6-9 Exploring V Codes

1. Family <u>history</u> of epilepsy with no evidence of seizures
   V17.2

2. Six-week postpartum <u>checkup</u>
   V24.2

3. Premarital physical (<u>exami</u>nation, marriage)
   V70.3

4. <u>Consult</u> with dietitian for patient with <u>diabetes</u> mellitus
   V65.3, 250.00

5. Rubella <u>screening</u>
   V73.3

EXERCISE 6-10 Coding HIV/AIDS and Fracture Cases

1. Patient is <u>HIV</u>-positive with no symptoms
   V08

2. <u>AIDS</u> patient treated for candidiasis
   042, 112.9

3. Open <u>fracture</u>, maxilla
   802.5

4. Greenstick <u>fracture</u>, third digit, right foot
   826.0

5. Multiple <u>fractures</u>, right femur, distal end
   821.29

EXERCISE 6-11 Coding Late Effects and Burns

1. <u>Malunion</u> due to fracture, right ankle, 9 months ago — 733.81, 905.4 (Late Effect)

2. Brain <u>damage</u> due to subdural <u>hematoma</u>, 18 months previously — 348.9, 438.9 (nontraumatic) or 907.0 (traumatic) (depending on documentation)

3. Second degree <u>burn</u>, anterior chest wall — 942.22, 948.00 (extent of body surface burned is 9 percent)

4. <u>Scalding</u> with <u>erythema</u>, right forearm and hand — 943.11, 944.10, 948.00

5. Third degree <u>burn</u>, back, 18 percent body surface — 942.34, 948.11

EXERCISE 6-12 Coding External Cause of Injury

> **NOTE:** Do not assign codes 695.1 (scaled skin syndrome), which is assigned for conditions due to allergies, etc.

1. Automobile <u>accident</u>, highway, passenger — E819.1 (Accident, motor vehicle)

2. Worker injured by <u>fall from</u> ladder — E881.0 (fall from ladder), E849.9 (unspecified place)

3. Accidental <u>drowning</u>, fell from power boat — 994.1 (drowning), E832.1 (fall from boat), E849.9

4. Soft tissue <u>injury</u>, right arm, due to snowmobile accident in patient's yard — 884.0, E820.9 (Accident, snow vehicle) and E849.0 (home)

5. Fall from playground equipment — E884.0 (fall), E849.4 (playground)

ANSWERS TO REVIEW

Infectious and Parasitic Diseases (including HIV)

1. Aseptic <u>meningitis</u> due to <u>AIDS</u> — 042, 047.8
2. Asymptomatic <u>HIV</u> infection — V08
3. <u>Septicemia</u> due to streptococcus — 038.0
4. <u>Dermatophytosis</u> of the foot — 110.4
5. <u>Measles</u>; no complications noted — 055.9
6. Nodular pulmonary <u>tuberculosis</u>; confirmed histologically — 011.15
7. Acute <u>cystitis</u> due to *E. coli* (<u>infection</u>) — 595.0, 041.4
8. Tuberculosis <u>osteomyelitis</u> of lower leg, confirmed by histology — 015.55, 730.86
9. Gas <u>gangrene</u> — 040.0

Neoplasms

> **NOTE:** Reference the ICD-9-CM Index to Diseases, and locate the condition documented in the diagnostic statement (e.g., melanoma). Then, follow the instructions to appropriately code each case (e.g., *see also* Neoplasm by site, malignant).

10. Malignant <u>melanoma</u> of skin of <u>scalp</u> — 172.4
11. <u>Lipoma</u> of <u>face</u> — 214.0
12. <u>Glioma</u> of the parietal lobe of the brain (<u>Neoplasm</u>, <u>brain</u>, <u>malignant</u>, <u>primary</u>) — 191.3
13. <u>Adenocarcinoma</u> of prostate (<u>Neoplasm</u>, <u>prostate</u>, <u>malignant</u>, <u>primary</u>) — 185
14. <u>Carcinoma</u> *in situ* of vocal cord (<u>Neoplasm</u>, <u>vocal cord</u>, <u>malignant</u>, <u>carcinoma in situ</u>) — 231.0

15. Hodgkin's granuloma of intra-abdominal lymph nodes and spleen   201.18

> **NOTE:** One code is reported when multiple sites are positive for Hodgkin's.

16. Paget's disease with infiltrating duct carcinoma of breast, nipple,   174.8
    and areola (Neoplasm, breast, malignant, primary)
17. Liver cancer (Neoplasm, liver, malignant)   155.2

> **NOTE:** One code is reported when multiple regions of the same organ are positive for cancer.

18. Metastatic adenocarcinoma from breast to brain (right mastectomy   174.9,
    performed five years ago) (Neoplasm, breast, malignant, primary, and   198.3 (in this
    Neoplasm, brain, malignant, secondary)   order)
19. Cancer of the pleura (primary site) (Neoplasm, pleura, malignant, primary)   163.9

Endocrine, Nutritional and Metabolic Diseases, and Immunity Disorders

20. Cushing's Syndrome   255.0
21. Hypokalemia   276.8
22. Type II diabetes mellitus, uncontrolled, with malnutrition   250.02, 263.9
23. Hypogammaglobulinemia   279.00
24. Hypercholesterolemia   272.0
25. Nephrosis due to type II diabetes   250.40, 581.81
26. Toxic diffuse goiter with thyrotoxic crisis   242.01
27. Cystic fibrosis   277.00
28. Panhypopituitarism   253.2
29. Rickets   268.0

Diseases of the Blood and Blood-forming Organs

30. Sickle cell disease with crisis   282.62
31. Iron deficiency anemia secondary to blood loss   280.0
32. Von Willebrand's disease   286.4
33. Chronic congestive splenomegaly   289.51
34. Congenital nonspherocytic hemolytic anemia   282.3
35. Essential thrombocytopenia   287.30
36. Malignant neutropenia   288.09
37. Fanconi's anemia   284.09
38. Microangiopathic hemolytic anemia   283.19
39. Aplastic anemia secondary to   284.89,
    antineoplastic medication for breast cancer   174.9, E933.1

Mental Disorders

40. Acute exacerbation of chronic undifferentiated schizophrenia   295.64
41. Reactive depressive psychosis due to the death of a child   298.0
42. Hysterical neurosis   300.10
43. Anxiety reaction manifested by fainting (do not code   300.00
    fainting because it is a symptom)
44. Alcoholic gastritis due to chronic alcoholism (episodic)   535.30, 303.92
45. Juvenile delinquency; patient was caught shoplifting   312.9

46. <u>Depression</u>	311
47. <u>Hypochondria</u>; patient also has continuous laxative habit	300.7, 305.91
48. Acute senile <u>dementia</u> with <u>Alzheimer's</u> disease (in this order)	331.0, 294.10
49. Epileptic <u>psychosis</u> with generalized grand mal <u>epilepsy</u>	294.8, 345.10

Diseases of the Nervous System and Sense Organs

50. *Neisseria* <u>meningitis</u>	036.0
51. Intracranial <u>abscess</u>	324.0

> **NOTE:** 342.9x is assigned to hemiplegia if *not* associated with old CVA.

52. Postvaricella <u>encephalitis</u>	052.0
53. <u>Hemiplegia</u> due to old CVA	438.20
54. <u>Encephalitis</u>	323.9
55. Retinal <u>detachment</u> with retinal defect	361.00
56. Congenital diplegic cerebral <u>palsy</u>	343.0
57. Tonic-clonic <u>epilepsy</u>	345.10
58. Infantile <u>glaucoma</u>	365.14
59. Mature <u>cataract</u>	366.9

Diseases of the Circulatory System

60. Congestive rheumatic heart <u>failure</u>	398.91
61. Mitral valve <u>stenosis</u> with aortic valve insufficiency	396.1
62. Acute rheumatic heart <u>disease</u>	391.9
63. <u>Hypertensive</u> cardiovascular disease, malignant	402.00
64. Congestive heart <u>failure</u>; benign <u>hypertension</u>	428.0, 401.1
65. Secondary benign <u>hypertension</u>; <u>stenosis</u> of renal artery	405.11, 440.1
66. Malignant <u>hypertensive</u> nephropathy with uremia (*Uremia* is renal failure, code 586, which is not assigned because it is included in 403.01)	403.01
67. Acute renal <u>failure</u>; essential <u>hypertension</u> (no cause-and-effect relationship between the renal failure and hypertension; therefore, two codes are reported)	584.9, 401.9
68. Acute myocardial <u>infarction</u> of inferolateral wall, initial episode of care	410.21
69. <u>Arteriosclerotic</u> heart disease (native coronary artery) with <u>angina pectoris</u>	414.01, 413.9

Diseases of the Respiratory System

70. Aspiration <u>pneumonia</u> due to regurgitated food	507.0
71. Streptococcal Group B <u>pneumonia</u>	482.32
72. Respiratory <u>failure</u> due to <u>myasthenia</u> gravis (in this order)	518.81, 358.00
73. Intrinsic <u>asthma</u> in status asthmaticus	493.11
74. COPD with <u>emphysema</u> (do not assign 496; see note at code 496 in ICD-9-CM Tabular List)	492.8

Diseases of the Digestive System

75. <u>Supernumerary</u> tooth	520.1
76. Unilateral femoral <u>hernia</u> with gangrene	551.00
77. <u>Cholesterolosis</u> of gallbladder	575.6
78. <u>Diarrhea</u>	787.91
79. Acute perforated peptic <u>ulcer</u>	533.10
80. Acute hemorrhagic <u>gastritis</u> with acute blood loss <u>anemia</u>	535.01, 285.1

81. Acute <u>appendicitis</u> with perforation and peritoneal abscess   540.1
82. Acute <u>cholecystitis</u> with cholelithiasis   574.00
83. Aphthous <u>stomatitis</u>   528.2
84. <u>Diverticulosis</u> and diverticulitis of colon   562.11
85. Esophageal <u>reflux</u> with esophagitis   530.11

Diseases of the Genitourinary System

86. Vesicoureteral <u>reflux</u> with bilateral reflux nephropathy   593.72
87. Acute <u>glomerulonephritis</u> with necrotizing glomerulolitis   580.4
88. Actinomycotic <u>cystitis</u>   039.8, 595.4 (in this order)
89. Subserosal uterine <u>leiomyoma</u>, cervical <u>polyp</u>, and <u>endometriosis</u> of uterus   218.2, 622.7, 617.0
90. <u>Dysplasia</u> of the cervix   622.10

Diseases of Pregnancy, Childbirth, and the Puerperium

91. <u>Defibrination</u> syndrome following termination of pregnancy (TOP) procedure two weeks ago (see *Excludes* note at 286.6 regarding TOP procedure)   639.1
92. <u>Miscarriage</u> at 19 weeks gestation   634.90
93. <u>Incompetent</u> cervix resulting in <u>miscarriage</u> and fetal death   634.91, 654.53
94. Postpartum <u>varicose</u> veins of legs   671.04
95. Spontaneous breech <u>delivery</u>   652.21
96. Triplet pregnancy, <u>delivered</u> spontaneously   651.11, V27.9
97. Retained placenta without hemorrhage, <u>delivery</u> this admission   667.02
98. <u>Pyrexia</u> of unknown origin during the puerperium (postpartum), delivery during previous admission   672.04
99. Late <u>vomiting</u> of pregnancy, undelivered   643.23
100. <u>Pre-eclampsia</u> complicating pregnancy, delivered this admission   642.41, V27.9

Diseases of the Skin and Subcutaneous Tissue

101. Diaper <u>rash</u>   691.0
102. <u>Acne</u> vulgaris   706.1
103. Post-infectional skin <u>cicatrix</u>   709.2
104. <u>Cellulitis</u> of the foot; culture reveals <u>staphylococcus</u>   682.7, 041.10
105. Infected <u>ingrowing</u> nail   703.0

Diseases of the Musculoskeletal System and Connective Tissue

106. <u>Displacement</u> of thoracic intervertebral disc   722.11
107. Primary localized <u>osteoarthrosis</u> of the hip   715.15
108. Acute juvenile rheumatoid <u>arthritis</u>   714.31
109. <u>Chondromalacia</u> of the patella   717.7
110. Pathologic <u>fracture</u> of the vertebra due to metastatic <u>carcinoma</u> of the bone from the lung   733.13, 198.5, 162.9

Congenital Anomalies

111. Congenital diaphragmatic <u>hernia</u>   756.6
112. Single liveborn male (born in the hospital) with <u>polydactyly</u> of fingers (newborn)   V30.00, 779.89, 755.01

113.	Unilateral <u>cleft</u> lip and palate	749.22
114.	<u>Patent</u> ductus arteriosus	747.0
115.	Congenital talipes equinovalgus	754.69

Certain Conditions Originating in the Perinatal Period

116.	<u>Erythroblastosis</u> fetalis	773.2
117.	<u>Hyperbilirubinemia</u> of prematurity, <u>prematurity</u> (birthweight 2,000 grams)	774.2, 765.18
118.	<u>Erb's</u> palsy	767.6
119.	<u>Hypoglycemia</u> in infant with diabetic mother	775.0
120.	<u>Premature "crack" baby</u> born in hospital to cocaine-dependent mother (birthweight 1,247 grams)	765.14, 760.75, 779.5, 304.20

Symptoms, Signs, and Ill-defined Conditions

121.	Abnormal cervical Pap smear	795.00
122.	Sudden infant death <u>syndrome</u>	798.0
123.	Sleep <u>apnea</u> with insomnia	780.51
124.	Fluid <u>retention</u> and <u>edema</u> (edema is coded because of *Excludes* note associated with 276.6)	276.6, 782.3
125.	<u>Elevated</u> blood pressure reading	796.2

Injury and Poisoning

Fractures, Dislocations, and Sprains

126.	Open frontal fracture with subarachnoid hemorrhage with brief loss of consciousness	800.72
127.	Supracondylar <u>fracture</u> of right humerus and <u>fracture</u> of olecranon process of the right ulna	812.41, 813.01
128.	Anterior <u>dislocation</u> of the elbow	832.01
129.	<u>Dislocation</u> of the first and second cervical vertebrae	839.08
130.	<u>Sprain</u> of lateral collateral ligament of knee	844.0

Open Wounds and Other Trauma

131.	Avulsion of eye	871.3
132.	<u>Traumatic</u> below-the-knee <u>amputation</u> with delayed healing	897.1
133.	Open <u>wound</u> of buttock	877.0
134.	Open <u>wound</u> of wrist involving tendons	881.22
135.	<u>Laceration</u> of external ear	872.00
136.	Traumatic subdural <u>hemorrhage</u> with open intracranial wound; loss of consciousness, 30 minutes	852.32
137.	<u>Concussion</u> without loss of consciousness	850.0
138.	Traumatic <u>laceration</u> of the liver, moderate	864.03
139.	Traumatic <u>hemothorax</u> with open wound into thorax and <u>concussion</u> with loss of consciousness	860.3, 850.5
140.	Traumatic duodenal <u>injury</u> (<u>internal</u>)	863.21

Burns

141.	Third-degree <u>burn</u> of lower leg and second-degree burn of thigh	945.34, 945.26
142.	Deep third-degree <u>burn</u> of forearm	943.41, 948.00
143.	Third-degree <u>burns</u> of back involving 20 percent of body surface	942.34, 948.22
144.	Thirty percent body <u>burns</u> with 10 percent third-degree	948.31
145.	First- and second-degree <u>burns</u> of palm	944.25

Foreign Bodies

146. <u>Coin</u> in the bronchus with bronchoscopy for removal of
the coin (<u>foreign body, entering through orifice</u>) — 934.1

147. <u>Foreign body</u> in the eye (<u>entering through orifice</u>) — 930.9

148. Marble in colon (<u>foreign body, entering through orifice</u>) — 936

149. Bean in nose (<u>foreign body, entering through orifice</u>) — 932

150. Q-tip stuck in ear (<u>foreign body, entering through orifice</u>) — 931

Complications

151. Infected ventriculoperitoneal shunt (<u>Complication, infection, ventricular shunt</u>) — 996.63

152. Displaced breast prosthesis (<u>Complication, mechanical, implant, prosthetic, in breast</u>) — 996.54

153. Leakage of mitral valve prosthesis (<u>Complication, mechanical, heart valve prosthesis</u>) — 996.02

154. <u>Postoperative</u> superficial <u>thrombophlebitis</u> of the right leg — 997.2, 451.0

155. Dislocated hip prosthesis (<u>Complication, orthopedic device, internal, mechanical</u>) — 996.42

V Codes

156. <u>Exposure</u> to tuberculosis — V01.1

157. Family <u>history</u> of colon carcinoma — V16.0

158. <u>Status (post)</u> unilateral kidney transplant, human <u>donor</u> — V59.4

159. Encounter for <u>removal</u> of cast (<u>plaster cast</u>) — V54.89

160. Admitted to donate bone marrow (<u>donor</u>) — V59.3

161. Encounter for <u>chemotherapy</u> for patient with Hodgkin's <u>lymphoma</u> — V58.11, 201.90

162. <u>Reprogramming</u> of cardiac pacemaker — V53.31

163. Replacement of <u>tracheostomy</u> tube (<u>Attention to</u>) — V55.0

164. Encounter for renal <u>dialysis</u> for patient in chronic renal <u>failure</u> — V56.0, 585.9

165. Encounter for speech <u>therapy</u> for patient with dysphasia secondary to an old CVA (<u>late effect</u>) — V57.3, 438.12

166. Encounter for <u>fitting</u> of artificial leg — V52.1

167. Encounter for <u>observation</u> of suspected malignant neoplasm of the cervix — V71.1

168. Visit to radiology department for barium swallow; abdominal <u>pain</u>; findings are negative; barium swallow performed and the findings are negative — 789.00

169. <u>Follow-up</u> examination of colon adenocarcinoma resected one year ago, no recurrence found (<u>history, personal, of</u>) — V67.09, V10.05

170. Routine general medical <u>examination</u> — V70.0

171. <u>Examination</u> of eyes — V72.0

172. Encounter for laboratory test; patient complains of <u>fatigue</u> — 780.79

173. Encounter for <u>physical therapy</u>; <u>status post</u> below-the-knee amputation six months ago — V57.1, V45.89

174. Kidney <u>donor</u> — V59.4

175. Encounter for <u>chemotherapy</u>; breast <u>carcinoma</u> (ICD-9-CM code V58.11 was added in 2006.) — V58.11, 174.9

Coding Late Effects

X 176. Hemiplegia due to previous cerebrovascular accident

X 177. Malunion of fracture, right femur

X 178. Scoliosis due to infantile paralysis

X **179.** Keloid secondary to injury nine months ago

180. Gangrene, left foot, following third-degree burn of foot two weeks ago

181. Cerebral thrombosis with hemiplegia

X **182.** Mental retardation due to previous viral encephalitis

183. Laceration of tendon of finger two weeks ago. Admitted now for tendon repair

> **NOTE:** Refer first to the ICD-9-CM Index to Diseases main term, Late (effect), for each diagnosis below. When the sequela (residual or resulting problem) is documented, report that code first followed by the late effect code.

184.	Residuals of <u>poliomyelitis</u>	138
185.	Sequela of old <u>crush</u> injury to left foot	906.4
186.	<u>Cerebrovascular accident</u> two years ago with late effects	438.9
187.	Effects of old gunshot <u>wound</u>, left thigh	906.1
188.	Disuse <u>osteoporosis</u> due to previous <u>poliomyelitis</u>	733.03, 138
189.	Brain <u>damage</u> following cerebral <u>abscess</u> seven months ago	348.9, 326
190.	<u>Hemiplegia</u> due to old <u>cerebrovascular accident</u>	438.20

> **NOTE:** Adverse reactions occur when patients take a prescribed medication, and a reaction develops. The first code reported is the adverse reaction (e.g., rash) and subsequent code(s) report the drug(s) taken, located in the Therapeutic Use column of the Table of Drugs and Chemicals. Poisonings occur when patients take a non-prescribed medication and/or combine prescribed with non-prescribed medications or drugs/alcohol. The first code reported is the poisoning code located in the first column of the Table of Drugs and Chemicals, and subsequent code(s) report the drug(s) and/or substance(s) (e.g., alcohol) (E-codes from the remaining columns in the Table of Drugs and Chemicals).

Adverse Reactions and Poisonings

191.	<u>Ataxia</u> due to interaction between prescribed <u>carbamazepine</u> and <u>erythromycin</u> (Adverse Reaction)	781.3, E936.3, E930.3
192.	<u>Vertigo</u> as a result of <u>dye</u> administered for a scheduled IVP (Adverse Reaction)	780.4, E947.8
193.	Accidental ingestion of mother's <u>oral contraceptives</u> (no signs or symptoms resulted) (Poisoning)	962.2, E858.0
194.	<u>Hemiplegia</u>; patient had an adverse reaction to prescribed <u>Enovid</u> one year ago (Late Effect of Adverse Reaction)	342.90, 909.5, E932.2
195.	<u>Stricture</u> of esophagus due to accidental lye ingestion three years ago (Late Effect of Adverse Reaction)	530.3, 909.1, E929.2
196.	<u>Listlessness</u> resulting from reaction between prescribed <u>Valium</u> and ingestion of a six-pack of beer (Poisoning)	969.4, 980.0, 780.79, E980.9, E980.3
197.	<u>Lead</u> poisoning (child had been discovered eating <u>paint</u> chips) (Poisoning)	984.0, E980.9
198.	Allergic reaction to <u>unspecified drug</u> (Adverse Reaction)	995.20, E935.9
199.	<u>Theophylline toxicity</u> (Adverse Reaction)	995.29, E944.1
200.	<u>Carbon monoxide</u> poisoning from car exhaust (<u>suicide attempt</u>) (Poisoning)	986, E952.0

CHAPTER 7   CPT Coding

ANSWERS TO CPT CODING EXERCISES

EXERCISE 7-1   Working with CPT Symbols and Conventions

> **NOTE:** The underlined words indicate key terms in the index. Words in parentheses are word substitutions to help you locate the procedure/service in the index, and they provide explanations of special coding situations.

1. *F*   <u>The Evaluation and Management and Anesthesia sections are excluded from the list. Nuclear medicine is a subsection of Radiology. Pathology should be listed as Pathology and Laboratory.</u>

2. *F*   The triangle <u>indicates a code description revision.</u>

3. *F*   CPT requires a <u>two-digit modifier</u> to be attached to the five-digit CPT code.

4. *T*   While parenthetical notes apply to specific codes or refer the reader to additional codes, blocked notes provide instruction for codes listed below the heading.

5. *T*   Semicolons save space in CPT where a series of related codes are found.

6. *F*   Qualifiers <u>may appear in the main and subordinate clauses.</u>

7. *F*   Parenthetical statements beginning with "eg" provide examples of terms that <u>may be in the health care provider's description of the service performed. These examples do not have to be included in the documentation.</u>

8. *T*   Horizontal triangles (▶◀) are found in revised guidelines, notes, and procedure descriptions.

9. *T*   The bullet (•) located to the left of a CPT code indicates a code new to that edition of CPT.

10. *F*   Code 50620 would be reported for a *ureterolithotomy performed on the* <u>middle one-third of the ureter.</u>

EXERCISE 7-2 Working with the CPT Index

1. Marsupialization means creating a pouch to exteriorize a cyst.

2. 47350   management of liver hemorrhage; simple suture of liver wound or injury

   47360   complex suture of liver wound or injury, with or without hepatic artery ligation

   47361   exploration of hepatic wound, extensive debridement, coagulation and/or suture, without packing of liver

   47362   re-exploration of hepatic wound for removal of packing

3. *T*

4. *F*   Main terms appear in boldface in the CPT index.

5. *F*   Inferred words do *not* appear in the CPT index.

EXERCISE 7-3 Assigning CPT Modifiers

1. Assistant surgeon reporting patient's cesarean section, delivery only.   −80

2. Cholecystectomy reported during postoperative period for treatment of leg fracture.   −79

3. Treatment for chronic conditions at same time preventative medicine is provided.   −25

4. Inpatient visit performed by surgeon, with decision to perform surgery tomorrow.   −57

5. Office consultation as preoperative clearance for surgery.   −56

6. Postoperative management of vaginal hysterectomy.   −55

7. Repeat gallbladder x-ray series, same physician.   −76

8. Arthroscopy of right elbow and closed fracture reduction of left wrist.   −51

9. Needle core biopsy of right and left breast.   −50

10. Consultation required by payer.   −32

EXERCISE 7-4 Finding Procedures in the Index

NOTE: CPT codes were updated using the AMA's downloadable CPT 2008 data file.

1. Closed treatment of wrist <u>dislocation</u>   25660, 25675, 25680

2. <u>Dilation</u> of cervix (*See* Dilation and Curettage)   57558, 57800

3. <u>Placement</u> of upper GI feeding tube (<u>Placement</u>, Nasogastric Tube)   43752

4. <u>Radiograph</u> and fluoroscopy of chest, four views
   (*See* Radiology, Diagnostic; x-ray)
   <u>x-ray, Chest</u>, Complete (Four Views), with Fluoroscopy   71034

5.	<u>Magnetic resonance imaging</u> (MRI), lower spine	72148-72158
6.	<u>Darrach</u> procedure (*See* Excision, Ulna, Partial)	25150-25151, 25240
7.	Manual <u>CBC</u> (*See* Blood Cell Count, Complete Blood Count [CBC])	85025-85027
8.	Electrosurgical <u>removal</u>, skin tags	11200-11201
9.	<u>Molar pregnancy</u> excision (*See* Hydatidiform Mole)	59100
10.	Muscle <u>denervation</u>, hip joint	27035

EXERCISE 7-5 Evaluation and Management Section

1.	<u>Home visit</u>, problem focused, established patient	99347
2.	ED service, new patient, low complexity (<u>Emergency Department Services</u>)	99282
3.	<u>Hospital</u> care, new patient, initial, high complexity	99223
4.	<u>Hospital</u> care, subsequent, detailed	99233
5.	ED care, problem focused, counseling 15 minutes; (<u>Emergency Department Services</u>)	99281
6.	Patient requested <u>consultation</u>, new patient, moderate complexity	99244
7.	Office <u>consultation</u>, high complexity, established patient, surgery scheduled tomorrow	99245
8.	Follow-up <u>consultation</u>, office, problem focused, counseling 15 minutes, encounter was 25 minutes. (There is no follow-up outpatient consult; use Est. Office Visit. Counseling becomes the key factor, selection is based on time.)	99214
9.	Follow-up <u>consultation</u>, inpatient, detailed, 35 minutes	99253
10.	Blood pressure check by nurse (established patient). (<u>Office and/or Other Outpatient Services</u>)	99211
11.	New patient, routine <u>preventive medicine</u>, age 11. Risk factor discussion, 20 minutes	99383
12.	Critical care, 1.5 hours (<u>Critical Care Services</u>)	99291, 99292
13.	<u>Nursing facility</u> visit, subsequent visit, expanded problem focused H&PE	99308
14.	Medical team <u>conference</u>, 50 minutes, nurse practitioner and discharge planner	99368
15.	<u>Follow-up</u> visit, ICU patient, stable, expanded problem focused H&PE (Patient is stable, use subsequent inpatient category)	99232
16.	<u>Resuscitation</u> of newborn, initial	99440
17.	<u>Telephone</u> E/M service by physician to established patient, 10 minutes	99441
18.	<u>Custodial care</u>, established patient, detailed H&PE, high complexity (CPT code 99336 was added in 2006.)	99336
19.	Pediatrician on <u>standby</u>, high-risk birth, 65 minutes	99360, 99360
20.	Heart risk factor education, group counseling, asymptomatic attendees, 65 minutes (<u>Preventative Medicine</u>)	99412

EXERCISE 7-6 Anesthesia Section

00144-AA-P2	1.	Anesthesiologist provided anesthesia services to a 77-year-old female patient who received a corneal transplant. The patient has a history of prior stroke.
00566-AA-P2	2.	Anesthesiologist provided anesthesia services to a 50-year-old diabetic patient who underwent direct coronary artery bypass grafting.
00834-AA-P1	3.	Anesthesiologist provided anesthesia services for hernia repair in the lower abdomen of an otherwise healthy 9-month-old infant.
00670-QX-P1	4.	CRNA provided anesthesia services under physician direction during an extensive procedure on the cervical spine of an otherwise healthy patient.
01744-QZ-P2	5.	CRNA provided anesthesia services to a morbidly obese female patient who underwent repair of malunion, humerus.

EXERCISE 7-7 Working with the Surgical Package

1. <u>Incision and drainage</u> (I&D), finger abscess   26010
2. Percutaneous I&D, <u>abscess, appendix</u>   44901
3. Anesthetic agent injection, L-5 <u>paravertebral nerve</u>   64475
4. Laparoscopic <u>cholecystectomy</u> with cholangiography   47563
5. Flexible esophagoscopy with removal of foreign body and radiologic supervision and interpretation (S&I) (Esophagus, Endoscopy, Removal, Foreign Body **or** Endoscopy, Esophagus, Removal, Foreign Body. See parenthetical note below 43215 for second code.)   43215, 74235

EXERCISE 7-8 Coding Separate and Multiple Procedures

1. Diagnostic <u>arthroscopy</u>, right wrist, with synovial biopsy   29840-RT
2. Simple vaginal mucosal <u>biopsy</u>   57100
3. Diagnostic nasal <u>endoscopy</u>, bilateral, and   31231
   facial <u>chemical peel</u>   15788-51
4. Diagnostic <u>thoracoscopy</u>, lungs and pleural space, with right lung biopsy   32602
5. Needle <u>biopsy</u> of testis   54500
6. Total abdominal <u>hysterectomy</u> with removal of ovaries   58150
   and anterior <u>colporrhaphy</u>   57240-51
7. <u>Laparoscopic</u> appendectomy and lumbar <u>hernia repair</u>   44970, 49540-51
8. <u>Biopsy</u> of larynx (indirect) via laryngoscopy and <u>laryngoplasty</u>   31510 31588-51
9. <u>Excision</u> of chest wall lesion with removal of ribs and plastic reconstruction   19271
10. Partial-thickness facial skin <u>debridement</u> and   11041
    full-thickness leg skin <u>debridement</u>   11040-51

EXERCISE 7-9 Radiology Coding

1. GI series (<u>x-ray</u>), with small bowel and air studies, without KUB   74249
2. Chest <u>x-ray</u>, PA & left lateral   71020
3. Cervical spine <u>x-ray</u>, complete, with flexion and extension (spine)   72052
4. <u>x-ray</u> pelvis, AP   72170
5. Abdomen, flat plate, AP (<u>x-ray</u>)   74000
6. BE, colon, with air (<u>x-ray</u> colon)   74280
7. Postoperative radiologic supervision and interpretation
   of <u>cholangiography</u> by radiologist   74305
8. <u>SPECT</u> exam of the liver   78205
9. Retrograde pyelography with KUB (<u>Urography</u>) via cystourethroscopy   52005, 74420
10. <u>SPECT</u> liver imaging   78205

EXERCISE 7-10 Pathology and Laboratory Coding

1. Hepatic function <u>panel</u>   80076
2. Hepatitis <u>panel</u>   80074
3. <u>TB</u> skin test, PPD   86580
4. UA (<u>Urinalysis</u>) by dip stick with micro, automated   81001
5. WBC count with Diff, automated   85004
6. Stool for <u>occult blood</u>   82272
7. Wet mount, vaginal <u>smear</u>   87210
8. <u>Glucose</u>/blood sugar, <u>quantitative</u>   82947
9. Sedimentation rate (need method for definitive code)   85651 or 85652

10. Throat <u>culture</u>, bacterial   87070
11. Urine <u>sensitivity, disk</u>   87184
12. Microhematocrit, spun (<u>Blood Cell Count</u>)   85013
13. <u>Monospot</u> test   86308
14. Strep test, rapid (<u>Streptococcus</u>, Group A, Direct Optical Observation)   87880

> **NOTE:** Identifying the correct CPT code for "strep" testing performed in an office setting often causes confusion. CPT code 87880 is reported for all immunologically based commercial Streptococcus Group A testing kits where the interpretation relies on a visual reaction that is observed by the naked eye.

15. One-year storage of <u>sperm</u>   89343

EXERCISE 7-11 Medicine Section

1. Cardiac catheterization, right side only, with conscious sedation, IV (<u>Catheter</u>, Cardiac, Right Heart)   93501
2. Routine <u>EKG</u>, tracing only   93005
3. <u>Spirometry</u>   94010
4. <u>CPR</u>, in office   92950
5. <u>Diagnostic psychiatric</u> examination   90801
6. Influenza <u>vaccine</u>, age 18 months   90471, 90657
7. <u>Whirlpool</u> and <u>paraffin bath</u> therapy   97022, 97018-51
8. WAIS-R and MMPI psychological tests and report, 1 hour (<u>Psychiatric Diagnosis</u>, Psychological Testing)   96101
9. Office services on emergency basis (<u>Office Medical Service</u>)   99058
10. Physical therapy <u>evaluation</u> (and management)   97001

ANSWERS TO REVIEW

> **NOTE:** Observation services are coded from either the (1) *Hospital Observation Services* subsection/category of E/M or (2) *Observation or Inpatient Care Services (Including Admission and Discharge Services)* subcategory in the Hospital Inpatient Services subsection/category. Designating a patient as receiving observation services has caused a great deal of confusion among providers and coders.
>
> *Observation services* are furnished by a hospital on its premises and include the use of a bed and periodic monitoring by the hospital's nursing or other staff as reasonable and necessary to evaluate an outpatient's condition or to determine the need for possible admission to the hospital as an inpatient. Observation services are classified as acute care services, and usually do not exceed one day (24 hours). Coverage for observation services is limited to no more than 48 hours, unless the third-party payer approves an exception. An inpatient admission ordered only because the patient is expected to remain in observation overnight is not considered medically necessary (and would not be reimbursed).
>
> *Inpatient services* are furnished when a hospital inpatient is formally admitted, as with the expectation of an overnight stay, and the severity of illness or intensity of services to be provided warrants hospital inpatient level of care.

Evaluation and Management Section

1. Office or Other Outpatient Services (refer to notes below the Office or Other Outpatient Services category).
2. FALSE.
3. Hospital Inpatient Services (refer to notes below the Hospital Inpatient Services category).
4. Consultation (refer to notes below the Consultations category).
5. FALSE (refer to the note below the Consultations category).
6. FALSE (refer to notes below the Office or Other Outpatient Consultations subcategory).
7. TRUE (refer to notes below the Initial Inpatient Consultations subcategory).
8. Subsequent Hospital Care (located within the Hospital Inpatient Services category/subsection). (refer to notes below the Follow up Inpatient Consultations subcategory)
9. The confirmatory consultations heading was deleted from CPT 2006. Modifier -32 is added to mandatory consultation codes.
10. FALSE (refer to notes below the Emergency Department Services category).

11. 99288 (refer to the Other Emergency Services subcategory).
12. According to CPT, "the physician is located in a hospital emergency or critical care department, and is in two-way voice communication with ambulance or rescue personnel outside the hospital. The physician directs the performance of necessary medical procedures. . . ."

> **NOTE:** For example, if you watch the television show *ER*, you've seen a nurse on a two-way radio with ambulance personnel. I realize she is not a physician on the show, but you get the idea. For those of you who have long memories, back in the 1970s there was a television show called *Emergency* that depicted a physician in two-way communication with paramedic rescue personnel.

13. FALSE (refer to notes below the Critical Care Services category).
14. 99291, 99292 × 3 (refer to the chart below the Critical Care Services category).
15. Nursing facilities (refer to notes below the Nursing Facility Services category).

> **NOTE:** SNF, skilled nursing facility, ICF, intermediate care facility, LTCF, long term care facility.

16. Domiciliary, Rest Home (e.g., Boarding Home), or Custodial Care Services.
17. Home Services (refer to notes below the Home Services category).
18. 99441
19. 99385 or 99395 (depending on whether the patient is new or established) (refer to Preventive Medicine Services category).
20. 99381 or 99391 (depending on whether the patient is new or established) (refer to the Preventive Medicine Services category).
    90471 (refer to Medicine Section, Immunization Administration of Vaccines/Toxoids category).
    90472
    90701 (refer to Medicine Section, Vaccines, Toxoids category).
    90712

> **NOTE:** If well-baby care was not provided in addition to the administration of vaccines, do not code 99381/99291.
>
> Note the sequencing of the Medicine Section codes above. Refer to the note below the Immunization Administration for Vaccines/Toxoids category that states, "Codes 90471–90472 must be reported in addition to the vaccine and toxoid code(s) 90476–90749." You might think this means to sequence codes 90471–90472 below codes 90476–90749. However, when reviewing codes 90476–90749, note that the symbol for modifier –51 Exempt ( ) is printed in front of each code. The symbol means that you do not attach modifier –51 to these codes; this means that codes 90476–90749 are sequenced below codes 90471–90472.

21. 99396 (refer to Preventive Medicine Services category).
22. 99234 or 99235 or 99236 (depending on level of service provided) (refer to notes below Observation or Inpatient Care Services category).

> **NOTE:** Assign codes 99218–99220 from the Hospital Observation Services category only when patients are admitted to and discharged from observation on different dates.

23. 99291, 99292 × 5 (refer to the chart in the Critical Care Services category), 99223.

> **NOTE:** Although the last 99292 code reflects just 16 minutes of critical care, it is reportable because it is ≥ 15 minutes.

24. 99455 (refer to Special Evaluation and Management Services category).

> **NOTE:** "Treating physician" is the patient's primary care physician.

25. Identify the CPT category and subcategory. *Hospital Inpatient Services, Initial Hospital Care*
    Identify the appropriate CPT code. *99221 (code selection requires 3/3 key components)*
26. Identify the CPT category and subcategory. *Consultations, Office or Other Outpatient Consultations*
    Identify the appropriate CPT code. *99242 (requirement of all three key components was met)*
27. Identify the CPT category. *Newborn Care*
    Identify the appropriate CPT code. *99433*

> **NOTE:** "Healthy newborn" was cared for by Dr. Choi.

28. Identify the CPT category and subcategory. *Office or Other Outpatient Services, Established Patient*
   Identify the appropriate CPT code. *99215*
29. Identify the CPT category and subcategory. *Hospital Inpatient Services, Subsequent Hospital Care*
   Identify the appropriate CPT code. *99232*

Surgery Section

30. <u>Pneumocentesis</u>; assistant surgeon reporting	32420-80
31. <u>Electrodesiccation</u>, basal cell carcinoma (1 cm), face	17281
32. Complicated bilateral repair of recurrent inguinal <u>hernia</u>	49520-22
33. <u>Biopsy</u> of anorectal wall via proctosigmoidoscopy	45305
34. <u>Mastectomy</u> for gynecomastia, bilateral	19300-50
35. Open reduction, right tibia/fibula shaft <u>fracture</u>, with insertion of screws	27758
36. Excision, <u>condylomata</u>, penis	54060
37. Replacement of breast <u>tissue expander</u> with breast prosthesis (permanent)	11970
38. Closed reduction of closed <u>fracture</u>, clavicle	23505
39. <u>Incision and drainage</u> infected bursa, wrist	25031
40. <u>Cystourethroscopy</u> with biopsy of urinary bladder	52204
41. <u>Endoscopic</u> (<u>nose</u>) right maxillary sinusotomy with partial polypectomy	31237
42. Insertion of non-tunnelled Hickman catheter (short-term) (age 70) (<u>Catheterization</u>, <u>Venous, Central Line</u>)	36556
43. <u>Avulsion</u> of four nail plates	11730, 11732 × 3

Radiology, Pathology and Laboratory, and Medicine Sections

44. <u>Arthrography</u> of the shoulder, supervision and interpretation	73040
45. Chest <u>x-ray</u>, frontal, single view (professional component only)	71010-26
46. Transabdominal ultrasound of pregnant uterus, first pregnancy (real time with image documentation), fetal and maternal evaluation, second trimester	76805
47. <u>Application</u> of radioactive needles (radioelement), intracavitary of uterus, intermediate	77762
48. Lipid panel <u>blood test</u>	80061
49. Drug screen for opiates (<u>outside laboratory</u> performed drug screen)	80101-90
50. <u>Hemogram</u> (manual) (complete CBC)	85014, 85018-51, 85032-51
51. Cervical cytopathology slides, manual screening under physician supervision	88150
52. Gross and microscopic examination of gallbladder (<u>Pathology</u>, <u>S</u>urgical)	88304
53. Complete echocardiography, transthoracic (real-time with image documentation [2D] with M-mode recording)	93307
54. Mumps vaccine <u>immunization</u>	90704, 90471
55. <u>Intermittent positive pressure breathing</u> of a newborn	94640
56. <u>Gait training</u>, first 30 minutes	97116 × 2
57. Medical <u>psychoanalysis</u>	90845
58. <u>Ultraviolet light</u> is used to treat a skin disorder	96900
59. <u>Chemotherapy</u>, IV infusion technique, 10 hours, requiring use of portable pump (including refill)	96414, 96521
60. Combined right <u>cardiac catheterization</u> and retrograde left heart catheterization	93526

Category II Codes

> **NOTE:** Refer to Performance Measures in the CPT index to locate Category II codes below.

61.	Initial prenatal care visit	0500F
62.	Assessment of tobacco use	1000F
63.	Recording of vital signs	2010F
64.	Documentation and review of spirometry results	3023F
65.	Inhaled bronchodilator prescribed for COPD patient	4025F

Category III Codes

66.	Destruction of macular drusen via photocoagulation	0017T
67.	Expired gas analysis spectroscopy	0064T
68.	Needle biopsy of prostate, saturation sampling for prostate mapping	0137T
69.	Pancreatic islet cell transplantation through portal vein, open approach	0142T
70.	Surgical laparoscopy with implantation of gastric stimulation electrodes, lesser curvature of the stomach, for patient diagnosed with morbid obesity	0155T

CHAPTER 8 HCPCS Level II Coding

ANSWERS TO HCPCS CODING EXERCISES

EXERCISE 8-1 HCPCS Index

	Code	**Index Entry**
1.	J3490	Key word(s): unclassified drug
2.	Q0114	Key word(s): fern test
3.	L3214	Key word(s): Benesch boot
4.	E0978	Key word(s): belt, safety
5.	A4913	Key word(s): dialysis, supplies

EXERCISE 8-2 Recognizing Payer Responsibility

local MAC: none
regional MAC: L3214, E0978
local MAC or regional MAC: A4913, J3490, Q0114

ANSWERS TO REVIEW

1.	a. Code: J3420	Modifier(s): -GA	Quantity: 1
	b. Code: E1031	Modifier(s): -NU -BP	Quantity: 1
	c. Code: A4253	Modifier(s): -KS	Quantity: 2
	d. Code: G0101 (modifier –QB was deleted in 2005.)	Modifier(s): none	Quantity: 1
	e. Code: E1392	Modifier(s): -RR	Quantity: 1
2.	a. Code: 28072	Modifier(s): -T2	Quantity: 1
	b. Code: 82951	Modifier(s): -QW	Quantity: 1
	c. Code: 27810	Modifier(s): -LT -GJ	Quantity: 1
	d. Code: 00162	Modifier(s): none	
	e. Code: 96118	Modifier(s): -AH	Quantity: 2

CHAPTER 9 CMS Reimbursement Methodologies

ANSWERS TO REVIEW

1. Submitted charge (based on provider's regular fee for office visit) $75
   Medicare physician fee schedule (PFS) $60
   Coinsurance amount (paid by patient or supplemental insurance) $12
   Medicare payment (80 percent of the allowed amount)   <u>$48</u>
   Medicare write-off (not to be paid by Medicare or the beneficiary)   <u>$15</u>
2. Submitted charge (based on provider's regular fee) $650
   NonPAR Medicare physician fee schedule allowed amount $450
   Limiting charge (115 percent of MPFS allowed amount)   <u>$517.50</u>
   Medicare payment (80 percent of the MPFS allowed amount)   <u>$360</u>
   Beneficiary is billed 20 percent plus the balance of the limiting charge $157.50
   ($450 × 20%) + ($517.50 − $450) = $90 + $67.50 = $157.50
   Medicare write-off (*not* to be paid by Medicare or the beneficiary)
   ($650 − $517.50)   <u>$132.50</u>
3. Submitted charge (based on provider's regular fee for office visit) $75
   Medicare allowed amount (according to the Medicare physician fee schedule) $60
   Nurse practitioner allowed amount (100 percent of MPFS)   <u>$60</u>
   Medicare payment (80 percent of the allowed amount)   <u>$48</u>
4. a
5. a
6. b
7. a
8. a
9. b
10. c
11. a
12. b
13. b
14. c
15. b
16. b
17. c
18. c
19. b
20. c

CHAPTER 10 Coding for Medical Necessity

ANSWERS TO EXERCISES

EXERCISE 10-1 Choosing the First-Listed Diagnosis

Review the list of symptoms, complaints, and disorders in each case and underline the first-listed diagnosis, which is reported as reference number in Block 21 of the CMS-1500 claim.

1. <u>Acute pharyngitis</u>
2. <u>Musculoligamentous sprain, left ankle</u>
3. <u>Benign prostatic hypertrophy (BPH) with urinary retention</u>
4. <u>Bacterial endocarditis</u>
5. <u>Partial drop foot gait, right</u>

EXERCISE 10-2 Linking Diagnoses with Procedures/Services

CASE 1

DIAGNOSIS POINTER	PROCEDURE/SERVICE
2	Hemoccult lab test
2	Proctoscopy with biopsy
3	Proctectomy

> **NOTE:** The hemoccult lab test and proctoscopy with biopsy are done because the patient presents with the symptom, blood in the stool. Occult blood is present in such minute amounts in stool that it is not visible to the naked eye. Patients who present with blood in their stools undergo the hemoccult lab test to determine the cause of the bleeding (e.g., colorectal cancer vs. hemorrhaging hemorrhoids). A positive hemoccult test would indicate a need for proctoscopy with biopsy, which (in this case) was done to determine the cause of the bleeding. While pathological diagnosis upon biopsy indicates Duke's C carcinoma of the colon, at the time the CMS-1500 claim was submitted, this diagnosis was unknown; therefore, link the proctoscopy with biopsy to the blood in the stool.

CASE 2

DIAGNOSIS POINTER	PROCEDURE/SERVICE
1	Office visit
1	Urinalysis
4	Rapid strep test

> **NOTE:** Urinary frequency with dysuria, sore throat with cough, and headaches are signs and symptoms; therefore, link all with the office visit. The urinalysis was specifically done because of the urinary frequency with dysuria. The rapid strep test was performed because of the sore throat with cough, but it came back positive; therefore, link "strep throat" with the test.

CASE 3

DIAGNOSIS POINTER	PROCEDURE/SERVICE
1	Office visit
1	Chest x-ray

> **NOTE:** Unlike pathological diagnoses, which can require several days prior to the establishment of a definitive diagnosis, a chest x-ray can be evaluated immediately upon completion and a diagnosis rendered. Because wheezing, congestion, and labored respirations are signs detected on physical examination, and pneumonia is a definitive diagnosis, report only the pneumonia on the CMS-1500 claim.

CASE 4

DIAGNOSIS POINTER	PROCEDURE/SERVICE
1	Nursing facility visit

> **NOTE:** Malaise and fatigue are assigned to the same ICD code number, so report the diagnosis pointer number just once.

CASE 5

DIAGNOSIS POINTER	PROCEDURE/SERVICE
3	Emergency department visit

> **NOTE:** Do not report signs and/or symptoms (e.g., chills and fever) on the CMS-1500 when a definitive diagnosis (e.g., acute diverticulitis) is documented.

EXERCISE 10-3 National Coverage Determinations

1. 93511 (left heart cardiac catheterization, cut-down); 414.00 (coronary artery disease); 413.9 (angina pectoris); 412 (status post myocardial infarction, four weeks ago). Review of the national coverage determination (NCD) about *Cardiac Catheterization Performed in Other than a Hospital Setting* indicates that this NCD is undergoing review. However, the original consideration stated that a "cardiac catheterization performed in a hospital setting for either inpatients or outpatients is a covered service. The procedure may also be covered when performed in a freestanding clinic when the carrier, in consultation with the appropriate quality improvement organization (QIO), determines that the procedure can be performed safely in all respects in the particular facility. Prior to approving Medicare payment for cardiac catheterizations performed in freestanding clinics, the carrier must request QIO review of the clinic."

2. 93798 (cardiac rehabilitation program); V57.89 (cardiac rehab); V45.82 (status post coronary angioplasty); V45.81 (status post coronary bypass); 411.1 (unstable angina). Review of the NCD about *Cardiac Rehabilitation Programs* indicates "Medicare coverage of cardiac rehabilitation programs are considered reasonable and necessary only for patients who (1) have a documented diagnosis of acute myocardial infarction within the preceding 12 months; or (2) have had coronary bypass surgery; or (3) have stable angina pectoris; or (4) have had heart valve repair/replacement; or (5) have had percutaneous transluminal coronary angioplasty (PTCA) or coronary stenting; or (6) have had a heart or heart–lung transplant.

> **NOTE:** This patient has unstable angina; therefore, Medicare will not cover a cardiac rehabilitation program.

3. 44388 (colonoscopy); V10.05 (history of colon cancer, treatment complete); 555.9 (Crohn's disease); 578.1 (blood in stool); 789.00 (abdominal pain). Review of the NCD about *Endoscopy* indicates that "endoscopic procedures are covered when reasonable and necessary for the individual patient."

> **NOTE:** A colonoscopy is an endoscopy.

4. 70450 (CT scan of head); 959.01 (closed head trauma); 920 (contusion of scalp). Review of the NCD about *Computerized Tomography* indicates that computerized tomography is covered if you find that the medical and scientific literature and opinion support the effective use of a scan for the condition, and the scan is: (1) reasonable and necessary for the individual patient; and (2) performed on a model of CT equipment that meets the criteria for approved models of CT equipment."

EXERCISE 10-4 Coding Case Scenarios

> **NOTE:** The underlined term in the Diagnoses column is the first-listed diagnosis or condition.

1.

Procedures	Codes	Diagnoses	Codes
Preventive medicine, established patient, age 66	99397	Annual exam	V70.0
Outpatient, established patient, level 4	99214-25	<u>Hypertension</u>	401.9
Vaccination, influenza	90658, 90471	Vaccination	V04.81

> **NOTE:** Do not code dizziness or tiredness, which are symptoms of hypertension.

2. | Procedures | Codes | Diagnoses | Codes |
|---|---|---|---|
| Arthroscopy, shoulder | 29805 | Pain, shoulder NOS | 719.41 |
| Outpatient, established patient, expanded problem focused | 99214-25 | Tired | 780.71 |
| | | Weakness | 780.79 |
| | | Depression | 311 |

3. | Procedure | Code | Diagnosis | Codes |
|---|---|---|---|
| *The emergency department physician reports the following codes:* | | | |
| ED visit, level 2 | 99292 | Ruptured appendix with abscess | 540.1 |
| *The surgeon reports the following codes:* | | | |
| E/M service, new patient (decision for surgery) | 99203-57 | Ruptured appendix with abscess | 540.1 |
| Laparoscopic appendectomy | 44970 | Ruptured appendix with abscess | 540.1 |

> **NOTE:** The diagnosis code is the same for both the emergency department physician and the surgeon.

4. | Procedure | Code | Diagnosis | Codes |
|---|---|---|---|
| *The emergency department physician reports the following codes:* | | | |
| ED visit, level 3 | 99283 | Acute Cholecystitis | 575.0 |
| *The surgeon reports the following codes:* | | | |
| Gallbladder ultrasound | 76705 | Acute Cholecystitis | 575.0 |
| E/M service, new patient (decision for surgery) | 99203-57 | Acute Cholecystitis | 575.0 |
| Laparosopic cholecystectomy | 47562 | Acute Cholecystitis | 575.0 |

> **NOTE:** The diagnosis code is the same for both the emergency department physician and the surgeon.

5. | Procedure | Code | Diagnosis | Codes |
|---|---|---|---|
| Postop care, appendectomy, open | 44950-55 | Aftercare, surgery | V58.32 |

> **NOTE:** Do not report an E/M office visit code. Modifier –55 is reported with the surgery code to obtain reimbursement for postoperative care. Do not code appendicitis; the appendix is no longer present.

EXERCISE 10-5 Coding SOAP Notes

	Diagnoses	ICD-9-CM Codes
1.	Atrophic gastritis	535.10
	Leg pain	729.5
2.	Aftercare, surgery	V58.42
	Diabetes mellitus	250.00

> **NOTE:** Do not assign 574.10 (cholecystitis with cholelithiasis) because the gallbladder has been removed, and this code was reported on the outpatient surgery claim. This is a postoperative office visit.

Diagnoses	ICD-9-CM Codes
3. Rheumatoid arthritis	714.0
Tenosynovitis, knee	727.09
4. Unstable angina	411.1
5. Exudative tonsillitis	463
6. Seizure disorder, onset	780.39

> **NOTE:** Lymphoma and COPD were not treated or medically managed.

EXERCISE 10-6 Coding Operative Reports

CASE 1

Diagnoses: Granulation, tissue, skin — 701.5
History, personal, malignant, skin — V10.83
Procedure: Excision, lesion, scalp, benign (0.3 cm) — 11420

CASE 2

Diagnosis: Atypical neoplasm, skin (uncertain behavior) — 238.2
(Pathology ordered the re-excision because of atypical cells)
Procedures: Excision, lesion, benign (return to O.R.) — 11406-58,
(5.0 cm, skin of back). Layered closure, intermediate. — 12032

CASE 3

Diagnoses: Neoplasm, benign, intestine, sigmoid — 211.3
Melanosis coli — 569.89
Procedure: Colonoscopy, with biopsy of polyp and fulguration — 45380,
of polyp — 45384-51

CASE 4

Diagnosis: Serous otitis media — 381.4
Procedure: Myringotomy (Tympanostomy) with insertion of — 69436-50
ventilating tubes (procedure performed bilaterally)

CASE 5

Diagnosis: Lesion, buccal mucosa (If working in the office, — 528.9
do not code diagnosis until biopsy report results are
received—results could indicate a malignant lesion.)
Procedure: Biopsy, buccal mucosa — 40812

CASE 6

Diagnosis: Pilonidal cyst (no mention of abscess) — 685.1
Procedure: Excision pilonidal cyst (no mention of extensive — 11770
or complicated excision)

CASE 7

Diagnosis: Femoral hernia, incarcerated (incarcerated equals — 552.00
strangulated)
Procedure: Herniorrhaphy, femoral (not stated as recurrent) — 49553

ANSWERS TO REVIEW
Comprehensive Coding Practice

		Diagnosis Code(s)	Procedure Code(s)
1.	Office visit	569.3	99204
	Friday surgery	V64.1	45378-53 (or 45378-73, depending on setting)
		569.3	
	Monday surgery	562.10	45385
		211.3	
2.		530.85	74241
3.		427.9	93312 (conscious sedation is not coded)
4.	May 5 (day)	473.9	99212
	May 5 (evening)	436	99223
	May 6	436	99291, 99292

Determining Medical Necessity (Case Studies: Set One) (5–8)

Answers to Case Studies: Set One are located in Section IV of this manual.

Coding and Determining Medical Necessity (Case Studies: Set Two) (9–14)

Answers to Case Studies: Set Two are located in Section IV of this manual.

Evaluation and Management Coding Practice

15. Identify the E/M category/subcategory: <u>Hospital Inpatient Services, Initial Hospital Care</u>
Determine the extent of history obtained: <u>Expanded problem focused</u>
RATIONALE FOR EXTENT OF HISTORY SELECTION: Upon review of the case study compared with the HCFA Documentation Guidelines (in your textbook appendix),
three elements were documented for the HPI = Brief HPI; seven elements were documented for the ROS = Extended ROS; and three elements were documented for the PFSH = Complete PFSH. Therefore, select expanded problem focused history because brief HPI (with only three elements documented) "drives" selection of lower level of extent of history.
Determine the extent of examination performed: <u>Expanded problem focused</u>
RATIONALE FOR EXTENT OF PE SELECTION: Upon review of the case study compared with the HCFA Documentation Guidelines (in your textbook appendix), seven elements were documented on PE. Therefore, expanded problem focused PE was documented.
Medical decision making: <u>Straightforward</u>
RATIONALE FOR MEDICAL DECISION MAKING SELECTION: This is a judgment call on my part; if you wanted to go with "low complexity," I would not have a problem with that. Code Number: <u>99221</u>

16. Identify the E/M category/subcategory: <u>Office or Other Outpatient Services, Established Patient</u>
Determine the extent of history obtained: <u>Detailed</u>
RATIONALE FOR EXTENT OF HISTORY SELECTION: Upon review of the case study compared with the HCFA Documentation Guidelines (in your textbook appendix), four elements were documented for the HPI = Extended HPI; eight elements were documented for the ROS = Extended ROS; and three elements were documented for the PFSH = complete PFSH. Therefore, select detailed history because extended HPI and extended ROS "drive" selection of extent of history. Determine the extent of examination performed: <u>Detailed</u>
RATIONALE FOR EXTENT OF PE SELECTION: Upon review of the case study compared with the HCFA Documentation Guidelines (in your textbook appendix), 19 elements were documented in the General Multisystem Exam.
Medical decision making: <u>Low complexity</u>
RATIONALE FOR MEDICAL DECISION MAKING SELECTION: This is a judgment call on my part; if you wanted to go with "straightforward," I would not have a problem with that. Code Number: <u>99214</u>

17. Identify the E/M category/subcategory: <u>Office or Other Outpatient Services, Established Patient</u>
Determine the extent of history obtained: <u>Expanded problem focused</u>
RATIONALE FOR EXTENT OF HISTORY SELECTION: Upon review of the case study compared with the HCFA Documentation Guidelines (in your textbook appendix), one element was documented for the HPI = Brief HPI: one element was documented for the ROS = problem pertinent; and no elements were documented for the PFSH = none. Therefore, select expanded problem focused history because no PFSH is required.
Determine the extent of examination performed: <u>Problem focused</u>
RATIONALE FOR EXTENT OF PE SELECTION: Upon review of the case study compared with the HCFA Documentation Guidelines (in your textbook appendix), just one element was documented in the General Multisystem Exam.
Medical decision making: <u>Low complexity</u>
Code Number: <u>99213</u>
RATIONALE: Only two of three key components are required to select the code.

18. Identify the E/M category/subcategory: <u>Office or Other Outpatient Services, Established Patient</u>
Determine the extent of history obtained: <u>Expanded problem focused</u>
RATIONALE FOR EXTENT OF HISTORY SELECTION: Upon review of the case study compared with the HCFA Documentation Guidelines (in your textbook appendix), two elements were documented for the HPI = Brief HPI; one element was documented for the ROS = problem pertinent; and no elements were documented for the PFSH = none. Therefore, select expanded problem focused history because no PFSH is required.
Determine the extent of examination performed: <u>Problem focused</u>
RATIONALE FOR EXTENT OF PE SELECTION: Upon review of the case study compared with the HCFA Documentation Guidelines (in your textbook appendix), three elements were documented in the General Multisystem Exam.
Medical decision making: <u>Straightforward</u>
Code Number: <u>99212</u> (just 2/3 key components "drives" code selection)

19. Identify the E/M category/subcategory: <u>Non-Face-to-Face Physician services, Telephone services</u>
Code Number: <u>99443</u>

Correcting Claims Submission Errors

20.

CODING ERROR	PROCEDURE CODE	DIAGNOSIS CODE
c	81003	599.0
		041.4

Select (c) because the coder should have reported code 788.1 for dysuria. There is no mention in the case of urinary tract infection (599.0) or *E. coli* (041.4) as a final diagnosis.

21.

CODING ERROR	PROCEDURE CODE	DIAGNOSIS CODE
c	71010	553.3

Code 786.05 (shortness of breath) should have been reported as the first-listed diagnosis because there were no acute findings suggesting a cause of the shortness of breath.

22.

CODING ERROR	PROCEDURE CODE	DIAGNOSIS CODE
a	99394	V70.3

Code 99395 should have been reported instead of 99394.

23.

CODING ERROR	PROCEDURE CODE	DIAGNOSIS CODE
e	66984	366.12
	69990-51	

Do not report code 69990-51 as a secondary procedure code. Code 66984 is a combination code reported for extracapsular cataract removal, microsurgery technique, and with insertion of intraocular lens prosthesis.

24. CODING ERROR	PROCEDURE CODE	DIAGNOSIS CODE
b	97001	438.2

Code 438.2 requires addition of a fifth digit to indicate which side was affected by hemiplegia. If this information is unknown, report 438.20 to indicate "unspecified side."

CHAPTER 11 Essential CMS-1500 Claim Instructions

ANSWERS TO EXERCISES

EXERCISE 11-1 Applying Optical Scanning Guidelines

1. GREEN JEFFERY L
2. 300 00
3. 12345 22 51
4. 123 456 7890
5. 123456789
6. Answers will vary but should be in MM DD YYYY format.

7.

8. 03 08 2000
9. Blank space in the upper left corner of the claim
10. Be sure all pin-fed borders are neatly removed and the individual claims are separated.
11. No handwritten information except signatures in Blocks 12, 13, and 31
12. Pica font and 10 characters per inch

EXERCISE 11-2 Entering Procedures in Block 24

24. A DATE(S) OF SERVICE From	To	B. PLACE OF SERVICE	C. EMG	D. PROCEDURES, SERVICES, OR SUPPLIES (Explain Unusual Circumstances) CPT/HCPCS	MODIFER	E. DIAGNOSIS POINTER	F. $ CHARGES	G. DAYS OR UNITS	H. EPSDT Family Plan	I. ID. QUAL.	J. RENDERING PROVIDER ID. #
1	10 10 YYYY			99213			65 00	1		NPI	
2	10 10 YYYY			99232			90 00	2		NPI	
3	10 12 YYYY			99231			35 00	1		NPI	
4	10 15 YYYY			72170			150 00	1		NPI	
5	11 09 YYYY			47600			900 00	1		NPI	
6	11 09 YYYY			29871	51		500 00	1		NPI	

EXERCISE 11-3 Completing Block 33

1. Goodmedicine Clinic
2. Dr. Blank
3. Dr. Jones PA

ANSWERS TO REVIEW

1. a		6. d	
2. a		7. d	
3. c		8. a	
4. c		9. b	
5. a		10. c	

CHAPTER 12 Commercial Insurance

ANSWERS TO EXERCISES

EXERCISES 12-1 and 12-2

Students should manually complete the commercial case studies in the order provided in the text. The commercial insurance case studies can also be entered using the Self Study mode of the CD-ROM program, which provides immediate feedback every time the enter key is struck.

Additional hints for using the CD-ROM can be found in the Preface of the text, as well as in the Resources section of the CD.

The completed claims can be found in Figures 12-4 and 12-5 of the textbook.

ANSWERS TO REVIEW

1.	a	**9.**	a
2.	c	**10.**	b
3.	b	**11.**	d
4.	a	**12.**	c
5.	d	**13.**	d
6.	b	**14.**	a
7.	d	**15.**	b
8.	a		

CHAPTER 13 Blue Cross Blue Shield

ANSWERS TO EXERCISES

EXERCISES 13-1 and 13-2 Completing the Mary S. Patient BCBS CMS-1500 Claim; Filing a Claim When a Patient Has Two BCBS Policies

The completed Mary S. Patient CMS-1500 claims can be found in Figures 13-7 and 13-8 of the textbook.

EXERCISE 13-3 Filing BCBS Secondary Claims

The completed Janet B. Cross CMS-1500 secondary claim can be found in Figure 13-10 of the textbook.

ANSWERS TO REVIEW

1.	b	**6.**	d
2.	c	**7.**	a
3.	b	**8.**	b
4.	a	**9.**	b
5.	a	**10.**	d

CHAPTER 14 Medicare

ANSWERS TO EXERCISES

EXERCISE 14-1 Medicare as Secondary Payer

1. **Billing order is:** The hospital plan can be billed at any time. The large group plan is primary, Medicare is secondary. Medigap is billed on the same CMS-1500 claim form as Medicare, if the provider participates in Medicare.

2. **Billing order is:** The liability plan is billed first. The other plans will not be billed unless the claim is refused by the liability company. If refused, the large group is primary, Medicare secondary, and the retirement plan billing will be electronically transferred by Medicare or billed last by the provider.

3. **Billing order is:** Cancer policy is billed at any time. Medicare is primary, retirement is supplemental.

4. **Billing order is:** Patient's large group plan is primary, Medicare is secondary. Medigap is billed on the Medicare claim if the provider is a PAR. Spouse's plan is not billed because there is no mention that the patient is covered by this plan. Small groups are also never primary to Medicare.

5. **Billing order is:** Medicare is primary. The employer plan has fewer than 100 employees.

EXERCISE 14-2 Completing the Mary S. Patient Medicare Primary CMS-1500 Claim

The completed Mary S. Patient primary Medicare CMS-1500 claim can be found in Figure 14-9 of the textbook.

EXERCISE 14-3 Medicare and Medigap Claims Processing

The completed John Q. Public Medicare/Medigap CMS-1500 claim can be found in Figure 14-10 of the textbook.

EXERCISE 14-4 Medicare–Medicaid Crossover Claims Processing

The completed Mary S. Patient Medicare/Medicaid crossover CMS-1500 claim can be found in Figure 14-11 of the textbook.

EXERCISE 14-5 Medicare Secondary Claims Processing

The completed Jack L. Neely MSP CMS-1500 claim can be found in Figure 14-13 of the textbook.

ANSWERS TO REVIEW

1.	b	**6.**	b
2.	a	**7.**	b
3.	a	**8.**	a
4.	c	**9.**	b
5.	b	**10.**	a

CHAPTER 15 Medicaid

ANSWERS TO EXERCISES

EXERCISE 15-1 Medicaid CMS-1500 Claims Processing

The completed Mary S. Patient primary Medicaid CMS-1500 claim form can be found in Figure 15-6 of the textbook.

ANSWERS TO REVIEW

1.	a	**6.**	a
2.	b	**7.**	a
3.	d	**8.**	c
4.	b	**9.**	c
5.	b	**10.**	a

CHAPTER 16 TRICARE

ANSWERS TO EXERCISES

EXERCISE 16-1 TRICARE CMS-1500 Claim

The completed Mary S. Patient primary TRICARE CMS-1500 claim can be found in Figure 16-5 of the textbook.

EXERCISE 16-2 Completion of TRICARE Secondary CMS-1500 Claim

The completed John R. Neely CMS-1500 secondary TRICARE claim can be found in Figure 16-7 of the textbook.

ANSWERS TO REVIEW

1. d	**6.** b
2. b	**7.** c
3. d	**8.** c
4. a	**9.** a
5. d	**10.** a

CHAPTER 17 Workers' Compensation

ANSWERS TO EXERCISES

EXERCISE 17-1 CMS-1500 Claims Completion

The completed Mary S. Patient CMS-1500 claim can be found in Figure 17-6 of the textbook.

ANSWERS TO REVIEW

1. d	**6.** b
2. c	**7.** d
3. a	**8.** a
4. d	**9.** a
5. b	**10.** b

SECTION III Chapter Exams and Answer Keys to Chapter Exams

EXAM–CHAPTER 1

Student Name _____

Multiple Choice

Circle the most appropriate response.

1. The concept that every procedure or service reported to a third-party payer must be linked to a condition that justifies the procedure or service is called medical
    a. condition.
    b. management.
    c. necessity.
    d. procedure.

2. Which codes supplement procedures, services, and supplies not classified in CPT?
    a. DSM
    b. HCPCS level II
    c. ICD
    d. modifiers

3. Which is a typical responsibility of a health insurance specialist?
    a. Assisting physicians with patient care
    b. Correcting claims processing errors
    c. Developing charges for procedures/services
    d. Establishing insurance program rules

4. Which organization offers a payer certification exam?
    a. AAPC
    b. AHIMA
    c. CMS
    d. NEBA

5. The mutual exchange of information between providers and payers is called electronic
    a. coding.
    b. data interchange.
    c. medical record.
    d. telemedicine.

6. Which is a reason an employer would contract with a managed care plan?
    a. Control the high costs associated with employee health care insurance
    b. Optimize employees' and dependents' access to medical care
    c. Require the employee to pay for services not considered necessary
    d. Shift the cost of health care insurance to employees

7. The abbreviation for the Healthcare Common Procedure Coding System is
    a. HCCPCS.
    b. HCPCS.
    c. HCPXCS.
    d. HPCS.

8. The document submitted by a provider to a third-party payer for the purpose of requesting reimbursement for services provided is a(n)
    a. bill.
    b. claim.
    c. edit.
    d. submission.

9. The process of classifying diagnoses, procedures, and services is called
    a. abstracting.
    b. billing.
    c. coding.
    d. posting.

10. The process of taking and passing credentialing exams (e.g., CPC) is called professional
    a. bonding.
    b. certification.
    c. indemnification.
    d. qualification.

11. Which coding system is used for reporting procedures and services in physician offices?

    a. CDT   c. DSM

    b. CPT   d. ICD-9-CM

12. Diagnoses are coded according to

    a. CMS.   c. HCPCS.

    b. CPT.   d. ICD-9-CM.

13. If reimbursement of a claim by a practice is not accepted by the payer, the claim can be

    a. appealed.   c. repealed.

    b. increased.   d. reversed.

14. Electronic data interchange is achieved by using

    a. a standardized, machine-readable format.   c. clerks who manually review claims.

    b. dial-up Internet connections only.   d. the same software by every payer.

15. Rules that govern the conduct of members of a profession are called

    a. ethics.   c. morals.

    b. laws.   d. regulations.

16. The notice received by a provider from a payer that contains payment information for a claim is the

    a. explanation of benefits.   c. remittance advice.

    b. letter of agreement.   d. statement of account.

17. A coding consultant who is paid by a practice to assist the coding and billing staff would most likely be classified as a(n)

    a. casual employee.   c. independent contractor.

    b. free agent.   d. *per diem* employee.

18. Which is another name for professional liability insurance?

    a. disability insurance   c. medical malpractice insurance

    b. errors and omissions insurance   d. workers' compensation insurance

19. Physician offices should bond employees who have which responsibility?

    a. clinical   c. financial

    b. coding   d. privacy

20. Which term is another word for stealing money?

    a. embezzling   c. securing

    b. guaranteeing   d. transferring

21. A customer was severely injured in a grocery store when a pallet of soda cans toppled onto him. Which insurance would be billed for the customer's medical care?
    a. liability
    b. medical malpractice
    c. property
    d. workers' compensation

22. Which type of insurance provides financial and medical benefits for an injured employee?
    a. errors and omissions
    b. personal liability
    c. private health
    d. worker's compensation

23. Claims assistance professionals who work directly for patients can achieve certification by successfully passing an exam offered by which professional association?
    a. AAPC
    b. AHIMA
    c. AMBA
    d. NEBA

24. The study of the body and its structures is
    a. anatomy.
    b. pathophysiology.
    c. pharmacology.
    d. physiology.

25. The study of disease processes and abnormalities of the body is
    a. anatomy.
    b. pathophysiology.
    c. pharmacology.
    d. physiology.

26. A claim was submitted for a left shoulder x-ray on an elderly patient, and the diagnosis reported on the claim was urinary tract infection. The claim was rejected because
    a. medical necessity was not met.
    b. the payer requires assignment of benefits.
    c. privacy standards were not met.
    d. the provider did not accept assignment.

27. A patient was diagnosed with asthma. Which coding system is used to report this condition on the claim?
    a. CPT
    b. DSM
    c. HCPCS level II
    d. ICD-9-CM

ANSWER KEY TO EXAM–CHAPTER 1

1. c	8. b	15. a	22. d
2. b	9. c	16. c	23. d
3. b	10. b	17. c	24. a
4. d	11. b	18. b	25. b
5. b	12. d	19. c	26. a
6. a	13. a	20. a	27. d
7. b	14. a	21. a	

EXAM—CHAPTER 2

Student Name _____

Multiple Choice

Circle the most appropriate response.

1. The type of health care that helps individuals avoid health and injury problems is
   a. acute.
   b. chronic.
   c. preventive.
   d. rehabilitative.

2. Payment for medical treatment of an injury will be denied by the liability payer if
   a. it is determined that there was no third-party negligence.
   b. the incident is not covered by the injured party's liability contract.
   c. the injured party did not file the claim with the liability payer first.
   d. the provider pays first.

3. During World War II, the government restricted the wages employers could offer employees; thus, employers began offering which of the following to their employees?
   a. benefits
   b. bonuses
   c. promotions
   d. vacations

4. When three or more doctors deliver health care and make joint use of equipment, supplies, and personnel, this is called a(n)
   a. association.
   b. bureau.
   c. group practice.
   d. partnership.

5. Which coding system is used to report procedures and services on physician office insurance claims?
   a. CDT
   b. CPT
   c. DSM
   d. ICD-9-CM

6. Which is a government-sponsored health program that provides benefits to indigent patients?
   a. CHAMPVA
   b. Medicaid
   c. Medicare
   d. TRICARE

7. The specified amount of annual out-of-pocket expenses for covered health care services that the insured must pay annually for health care is called the
   a. coinsurance.
   b. copayment.
   c. deductible.
   d. premium.

8. The standard claim developed by CMS and used to report procedures and services delivered by physicians is called the
   a. CMS-1450.
   b. CMS-1500.
   c. HCFA-1450.
   d. UB-04.

9. The World Health Organization originally developed which coding system in 1948?
   a. CPT
   b. HCPCS
   c. ICD
   d. ICD-9-CM

10. The Act passed in 1997 that resulted in the development of coding compliance programs by the federal government is the
    a. BBA.
    b. CLIA.
    c. COBRA.
    d. HIPAA.

11. The Act passed in 1996 that has had a great impact on confidentiality, electronic information transmission, and standardization is the
    a. BBA.
    b. CLIA.
    c. COBRA.
    d. HIPAA.

12. Which automobile insurance policy coverage can provide for expenses such as lost earnings, rehabilitation, and child care expenses, regardless of fault?
    a. collision
    b. comprehensive
    c. liability
    d. personal injury protection

13. The ambulatory payment classification prospective payment system is used to reimburse claims for what services?
    a. inpatient
    b. nursing facility
    c. outpatient
    d. rehabilitation

14. The percentage of costs a patient shares with the health plan is the
    a. coinsurance.
    b. copayment.
    c. deductible.
    d. premium.

15. Disability insurance typically provides what type of compensation to the injured person?
    a. financial
    b. financial and health care
    c. health care
    d. pain and suffering

16. To file a claim with a liability payer, which may serve as a substitute for an insurance claim?
    a. explanation of benefits
    b. patient billing statement
    c. remittance advice
    d. summary of benefits

17. What term describes the contractual right of a third-party payer to recover health care expenses from a liable party?
    a. compensation
    b. denial
    c. lien
    d. subrogation

18. What is the purpose of third-party administrators (TPAs)?
    a. Administer health care plans and process claims
    b. Correct mistakes on claims and resubmit claims for payment
    c. Develop and institute health care regulations
    d. Pay providers on behalf of the federal government

19. The federal legislation passed in 1981 that expanded the Medicare and Medicaid programs was
    a. ERISA.
    b. HIPAA.
    c. OBRA.
    d. TEFRA.

20. Which three components constitute the RBRVS payment system?
    a. fee schedule, practice expense, and malpractice expense
    b. physician work, practice expense, and geographical location
    c. physician work, practice expense, and malpractice insurance expense
    d. practice expense, malpractice insurance expense, and liability insurance expense

21. In which year was the first recognized commercial insurance company policy developed in the United States?
    a. 1860
    b. 1920
    c. 1939
    d. 1946

22. An official from Baylor University in Dallas developed what is recognized now as the first
_____ policy.

a. Blue Cross

b. disability

c. liability

d. Medicare

23. Insurance that is available through employers, labor unions, consumer health cooperatives, and other organizations is

a. group health insurance.

b. major medical insurance.

c. private insurance.

d. risk pool insurance.

24. The type of insurance that provides coverage for catastrophic or prolonged illnesses and injuries is

a. group health.

b. major medical.

c. private.

d. workers' compensation.

25. A provider's list of predetermined payments for health care services to patients is known as the

a. chargemaster.

b. coinsurance.

c. fee schedule.

d. relative value.

ANSWER KEY TO EXAM–CHAPTER 2

1. c	**8.** b	**15.** a	**22.** a
2. a	**9.** c	**16.** b	**23.** a
3. a	**10.** a	**17.** d	**24.** b
4. c	**11.** d	**18.** a	**25.** c
5. b	**12.** d	**19.** c	
6. b	**13.** c	**20.** c	
7. c	**14.** a	**21.** a	

EXAM—CHAPTER 3

Student Name _____

Multiple Choice

Circle the most appropriate response.

1. Managed care in the United States has been operational
   a. for the past 10 years.
   b. for nearly a century.
   c. since 1979.
   d. since indemnity insurance was started.

2. In what year was Kaiser-Permanente created?
   a. 1929
   b. 1938
   c. 1954
   d. 1955

3. Which term describes the process of developing patient care plans for the coordination and provision of care for complicated cases in a cost-effective manner?
   a. case management
   b. discharge planning
   c. preadmission review
   d. quality assurance

4. The National Committee on Quality Assurance is a nonprofit organization that
   a. determines the need for the addition, deletion, or revision of CPT codes.
   b. evaluates and accredits all types of health care entities and facilities.
   c. measures and evaluates the quality of an HMO's performance.
   d. provides utilization review services to physician offices.

5. Employees and dependents who join a managed care plan are called
   a. beneficiaries.
   b. customers.
   c. enlisted.
   d. subscribers.

6. Mandates are
   a. directives.
   b. laws.
   c. regulations.
   d. standards.

7. The review for appropriateness and necessity of care provided to patients, prior to the administration of care or retrospectively, is called
   a. preadmission review.
   b. preauthorization.
   c. precertification.
   d. utilization management.

8. Which type of HMO offers subscribers health care services by physicians who remain in their individual office setting?
   a. closed panel
   b. independent practice association
   c. network model
   d. staff model

9. Which act or amendment established an employee's right to continue health care coverage beyond a scheduled benefit termination date?
   a. COBRA of 1985
   b. ERISA
   c. MMA
   d. TEFRA

10. The 1988 amendment to the HMO Act of 1973 added which provision?

    a. Federally qualified HMOs could permit members to occasionally use non-HMO providers and be partially reimbursed.

    b. Savings accounts were formed so subscribers could use them to help offset the costs of copayments and coinsurance.

    c. Standards were created to assess managed care systems in terms of membership, utilization, quality, access, and financial indicators.

    d. The NCQA was formed by the Department of Health and Human Services to generate report cards for HMOs.

11. A *risk contract* is defined as an arrangement among health care providers

    a. stating that the HMO can provide services to Medicare beneficiaries only.

    b. that allows higher payments to the HMO if they treat Medicare beneficiaries.

    c. to make available capitated health care services to Medicare beneficiaries.

    d. to offer fee-for-service health care services to Medicare beneficiaries.

12. If an HMO has met the federal standards established in the HMO Act of 1973, the HMO can be

    a. federally qualified.

    b. qualified to accept subscribers without any specific membership requirements.

    c. qualified to set its own fees for Medicare patients.

    d. state qualified.

13. If a plan allows enrollees to seek care from non-network providers, what effect will this have on the enrollee who sees a non-network provider? The enrollee will:

    a. be limited to one visit per year.

    b. pay higher out-of-pocket costs.

    c. receive poor quality health care.

    d. seek care outside his or her geographic area.

14. Illegal wording in a managed care contract that prohibits a provider from discussing all possible treatment options with a patient is a _____ clause.

    a. gag

    b. incentive

    c. limit

    d. prohibit

15. Which type of managed care plan provides benefits to subscribers if they receive services only from network providers?

    a. exclusive provider organization

    b. health maintenance organization

    c. integrated delivery system

    d. preferred provider organization

16. A medical group that has been specially formed to serve a particular HMO is part of what type of HMO?

    a. closed panel

    b. direct contract model

    c. network model

    d. open panel

17. The newly emerging health plan that focuses on asking employees to be more responsible for health care decisions and cost-sharing is the _____ health plan.

    a. consumer-directed

    b. customer-directed

    c. defined-benefit

    d. employer-directed

18. Which plan was considered the earliest example of an independent practice association?

    a. American Medical Association
    b. Great Plains Regional Medical Center
    c. Kaiser Foundation Health Plan
    d. San Joaquin Medical Foundation

19. When a provider receives a fixed amount to provide only the care that an individual needs from that provider, this is known as a _____ payment.

    a. capitation
    b. fixed
    c. premium
    d. sub-capitation

20. When a number of people are grouped for insurance purposes, this is known as a(n)

    a. adverse selection.
    b. insurance pool.
    c. member group.
    d. risk pool.

21. A triple option plan can also be known as a cafeteria plan or a

    a. flexible benefit plan.
    b. flexible spending plan.
    c. health benefit plan.
    d. health spending plan.

22. Which combines health care delivery with financing of services provided?

    a. case management
    b. coordination of benefits
    c. managed care
    d. quality assurance

23. Which 2003 legislation allows tax deductions for amounts contributed to a health savings account?

    a. Balanced Budget Act (BBA)
    b. Health Insurance Portability and Accountability Act (HIPAA)
    c. Health Maintenance Organization Assistance Act (HMO Act)
    d. Medicare Modernization Act (MMA)

24. Managed care plans can contract with an outside vendor to establish and maintain a utilization management program. The plan can contract with a TPA or with a

    a. health maintenance organization.
    b. managed care organization.
    c. quality assurance organization.
    d. utilization review organization.

25. The voluntary process that a health care facility or organization undergoes to demonstrate that it has met requirements beyond those required by law is called

    a. accreditation.
    b. certification.
    c. regulation.
    d. standardization.

ANSWER KEY TO EXAM–CHAPTER 3

1. b	**8.** b	**15.** a	**22.** c
2. d	**9.** a	**16.** a	**23.** d
3. a	**10.** a	**17.** a	**24.** d
4. c	**11.** c	**18.** d	**25.** a
5. d	**12.** a	**19.** d	
6. b	**13.** b	**20.** d	
7. d	**14.** a	**21.** a	

EXAM—CHAPTER 4

Student Name _____

Multiple Choice

Circle the most appropriate response.

1. The patient's financial record, which can be found in automated or manual format, is the
   a. day sheet.
   b. encounter form.
   c. patient ledger.
   d. remittance advice.

2. The specified percentage of charges the patient must pay to the provider for each service received or for each visit is the
   a. coinsurance.
   b. copayment.
   c. deductible.
   d. premium.

3. The financial record source document used to record services rendered in a physician's office is the
   a. chargemaster.
   b. encounter form.
   c. patient ledger.
   d. remittance advice.

4. When the provider is required to receive as payment in full whatever amount the insurance reimburses for services, the provider is agreeing to
   a. accept assignment.
   b. assignment of benefits.
   c. authorize services.
   d. coordination of benefits.

5. Care rendered to a patient that was not properly approved (e.g., preapproved) by the insurance company is known as
   a. medical necessity.
   b. noncovered benefits.
   c. unapproved services.
   d. unauthorized services.

6. The maximum amount the payer will allow for each procedure or service, according to the patient's policy, is the
   a. allowed charge.
   b. chargemaster.
   c. denied charge.
   d. maximum charge.

7. Approximately how many insurance claims are filed each year?
   a. 100 million
   b. 600 million
   c. 5 billion
   d. more than 6 billion

8. The development of a claim begins at the
   a. clearinghouse.
   b. patient's place of employment.
   c. payer's office.
   d. provider's office.

9. In the development of a claim, data transmitted electronically or manually to payers or clearinghouses for processing is called claims
   a. adjudication.
   b. payment.
   c. processing.
   d. submission.

10. According to the national standards mandated by HIPAA for the electronic exchange of administrative and financial care transactions, which would be a covered entity?
    a. managed care organization
    b. multispecialty group practice that conducts only paper-based transactions
    c. provider who conducts only paper-based transactions
    d. small, self-administered health plan

11. The private, nonprofit organization that administers and coordinates the U.S. private-sector voluntary standardization system is
    a. ANSI.
    b. CMS.
    c. ERISA.
    d. HIPAA.

12. If a claim is found to contain all the data elements required for processing, it is known as a _____ claim.
    a. clean
    b. processed
    c. suspended
    d. valid

13. A procedure reported on a claim that is not included on the master benefit list will result in _____ of the claim.
    a. aging
    b. denial
    c. resubmission
    d. suspension

14. The remittance advice has what name in the Medicare program?
    a. Encounter Form
    b. Explanation of Benefits
    c. Medicare Summary Notice
    d. Provider Remittance Notice

15. The person responsible for paying the charges for services rendered by the provider is the
    a. beneficiary.
    b. guarantor.
    c. guardian.
    d. subscriber.

16. Which document is used to generate the patient's financial and medical record?
    a. encounter form
    b. patient insurance card
    c. patient ledger
    d. patient registration form

17. The rule stating that the policyholder whose birth month and day occur earlier in the calendar year holds the primary policy for dependent children is the _____ rule.
    a. birthday
    b. gender
    c. policy
    d. primary

18. To save the expense of mailing invoices to patients, the office may ask the patient to
    a. come back on payday and pay the patient's portion of the bill.
    b. leave a self-addressed, stamped envelope with the office.
    c. pay the patient's portion of the bill before treatment or before the patient leaves the office.
    d. set up an electronic funds transfer account.

19. How long must providers retain copies of government insurance claims?
    a. 30 days
    b. one year
    c. seven years
    d. permanently

20. What type of claim is generated for providers who do not accept assignment?
    a. delinquent
    b. rejected
    c. suspended
    d. unassigned

21. The process of submitting multiple CPT codes when one code should be submitted is
    a. downcoding
    b. segmenting
    c. unbundling
    d. upcoding

22. The insurance industry is regulated by whom?
    a. American Medical Association
    b. Centers for Medicare and Medicaid Services
    c. federal government
    d. individual states

23. The development of a claim typically consists of how many stages?

    a. four

    b. five

    c. seven

    d. six

24. Providers can communicate directly with payers by use of technology that emulates a system connection, known as a(n)

    a. dial-up connection.

    b. extranet.

    c. facsimile.

    d. magnetic tape.

25. When a provider performs a procedure for which no CPT or HCPCS level II code is available, what must be provided to the payer?

    a. additional ICD-9-CM codes

    b. patient's medical record

    c. practice's financial record

    d. supporting documentation

ANSWER KEY TO EXAM—CHAPTER 4

1. c	8. d	15. b	22. d
2. a	9. d	16. d	23. a
3. b	10. a	17. a	24. b
4. a	11. a	18. c	25. d
5. d	12. a	19. c	
6. a	13. b	20. d	
7. d	14. d	21. c	

EXAM–CHAPTER 5

Student Name _____

Multiple Choice

Circle the most appropriate response.

1. Federal and state statutes are
   a. also known as common law.
   b. based on court decisions.
   c. guidelines written by CMS.
   d. passed by legislative bodies.

2. Which term describes guidelines written by administrative agencies (such as CMS) that are based on laws passed by legislative bodies?
   a. interrogatories
   b. regulations
   c. statutes
   d. subpoenas

3. Case law is based on court decisions that establish precedent, and is also called _____ law.
   a. common
   b. mandated
   c. regulatory
   d. statutory

4. Which is the legal newspaper published weekly by the National Archives and Records Administration of the federal government?
   a. *EDI Xchange*
   b. *Federal Register*
   c. *Medicare Report*
   d. *The Pulse of CMS*

5. When a patient signs a release of medical information at a physician's office, that release is generally considered to be valid
   a. for six months.
   b. for a single visit to the physician.
   c. for one year from the date entered on the form.
   d. until the patient changes insurance companies.

6. Breach of confidentiality can result from
   a. discussing patient health care information with unauthorized sources.
   b. discussing the patient's case in the business office.
   c. sending medical information to non-health care entities with the patient's consent.
   d. sending patient health care information to the patient's insurance company.

7. Which term describes an individual's right to keep health care information from being disclosed to others?
   a. confidentiality
   b. privacy
   c. privilege
   d. security

8. Practices that submit hard-copy insurance claims may ask patients to sign which block on the CMS-1500 claim?
   a. accept assignment
   b. insured's name
   c. release of medical information
   d. reserved for local use

9. The safekeeping of patient information by controlling access to hard-copy and computerized records is a form of
   a. administrative simplification.
   b. electronic data interchange.
   c. privacy standards.
   d. security management.

10. A person who is legally designated to be in charge of a patient's affairs when the patient is a minor or a legally incompetent adult is a
    a. beneficiary.
    b. dependent.
    c. guardian.
    d. representative.

11. Information that is converted to a secure language format for electronic transmission is _____ data.
    a. decrypted
    b. electronic
    c. encrypted
    d. secure

12. Which federal legislation was enacted in 1995 to restrict the referral of patients to organizations in which providers have a financial interest?
    a. Federal Anti-Kickback Law
    b. Hill-Burton Act
    c. HIPAA
    d. Stark II laws

13. Testimony under oath taken outside the court (e.g., at the provider's office) is a(n)
    a. deposition.
    b. interrogatory.
    c. precedent.
    d. subpoena.

14. An organization that contracts with CMS to process claims and perform program integrity tasks for Medicare Part A is known as a Medicare
    a. administrative contractor.
    b. carrier.
    c. clearinghouse.
    d. fiscal intermediary.

15. In which year was the False Claims Act originally passed?
    a. 1863
    b. 1906
    c. 1965
    d. 1986

16. Which act of legislation requires Medicare administrative contractors to attempt the collection of overpayments made under the Medicare or Medicaid programs?
    a. False Claims Act
    b. Federal Claims Collection Act
    c. Payment Error Prevention Program
    d. Utilization Review Act

17. The general term that describes excessive charges for services, equipment, or supplies is called
    a. abuse.
    b. fraud.
    c. unbundling.
    d. upcoding.

18. The recognized difference between fraud and abuse is the
    a. cost.
    b. intent.
    c. payer.
    d. timing.

19. When a Medicare provider commits fraud, which entity conducts the investigation?
    a. Centers for Medicare and Medicaid Services
    b. Medicare administrative contractor
    c. Office of the Inspector General
    d. U.S. Attorney General

20. A provider or beneficiary can receive a waiver of recovery of overpayment in which situation?

    a. The beneficiary was without fault with respect to the overpayment and recovery would cause financial hardship.

    b. The overpaid physician was found to be at fault, but the overpayment amount was nominal.

    c. The overpayment was discovered two years or more after the year of payment.

    d. The provider was not informed by the office manager that a demand letter had been received by the office.

21. As part of the administrative simplification provision of HIPAA, which of the following unique identifiers is assigned to third-party payers?

    a. National Health PlanID (PlanID)

    b. National Individual Identifier

    c. National Provider Identifier (NPI)

    d. National Standard Employer Identifier Number (EIN)

22. Which two classifications of patients are exempt from the required authorization for release of medical information to payers?

    a. Medicaid and Medicare   c. workers' compensation and Blue Cross

    b. Medicaid and workers' compensation   d. workers' compensation and Medicare

23. Special rules apply to the release of medical information for patients with which diagnosis listed?

    a. congestive heart failure   c. motor vehicle accident

    b. metastatic cancer   d. schizophrenia

24. What is the best way to verify the identity of a caller who is requesting medical information?

    a. Ask the caller to spell the patient's full name.

    b. Ask the caller to verify the patient's social security number.

    c. Inform the caller of the patient's diagnoses and have the caller confirm the diagnoses.

    d. Use the call-back method.

25. The purpose of the Correct Coding Initiative is to

    a. determine the skill level of the provider's coding staff.

    b. make it more difficult for the practice to earn a profit.

    c. reduce Medicare program expenditures.

    d. reduce the number of codes used on Medicare claims.

ANSWER KEY TO EXAM—CHAPTER 5

1. d	**8.** c	**15.** a	**22.** b
2. b	**9.** d	**16.** b	**23.** d
3. a	**10.** c	**17.** a	**24.** d
4. b	**11.** c	**18.** b	**25.** c
5. c	**12.** d	**19.** c	
6. a	**13.** a	**20.** a	
7. b	**14.** a	**21.** a	

EXAM—CHAPTER 6   Student Name _____

Multiple Choice

Circle the most appropriate response.

1. The ICD-9-CM system classifies
   - a. morbidity.
   - b. mortality data.
   - c. provider services.
   - d. supplies and services.

2. Qualified diagnoses are a necessary part of the patient's hospital and office record; however, physician offices are required to report
   - a. qualified diagnoses for inpatients and outpatients.
   - b. qualified diagnoses related to outpatient procedures.
   - c. signs and symptoms in addition to qualified diagnoses.
   - d. signs and symptoms instead of qualified diagnoses.

3. ICD-9-CM Supplemental Classifications classify
   - a. factors influencing health status.
   - b. hypertension.
   - c. infectious organisms.
   - d. neoplasms.

4. In ICD-9-CM, italicized codes signify that
   - a. a fifth digit must be added to the code number for the diagnosis.
   - b. more than one code is required to fully describe a diagnosis.
   - c. the italicized code is reported first when listing multiple diagnoses.
   - d. the provider should be asked to clarify the diagnosis.

5. The ICD-9-CM Convention, "Code First Underlying Condition," means that the
   - a. cause of the condition must be coded and reported before the manifestation code.
   - b. code is to be assigned for synonyms or similar conditions.
   - c. condition code was enclosed in slanted square brackets in Volume II.
   - d. diagnosis is not elsewhere classifiable or not otherwise specified.

6. In the diagnosis "acute myocardial infarction," which is the main term to be located in the ICD-9-CM *Index to Diseases?*
   - a. acute
   - b. heart
   - c. infarction
   - d. myocardial

7. The diagnostic statement "urinary tract infection due to *E. coli*" requires_____code(s) to be assigned.
   - a. one
   - b. two
   - c. three
   - d. four

8. ICD-9-CM (disease) category codes contain_____digits.
   - a. two
   - b. three
   - c. four
   - d. five

9. Main terms in the ICD-9-CM alphabetic index are in
   - a. boldface.
   - b. italics.
   - c. parentheses.
   - d. upper case.

10. ICD-9-CM (disease) subclassification codes contain_____digits.
    - a. two
    - b. three
    - c. four
    - d. five

11. The reporting of diagnosis codes on the CMS-1500 claim is necessary to demonstrate
    a. accuracy of the procedure code.
    b. higher payment.
    c. medical necessity.
    d. quality of care.

12. The diagnosis that is the most significant condition for which procedures/services were provided is the
    a. first-listed diagnosis.
    b. primary diagnosis.
    c. principal diagnosis.
    d. principal procedure.

13. Which of the following is considered a qualified diagnosis?
    a. carpal tunnel syndrome
    b. congestive heart failure
    c. rule out myocardial infarction
    d. type II diabetes mellitus

14. Diabetic neuropathy is an example of a(n)
    a. comorbidity.
    b. eponym.
    c. manifestation.
    d. sequela.

15. Which convention is used to display a series of terms that can modify the statement to its right?
    a. braces
    b. brackets
    c. colon
    d. parentheses

Coding

Circle the most appropriate response.

16. Urinary tract infection due to *E. coli*
    a. 041.4
    b. 041.4, 599.0
    c. 599.0
    d. 599.0, 041.4

17. Diabetic cataract
    a. 250.50
    b. 250.50, 366.41
    c. 366.41
    d. 366.41, 250.50

18. Hemiplegia resulting from cerebrovascular accident that occurred one year ago
    a. 342.90
    b. 344.89
    c. 436
    d. 438.20

19. Sore throat; rule out strep throat (patient treated in physician's office)
    a. 034.0
    b. 034.0, 462
    c. 462
    d. 462, 034.0

20. Metastatic osteosarcoma of the lung. Lung cancer was treated.
    a. 170.9
    b. 170.9, 197.0
    c. 197.0
    d. 197.0, 170.9

21. HIV-positive
    a. 042
    b. 042, V08
    c. 079.53
    d. V08

22. Marble lodged in right nostril
    a. 508.9
    b. 756.52
    c. 782.61
    d. 932

23. Facial laceration
    a. 873.40
    b. 873.49
    c. 873.50
    d. 873.59

24. Well-child visit
    a. V20.2
    b. V21.0
    c. V61.20
    d. V70.0

25. Annual physical examination
    a. V57.1
    b. V67.9
    c. V69.0
    d. V70.0

ANSWER KEY TO EXAM—CHAPTER 6

1. a	8. b	15. a	22. d
2. d	9. a	16. d	23. a
3. a	10. d	17. b	24. a
4. b	11. c	18. d	25. d
5. a	12. a	19. c	
6. c	13. c	20. d	
7. b	14. c	21. d	

EXAM—CHAPTER 7   Student Name _____

Multiple Choice

Circle the most appropriate response.

1. CPT-4 is published annually by
   a. AMA.   c. WHO.
   b. CMS.   d. Medicare.

2. The hospital assigns CPT codes to report
   a. inpatient ancillary services.   c. inpatient surgical procedures.
   b. inpatient and outpatient surgery.   d. outpatient services and procedures.

3. CPT Category I contains _____ sections.
   a. four   c. six
   b. five   d. seven

4. When reporting CPT codes on the CMS-1500 claim, medical necessity is proven by
   a. attaching a special report to the CMS-1500 claim.
   b. linking the CPT code to its ICD-9-CM counterpart.
   c. reporting ICD-9-CM codes for the patient's condition.
   d. sequencing CPT codes in a logical, chronological order.

5. New CPT codes go into effect
   a. twice each year, on January 1 and July 1.   c. once each year, on October 1.
   b. twice each year, on October 1 and April 1.   d. once each year, on December 1.

6. CPT Appendix A contains information about
   a. deleted codes.   c. new code descriptions.
   b. modifiers.   d. revised codes.

7. Modifiers are reported to
   a. alter or change the meaning of the code reported on the CMS-1500 claim.
   b. decrease the reimbursement amount to be processed by the payer.
   c. increase the reimbursement amount to be processed by the payer.
   d. indicate an alteration in the description of the procedure service performed.

8. A black triangle located to the left of a CPT code indicates that the code
   a. has been deleted and should not be used.
   b. has been revised from previous CPT publications.
   c. has special rules that apply to its use.
   d. is new to this edition of CPT.

9. A bullet or black dot located to the left of a CPT code indicates
   a. a deleted CPT code that should not be used.
   b. a new, never previously published CPT code.
   c. a revised CPT code from an earlier publication.
   d. that special rules apply to the use of this code.

10. CPT index terms that are printed in boldface are called
    a. descriptors.   c. main terms.
    b. essential modifiers.   d. subterms.

11. To save space in the CPT index when referencing subterms, the practice of _____ words is used.
    a. abbreviated
    b. boldfaced
    c. inferred
    d. italicized

12. When coding fracture treatments, the term *manipulation* is used the same as the word
    a. exploration.
    b. fixation.
    c. reduction.
    d. splinting.

13. Critical care services codes are based on the
    a. length of time the patient is in the critical care unit.
    b. number of services provided to the patient.
    c. total number of consecutive days the physician cares for the patient.
    d. total time a physician spends in constant attendance with the patient.

14. Prolonged services codes are assigned in addition to other E/M services when treatment exceeds the time included in the CPT description by _____ minutes.
    a. 10
    b. 15
    c. 20
    d. 30

15. Which type of code can be used for a physician who is required to spend a prolonged period of time without patient contact waiting for an event to occur that will require the physician's services?
    a. case management services
    b. physician standby services
    c. preventive medicine services
    d. prolonged services

Coding

Circle the most appropriate response.

16. Initial office visit for a patient with left knee pain. Detailed history and examination was documented, along with low-complexity medical decision making.
    a. 99202
    b. 99203
    c. 99204
    d. 99213

17. 45-year-old patient seen for annual physical examination by his physician.
    a. 99368
    b. 99412
    c. 99386
    d. 99396

18. Anesthesia administered for vaginal hysterectomy. The patient is a healthy 55-year-old woman.
    a. 00944-P1
    b. 00944-P2
    c. 58552-P1
    d. 58200-P2

19. Excision of 1.0-cm malignant lesion of the nose, with simple closure.
  a. 11440
  b. 11601
  c. 11621
  d. 11641

20. Closed reduction of humeral shaft fracture, with skeletal traction.
  a. 23600
  b. 23625
  c. 24500
  d. 24505

21. Thyroid scan, with uptake (single determination).
  a. 78000
  b. 78001
  c. 78003
  d. 78006

22. Lipid panel, performed by outside lab.
  a. 80061-90
  b. 82465-90, 83718-90, 84478-90
  c. 83721-90
  d. 83718-90

23. Surgical pathology, gallbladder
  a. 88300
  b. 88302
  c. 88304
  d. 88305

24. DTP vaccine, intramuscular.
  a. 90471
  b. 90471, 90472, 90701
  c. 90471, 90701
  d. 90701

25. Chemotherapy administration, intravenous, push technique, 45 minutes.
  a. 96409, 96413-51
  b. 96409
  c. 96413
  d. 96411
  (CPT codes 96409, 96411, and 96416 were added in 2006.)

ANSWER KEY TO EXAM—CHAPTER 7

1. a	**8.** b	**15.** b	**22.** a
2. d	**9.** b	**16.** b	**23.** c
3. c	**10.** c	**17.** d	**24.** c
4. b	**11.** c	**18.** a	**25.** b
5. a	**12.** c	**19.** d	
6. b	**13.** d	**20.** d	
7. d	**14.** d	**21.** d	

EXAM–CHAPTER 8   Student Name _____

Multiple Choice

Circle the most appropriate response.

1. HCPCS is a multilevel coding system that contains _____ levels.

   a. one   c. three

   b. two   d. four

2. Which resources should be referenced when determining the potential for Medicare reimbursement?

   a. CPT coding manual

   b. HCPCS coding manual

   c. ICD-9-CM coding manual

   d. Medicare Carriers Manual and Coverage Issues Manual

3. Level II HCPCS codes are created by the

   a. AMA.   c. DMERCs.

   b. CMS.   d. MACs.

4. Level I HCPCS codes are created by the

   a. AMA.   c. DMERCs.

   b. CMS.   d. MACs.

5. HCPCS national codes include many codes for equipment, services, procedures, supplies, injectables, prosthetics, and orthotics; CPT has just one code for supplies. The CPT code is

   a. 99070.   c. 99199.

   b. 99080.   d. 99600.

6. HCPCS "J codes" classify medications according to

   a. generic or chemical name of drug, route of administration, and dosage.

   b. generic or chemical name of drug, approval for Medicare coverage, and cost.

   c. product name of drug, method of delivery, and cost.

   d. product name of drug, route of administration, and dosage.

7. The purpose of the creation of HCPCS codes was to furnish health care providers with a:

   a. mandate to use electronic claims submission.

   b. method for obtaining higher reimbursement from Medicare.

   c. standardized language for reporting professional services, procedures, supplies, and equipment.

   d. standardized way of reporting inpatient and outpatient diagnoses.

8. Which statement is true of durable medical equipment?

   a. It can withstand repeated use.

   b. It is primarily used to serve a purpose of convenience.

   c. It is routinely purchased by individuals who are not suffering from an illness or injury.

   d. It is used by the patient in an outpatient rehabilitation facility.

9. Which special codes allow payers the flexibility of establishing codes if they are needed before the next January 1 annual update?

   a. level III   c. permanent

   b. miscellaneous   d. temporary

10. Which organization is responsible for the modification, deletion, or addition of dental codes?
    a. American Dental Association
    b. American Medical Association
    c. Centers for Medicare and Medicaid Services
    d. HCPCS National Panel

11. Temporary additional payments over and above the OPPS payment made for certain innovative medical devices, drugs, and biologicals provided to Medicare beneficiaries are known as _____ payments.
    a. pass-through
    b. temporary pass-through
    c. transitional additional
    d. transitional pass-through

12. Q codes are used
    a. to identify services that would not ordinarily be assigned a CPT code (e.g., drugs, biologicals, and other types of medical equipment or services).
    b. to identify professional health care procedures and services that do not have codes identified in CPT.
    c. by state Medicaid agencies when no HCPCS level II permanent codes exist but are needed to administer the Medicaid program.
    d. by regional MACs when existing permanent national codes do not include codes needed to implement a regional MAC medical review coverage policy.

13. Modifiers are used with HCPCS codes to
    a. change the original description of the service, procedure, or supply item.
    b. decrease payment from Medicare.
    c. increase payment from Medicare.
    d. provide additional information regarding the product or service identified.

14. HCPCS level II modifiers consist of two characters that are
    a. alphabetic only.
    b. alphabetic or alphanumeric.
    c. alphanumeric only.
    d. one letter and one symbol.

15. Which organization is responsible for providing suppliers and manufacturers with assistance in determining HCPCS codes to be used?
    a. American Medical Association
    b. Centers for Medicare and Medicaid Services
    c. durable medical equipment, prosthetic, and orthotic supplies dealers
    d. statistical analysis Medicare administrative contractor

Coding

Circle the most appropriate response.

16. Surgical stocking, above knee (patient underwent left knee arthroscopy).
    a. A4490
    b. A4495
    c. A4500
    d. A4510

17. Standard wheelchair with fixed full-length arms and fixed detachable foot rests.
    a. E1130
    b. E1140
    c. E1150
    d. E1160

18. Behavioral health screening to determine eligibility for admission to treatment program.
    a. H0002
    b. H0003
    c. H0004
    d. H0005

19. Tetracycline, 200 mg injection.
    a. J0120
    b. J0900
    c. J1080
    d. J3140

20. Thoracic hip-knee-ankle orthosis (THKAO) standing frame.
    a. L1499
    b. L1500
    c. L1510
    d. L1520

21. Prolotherapy.
    a. D3230
    b. E0691
    c. M0076
    d. P2031

22. Screening Pap smear (cervical or vaginal), up to three smears, requiring physician interpretation.
    a. P3000
    b. P3001
    c. P7001
    d. Q0091

23. Polishing and resurfacing of ocular prosthesis.
    a. V2623
    b. V2624
    c. V2625
    d. V2626

24. Speech screening.
    a. V5336
    b. V5362
    c. V5363
    d. V5364

25. Venipuncture for specimen collection (one homebound patient).
    a. A4257
    b. A4258
    c. S9504
    d. S9529

ANSWER KEY TO EXAM—CHAPTER 8

1. b	8. a	15. d	22. b
2. d	9. d	16. a	23. b
3. b	10. a	17. a	24. b
4. a	11. d	18. a	25. d
5. a	12. a	19. a	
6. a	13. d	20. c	
7. c	14. b	21. c	

EXAM—CHAPTER 9

Student Name _____

Multiple Choice

Circle the most appropriate response.

1. RBRVS contains relative value components that consist of
    a. geographic cost, work expense, expense to the practice.
    b. intensity of work, expense to perform services, geographic location.
    c. liability and work expense, along with intensity of work.
    d. work expense, practice expense, malpractice expense.

2. Each relative value component is multiplied by the geographic cost practice index (GCPI), and then each is further multiplied by a variable figure called the
    a. common denominator.
    b. conversion factor.
    c. related work total.
    d. relative value unit.

3. Nonparticipating (nonPAR) providers are restricted to billing at or below the
    a. fee-for-service scale.
    b. limiting charge.
    c. physician fee schedule.
    d. relative value scale.

4. Medicare administrative contractors must keep Medicare fees within a $20 million spending ceiling, as stated in the Balanced Billing Act (BBA). This is called
    a. balanced budget rule.
    b. budget neutrality.
    c. Medicare spend-down.
    d. the Medicare spending limit.

5. Medicare participating providers commonly report actual fees to Medicare but adjust fees after payment is received. The difference between the fee reported and the payment received is a
    a. fee adjustment.
    b. limiting charge.
    c. neutral charge.
    d. write-off.

6. When other insurers are initially liable for payment on a medical service or supply provided to a patient, Medicare classifies them as the _____ payer.
    a. Medicare secondary
    b. primary
    c. secondary
    d. supplemental

7. "Incident to" relates to services provided by nonPARs that are defined as services
    a. provided incidental to other services provided by a physician.
    b. provided solely for the comfort and best interest of the beneficiary.
    c. provided without the nonparticipating provider's supervision.
    d. that would otherwise not be reimbursed by the Medicare carrier.

8. When office-based services are performed at a facility other than the physician's office, Medicare payments are reduced because the physician did not provide the supplies, drugs, utilities, or overhead. This payment reduction is called a(n)
    a. ambulatory payment classification.
    b. facility write-off.
    c. outpatient fee reduction.
    d. site-of-service differential.

9. The prospective payment system providing a lump-sum payment that is dependent on the patient's principal diagnosis, comorbidities, complications, and principal and secondary procedures is
    a. ambulatory payment classifications (APCs).
    b. diagnosis-related groups (DRGs).
    c. Medicare Physician Fee Schedule (MPFS).
    d. resource-based relative value scale (RBRVS).

10. Prospective price-based rates are established by the
    a. actual charges for inpatient care reported to payers after discharge of the patient from the hospital.
    b. American Medical Association.
    c. payer, based on a particular category of patient.
    d. reported health care costs from which a *per diem* rate has been determined.

11. A state-licensed, Medicare-certified supplier of surgical health care services that must accept assignment on Medicare claims is a(n)
    a. ambulatory surgery center.
    b. certified surgery center.
    c. Medicare administrative contractor.
    d. provider office surgical center.

12. What term is used to describe the types and categories of patients treated by a health care facility or provider?
    a. adverse selection
    b. case mix
    c. covered population
    d. medical diagnostic category

13. The inpatient prospective payment system (IPPS) was designed to:
    a. decrease the amount of money being paid to hospitals by the Medicare program.
    b. discourage hospitals from accepting Medicare patients.
    c. increase the amount of money being paid to hospitals by the Medicare program.
    d. provide hospitals with an incentive to manage their operations more efficiently without affecting quality of care.

14. Anesthesia services payments are based on the American Society of Anesthesiologists' relative value system and the
    a. actual time an anesthesiologist spends with a patient.
    b. location where anesthesia services were performed.
    c. surgical patient's length of stay.
    d. type of anesthetic administered to the patient.

15. The document formerly known as the Explanation of Medicare Benefits is now known as the
    a. Advance Beneficiary Notice.
    b. Medicare Payment Notice.
    c. Medicare Remittance Advice.
    d. Medicare Summary Notice.

16. The Medicare physician fee schedule amount for code 99213 is $100. Calculate the nonPAR allowed charge.
    a. $20
    b. $80
    c. $95
    d. $109.25

17. The Medicare physician fee schedule amount for code 99213 is $100. Calculate the nonPAR limiting charge.
    a. $20
    b. $80
    c. $95
    d. $109.25

18. The Medicare physician fee schedule amount for code 99213 is $100. The participating provider's usual charge for this service is $125. Calculate the Medicare reimbursement amount.
    a. $76
    b. $80
    c. $109.25
    d. $115

19. The Medicare physician fee schedule amount for code 99213 is $100. The participating provider's usual charge for this service is $125. Calculate the patient's coinsurance amount.

   a. $20
   b. $25

   c. $76
   d. $80

20. The Medicare physician fee schedule amount for code 99213 is $100. The nonparticipating provider's usual charge for this service is $150. Calculate the Medicare reimbursement amount.

   a. $76
   b. $80

   c. $95
   d. $109.25

21. The Medicare physician fee schedule amount for code 99213 is $100. The nonparticipating provider's usual charge for this service is $150. Calculate the amount the patient owes the nonPAR.

   a. $20
   b. $33.25

   c. $76
   d. $95

22. The Medicare physician fee schedule amount for code 99213 is $100. The participating provider's usual charge for this service is $125. The nonparticipating provider's charge for this service is $150. Calculate the difference in the amount paid by the patient to the PAR and the nonPAR.

   a. $13.25
   b. $20

   c. $33.25
   d. $76

23. The Medicare physician fee schedule amount for code 32562 is $2500. The nonparticipating provider usually charges $3200 for this procedure. Calculate the nonPAR allowed charge.

   a. $2185
   b. $2375

   c. $2500
   d. $2731.25

24. The Medicare physician fee schedule amount for code 32562 is $2500. The nonparticipating provider usually charges $3200 for this procedure. Calculate the nonPAR limiting charge.

   a. $2185
   b. $2375

   c. $2500
   d. $2731.25

25. The Medicare physician fee schedule amount for code 32562 is $2500. The nonparticipating provider usually charges $3200 for this procedure. Calculate the Medicare reimbursement amount.

   a. $1900
   b. $2375

   c. $2500
   d. $3200

ANSWER KEY TO EXAM–CHAPTER 9

1. d	8. d	15. d	22. a
2. b	9. b	16. c	23. b
3. b	10. c	17. d	24. d
4. b	11. a	18. b	25. a
5. d	12. b	19. a	
6. b	13. d	20. a	
7. a	14. a	21. b	

EXAM—CHAPTER 10

Student Name _____

Multiple Choice

Circle the most appropriate response.

1. The first-listed diagnosis reported on a CMS-1500 claim form is the
   a. diagnosis with the highest potential reimbursement.
   b. first condition the physician addressed with the patient.
   c. major reason the patient sought medical care.
   d. most important condition troubling the patient.

2. The concept of linking diagnosis codes with procedure/service codes is called
   a. medical matching.
   b. medical necessity.
   c. prospective payment.
   d. reimbursement.

3. A patient is seen in the office and is diagnosed with a sprained wrist. He complains of pain and upon examination, the provider notes bruising and edema of the wrist. Which should be reported to the third-party payer?
   a. bruising and edema
   b. rule out wrist fracture
   c. sprained wrist
   d. sprained wrist, bruising, and edema

4. When a provider documents justification for a patient seeking health care services, but no disorder is documented, the health insurance specialist usually assigns a(n)
   a. E code.
   b. qualified diagnosis code.
   c. unlisted code.
   d. V code.

5. HCPCS level II modifiers are added to which codes?
   a. CPT and HCPCS codes
   b. DSM codes
   c. HCPCS codes only
   d. ICD-9-CM codes

Coding

Circle the most appropriate response.

6. The patient is a 25-year-old white female who is at 13 weeks gestation right now and EDC of February 3, YYYY. She had a history of 23-1/2 week loss of twins secondary to cervical incompetence. Because of her cervix having fingertip dilation now, the decision was made with the patient to go along with cervical cerclage in hopes of salvaging the pregnancy. The patient was admitted to the ambulatory surgery center where she underwent suture placement of the cervix, in a McDonald cerclage fashion. There were no complications associated with the procedure and the patient was discharged later that day.
   a. 622.5; 59320
   b. 654.53; 57700
   c. 654.53; 59320
   d. 59320

7. The patient is a 39-year-old female on lithium who is unable to discontinue the medication and who does not desire to become pregnant while on the medication. The patient therefore desires surgical sterilization. The patient was admitted to the ambulatory surgery center where she underwent bilateral tubal ligation with placement of Falope rings. The patient tolerated the procedure well and was discharged from the surgery center on the evening of the procedure.
   a. V25.2; 58671
   b. V25.2; 58673
   c. V25.8; 58671
   d. V26.51; 58673

8. The patient is a 28-year-old married female with history of trying to conceive for the past four years. The patient also complains of chronic pelvic pain for the past 10 years, worsening over the last three to four years. The patient was admitted to the ambulatory surgery center for examination under anesthesia, diagnostic laparoscopy, and hydrotubation. The patient successfully underwent the above procedures, with the findings of normal-appearing ovaries and patent fallopian tubes on chromotubation. She was discharged in satisfactory condition on the afternoon of admission.

   a. 625.9; 58679

   b. 628.9, 625.9; 49320, 58350-51

   c. 628.9, 625.9; 58679

   d. 628.9; 49320, 58350-51

9. The patient is a 52-year-old, deaf, white female who has had bilateral carpal tunnel syndrome for an undetermined period of time. The carpal tunnel syndrome is noted to be slightly greater in the left than the right. The patient also has bilateral thumb arthritis. It was elected not to address the latter problem at the present time. The patient has had quite classic symptoms without any history of rheumatoid arthritis. The patient underwent carpal tunnel release on the left in June of this year, and was admitted today for the procedure on the right. Subsequently, the patient underwent decompression of the right carpal tunnel with epineurolysis of the median nerve, individual motor branch decompression, and multiple flexor tenosynovectomies of the palm and wrist. At the completion of the procedure, the patient's wound was closed and a Xeroform bulky gauze dressing was applied, along with a volar splint out to the PIP joints, placing the wrist in neutral position. The patient tolerated the procedure well and was discharged to the ambulatory surgery recovery area in good condition.

   a. 354.0, 64721, 26145

   b. 354.0, 64721-RT, 26145-51-RT, 25115-51

   c. 354.00, 64721-RT, 26145-51-RT, 25115-51

   d. 354.2, 64721-RT, 26145-51-RT, 25115-51

10. The patient is a 23-year-old, G0, P0, who had a Pap smear in April YYY showing slight cervical dysplasia. She had colposcopy performed on June 2, YYYY, with biopsy showing extensive lesion with slight dysplasia. She was also noted to have a large right vaginal wall cyst, cultures from which were negative. The patient is being admitted to the ambulatory surgery center today for cervical laser ablation and incision and drainage of the vaginal wall cyst. The patient was taken to the operating room where general anesthesia was administered. Exam under anesthesia revealed a right vaginal wall cyst measuring 3 × 5 cm. The uterus was within normal limits. The adnexa were normal; no masses were palpated. Upon examination of the cervix, the patient was noted to have an area of dysplasia of approximately 1 cm around the cervical os. The area of cervical dysplasia was ablated 7 cm deep using CO_2 laser at 40 watts. Colpotomy was performed for incision and drainage of the vaginal wall cyst. Blood loss was minimal. The anesthesia was reversed and the patient was taken to the post anesthesia care unit in satisfactory condition.

    a. 622.1, 623.8; 57513, 57010-51

    b. 622.10, 623.8; 57513, 57010

    c. 622.10, 623.8; 57513, 57010-51

    d. 623.8; 57513, 57010-51

11. The patient is an 82-year-old male who injured his lower back lifting his wife on May 15 of this past year. He was diagnosed with right L3-4 radiculopathy, with secondary myofascial pain in the right lower lumbar paraspinal muscles. The patient has tried conservative treatment with physical therapy, pain medication, and use of a TENS unit with no significant pain relief. The patient is therefore admitted today to undergo an epidural (caudal) block at the L4-5 level. The procedure was carried out without any complications, and the patient is to follow up in the office next week.

    a. 724.4, 729.1; 62310

    b. 724.4, 729.1; 62311

    c. 724.4, 729.1; 62311, 97039

    d. 724.4; 62311

12. The patient is a 35-year-old divorced female who has a history of papillomatosis with lesions excised in 1988. In May of this year, papillomatous lesions were noted on examination extending from the clitoris on the left inferiorly, approximately 2 cm and 0.5 cm wide. Biopsies were obtained which confirmed condyloma and marked dysplasia extending to the lateral margins. The patient was admitted today for further excision of these lesions. The patient was placed in the dorsolithotomy position and was prepped and draped in the usual fashion. After induction of local anesthetic, the area of the lesion was excised in an elliptical fashion with a 5 mm margin on either side. Hemostasis was easily achieved with the Bovie, and the patient was transferred to the recovery area in good condition.

a. 078.10; 11421

b. 078.10; 11422

c. 078.19; 11421

d. 078.19; 11422

13. The patient is a 25-year-old married female, gravida 1, para 1, with persistent ovarian cyst throughout her recent pregnancy. On previous ultrasound, the cyst was measured to be 6.4 × 5.1 × 4.8 cm in size. On postpartum examination, the cyst was still present; therefore, laparoscopy was planned. The patient was admitted today with the plan to undergo operative laparoscopy with left cystectomy. The procedure was performed and the cyst was removed without incident. After the procedure was complete, the patient was transferred to the recovery room in satisfactory condition, to be discharged early this evening.

a. 620.2; 58920-LT

b. 620.2; 58925-LT

c. 620.2; 58925-LT, 76830-LT

d. 620.20; 58925-LT

14. The patient is a 73-year-old male who underwent right hip osteotomy with placement of plate and screws in the right hip for fracture suffered three years ago. Approximately six weeks ago, the patient began to experience pain in the right hip which increased in intensity and severity despite a cortisone shot and oral analgesics. A right hip x-ray was performed and it was noted that one of the screws was displaced, pressing on a major nerve. The previous fracture had healed successfully, and it was felt that the hardware could be removed fully. The patient was then scheduled for removal of the internal fixation device of the right hip, under spinal anesthesia. The patient successfully underwent hardware removal and the procedure was well tolerated. The patient was transferred to the orthopedic surgery recovery unit in stable condition.

a. V54.0; 20680

b. V54.01; 20670

c. V54.01; 20680-RT

d. V54.09; 20670

15. The patient is a 39-year-old pharmacist who was seen in the office for progressive tightness and contracture of the left middle finger. The patient was diagnosed with trigger finger of the left middle finger, and was scheduled to undergo trigger finger release at this ambulatory surgery center. The patient was admitted, and under satisfactory local block anesthesia, a transverse incision was made parallel to the distal palmar crease overlying the middle finger, and the wound was then deepened by sharp and blunt dissection. The flexor tendon sheath was identified and divided longitudinally. Subsequently, there was good gliding motion of the flexor tendon passively without any obstruction. The wound was closed and bulky dressing was applied. The patient tolerated the procedure well and was transferred to the recovery area in good condition.

a. 727.03; 26055-F1

b. 727.03; 26055-F2

c. 727.05; 26055-F1

d. 727.05; 26055-F2

16. SUBJECTIVE: The patient is a 46-year-old, twice-divorced, Navy veteran who has been suffering from bipolar disorder, manic type, and takes lithium 500 mg, which seems effective. OBJECTIVE: Mental status exam: (Thirty minutes of psychotherapy was provided.) He has been doing very well with the current medication. No evidence of memory loss or any psychotic behavior. His affect is appropriate and mood is stable. Insight and judgment are good. He is not considered a danger to self or others. ASSESSMENT: Bipolar disorder, manic type. PLAN: Continue lithium 500 mg per day.

a. 296.4; 90805

b. 296.40; 90804

c. 296.40; 90805

d. 296.46; 90805

17. Thirty minutes of psychotherapy was provided to a patient who is undergoing treatment for Crohn's disease with prednisone, which she began taking recently for flareup of symptoms. She is presently taking 15 mg b.i.d. The patient is knowledgeable about her disease and is followed by Dr. Weaver. The patient was referred today because of strong feelings of anger toward kids whom she knows are responsible for breaking into her cabin last weekend, taking a video camera. She explains that these feelings may be aggravated by the prednisone. However, she explains that the police will not do anything because there is no evidence that these people are responsible for the theft. The patient states that these same kids have been vandalizing homes over the past year, and everyone knows who it is. However, even though it is in the hands of the police, they are still not doing enough, which angers her. She tells me she would like to get a shotgun for protective purposes, and she thinks these people will probably try to come around on the weekend, thinking that her family is not there. She would like to surprise these people and perhaps use the shotgun if she feels her life is in danger. We talked at length about the situation, and I advocated that if she waits at the cabin on the weekend, hoping that these people will show up, that she have her husband or her girlfriend with her. She agreed. Later that day, I attempted to call the patient's husband, but he was never at the location. I asked the patient to have her husband call me; however, he has not as of yet. On the day following the patient's visit, I called the patient and she stated she was feeling less angry and more calmed down. A friend who is well acquainted with the situation was there, and I spoke with her. The friend explained that the patient was very angry the day before, but seemed to be calmer today. She stated she will stay with the patient and will not allow the patient to stay alone, especially with a gun, until the situation is resolved. The friend will also discuss the situation with the patient's husband. ASSESSMENT: Adjustment reaction. Crohn's disease. PLAN: The patient will return in two weeks or sooner if any additional problems arise.

    a. 309.9; 90805

    b. 555.0, 309.9; 90805

    c. 555.9, 309.9; 90805

    d. 555.9, 312.00; 90805

18. The patient is appearing more spirited and less troubled by feelings of depression. She states that things are not so gloomy. She seems upbeat about her life. She recently graduated and obtained an associate's degree and wishes to go on further with her education. She is trying to work on getting her husband more involved in their life. She still manifests tearfulness at times, but she is more focused on her needs at this time, which is healthy. She sees the marriage as something to continue to work on despite her own ambitions. The meds are very helpful to her and she is feeling less depressed. She complains of tiredness today, and I have recommended her to cut back on the dosage, which she is in agreement with. She is also seeing a therapist for psychotherapy, which is very helpful. She is going through her menopause and being inactive sexually, she does not worry about getting pregnant, in view of taking meds. She is alert, oriented × 3, no abnormalities of thought content or thought process. She states that she has never had any suicidal thoughts. Return to clinic in two months.

    a. 309.0; 99212

    b. 311; 90804

    c. 311; 99205

    d. 311; 99212

19. The patient has the following problems: hyperlipidemia, coronary artery disease, cerebrovascular disease, esophageal reflux, and anxiety with depression. HISTORY OF PRESENT ILLNESS: The patient is an 80-year-old white male who was last seen in June of this year by Dr. Hank Himmel for the above problems. At that time the patient was placed on cimetidine twice a day and fluoxetine 10 mg a day by Dr. Carl Custer for psychiatry. The patient had been followed up in the past by a private doctor in Fairport. However, he no longer sees him and is using us now as his primary care providers. There have been no labs done on this patient as of yet. He comes in today without any new complaints, except for his original complaint of feeling tired all of the time and no energy. PHYSICAL EXAMINATION: Today on examination the patient was 57 inches tall, weighed 184 pounds. Blood pressure 122/70. Pulse: 60 per minute. Respiration: 18 per minute. HEENT: Basically within normal limits. He wears glasses for visual acuity. He has hearing aids bilaterally. NECK: Supple. Trachea is midline. Thyroid not palpable. LUNGS: Clear to A&P. Heart sounds were regular without murmur or ectopic beat noted. ABDOMEN: Slightly obese. It was nontender. There was no gross organomegaly noted. His bowel sounds were normal. EXTREMITIES: Pulses in the lower extremities were present. He had good circulation with some

very mild edema around the ankles. ASSESSMENT: As stated above in the problem list. PLAN: I would like to see this patient back in three months time. Before leaving today he will be referred and taken to psychiatry where he can have a new appointment set up and have his medications renewed. He will have labs requested in the next two to three weeks. We will check his chemistries, as well as hemogram. I also want to get fecal occult times three. I will see him in three months. He will continue his medications of cimetidine 400 mg. However, he will take just once a day at nighttime. He is also taking lovastatin for his hyperlipidemia, 40 mg a day. He has used blocks under the bed to elevate the head of his bed, which has relieved his nighttime heartburn. I would advise him to continue doing this, as well as taking the cimetidine at bedtime. He is being referred as stated to psychiatry for follow-up, and I will see him in three months.

a. 272.4, 300.4, 414.00, 437.9, 530.81; 99213

b. 300.4, 414.9, 414.00, 530.81, 272.4; 99213

c. 300.4, 414.9, 414.00, 530.81, 272.4; 99214

d. 300.4; 414.9, 414.00, 272.4; 99213

20. The patient was seen for regular appointment today. He is pleasant, cooperative, and coherent. Reports he is still having some problems with balance. He walks with a cane, which is helpful. He is oriented × 3. No evidence of delusions, hallucinations, or dangerous behavior. Still reports he feels kind of depressed at times. However, he has been handling his home situation fairly well. The patient has a good memory; insight and judgment seem very good. Takes the medication as prescribed which seems fairly effective. DIAGNOSIS: Dysthymia. PLAN: Sertraline 50 mg every morning.

a. 300.4; 99214

b. 300.4; 99212

c. 300.4, 781.2; 99212

d. 311; 99212

21. SUBJECTIVE: No change in gait instability; when he had head CT and had to lie quietly with neck extended, gait instability much more for 20-30 minutes after test. Medications are warfarin, digoxin, and verapamil. OBJECTIVE: Alert. Ataxic gait with foot slapping and instability on tandem. Mild distal weakness and wasting, barely detectable DTRs, impaired vibration below hips, impaired position sense in toes. Head CT showed diffuse atrophic changes. EMG revealed distal demyelinating axonal neuropathy. GHb and TSH unremarkable. ASSESSMENT: Gait disorder with central/peripheral components in context of cervical spondylosis and peripheral neuropathy. PLAN: B12 folate [I can find no evidence in chart these have ever been done]; revisit one month.

a. 781.2, 721.0, 356.9; 99212-21

b. 781.2, 721.0, 356.9; 99213

c. 781.2, 721.1, 356.9; 99212-21

d. 781.3, 721.0, 356.9; 99212-21

22. SUBJECTIVE: Tremor remains under control; manifests mainly during fine manipulations. No symptoms of TIA. Scheduled for right knee replacement at SMH next month. Medications are fexophenadine, ASA b.i.d., clonazepam 1 mg q.i.d., desipramine 150 mg daily, trazodone 100 mg h.s., terazosin, nifedipine, lovastatin, captopril, beclomethasone, and timolol drops. OBJECTIVE: BP 144/90. Alert. Impaired tongue mobility. Antalgic gait. Impaired RAMs (left to right), no tremor. Left hyperreflexia. Positive snout and jaw jerk. ASSESSMENT: Essential tremor, responsive to primidone. Bilateral subcortical infarcts secondary to hypertensive vascular disease. PLAN: Continue primidone 125 mg b.i.d. Revisit in four months.

a. 332.0, 401.9, 434.91; 99212

b. 333.1, 401.1, 434.91; 99212

c. 333.1, 401.9, 433.91; 99212

d. 333.1, 401.9, 434.91; 99212

23. This is a 78-year-old white male veteran who has a longstanding history of schizophrenia. His condition has been stable. He used to complain about a sleeping problem, but no longer complains of sleeping problems since he has been on temazepam, which was switched to oxazepam today. He is pleasant, cooperative. He has some hearing difficulties, but his memory is good. He understands clearly what is going on. There are no acute psychotic symptoms. No delusions or hallucinations noted. He denies any suicidal or homicidal ideation, intention, or plans. His affect is appropriate, mood is stable. Insight and judgment are fairly good. Taking medication as prescribed, with no side effects. DIAGNOSIS: Schizoaffective disorder, chronic, in partial remission. PLAN: Continue Haldol 2 mg h.s., trazodone 100 mg h.s., oxazepam 15 mg 1 or 2 h.s. p.r.n.

    a. 295.72; 99211   c. 295.72; 99212-21

    b. 295.72; 99212   d. 295.82; 99212

24. SUBJECTIVE: Some improvement in paresthesias since amitriptyline was started, though he is using it only sporadically. OBJECTIVE: As per previous visit, most notable findings being moderate distal weakness in the right lower extremity, antalgic gait, impaired vibratory sensation below the knees, and low-stocking sensory impairment. ASSESSMENT: Distal sensorimotor neuropathy, symptomatic response to amitriptyline. PLAN: Suggested he take the amitriptyline q.h.s. as originally prescribed. Reassess in four months.

    a. 355.9; 99211   c. 355.90; 99212

    b. 355.9; 99212   d. 782.0; 99212

25. Follow-up diabetic maintenance care was provided with debridement of six mycotic toenails and paring of digital hyperkeratoses, third and fourth toes, right foot. The patient has an ulcer on the right heel, which is under the care of Dr. Hoffman. When first examining the patient this morning, dried blood was noted on all toes of the left foot. The patient admits to attempting nail care yesterday evening and apparently created a mild laceration of the second toenail, left foot. There is an intact scab formation this morning. No further treatment is needed. The Plastizote chukka-style boots that were dispensed in April are comfortable, and patient likes them very much. No other concerns. DIAGNOSES: Onychomycosis, diabetes type I with neuropathy, hyperkeratoses. PLAN: Return to clinic in six weeks.

    a. 110.1, 250.01, 357.2; 11720, 11056-51   c. 110.1, 250.61, 357.2; 11721, 11056-51

    b. 110.1, 250.61, 357.2; 11721, 11056   d. 110.4, 250.61, 357.4; 11750, 11056

ANSWER KEY TO EXAM—CHAPTER 10

1. c	8. c	15. b	22. d
2. b	9. b	16. c	23. b
3. c	10. c	17. c	24. b
4. d	11. b	18. d	25. c
5. a	12. b	19. b	
6. c	13. b	20. b	
7. a	14. c	21. a	

EXAM – CHAPTER 11   Student Name _____

Multiple Choice

Circle the most appropriate response.

1. When a patient is seen by his surgeon for postoperative complications, any services provided are
   a. billed separately from the global surgery performed.
   b. identified on the CMS-1500 claim with a 5-digit modifier.
   c. included as part of the global surgery and not billed separately.
   d. not submitted to the third-party payer for reimbursement.

2. According to optical scanning guidelines, the punctuation that is acceptable when it is part of the patient's name is a(n)
   a. accent mark   c. hyphen.
   b. apostrophe.   d. tilde

3. Birth dates are entered as _____ on the CMS-1500 claim depending on block instructions.
   a. DD MM YYYY or DDMMYYYY   c. MM DD YY or MMDDYY
   b. MM DD YYYY or MMDDYYYY   d. YYYY MM DD or YYYYMMDD

4. The diagnosis code reported in item 1, Block 21, of the CMS-1500 claim is the
   a. comorbidity.   c. first-listed diagnosis.
   b. complication.   d. principal diagnosis.

5. Items 1–4 in Block 21 of the CMS-1500 claim link the listed diagnosis codes to their appropriate procedure/service codes reported in Block 24. These items are known as _____ numbers.
   a. location   c. ranking
   b. orientation   d. reference

6. The legal business name of the practice is also called the
   a. administrative contractor.   c. provider identity.
   b. billing entity.   d. third-party payer.

7. The unique identifier that CMS will assign to providers as part of HIPAA requirements is called the
   a. Grp #.   c. PIN.
   b. NPI.   d. UPIN.

8. The maximum number of CPT and/or HCPCS modifiers that can be reported in Block 24 of the CMS-1500 claim is
   a. one.   c. three.
   b. two.   d. four.

9. Block 25 of the CMS-1500 claim requires entry of either the provider's social security number or the
   a. EIN.   c. PIN.
   b. Grp #.   d. UPIN.

10. Which character is entered in the boxes of Block 8 of the CMS-1500 claim to indicate patient status?
    a. X   c. /
    b. √   d. *

11. When entering the diagnosis codes in Block 21 of the CMS-1500, which is entered instead of the decimal?
    a. comma
    b. hyphen
    c. slash
    d. space

12. A patient whose birthday is January 5, 1965, would be entered on the CMS-1500 as
    a. 01 05 1965
    b. 1 5 65
    c. 01 05 65
    d. 1 05 1965

13. A total charge of $900 would be entered on the CMS-1500 as
    a. 900
    b. 900 00
    c. 900.00
    d. $900.00

14. What is reported in Block 24E of the CMS-1500?
    a. CPT or HCPCS modifiers
    b. diagnosis code(s)
    c. ICD-9-CM procedure codes
    d. diagnosis pointer number

15. When reporting anesthesia time in Block 24G, how must the time be entered?
    a. by hours, rounding up as needed
    b. fractions of hours
    c. start of the anesthesia in military time
    d. total minutes

16. Provider services for inpatient medical cases are billed on what basis?
    a. fee-for-service
    b. global fee
    c. OPPS
    d. services not billed

17. Which prohibits a payer from notifying a provider about payment or rejections on unassigned claims?
    a. Balanced Budget Act of 1997
    b. Consolidated Omnibus Budget Reconciliation Act of 1985
    c. Federal Privacy Act of 1974
    d. Health Insurance Portability and Accountability Act of 1996

18. Medicare Conditions of Participation (CoP) require providers to maintain copies of government insurance claims and attachments submitted for what period of time?
    a. 5 years
    b. 6 months
    c. 6 years
    d. indefinitely

19. When the patient signs Block 13 of the CMS-1500, allowing payment to go directly to the provider, this is known as
    a. accepting assignment.
    b. assignment of benefits.
    c. conditions of participation.
    d. provider reimbursement.

20. When an "X" is entered in one or more of the YES boxes in Block 10 of the CMS-1500 claim, this may indicate that
    a. payment on the claim may be the responsibility of a liability payer.
    b. the patient wishes to have payment for the claim sent directly to the provider.
    c. the provider has not included sufficient information for the payer to reimburse the claim.
    d. the provider will accept assignment on the claim.

21. When is it appropriate to file a patient's secondary insurance claim?
    a. after a copy of the explanation of benefits is received by the practice
    b. after the explanation of benefits is received by the patient
    c. after the remittance advice is received by the medical practice
    d. at the same time the primary insurance claim is filed, if primary and secondary payers are different

22. An example of a supplemental insurance plan is
    a. CHAMPUS.
    b. Medicaid.
    c. Medigap.
    d. TRICARE.

23. To prevent breach of patient confidentiality, the patient must either sign an "Authorization for Release of Medical Information" (ROMI) statement, or
    a. Block 12 of the CMS-1500 claim.
    b. have the health insurance specialist sign on behalf of the patient.
    c. sign the encounter form at the conclusion of the visit.
    d. verbally authorize the practice to submit the claim.

24. Which diagnosis is considered a chronic condition that would always affect patient care?
    a. conjunctivitis
    b. diabetes mellitus
    c. hip fracture
    d. influenza

25. In Block 24G, _____ units would be entered based on the following statement: Three-view sinus series.
    a. 1
    b. 1, 1, 1
    c. 3
    d. 3V

ANSWER KEY TO EXAM—CHAPTER 11

1. a	8. c	15. d	22. c
2. c	9. a	16. a	23. a
3. b	10. a	17. c	24. b
4. c	11. d	18. a	25. a
5. d	12. a	19. b	
6. b	13. b	20. a	
7. b	14. d	21. c	

EXAM–CHAPTER 12

Student Name _____

Multiple Choice

Circle the most appropriate response.

1. Which would result in the least out-of-pocket expense for the patient?

    a. coverage by both the patient's and the spouse's employer group health plans

    b. coverage by the patient's primary employer group health plan

    c. coverage by the spouse's secondary employer group health plan

    d. coverage by the spouse's employer group health plan and the patient's supplemental health plan

2. When the patient signs a special form that has been placed in the financial or medical record, it is acceptable to enter what phrase in Block 12 and/or Block 13 of the CMS-1500 claim?

    a. PLEASE SEE RELEASE

    b. SEE PREVIOUS

    c. SIGNATURE IS AVAILABLE

    d. SIGNATURE ON FILE

3. The "birthday rule" applies when dependent children living at home are covered by more than one health insurance policy. The primary policy is determined by the parent

    a. who acquired the insurance policy first.

    b. who has a birthday that occurs first in the year.

    c. who has been employed longest.

    d. whose birth year occurs first.

4. The patient is covered by two health insurance policies, his own employer's group health plan and his spouse's employer's group health plan. Which plan is primary for the patient?

    a. The patient's own employer's group health plan is primary.

    b. The plan of the spouse whose birth year is first is primary.

    c. The plan of the spouse whose birthday occurs first in the year is primary.

    d. The spouse's employer's group health plan is primary.

5. When a patient is covered by a government health program (e.g., Medicare) and an employer group health plan, which is considered primary?

    a. employer group health plan

    b. government health program

    c. plan that has been in effect the longest

    d. plan that has the highest reimbursement rate

6. When a patient is listed as a dependent on her spouse's employer group health plan (EGHP) and is covered by an EGHP of her own, the spouse's plan is considered

    a. invalid.

    b. primary.

    c. secondary.

    d. supplemental.

7. The patient's birth date is January 5, 1967. This is entered in Block 3 of the CMS-1500 claim as

    a. 01 05 67

    b. 01 05 1967

    c. 1 5 1967

    d. 01051967

8. When the patient and policyholder are identical, Block 4 of the CMS-1500 claim will contain

    a. either the word SAME or the patient's name/address as entered in Block 2.

    b. the patient's name and address as they were entered in Block 2.

    c. the phrase SAME AS BEFORE.

    d. the word SAME.

9. For patients between the ages of 19 and 23 who are named as dependents on a family policy, and who are full-time students, enter an X in the appropriate box of Block 9 on the CMS-1500 and attach

   a. a written notice of the student's school status (filed each semester).

   b. the school acceptance letter sent to the student (patient).

   c. the student's final grade report (GPA must be at least 2.0).

   d. the student's semester course schedule.

10. When an X appears in the YES box in Block 10a of the CMS-1500 claim, this indicates

    a. it is possible that homeowner's insurance will be liable for services charged.

    b. the services provided were related to an on-the-job injury.

    c. the services provided were related to an auto accident injury.

    d. workers' compensation denied payment for services reported on the claim.

11. Deductibles, copayments, and coinsurance expenses are usually covered by what type of plan?

    a. government

    b. liability

    c. secondary EGHP

    d. supplemental

12. When a patient is referred to a consultant, what is entered in Block 17 of the CMS-1500 claim?

    a. ID number of the referring provider

    b. the complete name and credentials of the referring provider

    c. the name of the practice with which the referring provider is affiliated

    d. the type of specialty of the referring provider

13. If laboratory procedures are performed in the provider's office, how is this indicated on the CMS-1500 claim?

    a. by entering an X in the NO box of Block 20 of the CMS-1500

    b. by entering an X in the YES box of Block 20 on the CMS-1500

    c. by entering the name of the laboratory technician in Block 19 of the CMS-1500

    d. by leaving Block 20 of the CMS-1500 blank

14. If the provider's employer tax identification number (EIN) is unavailable, what is acceptable to enter in Block 25 of the CMS-1500?

    a. no other entry is permitted

    b. the address of the provider's office

    c. the provider identification number

    d. the provider's social security number

15. Which of the following is considered a commercial health insurance company?

    a. Aetna

    b. Medicaid

    c. Medicare

    d. TRICARE

16. An intensive outpatient program is a multifaceted, highly comprehensive program designed to help what type of individuals?

    a. nursing facility residents

    b. patients with organic psychiatric diseases

    c. physical rehabilitation patients

    d. those with chemical dependencies and/or abuse issues

17. If an attachment such as a discharge summary, operative report, or other document will accompany a claim to clarify patient services, this is indicated on the CMS-1500 by entering the word(s)

    a. ATTACHMENT in Block 19 of the CMS-1500 claim.

    b. ATTACHMENT in the upper-right corner of the CMS-1500 claim.

    c. SEE ATTACHED in Block 24K of the CMS-1500 claim.

    d. SEE ATTACHED in the bottom-left corner of the CMS-1500 claim.

18. An outside laboratory can also be referred to as a(n) _____ laboratory.
    a. approved
    b. reference
    c. referral
    d. required

19. In Block 24E of the CMS-1500, multiple diagnosis pointer numbers are each separated by a
    a. blank space.
    b. comma.
    c. hyphen.
    d. slash.

20. If the same payer provides both the primary and secondary coverage, submit _____ CMS-1500 claim(s).
    a. one
    b. one, plus an attachment to indicate that the patient is covered by two policies issued by the same payer
    c. one, plus copies of the patient's insurance cards attached with every claim
    d. two

21. When filing commercial insurance claims, what information from a nonPAR is required in Block 33 of the CMS-1500?
    a. The billing entity's name, address, telephone number, group number, and PIN
    b. The nonPAR's telephone number, official name of the billing entity, and mailing address (including zip code)
    c. The nonPAR's telephone number, official name of the billing entity, full mailing address, and group number
    d. The provider's name, PIN number, and group number

22. In which Block on the CMS-1500 is a prior authorization number for procedures or services entered?
    a. Block 10d
    b. Block 11
    c. Block 19
    d. Block 23

23. Which item is considered a place of service for purposes of Block 24B on the CMS-1500?
    a. diagnostic radiology
    b. kidney donor
    c. nursing facility
    d. physical therapy

24. If the patient authorizes payment to be sent directly to the provider who performed the service or procedure, this is known as
    a. accepting assignment.
    b. accepting benefits.
    c. assignment of benefits.
    d. coordination of benefits.

25. Under what circumstance will the health insurance plan pay the claim when an X is entered in any of the YES boxes in Block 10a through 10c?
    a. Documentation is submitted to the health insurance plan proving that the other liable party has denied the claim.
    b. The patient fails to make a follow-up appointment for treatment.
    c. The patient states that the claim has not been paid by the other liable party.
    d. The patient submits the explanation of benefits to the health insurance plan.

ANSWER KEY TO EXAM–CHAPTER 12

1. a	8. d	15. a	22. d
2. d	9. a	16. d	23. c
3. b	10. d	17. a	24. c
4. a	11. d	18. b	25. a
5. a	12. a	19. a	
6. c	13. a	20. a	
7. b	14. d	21. b	

EXAM—CHAPTER 13   Student Name _____

Multiple Choice

Circle the most appropriate response.

1. A participating provider is one who enters into a contract with a BCBS corporation and agrees to
   a. bill patients for only deductible and copay/coinsurance amounts.
   b. provide free billing manuals to Blue Cross/Blue Shield subscribers.
   c. require BCBS subscribers to submit health care insurance claims.
   d. resolve health care claims disputes with BCBS on behalf of subscribers.

2. A BCBS program that requires participating providers to adhere to managed care provisions is called a(n)
   a. Away from Home Care® Program
   b. government-wide service benefit plan.
   c. point-of-service plan (POS).
   d. preferred provider network (PPN).

3. A BCBS special accidental injury rider covers _____ percent of nonsurgical care sought and rendered within 24 to 72 hours of the accidental injury.
   a. 20
   b. 50
   c. 80
   d. 100

4. For BCBS to cover care rendered under a medical emergency care rider, the insurance specialist must
   a. determine that outpatient follow-up care was provided to the patient.
   b. document medical necessity for emergency care of unexpected conditions.
   c. link diagnoses reported in Block 21 with services reported in Block 24.
   d. ensure that immediate treatment was sought for sudden, severe conditions.

5. Which health insurance contract covers company employees who are located in more than one geographic area?
   a. Away from Home Care® Program
   b. BCBS Program
   c. BlueCard® Program
   d. Healthcare Anywhere

6. Which is a BCBS managed care program?
   a. Away from Home Care® Program
   b. BlueCard® Program
   c. fee-for-service plan
   d. point-of-service plan

7. A contract between an insurer and a health care provider or group of providers who agree to provide services to persons covered under the contract is called a
   a. preferred provider arrangement.
   b. point-of-service plan.
   c. health maintenance organization.
   d. fee-for-service plan.

8. Which concept applies when BCBS directly reimburses participating providers for health care services rendered to subscribers?
   a. accept assignment
   b. assignment of benefits
   c. indemnity coverage
   d. prospective authorization

9. A third-party administrator is a company that
   a. pays providers for services rendered, on behalf of BCBS.
   b. preauthorizes certain health care services for subscribers.
   c. processes health insurance claims for providers.
   d. provides administrative services to health care plans.

10. A health care system that assumes or shares the financial and health care delivery risks associated with providing comprehensive medical services to subscribers, in return for a fixed, prepaid fee, is a(n)

    a. exclusive provider organization.

    b. health maintenance organization.

    c. point-of-service plan.

    d. preferred provider organization.

11. Business entities that pay taxes on profits generated by the corporation and distribute after-tax profits to shareholders and officers are _____ organizations.

    a. charitable

    b. for-profit

    c. nonprofit

    d. taxable

12. In exchange for tax relief for any of the nonprofit BCBS plans, the nonprofit plans are forbidden by state law from

    a. canceling coverage of an individual based on poor health or if payments to the provider have far exceeded the average.

    b. canceling coverage if the plan can prove that fraudulent statements were made on the application for coverage.

    c. canceling coverage when premiums have not been paid.

    d. converting to for-profit status.

13. From whom must BCBS plans receive approval before instituting benefit changes or rate increases in each individual state?

    a. governor's office

    b. state attorney general

    c. state hospital association

    d. state insurance commissioner

14. The BCBS preferred provider network rate is generally how much lower than the PAR allowed rate?

    a. 5 percent

    b. 10 percent

    c. 15 percent

    d. 20 percent

15. The amount commonly charged for a specific medical service by providers within a particular geographic region is known as the

    a. allowable fee.

    b. capitation.

    c. deductible.

    d. usual, customary, and reasonable rate.

16. When a nonPAR agrees to file a claim on behalf of a BCBS patient, the payment is sent to the

    a. facility where treatment was rendered.

    b. patient.

    c. provider.

    d. third-party administrator.

17. A special clause written into a contract that stipulates additional coverage over and above the standard contract is a(n)

    a. addendum.

    b. agreement.

    c. benefit.

    d. rider.

18. What may occur if a patient neglects to follow the mandatory second surgical opinion requirement of her BCBS plan?

    a. The patient may receive substandard surgical care.

    b. The patient's out-of-pocket expenses may be greatly increased.

    c. The patient's policy will be canceled.

    d. The provider will be removed from participating provider status.

19. The customary deadline for filing BCBS claims is how long from the patient's date of service?

    a. 30 days

    b. 6 months

    c. 90 days

    d. one year

20. Approximately how many Americans are covered by a BCBS plan?
    a. 45 million
    b. 450 million
    c. 5 million
    d. 80 million

21. A BCBS preferred provider network is operated similarly to what type of managed care design?
    a. exclusive provider organization
    b. health maintenance organization
    c. point-of-service plan
    d. preferred provider organization

22. What type of BCBS claims may require forwarding to a third-party administrator?
    a. elective, nonemergency surgery
    b. mental health
    c. nursing facility
    d. outpatient physical rehabilitation

23. Which feature makes a BCBS plan different from other commercial plans?
    a. BCBS allows access to a Web site for providers to keep up-to-date with insurance procedures and changes.
    b. BCBS has providers send claims through a TPA before claims are processed by BCBS.
    c. BCBS plans are available throughout the United States.
    d. BCBS provides billing manuals and newsletters to keep PARs up-to-date on insurance procedures.

24. When filing a claim for a patient who is enrolled in the Federal Employee Program, what number is used for the group ID number on the claim?
    a. enrollee identification number
    b. patient's date of birth
    c. provider identification number
    d. three-digit enrollment code

25. If the total charges due from the patient's encounter amount to $142.75, how must this amount be reported in Block 28?
    a. 142 75
    b. 142.75
    c. $142.75
    d. 143.00

ANSWER KEY TO EXAM—CHAPTER 13

1. a	8. b	15. d	22. b
2. d	9. d	16. b	23. d
3. d	10. b	17. d	24. d
4. c	11. b	18. b	25. a
5. d	12. a	19. d	
6. d	13. d	20. d	
7. a	14. b	21. d	

EXAM—CHAPTER 14   Student Name _____

Multiple Choice

Circle the most appropriate response.

1. Medicare is available to an individual who has worked at least
    a. 5 years in Medicare-covered employment, is at least 65 years old, and is a permanent resident of the United States.
    b. 10 years in Medicare-covered employment, is at least 62 years old, and is a citizen of the United States.
    c. 10 years in Medicare-covered employment, is at least 65 years old, and is a citizen or permanent resident of the United States.
    d. 25 years in Medicare-covered employment, is at least 62 years old, and is a citizen of the United States.

2. Upon applying for Medicare Part A and Part B, an initial enrollment period of _____ months begins.
    a. 3   c. 7
    b. 6   d. 12

3. The general enrollment period for Medicare Part B coverage
    a. begins on the beneficiary's birthday and continues for a period of 90 days.
    b. is held from January 1 through March 31 each year.
    c. is open, which means eligible individuals can enroll at any time.
    d. is the same as that for the initial enrollment period.

4. A Medicare benefit period begins
    a. after the Medicare patient's spell of illness has ended but before any subsequent inpatient hospitalizations.
    b. each time a Medicare patient is admitted to the hospital, regardless of the number of days the patient has been out of the hospital.
    c. just once each year, on January 1, whether or not the patient is admitted to the hospital.
    d. with the first day of hospitalization and ends when the patient has been out of the hospital for 60 consecutive days.

5. Lifetime reserve days
    a. accrue each year, until the Medicare beneficiary has earned 90 days, which can then be used as needed.
    b. include a total of 60 days that are to be used all at once, on a continuous basis, by the Medicare patient.
    c. may be used only once during a patient's lifetime and are usually used during the patient's final, terminal hospital stay.
    d. renew on January 1 of each year for each Medicare patient, and can be used by the beneficiary as needed.

6. The limiting charge is the maximum fee a nonPAR may charge for a covered service. If the Medicare allowed fee for a service is $100, the nonPAR limiting charge would be
    a. $76.   c. $95.
    b. $80.   d. $115.

7. The Privacy Act of 1979 allows MACs to release unassigned claim status information to nonPARs, as follows:

   a. amount paid on the claim and the approved charge information

   b. date the claim was paid by the MAC and approved charge information

   c. date the claim was received by the MAC; date the claim was paid, denied, or suspended; and general reason the claim was suspended

   d. date the claim was received by the MAC; date the claim was paid, denied, or suspended; and the amount paid on the claim

8. A Medicare private contract is an agreement between the Medicare beneficiary and a physician who has "opted out" of Medicare for two years. This means that

   a. claims submitted to Medicare will be processed along with claims submitted to supplemental insurance (Medigap).

   b. Medicare payments will be made for services and procedures provided to patients.

   c. the patient is not required to pay physician charges, and the physician is not limited as to charges submitted to Medicare.

   d. The physician cannot bill for any service or supplies provided to any Medicare beneficiary for at least two years.

9. The patient has the following health care plans: Medicare, Medigap, and an employer large group health plan (EGHP). The billing order for this patient would be:

   a. EGHP, Medicare, Medigap.   c. Medicare, Medigap, EGHP.

   b. Medigap, Medicare, EGHP.   d. Medicare, EGHP, Medigap.

10. Individuals automatically enrolled in Medicare Part A are those who

   a. already receive Social Security, Railroad Retirement Board, or disability benefits and are not yet age 65.

   b. qualify for both Part A and Part B.

   c. have an annual income that falls below the federal poverty level.

   d. turn 65 years of age as of March 1 of any given year.

11. Under which program does the federal government require state Medicaid programs to pay Medicare Part B premiums, patient deductibles, and coinsurance for individuals who have Medicare Part A, a low monthly income, limited resources, and are not otherwise eligible for Medicaid?

   a. Qualified Disabled Working Individual   c. Qualifying Individual

   b. Qualified Medicare Beneficiary   d. Special Low-Income Medicare Beneficiary

12. Hospice provides which services for patients?

   a. medical care in the home with the goal of keeping the patient out of the acute or long-term care setting

   b. medical care, as well as psychological, sociological, and spiritual care

   c. no copay if the patient has had a three-day minimum qualifying stay in an acute care facility

   d. temporary hospitalization for a terminally ill, dependent patient for the purpose of providing relief from duty for the nonpaid caregiver of that patient

13. A managed care organization that is owned and operated by a network of physicians and hospitals rather than an insurance company is a

   a. health maintenance organization.   c. preferred provider organization.

   b. management service organization.   d. provider sponsored organization.

14. Which Medicare plans provide care under contract to Medicare (in the form of managed care plans and private fee-for-service plans) and may include benefits such as coordination of care, reductions in out-of-pocket expenses, and prescription drugs?

    a. Medicare Advantage

    b. Medicare Part B

    c. Medicare Part D

    d. Medicare Savings Accounts

15. Which type of account provides a means for individuals without Medicare to set aside money for current medical expenses as well as future medical expenses, with the benefit of tax-favored treatment of the funds?

    a. extra coverage plan

    b. health savings account

    c. Medicare savings account

    d. Program of All-Inclusive Care for the Elderly

16. Medicare Supplementary Insurance is also known as

    a. Medicaid.

    b. Medicare Advantage.

    c. Medicare SELECT.

    d. Medigap.

17. Which of the following providers are required to accept assignment on all Medicare covered services, regardless of their participating status?

    a. anesthesiologists

    b. ophthalmologists

    c. psychiatrists

    d. psychologists

18. Prior to performing an elective procedure or a noncovered procedure on a Medicare beneficiary, a nonPAR must do what?

    a. Collect a deposit toward the cost of the procedure.

    b. Have the beneficiary sign and date a surgical disclosure notice.

    c. Have the patient sign a waiver-of-liability form.

    d. Obtain a copy of the beneficiary's living will.

19. The act of billing the patient for the difference between the charged fee and the Medicare allowed fee (which is restricted in many states) is known as

    a. accepting assignment.

    b. balance billing.

    c. collecting coinsurance.

    d. roster billing.

20. An agreement between a Medicare beneficiary and a physician or other practitioner who has "opted out" of Medicare for two years is known as

    a. a Medicare private contract.

    b. a participating provider agreement.

    c. accepting assignment.

    d. assignment of benefits.

21. The purpose of the advance beneficiary notice is to alert the patient that

    a. a service is unlikely to be reimbursed by Medicare and that the patient must guarantee payment for services.

    b. if the patient has the service or procedure performed, the patient will no longer qualify for Medicare benefits.

    c. the provider is a nonparticipating provider and the patient will be responsible for payment.

    d. the service performed is experimental and successful outcome is not guaranteed.

22. Medicare is considered primary when the patient is also covered by

    a. a third-party liability policy.

    b. a workers' compensation program.

    c. the Federal Black Lung Program.

    d. TRICARE.

23. Which is sent to Medicare beneficiaries on a monthly basis and lists health insurance claims information?

a. advance beneficiary notice

b. Medicare remittance advice

c. Medicare Summary Notice

d. Notice of Exclusion of Medicare Benefits

24. The deadline for filing Medicare claims is

a. six months from the date of service.

b. one year from the date of service.

c. December 31 of the year following the date of service.

d. December 31 of the year in which the service was provided.

25. How many days must be allowed to pass before a provider can resubmit a paper CMS-1500 claim to Medicare?

a. 0, because paper claims cannot be resubmitted

b. 21

c. 30

d. 45

ANSWER KEY TO EXAM—CHAPTER 14

1. c	**8.** d	**15.** b	**22.** d
2. c	**9.** a	**16.** d	**23.** c
3. b	**10.** a	**17.** d	**24.** c
4. d	**11.** b	**18.** b	**25.** d
5. c	**12.** b	**19.** b	
6. d	**13.** d	**20.** a	
7. c	**14.** a	**21.** a	

EXAM–CHAPTER 15

Student Name _____

Multiple Choice

Circle the most appropriate response.

1. The spousal impoverishment protection legislation was originally part of the
   a. Balanced Budget Act of 1997.
   b. Health Insurance Portability and Accountability Act.
   c. Medicare Catastrophic Coverage Act.
   d. Tax Equity and Fiscal Responsibility Act.

2. Medicare beneficiaries with low incomes and limited resources may be eligible for Medicaid benefits; as a result, beneficiaries will receive additional services (not covered by Medicare), such as
   a. ambulatory surgery services, emergency department services, and outpatient care.
   b. inpatient hospitalizations, home health care, and hospice care services.
   c. nursing facility care beyond 100 days, prescription drugs, eyeglasses, and hearing aids.
   d. physician office services, urgent care, and durable medical equipment.

3. Certain individuals who have resources at or below twice the standard allowed under the SSI program and income at or below 100 percent of the FPL do not have to pay their monthly Medicare premiums, deductibles, and coinsurance; they are categorized as
   a. qualified disabled and working individuals.
   b. qualified Medicare beneficiaries.
   c. qualifying individuals.
   d. specified low-income Medicare beneficiaries.

4. Medicaid will conditionally subrogate claims
   a. because Medicaid eligibility is determined by income.
   b. on Medicare/Medicaid crossover cases.
   c. until preauthorization is obtained for nonemergency admissions.
   d. when there is liability insurance to cover a person's injuries.

5. Preauthorization guidelines for Medicaid recipients are required for which of the following?
   a. admission for preoperative testing and prenatal care
   b. elective admissions and extension of inpatient days
   c. outpatient procedures and prescription medications
   d. routine physician office visits and emergency outpatient treatment

6. Medicaid provides medical and health-related services for individuals and families with low incomes and limited resources, who are collectively known as
   a. categorically needy.
   b. dual eligibles.
   c. medically disabled.
   d. medically indigent.

7. The Medicaid program that makes cash assistance available on a time-limited basis for children deprived of support because of a parent's death, incapacity, absence, or unemployment is the
   a. Early and Periodic Screening, Diagnostic, and Treatment program.
   b. State Children's Health Insurance Program.
   c. Temporary Assistance to Needy Families.
   d. Ticket to Work and Work Incentives Improvement Act of 1999.

8. How long does Medicaid coverage continue for an infant born to a Medicaid-eligible woman?

    a. six months after birth

    b. through the first year of the infant's life

    c. until the child's second birthday

    d. until the mother is no longer eligible for Medicaid

9. The spousal impoverishment protection legislation exempts which items from the couple's combined countable resources?

    a. boat, hunting camp, savings account, and investment dividends

    b. primary home, household goods, automobile, and burial funds

    c. rental property, retirement income, certificates of deposit, and employment income

    d. summer home, stocks, bonds, and SSI income

10. How frequently should a patient's Medicaid eligibility be verified?

    a. at the time of the patient's annual wellness checkup

    b. on a monthly basis

    c. when the patient notifies you of any changes in Medicaid coverage

    d. with each visit to the provider

11. Which service is considered optional in the Medicaid program?

    a. pediatric nurse practitioner services   c. physician services

    b. physical therapy   d. prenatal care

12. The ultimate purpose of the Programs of All-Inclusive Care for the Elderly is to

    a. decrease the burden of home health care agencies.

    b. help the person maintain independence, dignity, and quality of life.

    c. prevent a patient from being admitted to a nursing facility.

    d. replace the services of home health care and day health centers.

13. A disproportionate share hospital is one that treats a disproportionate number of what type of patient?

    a. Medicaid   c. self-pay

    b. Medicare   d. veterans

14. States rarely require Medicaid recipients to pay a

    a. coinsurance.   c. deductible.

    b. copayment.   d. premium.

15. Each state's annual federal medical assistance percentage is determined by using a formula that

    a. calculates an appropriate dollar amount based on each state's population.

    b. calculates the amount to be awarded based on the number of uninsured and unemployed individuals in each state.

    c. compares each state's annual Medicaid expenditures and calculates the percentage each will receive.

    d. compares the state's average per capita income level with the national average.

16. A Medicaid claim that has been corrected, resulting in additional payment(s) to the provider, is a(n) _____ claim.

    a. adjusted   c. suspended

    b. rejected   d. voided

17. Medicaid remittance advice documents should be maintained for how long?
    a. according to the federal statute of limitations
    b. according to the statute of limitations of the state in which the provider practices
    c. indefinitely
    d. until the patient no longer qualifies for Medicaid coverage

18. The unit in charge of safeguarding the state's Medicaid program against unnecessary or inappropriate use of services is the
    a. Office of Inspector General.
    b. state insurance commissioner.
    c. Surveillance and Utilization Review System.
    d. U.S. Attorney General.

19. What special handling of the CMS-1500 claim is required when there is more than one preauthorization number to be reported in Block 23?
    a. A semicolon must be placed between the preauthorization numbers.
    b. A separate CMS-1500 claim form must be generated.
    c. An attachment must be provided that lists the preauthorization numbers.
    d. The claim must be mailed rather than transmitted electronically.

20. What coverage does a Medicaid "Baby Your Baby" program provide?
    a. delivery and nursery care services for the newborn
    b. Medicaid coverage through the first year of the infant's life
    c. prenatal care only for the pregnant mother.
    d. specialized care for a high-needs newborn, such as neonatal intensive care unit services

21. Which program modernized the employment services system for people with disabilities, making it possible for them to join the work force without fear of losing Medicaid or Medicare coverage?
    a. Medicare Catastrophic Coverage Act of 1988
    b. State Children's Health Insurance Program
    c. Temporary Assistance to Needy Families
    d. The Ticket to Work and Work Incentives Improvement Act of 1999

22. Which of the following practices is prohibited by law?
    a. balance billing of Medicaid patients
    b. billing a Medicaid patient for a service that is not a covered benefit
    c. billing the patient directly for a service provided when the individual's Medicaid eligibility has changed
    d. charging the Medicaid patient a copayment for a service

23. When an enrollee has a primary care provider who authorizes access to specialty care but is not at risk for the cost of the care provided, the beneficiary is enrolled in a(n)
    a. Medicaid health maintenance organization.   c. optional categorically needy group.
    b. Medicare/Medicaid crossover plan.   d. primary care case management plan.

24. Children under the age of six and pregnant women whose family income is at or below 133 percent of the federal poverty level qualify for Medicaid benefits as part of the
    a. basic coverage group.
    b. mandatory categorically needy eligibility group.
    c. optional categorically related group.
    d. State Children's Health Insurance Program.

25. If a service provided can be categorized as both EPSDT and family planning, what is entered in Block 24H on the CMS-1500 claim form?

a. B

b. E

c. E, F

d. F

ANSWER KEY TO EXAM—CHAPTER 15

1. c	**8.** b	**15.** d	**22.** a
2. c	**9.** b	**16.** a	**23.** d
3. b	**10.** d	**17.** a	**24.** b
4. d	**11.** b	**18.** c	**25.** a
5. b	**12.** b	**19.** b	
6. d	**13.** a	**20.** c	
7. c	**14.** d	**21.** d	

EXAM—CHAPTER 16

Student Name _____

Multiple Choice

Circle the most appropriate response.

1. TRICARE is a health care program for
   a. active duty members of the military and their qualified family members.
   b. dependents of veterans who have been rated by VA as having a disability.
   c. survivors of veterans who died from VA-rated service-connected conditions.
   d. survivors of persons who died in the line of duty and not due to misconduct.

2. The office that coordinates and administers the TRICARE program is called
   a. Military Health Services System.
   b. Program Integrity Office.
   c. TRICARE Management Activity.
   d. TRICARE Service Centers.

3. A group of civilian practitioners organized by TRICARE contractors to supplement military direct care is called a
   a. health maintenance organization.
   b. point-of-service plan.
   c. preferred provider network.
   d. primary care manager.

4. TRICARE deductibles are applied to the government's fiscal year, which runs from
   a. June 1 to May 31.
   b. September 1 to August 31.
   c. October 1 to September 30.
   d. January 1 to December 31.

5. TRICARE beneficiaries are protected from devastating financial loss due to serious illness or long-term treatment through a catastrophic cap benefit that
   a. allows for unlimited out-of-pocket costs each year for covered services.
   b. establishes limits over which payment for services is not required.
   c. prohibits providers from billing for charges not reimbursed by TRICARE.
   d. requires the member to pay a percentage of the expenses for medical.

6. The amount the TRICARE Standard member pays each year toward outpatient care before TRICARE begins sharing the cost of medical care is called a
   a. coinsurance.
   b. copayment.
   c. premium.
   d. deductible.

7. A registered nurse or physician's assistant who assists primary care managers with preauthorizations and referrals to health care services in the military treatment facility or the civilian provider network is called a
   a. beneficiary service representative.
   b. health care finder.
   c. nurse advisor.
   d. primary care manager.

8. A certificate issued by a military treatment facility stating that the facility cannot provide needed care is called a _____ statement.
   a. denial
   b. nonavailability
   c. preauthorization
   d. referral

9. Which of the following would qualify as a TRICARE sponsor?
   a. dependent of a deceased active-duty serviceman
   b. dependent of a veteran who has been rated by the VA as having a total and permanent disability
   c. retired uniformed service personnel
   d. survivor of a veteran who died in the line of duty and not from misconduct

10. The function of the TRICARE Service Centers is to
    a. assist TRICARE sponsors with health care needs and answer questions about the program.
    b. manage the TRICARE programs and demonstration projects.
    c. monitor for fraud and abuse activities worldwide involving purchased care for beneficiaries in the Military Health Services System.
    d. provide nonemergency care to eligible beneficiaries and arrange referrals for specialty care if needed.

11. Which TRICARE program offers families a standardized obstetric benefit?
    a. Family Centered Care
    b. TRICARE for Life
    c. TRICARE Overseas Program
    d. TRICARE Plus

12. Which place of service is the least costly when using the TRICARE pharmacy program to obtain medications?
    a. military treatment facility
    b. non-network pharmacies
    c. TRICARE mail-order pharmacy
    d. TRICARE retail networks

13. A research study that helps to find ways to diagnose, prevent, or treat illnesses and improve health care is called a(n)
    a. clinical trial.
    b. critical pathway.
    c. demonstration project.
    d. investigative trial.

14. What system is used to confirm TRICARE eligibility for sponsors and their dependents?
    a. Defense Enrollment Eligibility Reporting System
    b. Health Care Finder
    c. TRICARE Management Activity
    d. Program Integrity Office

15. Active duty personnel must enroll in the _____ program to receive guaranteed access to care at MTFs.
    a. TRICARE Extra
    b. TRICARE for Life
    c. TRICARE Prime
    d. TRICARE Standard

16. The health insurance specialist submits TRICARE claims to
    a. Military Health Services System.
    b. military treatment facilities.
    c. TRICARE contractors.
    d. TRICARE Management Activity.

17. If a TRICARE sponsor and spouse divorce, what effect will this have on the TRICARE status of the children?
    a. The children lose their TRICARE eligibility.
    b. The children may recover their TRICARE benefits if the civilian spouse marries another TRICARE sponsor.
    c. The children may remain eligible for TRICARE for an additional premium charge.
    d. The children remain eligible for TRICARE even if the parents divorce or remarry.

18. How many regions are in the TRICARE system?
    a. 3
    b. 4
    c. 5
    d. 11

19. Decision-making tools used by providers to determine appropriate health care for specific clinical circumstances are known as
    a. clinical trials.
    b. critical pathways.
    c. practice guidelines.
    d. preauthorizations.

20. Which TRICARE program requires an enrollment fee?

    a. TRICARE Extra   c. TRICARE Prime

    b. TRICARE Plus   d. TRICARE Standard

21. Who is available to assist providers in recovering charges if a beneficiary fails to pay the deductible or cost share (e.g., copayment)?

    a. beneficiary services representative

    b. Defense Enrollment Eligibility Reporting System

    c. health care finder

    d. TRICARE Management Activity

22. If the patient is being transferred within the next six months, TRICARE suggests that the

    a. claim be submitted via overnight mail to ensure that it is paid quickly.

    b. insurance specialist should enter the word TRANSFER in Block 19.

    c. office collect the fee for services provided and then reimburse the enrollee after payment from TRICARE has been received.

    d. provider should accept assignment to prevent collection problems.

23. The purpose of the good faith policy established by TRICARE is to allow

    a. beneficiaries to be seen without presenting an ID card.

    b. contract providers to treat patients without any oversight from TRICARE.

    c. the provider a means to recover payment when the enrollee has presented an invalid ID card.

    d. TRICARE to reduce reimbursement rates if the provider does not show good faith in treating enrollees.

24. What special handling is required for all injuries that have been assigned ICD codes in the 800 to 959 range?

    a. A "Personal Injury-Possible Third-Party Liability" statement should accompany the claim.

    b. Only a TRICARE emergency department provider is permitted to treat the enrollee.

    c. The phrase THIRD-PARTY LIABILITY should be entered in Block 19 of the CMS-1500 claim form.

    d. TRICARE will not pay for services in this code range.

25. Block 31 of the CMS-1500 claim submitted to TRICARE must contain the

    a. full typewritten name and credentials of the provider.

    b. health insurance specialist's signature on behalf of the provider.

    c. provider's actual signature or use of a signature stamp.

    d. words SIGNATURE ON FILE.

ANSWER KEY TO EXAM—CHAPTER 16

1. a	8. b	15. c	22. d
2. c	9. c	16. c	23. c
3. c	10. a	17. d	24. a
4. c	11. a	18. b	25. c
5. b	12. a	19. c	
6. d	13. a	20. c	
7. b	14. a	21. a	

EXAM—CHAPTER 17

Student Name _____

Multiple Choice

Circle the most appropriate response.

1. The legislation that provides workers' compensation for nonmilitary federal employees is called the
   a. Federal Employment Compensation Act.
   b. Federal Employment Liability Act.
   c. Longshore and Harbor Act.
   d. Merchant Marine Act (or Jones Act).

2. The government agency that functions as the insuring body to cover workers' compensation claims is called the
   a. Federal Employees' Compensation Act.
   b. Federal Employment Liability Act.
   c. State Insurance Fund.
   d. Workers' Compensation Board.

3. The workers' compensation *First Report of Injury* form is completed when the
   a. employer authorizes treatment of the injury.
   b. patient claims a first work-related injury or illness, not for subsequent work-related injuries or illnesses.
   c. patient has given consent for filing of compensation claims and reports.
   d. patient signs the *First Report of Injury* form.

4. The filing deadline for the *First Report of Injury* form is determined by
   a. individual physicians.
   b. OSHA.
   c. state law.
   d. the fiscal agent.

5. State compensation boards establish a schedule of approved workers' compensation fees based on the _____ unit value scale.
   a. APC
   b. DRG
   c. RBRVS
   d. RVS

6. Providers are required to accept the compensation payment as payment in full; this is called
   a. accept assignment.
   b. adjudication.
   c. arbitration.
   d. assignment of benefits.

7. Employees of the federal government, coal miners, longshoremen, and harbor workers
   a. are covered by state-sponsored workers' compensation laws.
   b. are not eligible for workers' compensation coverage by any organization.
   c. must be permanently disabled to receive workers' compensation.
   d. receive workers' compensation coverage through the federal government.

8. According to OSHA regulations, comprehensive records of all vaccinations given and any accidental exposure incidents, such as needle sticks, must be maintained for _____ years.
   a. 5
   b. 10
   c. 7
   d. 20

9. What is the definition of *temporary partial disability*?
   a. Part of the employee's wage-earning capacity has been permanently lost.
   b. The employee's wage-earning capacity is partially lost, but only on a temporary basis.
   c. The employee's wage-earning capacity is permanently and totally lost.
   d. The employee's wage-earning capacity is totally lost, but only on a temporary basis.

10. What agency can a worker contact to appeal a denied claim?

    a. Occupational Health and Safety Administration

    b. Office of Workers' Compensation Programs

    c. State Insurance Fund

    d. State Workers' Compensation Board

11. The type of workers' compensation claim that is easiest to process is

    a. medical treatment.
             c. temporary disability.

    b. permanent disability.
           d. vocational rehabilitation.

12. The person responsible for completing the *First Report of Injury* is the:

    a. employer.
               c. injured employee.

    b. health insurance specialist.
      d. treating physician.

13. An employee twisted his ankle at work on December 1 and called in sick to work on December 2 and December 3. The employee saw his family physician on December 4. The date to be entered in Item 4 of the *First Report of Injury* is

    a. December 1.
              c. December 3.

    b. December 2.
             d. December 4.

14. Item 6 of the *First Report of Injury* form requires the employee's word-for-word description of the accident. If the space in Item 6 is not sufficient, what should the provider do?

    a. Attach an additional page to the form.

    b. Enter AVAILABLE UPON REQUEST in Item 6.

    c. Paraphrase the employee's description to make sure it fits in the space provided for Item 6.

    d. Write in the margins of the page to keep all of the information on one page.

15. A workers' compensation progress report is filed when

    a. a private payer is erroneously billed for the workers' compensation claim.

    b. the employer requests the injured worker be released to return to work.

    c. the injured worker fails to keep a medical appointment.

    d. there is any significant change in the worker's medical or disability status.

16. An employee willfully misrepresents a physical condition to obtain benefits from the state compensation fund. This is an example of

    a. employee fraud.
            c. provider abuse.

    b. employer fraud.
           d. provider fraud.

17. What group of government employees is excluded from federal workers' compensation programs?

    a. coal miners
              c. postal workers

    b. maritime workers
         d. uniformed services

18. An employee will lose the right to workers' compensation coverage if the injury results solely from

    a. carelessness.
             c. inadequate training.

    b. drug or alcohol intoxication.
   d. unprofessional behavior.

19. Workers' compensation premiums are paid by the

    a. employee.
              c. injured worker.

    b. employer.
             d. state insurance fund.

20. A dispute resolution process in which a final determination is made by an impartial person who may not have judicial powers is known as
    a. accepting assignment.
    b. adjudication.
    c. arbitration.
    d. deposition.

21. Which of the following entities can be a designated fiscal agent?
    a. Federal Employees' Compensation Act Program
    b. Office of Workers' Compensation Programs
    c. State Insurance Compensation Board
    d. State Insurance Compensation Fund

22. What information is entered in Block 11 of the CMS-1500 claim form for a workers' compensation case?
    a. Nothing is entered in Block 11 of the CMS-1500. The block is left blank.
    b. The group number of the patient's private insurance plan is entered in Block 11 of the CMS-1500.
    c. The patient's social security number is entered in Block 11 of the CMS-1500.
    d. The workers' compensation claim number is entered in Block 11 of the CMS-1500.

23. The diagnosis *pneumoconiosis* is associated with which federal compensation program?
    a. Energy Employees Occupational Illness Compensation Program
    b. Federal Black Lung Program
    c. Longshore and Harbor Workers' Compensation Program
    d. Mine Safety and Health Administration

24. Workers' compensation laws protect the employer by
    a. limiting the award an injured employee can recover from an employer.
    b. prohibiting the employee from suing the employer for hazardous working conditions.
    c. providing the employer an option to terminate an employee because of a workers' compensation claim.
    d. requiring the injured worker to return to the job at the request of the employer.

25. When an injured employee has suffered a loss of eyesight, hearing, or a part of the body or its use, benefits are payable
    a. according to a payment schedule set by law.
    b. based on the employee's earning capacity at the time of illness or injury.
    c. based on the injured employee's diminished wage-earning capacity only; no medical benefits are provided.
    d. for medical treatment only.

ANSWER KEY TO EXAM–CHAPTER 17

1. a	8. d	15. d	22. d
2. c	9. b	16. a	23. b
3. a	10. d	17. d	24. a
4. c	11. a	18. b	25. a
5. d	12. d	19. b	
6. a	13. a	20. c	
7. d	14. a	21. d	

APPENDIX I Completed Claims for Case Studies: Set One

1500

HEALTH INSURANCE CLAIM FORM

APPROVED BY NATIONAL UNIFORM CLAIM COMMITTEE 08/05

| | PICA | | | | | | | | | | | PICA | |

1. MEDICARE (Medicare #)	MEDICAID (Medicaid #)	TRICARE CHAMPUS (Sponsor's SSN)	CHAMPVA (Member ID#)	GROUP HEALTH PLAN (SSN or ID)	FECA BLK LUNG (SSN)	OTHER [X] (ID)	1a. INSURED'S I.D. NUMBER (For Program in Item 1)

1a. INSURED'S I.D. NUMBER (For Program in Item 1): 272034109

2. PATIENT'S NAME (Last Name, First Name, Middle Initial): HIGHTOWER, MARY, S

3. PATIENT'S BIRTH DATE: 08 07 1951 **SEX** M F [X]

4. INSURED'S NAME (Last Name, First Name, Middle Initial): HIGHTOWER, WALTER, W

5. PATIENT'S ADDRESS (No., Street): 61 WATER TOWER STREET

6. PATIENT'S RELATIONSHIP TO INSURED: Self Spouse [X] Child Other

7. INSURED'S ADDRESS (No., Street): 61 WATER TOWER STREET

CITY: ANYWHERE **STATE**: NY

8. PATIENT STATUS: Single Married [X] Other

CITY: ANYWHERE **STATE**: NY

ZIP CODE: 12345-1234 **TELEPHONE (Include Area Code)**: (101)2016987

Employed Full-Time Student Part-Time Student

ZIP CODE: 12345-1234 **TELEPHONE (Include Area Code)**: (101)2016987

9. OTHER INSURED'S NAME (Last Name, First Name, Middle Initial):

10. IS PATIENT'S CONDITION RELATED TO:

11. INSURED'S POLICY GROUP OR FECA NUMBER: NPW

a. OTHER INSURED'S POLICY OR GROUP NUMBER:

a. EMPLOYMENT? (Current or Previous): YES NO [X]

a. INSURED'S DATE OF BIRTH: 04 09 1951 **SEX** M [X] F

b. OTHER INSURED'S DATE OF BIRTH: MM DD YY **SEX** M F

b. AUTO ACCIDENT?: YES NO [X] PLACE (State)

b. EMPLOYER'S NAME OR SCHOOL NAME: ANYWHERE WATER CO

c. EMPLOYER'S NAME OR SCHOOL NAME:

c. OTHER ACCIDENT?: YES NO [X]

c. INSURANCE PLAN NAME OR PROGRAM NAME: AETNA

d. INSURANCE PLAN NAME OR PROGRAM NAME:

10d. RESERVED FOR LOCAL USE:

d. IS THERE ANOTHER HEALTH BENEFIT PLAN?: YES NO [X] *If yes*, return to and complete item 9 a-d.

READ BACK OF FORM BEFORE COMPLETING & SIGNING THIS FORM.

12. PATIENT'S OR AUTHORIZED PERSON'S SIGNATURE I authorize the release of any medical or other information necessary to process this claim. I also request payment of government benefits either to myself or to the party who accepts assignment below.

SIGNED **SIGNATURE ON FILE** DATE

13. INSURED'S OR AUTHORIZED PERSON'S SIGNATURE I authorize payment of medical benefits to the undersigned physician or supplier for services described below.

SIGNED **SIGNATURE ON FILE**

14. DATE OF CURRENT: ILLNESS (First symptom) OR INJURY (Accident) OR PREGNANCY (LMP): 01 10 YYYY

15. IF PATIENT HAS HAD SAME OR SIMILAR ILLNESS, GIVE FIRST DATE MM DD YY

16. DATES PATIENT UNABLE TO WORK IN CURRENT OCCUPATION: FROM TO

17. NAME OF REFERRING PROVIDER OR OTHER SOURCE: IM GOODDOC MD

17a. 17b. NPI 5678901234

18. HOSPITALIZATION DATES RELATED TO CURRENT SERVICES: FROM 01 10 YYYY TO 01 10 YYYY

19. RESERVED FOR LOCAL USE:

20. OUTSIDE LAB?: YES NO [X] $ CHARGES

21. DIAGNOSIS OR NATURE OF ILLNESS OR INJURY (Relate Items 1, 2, 3 or 4 to Item 24E by Line)

1. 414 05
2.
3.
4.

22. MEDICAID RESUBMISSION CODE ORIGINAL REF. NO.

23. PRIOR AUTHORIZATION NUMBER

24. A DATE(S) OF SERVICE From / To MM DD YY MM DD YY	B. PLACE OF SERVICE	C. EMG	D. PROCEDURES, SERVICES, OR SUPPLIES (Explain Unusual Circumstances) CPT/HCPCS / MODIFIER	E. DIAGNOSIS POINTER	F. $ CHARGES	G. DAYS OR UNITS	H. EPSDT Family Plan	I. ID. QUAL.	J. RENDERING PROVIDER ID. #
1	01 10 YYYY		22	93510	1	2000 00	1		NPI
2	01 10 YYYY		22	93540	1	250 00	1		NPI
3	01 10 YYYY		22	93556	1	750 00	1		NPI
4									NPI
5									NPI
6									NPI

25. FEDERAL TAX I.D. NUMBER: 117654312 SSN EIN [X]

26. PATIENT'S ACCOUNT NO.: 1-1

27. ACCEPT ASSIGNMENT? (For govt. claims, see back): [X] YES NO

28. TOTAL CHARGE: $ 3000 00

29. AMOUNT PAID: $

30. BALANCE DUE: $ 3000 00

31. SIGNATURE OF PHYSICIAN OR SUPPLIER INCLUDING DEGREES OR CREDENTIALS (I certify that the statements on the reverse apply to this bill and are made a part thereof.)

IRMINA M BRILLIANT MD

SIGNED DATE MMDDYYYY

32. SERVICE FACILITY LOCATION INFORMATION

GOODMEDICINE HOSPITAL
1 PROVIDER STREET
ANYWHERE NY 12345

a. 1123456789 b.

33. BILLING PROVIDER INFO & PH #: (101)2013145

IRMINA M BRILLIANT MD
25 MEDICAL DRIVE
INJURY NY 12347

a. 2345678901 b.

NUCC Instruction Manual available at: www.nucc.org

APPROVED OMB-0938-0999 FORM CMS-1500 (08/05)

1500

HEALTH INSURANCE CLAIM FORM

APPROVED BY NATIONAL UNIFORM CLAIM COMMITTEE 08/05

| | PICA | | PICA | |

1. MEDICARE	MEDICAID	TRICARE CHAMPUS	CHAMPVA	GROUP HEALTH PLAN	FECA BLK LUNG	OTHER	1a. INSURED'S I.D. NUMBER (For Program in Item 1)
(Medicare #)	(Medicaid #)	(Sponsor's SSN)	(Member ID#)	(SSN or ID)	(SSN)	X (ID)	210010121

2. PATIENT'S NAME (Last Name, First Name, Middle Initial)	3. PATIENT'S BIRTH DATE	SEX	4. INSURED'S NAME (Last Name, First Name, Middle Initial)
GAYLE, IMA	09 30 1945 M	F X	GAYLE, IMA

5. PATIENT'S ADDRESS (No., Street)	6. PATIENT'S RELATIONSHIP TO INSURED	7. INSURED'S ADDRESS (No., Street)
101 HAPPY DRIVE	Self X Spouse Child Other	101 HAPPY DRIVE

CITY	STATE	8. PATIENT STATUS	CITY	STATE
ANYWHERE	NY	Single X Married Other	ANYWHERE	NY

ZIP CODE	TELEPHONE (Include Area Code)		ZIP CODE	TELEPHONE (Include Area Code)
12345-1234	(101)1119876	Employed X Full-Time Student Part-Time Student	12345-1234	(101)1119876

9. OTHER INSURED'S NAME (Last Name, First Name, Middle Initial)	10. IS PATIENT'S CONDITION RELATED TO:	11. INSURED'S POLICY GROUP OR FECA NUMBER
		101

a. OTHER INSURED'S POLICY OR GROUP NUMBER	a. EMPLOYMENT? (Current or Previous) YES X NO	a. INSURED'S DATE OF BIRTH 09 30 1945 SEX M F X
b. OTHER INSURED'S DATE OF BIRTH MM DD YY SEX M F	b. AUTO ACCIDENT? PLACE (State) YES X NO	b. EMPLOYER'S NAME OR SCHOOL NAME MAIL BOXES INC
c. EMPLOYER'S NAME OR SCHOOL NAME	c. OTHER ACCIDENT? YES X NO	c. INSURANCE PLAN NAME OR PROGRAM NAME CONN GENERAL
d. INSURANCE PLAN NAME OR PROGRAM NAME	10d. RESERVED FOR LOCAL USE	d. IS THERE ANOTHER HEALTH BENEFIT PLAN? YES X NO If yes, return to and complete item 9 a-d.

READ BACK OF FORM BEFORE COMPLETING & SIGNING THIS FORM.

12. PATIENT'S OR AUTHORIZED PERSON'S SIGNATURE I authorize the release of any medical or other information necessary to process this claim. I also request payment of government benefits either to myself or to the party who accepts assignment below.

SIGNED SIGNATURE ON FILE   DATE _____

13. INSURED'S OR AUTHORIZED PERSON'S SIGNATURE I authorize payment of medical benefits to the undersigned physician or supplier for services described below.

SIGNED SIGNATURE ON FILE

14. DATE OF CURRENT: ILLNESS (First symptom) OR INJURY (Accident) OR PREGNANCY (LMP) 03 01 YYYY	15. IF PATIENT HAS HAD SAME OR SIMILAR ILLNESS. GIVE FIRST DATE MM DD YY	16. DATES PATIENT UNABLE TO WORK IN CURRENT OCCUPATION FROM MM DD YY TO MM DD YY
17. NAME OF REFERRING PROVIDER OR OTHER SOURCE	17a. / 17b. NPI	18. HOSPITALIZATION DATES RELATED TO CURRENT SERVICES FROM MM DD YY TO MM DD YY
19. RESERVED FOR LOCAL USE		20. OUTSIDE LAB? YES X NO $ CHARGES

21. DIAGNOSIS OR NATURE OF ILLNESS OR INJURY (Relate Items 1, 2, 3 or 4 to Item 24E by Line)

1. 782 . 0   3. |___|.|___|

2. 715 . 96   4. |___|.|___|

22. MEDICAID RESUBMISSION CODE   ORIGINAL REF. NO.

23. PRIOR AUTHORIZATION NUMBER

24. A DATE(S) OF SERVICE From MM DD YY To MM DD YY	B. PLACE OF SERVICE	C. EMG	D. PROCEDURES, SERVICES, OR SUPPLIES (Explain Unusual Circumstances) CPT/HCPCS MODIFIER	E. DIAGNOSIS POINTER	F. $ CHARGES	G. DAYS OR UNITS	H. EPSDT Family Plan	I. ID. QUAL.	J. RENDERING PROVIDER ID. #
1 03 01 YYYY	11		99213	1	60 00	1		NPI	
2 03 01 YYYY	11		20552	1	75 00	1		NPI	
3								NPI	
4								NPI	
5								NPI	
6								NPI	

25. FEDERAL TAX I.D. NUMBER SSN EIN	26. PATIENT'S ACCOUNT NO.	27. ACCEPT ASSIGNMENT? (For govt. claims, see back)	28. TOTAL CHARGE	29. AMOUNT PAID	30. BALANCE DUE
111397992 X	1-2	X YES NO	$ 135 00	$ 50 00	$ 85 00

31. SIGNATURE OF PHYSICIAN OR SUPPLIER INCLUDING DEGREES OR CREDENTIALS (I certify that the statements on the reverse apply to this bill and are made a part thereof.) SEJAL RAJA MD SIGNED DATE MMDDYYYY	32. SERVICE FACILITY LOCATION INFORMATION a. NPI b.	33. BILLING PROVIDER INFO & PH # (101)2022923 SEJAL RAJA MD 1 MEDICAL DRIVE INJURY NY 12347 a. 7890123456 b.

NUCC Instruction Manual available at: www.nucc.org

APPROVED OMB-0938-0999 FORM CMS-1500 (08/05)

1500

HEALTH INSURANCE CLAIM FORM

APPROVED BY NATIONAL UNIFORM CLAIM COMMITTEE 08/05

☐☐☐ PICA   PICA ☐☐☐

1. MEDICARE MEDICAID TRICARE CHAMPUS CHAMPVA GROUP HEALTH PLAN FECA BLK LUNG OTHER	1a. INSURED'S I.D. NUMBER (For Program in Item 1)
☐(Medicare #) ☐(Medicaid #) ☐(Sponsor's SSN) ☐(Member ID#) ☐(SSN or ID) ☐(SSN) ☒(ID)	5623569

2. PATIENT'S NAME (Last Name, First Name, Middle Initial)	3. PATIENT'S BIRTH DATE SEX	4. INSURED'S NAME (Last Name, First Name, Middle Initial)
SPENCER, SANDY	08 05 1985 M☐ F☒	SPENCER, SANDY

5. PATIENT'S ADDRESS (No., Street)	6. PATIENT'S RELATIONSHIP TO INSURED	7. INSURED'S ADDRESS (No., Street)
101 HIGH STREET	Self ☒ Spouse ☐ Child ☐ Other ☐	101 HIGH STREET
CITY STATE	8. PATIENT STATUS	CITY STATE
ANYWHERE NY	Single ☒ Married ☐ Other ☐	ANYWHERE NY
ZIP CODE TELEPHONE (Include Area Code)	Employed ☒ Full-Time Student ☐ Part-Time Student ☐	ZIP CODE TELEPHONE (Include Area Code)
12345-1234 (101)5555698		12345-1234 (101)5555698

9. OTHER INSURED'S NAME (Last Name, First Name, Middle Initial)	10. IS PATIENT'S CONDITION RELATED TO:	11. INSURED'S POLICY GROUP OR FECA NUMBER
a. OTHER INSURED'S POLICY OR GROUP NUMBER	a. EMPLOYMENT? (Current or Previous) ☐ YES ☒ NO	a. INSURED'S DATE OF BIRTH SEX 08 05 1985 M☐ F☒
b. OTHER INSURED'S DATE OF BIRTH SEX M☐ F☐	b. AUTO ACCIDENT? PLACE (State) ☐ YES ☒ NO	b. EMPLOYER'S NAME OR SCHOOL NAME GOODMEDICINE MEDICAL CLINIC
c. EMPLOYER'S NAME OR SCHOOL NAME	c. OTHER ACCIDENT? ☐ YES ☒ NO	c. INSURANCE PLAN NAME OR PROGRAM NAME AFLAC
d. INSURANCE PLAN NAME OR PROGRAM NAME	10d. RESERVED FOR LOCAL USE	d. IS THERE ANOTHER HEALTH BENEFIT PLAN? ☐ YES ☒ NO If yes, return to and complete item 9 a-d.

READ BACK OF FORM BEFORE COMPLETING & SIGNING THIS FORM.

12. PATIENT'S OR AUTHORIZED PERSON'S SIGNATURE I authorize the release of any medical or other information necessary to process this claim. I also request payment of government benefits either to myself or to the party who accepts assignment below.	13. INSURED'S OR AUTHORIZED PERSON'S SIGNATURE I authorize payment of medical benefits to the undersigned physican or supplier for services described below.
SIGNED SIGNATURE ON FILE DATE	SIGNED SIGNATURE ON FILE

14. DATE OF CURRENT: ILLNESS (First symptom) OR INJURY (Accident) OR PREGNANCY (LMP) 10 15 YYYY	15. IF PATIENT HAS HAD SAME OR SIMILAR ILLNESS. GIVE FIRST DATE MM DD YY	16. DATES PATIENT UNABLE TO WORK IN CURRENT OCCUPATION FROM TO
17. NAME OF REFERRING PROVIDER OR OTHER SOURCE	17a. 17b. NPI	18. HOSPITALIZATION DATES RELATED TO CURRENT SERVICES FROM TO
19. RESERVED FOR LOCAL USE		20. OUTSIDE LAB? $ CHARGES ☐ YES ☒ NO

21. DIAGNOSIS OR NATURE OF ILLNESS OR INJURY (Relate Items 1, 2, 3 or 4 to Item 24E by Line)	22. MEDICAID RESUBMISSION CODE ORIGINAL REF. NO.
1. 401 9 3.	23. PRIOR AUTHORIZATION NUMBER
2. 4.	

24. A. DATE(S) OF SERVICE From — To MM DD YY MM DD YY	B. PLACE OF SERVICE	C. EMG	D. PROCEDURES, SERVICES, OR SUPPLIES (Explain Unusual Circumstances) CPT/HCPCS MODIFIER	E. DIAGNOSIS POINTER	F. $ CHARGES	G. DAYS OR UNITS	H. EPSDT Family Plan	I. ID. QUAL.	J. RENDERING PROVIDER ID. #
1 1015 YYYY	11		99214	1	100 00	1		NPI	
2								NPI	
3								NPI	
4								NPI	
5								NPI	
6								NPI	

25. FEDERAL TAX I.D. NUMBER SSN EIN	26. PATIENT'S ACCOUNT NO.	27. ACCEPT ASSIGNMENT? (For govt. claims, see back)	28. TOTAL CHARGE	29. AMOUNT PAID	30. BALANCE DUE
117654312 ☒	1-3	☒ YES ☐ NO	$ 100 00	$	$ 100 00

31. SIGNATURE OF PHYSICIAN OR SUPPLIER INCLUDING DEGREES OR CREDENTIALS (I certify that the statements on the reverse apply to this bill and are made a part thereof.)	32. SERVICE FACILITY LOCATION INFORMATION	33. BILLING PROVIDER INFO & PH # (101)2013145
IRMINA M BRILLIANT MD		IRMINA M BRILLIANT MD 25 MEDICAL DRIVE INJURY NY 12347
SIGNED DATE MMDDYYYY	a. NPI b.	a. 2345678901 b.

NUCC Instruction Manual available at: www.nucc.org   APPROVED OMB-0938-0999 FORM CMS-1500 (08/05)

CARRIER

PATIENT AND INSURED INFORMATION

PHYSICIAN OR SUPPLIER INFORMATION

1500

HEALTH INSURANCE CLAIM FORM

APPROVED BY NATIONAL UNIFORM CLAIM COMMITTEE 08/05

| | PICA | | PICA | |

1. MEDICARE (Medicare #) / MEDICAID (Medicaid #) / TRICARE CHAMPUS (Sponsor's SSN) / CHAMPVA (Member ID#) / GROUP HEALTH PLAN (SSN or ID) / FECA BLK LUNG (SSN) / OTHER [X] (ID)

1a. INSURED'S I.D. NUMBER (For Program in Item 1)
ZJW334444

2. PATIENT'S NAME (Last Name, First Name. Middle Initial)
TIGER, KATLYN

3. PATIENT'S BIRTH DATE MM DD YY
01 03 1954 SEX M☐ F[X]

4. INSURED'S NAME (Last Name, First Name, Middle Initial)
TIGER, KATLYN

5. PATIENT'S ADDRESS (No., Street)
2 JUNGLE ROAD

6. PATIENT'S RELATIONSHIP TO INSURED
Self [X] Spouse ☐ Child ☐ Other ☐

7. INSURED'S ADDRESS (No., Street)
2 JUNGLE ROAD

CITY NOWHERE STATE NY

8. PATIENT STATUS
Single [X] Married ☐ Other ☐

CITY NOWHERE STATE NY

ZIP CODE 12346-1234 TELEPHONE (Include Area Code) (101)1112222

Employed [X] Full-Time Student ☐ Part-Time Student ☐

ZIP CODE 12346-1234 TELEPHONE (Include Area Code) (101)1112222

9. OTHER INSURED'S NAME (Last Name, First Name, Middle Initial)

10. IS PATIENT'S CONDITION RELATED TO:

11. INSURED'S POLICY GROUP OR FECA NUMBER
W310

a. OTHER INSURED'S POLICY OR GROUP NUMBER

a. EMPLOYMENT? (Current or Previous)
YES ☐ NO [X]

a. INSURED'S DATE OF BIRTH MM DD YY
01 03 1954 SEX M☐ F[X]

b. OTHER INSURED'S DATE OF BIRTH MM DD YY SEX M☐ F☐

b. AUTO ACCIDENT? PLACE (State)
YES ☐ NO [X]

b. EMPLOYER'S NAME OR SCHOOL NAME
JOHN LION CPA

c. EMPLOYER'S NAME OR SCHOOL NAME

c. OTHER ACCIDENT?
YES ☐ NO [X]

c. INSURANCE PLAN NAME OR PROGRAM NAME
BCBS

d. INSURANCE PLAN NAME OR PROGRAM NAME

10d. RESERVED FOR LOCAL USE

d. IS THERE ANOTHER HEALTH BENEFIT PLAN?
YES ☐ NO ☐ If yes, return to and complete item 9 a-d.

READ BACK OF FORM BEFORE COMPLETING & SIGNING THIS FORM.
12. PATIENT'S OR AUTHORIZED PERSON'S SIGNATURE I authorize the release of any medical or other information necessary to process this claim. I also request payment of government benefits either to myself or to the party who accepts assignment below.

SIGNED SIGNATURE ON FILE DATE

13. INSURED'S OR AUTHORIZED PERSON'S SIGNATURE I authorize payment of medical benefits to the undersigned physician or supplier for services described below.

SIGNED

14. DATE OF CURRENT: MM DD YY
02 28 YYYY ILLNESS (First symptom) OR INJURY (Accident) OR PREGNANCY (LMP)

15. IF PATIENT HAS HAD SAME OR SIMILAR ILLNESS, GIVE FIRST DATE MM DD YY

16. DATES PATIENT UNABLE TO WORK IN CURRENT OCCUPATION MM DD YY
FROM TO

17. NAME OF REFERRING PROVIDER OR OTHER SOURCE
17a.
17b. NPI

18. HOSPITALIZATION DATES RELATED TO CURRENT SERVICES MM DD YY
FROM 02 28 YYYY TO 03 01 YYYY

19. RESERVED FOR LOCAL USE

20. OUTSIDE LAB? $ CHARGES
YES ☐ NO [X]

21. DIAGNOSIS OR NATURE OF ILLNESS OR INJURY (Relate Items 1, 2, 3 or 4 to Item 24E by Line)
1. 485
2.
3.
4.

22. MEDICAID RESUBMISSION CODE ORIGINAL REF. NO.

23. PRIOR AUTHORIZATION NUMBER

24. A. DATE(S) OF SERVICE

	A. DATE(S) OF SERVICE From MM DD YY	To MM DD YY	B. PLACE OF SERVICE	C. EMG	D. PROCEDURES, SERVICES, OR SUPPLIES (Explain Unusual Circumstances) CPT/HCPCS	MODIFIER	E. DIAGNOSIS POINTER	F. $ CHARGES	G. DAYS OR UNITS	H. EPSDT Family Plan	I. ID. QUAL.	J. RENDERING PROVIDER ID. #
1	02 28 YYYY		21		99220		1	175 00			NPI	
2	03 01 YYYY		21		99217		1	65 00			NPI	
3											NPI	
4											NPI	
5											NPI	
6											NPI	

25. FEDERAL TAX I.D. NUMBER SSN EIN
111234632 ☐ [X]

26. PATIENT'S ACCOUNT NO.
1-4

27. ACCEPT ASSIGNMENT? (For govt. claims, see back)
[X] YES ☐ NO

28. TOTAL CHARGE
$ 240 00

29. AMOUNT PAID
$

30. BALANCE DUE
$

31. SIGNATURE OF PHYSICIAN OR SUPPLIER INCLUDING DEGREES OR CREDENTIALS (I certify that the statements on the reverse apply to this bill and are made a part thereof.)
ARNOLD J YOUNGLOVE MD
SIGNED DATE MMDDYYYY

32. SERVICE FACILITY LOCATION INFORMATION
GOODMEDICINE HOSPITAL
1 PROVIDER STREET
ANYWHERE NY 12345
a. 1123456789 b.

33. BILLING PROVIDER INFO & PH # (101)2027754
ARNOLD J YOUNGLOVE MD
21 PROVIDER ST
INJURY NY 12347
a. 0123456789 b.

NUCC Instruction Manual available at: www.nucc.org

APPROVED OMB-0938-0999 FORM CMS-1500 (08/05)

1500

HEALTH INSURANCE CLAIM FORM

APPROVED BY NATIONAL UNIFORM CLAIM COMMITTEE 08/05

| | PICA | | | | | | | | | | PICA | | |

1. MEDICARE (Medicare #)	MEDICAID (Medicaid #)	TRICARE CHAMPUS (Sponsor's SSN)	CHAMPVA (Member ID#)	GROUP HEALTH PLAN (SSN or ID)	FECA BLK LUNG (SSN)	OTHER [X] (ID)	1a. INSURED'S I.D. NUMBER (For Program in Item 1)

1a. INSURED'S I.D. NUMBER (For Program in Item 1)
XWV7794483

2. PATIENT'S NAME (Last Name, First Name, Middle Initial)
GREEN, JEFFREY, A

3. PATIENT'S BIRTH DATE   MM 02 DD 03 YY 1997 SEX M [X] F [ ]

4. INSURED'S NAME (Last Name, First Name, Middle Initial)
GREEN, JEFFREY, G

5. PATIENT'S ADDRESS (No., Street)
103 MOUNTAIN VIEW ROAD

6. PATIENT'S RELATIONSHIP TO INSURED
Self [ ] Spouse [ ] Child [X] Other [ ]

7. INSURED'S ADDRESS (No., Street)
103 MOUNTAIN VIEW ROAD

CITY
NOWHERE   STATE NY

8. PATIENT STATUS
Single [X] Married [ ] Other [ ]

CITY
NOWHERE   STATE NY

ZIP CODE
12346-1234   TELEPHONE (Include Area Code) (101)1178765

Employed [ ] Full-Time Student [ ] Part-Time Student [ ]

ZIP CODE
12346-1243   TELEPHONE (Include Area Code) (101)1178765

9. OTHER INSURED'S NAME (Last Name, First Name, Middle Initial)

10. IS PATIENT'S CONDITION RELATED TO:

11. INSURED'S POLICY GROUP OR FECA NUMBER
876

a. OTHER INSURED'S POLICY OR GROUP NUMBER

a. EMPLOYMENT? (Current or Previous)
YES [ ] NO [X]

a. INSURED'S DATE OF BIRTH   MM 07 DD 01 YY 1955   SEX M [X] F [ ]

b. OTHER INSURED'S DATE OF BIRTH MM DD YY   SEX M [ ] F [ ]

b. AUTO ACCIDENT?   PLACE (State)
YES [ ] NO [X]

b. EMPLOYER'S NAME OR SCHOOL NAME
AFLAC

c. EMPLOYER'S NAME OR SCHOOL NAME

c. OTHER ACCIDENT?
YES [ ] NO [X]

c. INSURANCE PLAN NAME OR PROGRAM NAME
BCBS

d. INSURANCE PLAN NAME OR PROGRAM NAME

10d. RESERVED FOR LOCAL USE

d. IS THERE ANOTHER HEALTH BENEFIT PLAN?
YES [ ] NO [ ] **If yes,** return to and complete item 9 a-d.

READ BACK OF FORM BEFORE COMPLETING & SIGNING THIS FORM.
12. PATIENT'S OR AUTHORIZED PERSON'S SIGNATURE I authorize the release of any medical or other information necessary to process this claim. I also request payment of government benefits either to myself or to the party who accepts assignment below.

SIGNED SIGNATURE ON FILE   DATE

13. INSURED'S OR AUTHORIZED PERSON'S SIGNATURE I authorize payment of medical benefits to the undersigned physcian or supplier for services described below.

SIGNED

14. DATE OF CURRENT: MM 03 DD 10 YY YYYY   ILLNESS (First symptom) OR INJURY (Accident) OR PREGNANCY (LMP)

15. IF PATIENT HAS HAD SAME OR SIMILAR ILLNESS, GIVE FIRST DATE MM DD YY

16. DATES PATIENT UNABLE TO WORK IN CURRENT OCCUPATION
FROM MM DD YY TO MM DD YY

17. NAME OF REFERRING PROVIDER OR OTHER SOURCE

17a.
17b. NPI

18. HOSPITALIZATION DATES RELATED TO CURRENT SERVICES
FROM MM DD YY TO MM DD YY

19. RESERVED FOR LOCAL USE

20. OUTSIDE LAB? $ CHARGES
YES [ ] NO [X]

21. DIAGNOSIS OR NATURE OF ILLNESS OR INJURY (Relate Items 1, 2, 3 or 4 to Item 24E by Line)
1. 466.0
2. 472.0
3.
4.

22. MEDICAID RESUBMISSION CODE   ORIGINAL REF. NO.

23. PRIOR AUTHORIZATION NUMBER

24. A. DATE(S) OF SERVICE From MM DD YY To MM DD YY	B. PLACE OF SERVICE	C. EMG	D. PROCEDURES, SERVICES, OR SUPPLIES (Explain Unusual Circumstances) CPT/HCPCS	MODIFIER	E. DIAGNOSIS POINTER	F. $ CHARGES	G. DAYS OR UNITS	H. EPSDT Family Plan	I. ID. QUAL.	J. RENDERING PROVIDER ID. #
1 03 10 YYYY	11		99212		1	26 00	1		NPI	
2									NPI	
3									NPI	
4									NPI	
5									NPI	
6									NPI	

25. FEDERAL TAX I.D. NUMBER   SSN [ ] EIN [X]
111397992

26. PATIENT'S ACCOUNT NO.
1-5

27. ACCEPT ASSIGNMENT? (For govt. claims, see back)
YES [X] NO [ ]

28. TOTAL CHARGE
$ 26 00

29. AMOUNT PAID
$

30. BALANCE DUE
$

31. SIGNATURE OF PHYSICIAN OR SUPPLIER INCLUDING DEGREES OR CREDENTIALS (I certify that the statements on the reverse apply to this bill and are made a part thereof.)

SEJAL RAJA MD
SIGNED   DATE MMDDYYYY

32. SERVICE FACILITY LOCATION INFORMATION

a. NPI   b.

33. BILLING PROVIDER INFO & PH # (101)2022923
SEJAL RAJA MD
1 MEDICAL DRIVE
INJURY NY 12347
a. 7890123456   b.

NUCC Instruction Manual available at: www.nucc.org

APPROVED OMB-0938-0999 FORM CMS-1500 (08/05)

1500

HEALTH INSURANCE CLAIM FORM

APPROVED BY NATIONAL UNIFORM CLAIM COMMITTEE 08/05

	PICA	PICA		

1. MEDICARE (Medicare #) ☐ | MEDICAID (Medicaid #) ☐ | TRICARE CHAMPUS (Sponsor's SSN) ☐ | CHAMPVA (Member ID#) ☐ | GROUP HEALTH PLAN (SSN or ID) ☐ | FECA BLK LUNG (SSN) ☐ | OTHER (ID) [X]

1a. INSURED'S I.D. NUMBER (For Program in Item 1)
ZJW35834

2. PATIENT'S NAME (Last Name, First Name, Middle Initial)
NOEL, CHRISTINE

3. PATIENT'S BIRTH DATE MM DD YY
09 03 1977 M ☐ F [X]

4. INSURED'S NAME (Last Name, First Name, Middle Initial)
NOEL, HENRY

5. PATIENT'S ADDRESS (No., Street)
100 CHRISTMAS TREE LN

6. PATIENT'S RELATIONSHIP TO INSURED
Self ☐ Spouse [X] Child ☐ Other ☐

7. INSURED'S ADDRESS (No., Street)
100 CHRISTMAS TREE LN

CITY ANYWHERE **STATE** NY

8. PATIENT STATUS
Single ☐ Married [X] Other ☐

CITY ANYWHERE **STATE** NY

ZIP CODE 12345-1234 **TELEPHONE** (Include Area Code) (101)1158123

Employed ☐ Full-Time Student [X] Part-Time Student ☐

ZIP CODE 12345-1234 **TELEPHONE** (Include Area Code) (101)1158123

9. OTHER INSURED'S NAME (Last Name, First Name, Middle Initial)
NOEL, CHRISTINE

10. IS PATIENT'S CONDITION RELATED TO:

11. INSURED'S POLICY GROUP OR FECA NUMBER
624

a. OTHER INSURED'S POLICY OR GROUP NUMBER
123W476 X23

a. EMPLOYMENT? (Current or Previous)
☐ YES [X] NO

a. INSURED'S DATE OF BIRTH MM DD YY
02 21 1975 M [X] F ☐

b. OTHER INSURED'S DATE OF BIRTH MM DD YY
09 03 1977 M ☐ F [X]

b. AUTO ACCIDENT? PLACE (State)
☐ YES [X] NO

b. EMPLOYER'S NAME OR SCHOOL NAME
WORLD UNIVERSITY

c. EMPLOYER'S NAME OR SCHOOL NAME
WORLD UNIVERSITY

c. OTHER ACCIDENT?
☐ YES [X] NO

c. INSURANCE PLAN NAME OR PROGRAM NAME
BCBS

d. INSURANCE PLAN NAME OR PROGRAM NAME
BCBS

10d. RESERVED FOR LOCAL USE

d. IS THERE ANOTHER HEALTH BENEFIT PLAN?
☐ YES ☐ NO **If yes,** return to and complete item 9 a-d.

READ BACK OF FORM BEFORE COMPLETING & SIGNING THIS FORM.

12. PATIENT'S OR AUTHORIZED PERSON'S SIGNATURE I authorize the release of any medical or other information necessary to process this claim. I also request payment of government benefits either to myself or to the party who accepts assignment below.

SIGNED SIGNATURE ON FILE DATE

13. INSURED'S OR AUTHORIZED PERSON'S SIGNATURE I authorize payment of medical benefits to the undersigned physcian or supplier for services described below.

SIGNED

14. DATE OF CURRENT: MM DD YY
03 01 YYYY
ILLNESS (First symptom) OR INJURY (Accident) OR PREGNANCY (LMP)

15. IF PATIENT HAS HAD SAME OR SIMILAR ILLNESS, GIVE FIRST DATE MM DD YY

16. DATES PATIENT UNABLE TO WORK IN CURRENT OCCUPATION MM DD YY MM DD YY
FROM TO

17. NAME OF REFERRING PROVIDER OR OTHER SOURCE
17a.
17b. NPI

18. HOSPITALIZATION DATES RELATED TO CURRENT SERVICES MM DD YY MM DD YY
FROM TO

19. RESERVED FOR LOCAL USE

20. OUTSIDE LAB? $ CHARGES
☐ YES [X] NO

21. DIAGNOSIS OR NATURE OF ILLNESS OR INJURY (Relate Items 1, 2, 3 or 4 to Item 24E by Line)
1. 462
2. 788 41
3. ____
4. ____

22. MEDICAID RESUBMISSION CODE ORIGINAL REF. NO.

23. PRIOR AUTHORIZATION NUMBER

24. A DATE(S) OF SERVICE From MM DD YY	To MM DD YY	B. PLACE OF SERVICE	C. EMG	D. PROCEDURES, SERVICES, OR SUPPLIES (Explain Unusual Circumstances) CPT/HCPCS	MODIFIER	E. DIAGNOSIS POINTER	F. $ CHARGES	G. DAYS OR UNITS	H. EPSDT Family Plan	I. ID. QUAL.	J. RENDERING PROVIDER ID. #
1	03 01 YYYY		11		99212		1	45 00	1		NPI	
2	03 01 YYYY		11		81000		2	8 00	1		NPI	
3	03 01 YYYY		11		87880		1	12 00	1		NPI	
4											NPI	
5											NPI	
6											NPI	

25. FEDERAL TAX I.D. NUMBER SSN EIN
111234632 ☐ [X]

26. PATIENT'S ACCOUNT NO.
1-6

27. ACCEPT ASSIGNMENT? (For govt. claims, see back)
[X] YES ☐ NO

28. TOTAL CHARGE
$ 65 00

29. AMOUNT PAID
$

30. BALANCE DUE
$

31. SIGNATURE OF PHYSICIAN OR SUPPLIER INCLUDING DEGREES OR CREDENTIALS (I certify that the statements on the reverse apply to this bill and are made a part thereof.)
ARNOLD J YOUNGLOVE MD
SIGNED DATE MMDDYYYY

32. SERVICE FACILITY LOCATION INFORMATION
a. NPI b.

33. BILLING PROVIDER INFO & PH # (101)2027754
ARNOLD J YOUNGLOVE MD
21 PROVIDER ST
INJURY NY 12347
a. 0123456789 b.

NUCC Instruction Manual available at: www.nucc.org

APPROVED OMB-0938-0999 FORM CMS-1500 (08/05)

1500

HEALTH INSURANCE CLAIM FORM

APPROVED BY NATIONAL UNIFORM CLAIM COMMITTEE 08/05

	PICA												PICA	

1. MEDICARE	MEDICAID	TRICARE CHAMPUS	CHAMPVA	GROUP HEALTH PLAN	FECA BLK LUNG	OTHER	1a. INSURED'S I.D. NUMBER	(For Program in Item 1)
X (Medicare #)	(Medicaid #)	(Sponsor's SSN)	(Member ID#)	(SSN or ID)	(SSN)	(ID)	101891701A	

2. PATIENT'S NAME (Last Name, First Name, Middle Initial)
PHISH, GLADYS

3. PATIENT'S BIRTH DATE MM 11 DD 21 YY 1930 **SEX** M F X

4. INSURED'S NAME (Last Name, First Name, Middle Initial)

5. PATIENT'S ADDRESS (No., Street)
21 WINDWHISPER DR

6. PATIENT'S RELATIONSHIP TO INSURED
Self X Spouse Child Other

7. INSURED'S ADDRESS (No., Street)

CITY INJURY **STATE** NY

8. PATIENT STATUS
Single Married X Other

CITY **STATE**

ZIP CODE 12347-1234 **TELEPHONE (Include Area Code)** (101)1112397

Employed Full-Time Student Part-Time Student

ZIP CODE **TELEPHONE (Include Area Code)** ( )

9. OTHER INSURED'S NAME (Last Name, First Name, Middle Initial)

10. IS PATIENT'S CONDITION RELATED TO:

11. INSURED'S POLICY GROUP OR FECA NUMBER
NONE

a. OTHER INSURED'S POLICY OR GROUP NUMBER

a. EMPLOYMENT? (Current or Previous)
YES X NO

a. INSURED'S DATE OF BIRTH MM DD YY **SEX** M F

b. OTHER INSURED'S DATE OF BIRTH MM DD YY **SEX** M F

b. AUTO ACCIDENT? **PLACE (State)**
YES X NO

b. EMPLOYER'S NAME OR SCHOOL NAME

c. EMPLOYER'S NAME OR SCHOOL NAME

c. OTHER ACCIDENT?
YES X NO

c. INSURANCE PLAN NAME OR PROGRAM NAME

d. INSURANCE PLAN NAME OR PROGRAM NAME

10d. RESERVED FOR LOCAL USE

d. IS THERE ANOTHER HEALTH BENEFIT PLAN?
YES NO **If yes,** return to and complete item 9 a-d.

READ BACK OF FORM BEFORE COMPLETING & SIGNING THIS FORM.
12. PATIENT'S OR AUTHORIZED PERSON'S SIGNATURE I authorize the release of any medical or other information necessary to process this claim. I also request payment of government benefits either to myself or to the party who accepts assignment below.

SIGNED SIGNATURE ON FILE DATE

13. INSURED'S OR AUTHORIZED PERSON'S SIGNATURE I authorize payment of medical benefits to the undersigned physician or supplier for services described below.

SIGNED

14. DATE OF CURRENT: MM 03 DD 10 YY YYYY ILLNESS (First symptom) OR INJURY (Accident) OR PREGNANCY (LMP)

15. IF PATIENT HAS HAD SAME OR SIMILAR ILLNESS. GIVE FIRST DATE MM DD YY

16. DATES PATIENT UNABLE TO WORK IN CURRENT OCCUPATION FROM MM DD YY TO MM DD YY

17. NAME OF REFERRING PROVIDER OR OTHER SOURCE
IM GOODDOC MD

17a.
17b. NPI 5678901234

18. HOSPITALIZATION DATES RELATED TO CURRENT SERVICES FROM MM 03 DD 10 YY YYYY TO MM 03 DD 10 YY YYYY

19. RESERVED FOR LOCAL USE

20. OUTSIDE LAB?
YES X NO **$ CHARGES**

21. DIAGNOSIS OR NATURE OF ILLNESS OR INJURY (Relate Items 1, 2, 3 or 4 to Item 24E by Line)
1. 682.4
2.
3.
4.

22. MEDICAID RESUBMISSION CODE ORIGINAL REF. NO.

23. PRIOR AUTHORIZATION NUMBER

24. A. DATE(S) OF SERVICE From MM DD YY To MM DD YY	B. PLACE OF SERVICE	C. EMG	D. PROCEDURES, SERVICES, OR SUPPLIES (Explain Unusual Circumstances) CPT/HCPCS MODIFIER	E. DIAGNOSIS POINTER	F. $ CHARGES	G. DAYS OR UNITS	H. EPSDT Family Plan	I. ID. QUAL.	J. RENDERING PROVIDER ID. #
1	03 10 YYYY	22		10060	1	450 00	1		NPI
2									NPI
3									NPI
4									NPI
5									NPI
6									NPI

25. FEDERAL TAX I.D. NUMBER SSN EIN
111982342 X

26. PATIENT'S ACCOUNT NO.
1-7

27. ACCEPT ASSIGNMENT? (For govt. claims, see back)
X YES NO

28. TOTAL CHARGE
$ 450 00

29. AMOUNT PAID
$

30. BALANCE DUE
$

31. SIGNATURE OF PHYSICIAN OR SUPPLIER INCLUDING DEGREES OR CREDENTIALS (I certify that the statements on the reverse apply to this bill and are made a part thereof.)
ANGELA DILALIO MD
SIGNED DATE MMDDYYYY

32. SERVICE FACILITY LOCATION INFORMATION
GOODMEDICINE HOSPITAL
1 PROVIDER ST
ANYWHERE NY 12345
a. 1123456789 b.

33. BILLING PROVIDER INFO & PH # (101)2014321
ANGELA DILALIO MD
99 PROVIDER DR
INJURY NY 12347
a. 4567890123 b.

NUCC Instruction Manual available at: www.nucc.org

APPROVED OMB-0938-0999 FORM CMS-1500 (08/05)

1500

HEALTH INSURANCE CLAIM FORM

APPROVED BY NATIONAL UNIFORM CLAIM COMMITTEE 08/05

☐☐ PICA | PICA ☐☐

1. MEDICARE [X] (Medicare #) MEDICAID ☐ (Medicaid #) TRICARE CHAMPUS ☐ (Sponsor's SSN) CHAMPVA ☐ (Member ID#) GROUP HEALTH PLAN ☐ (SSN or ID) FECA BLK LUNG ☐ (SSN) OTHER ☐ (ID)

1a. INSURED'S I.D. NUMBER (For Program in Item 1)
102623434B

2. PATIENT'S NAME (Last Name, First Name, Middle Initial)
BLUEBERRY, ELAINE

3. PATIENT'S BIRTH DATE SEX
MM 10 DD 02 YY 1925 M ☐ F [X]

4. INSURED'S NAME (Last Name, First Name, Middle Initial)

5. PATIENT'S ADDRESS (No., Street)
101 BUST ST

6. PATIENT'S RELATIONSHIP TO INSURED
Self ☐ Spouse ☐ Child ☐ Other ☐

7. INSURED'S ADDRESS (No., Street)

CITY
ANYWHERE
STATE
NY

8. PATIENT STATUS
Single [X] Married ☐ Other ☐

CITY   STATE

ZIP CODE
12345-1234
TELEPHONE (Include Area Code)
(101)5555689

Employed ☐ Full-Time Student ☐ Part-Time Student ☐

ZIP CODE   TELEPHONE (Include Area Code)
( )

9. OTHER INSURED'S NAME (Last Name, First Name, Middle Initial)

10. IS PATIENT'S CONDITION RELATED TO:

11. INSURED'S POLICY GROUP OR FECA NUMBER

a. OTHER INSURED'S POLICY OR GROUP NUMBER

a. EMPLOYMENT? (Current or Previous)
☐ YES [X] NO

a. INSURED'S DATE OF BIRTH
MM DD YY SEX M ☐ F ☐

b. OTHER INSURED'S DATE OF BIRTH
MM DD YY SEX M ☐ F ☐

b. AUTO ACCIDENT? PLACE (State)
☐ YES [X] NO

b. EMPLOYER'S NAME OR SCHOOL NAME

c. EMPLOYER'S NAME OR SCHOOL NAME

c. OTHER ACCIDENT?
☐ YES [X] NO

c. INSURANCE PLAN NAME OR PROGRAM NAME

d. INSURANCE PLAN NAME OR PROGRAM NAME

10d. RESERVED FOR LOCAL USE

d. IS THERE ANOTHER HEALTH BENEFIT PLAN?
☐ YES ☐ NO **If yes,** return to and complete item 9 a-d.

READ BACK OF FORM BEFORE COMPLETING & SIGNING THIS FORM.
12. PATIENT'S OR AUTHORIZED PERSON'S SIGNATURE I authorize the release of any medical or other information necessary to process this claim. I also request payment of government benefits either to myself or to the party who accepts assignment below.

SIGNED SIGNATURE ON FILE DATE

13. INSURED'S OR AUTHORIZED PERSON'S SIGNATURE I authorize payment of medical benefits to the undersigned physcian or supplier for services described below.

SIGNED

14. DATE OF CURRENT: ILLNESS (First symptom) OR INJURY (Accident) OR PREGNANCY (LMP)
MM 03 DD 01 YY YYYY

15. IF PATIENT HAS HAD SAME OR SIMILAR ILLNESS, GIVE FIRST DATE MM DD YY

16. DATES PATIENT UNABLE TO WORK IN CURRENT OCCUPATION
FROM MM DD YY TO MM DD YY

17. NAME OF REFERRING PROVIDER OR OTHER SOURCE
IM GOODDOC MD
17a.
17b. NPI 5678901234

18. HOSPITALIZATION DATES RELATED TO CURRENT SERVICES
FROM MM 03 DD 01 YY YYYY TO MM 03 DD 05 YY YYYY

19. RESERVED FOR LOCAL USE

20. OUTSIDE LAB? $ CHARGES
☐ YES [X] NO

21. DIAGNOSIS OR NATURE OF ILLNESS OR INJURY (Relate Items 1, 2, 3 or 4 to Item 24E by Line)
1. 578 . 9   3. ___ . ___
2. 691 . 0   4. ___ . ___

22. MEDICAID RESUBMISSION CODE ORIGINAL REF. NO.

23. PRIOR AUTHORIZATION NUMBER

24. A DATE(S) OF SERVICE From MM DD YY	To MM DD YY	B. PLACE OF SERVICE	C. EMG	D. PROCEDURES, SERVICES, OR SUPPLIES (Explain Unusual Circumstances) CPT/HCPCS	MODIFIER	E. DIAGNOSIS POINTER	F. $ CHARGES	G. DAYS OR UNITS	H. EPSDT Family Plan	I. ID. QUAL.	J. RENDERING PROVIDER ID. #
1	03 01 YYYY		21		99253		1	125 00	1		NPI	
2											NPI	
3											NPI	
4											NPI	
5											NPI	
6											NPI	

25. FEDERAL TAX I.D. NUMBER SSN EIN
117654312 ☐ [X]

26. PATIENT'S ACCOUNT NO.
1-8

27. ACCEPT ASSIGNMENT? (For govt. claims, see back)
[X] YES ☐ NO

28. TOTAL CHARGE
$ 125 00

29. AMOUNT PAID
$

30. BALANCE DUE
$

31. SIGNATURE OF PHYSICIAN OR SUPPLIER INCLUDING DEGREES OR CREDENTIALS (I certify that the statements on the reverse apply to this bill and are made a part thereof.)
IRMINA M BRILLIANT MD
SIGNED DATE MMDDYYYY

32. SERVICE FACILITY LOCATION INFORMATION
GOODMEDICINE HOSPITAL
1 PROVIDER STREET
ANYWHERE NY 12345
a. 112345 6789 NPI b.

33. BILLING PROVIDER INFO & PH # (101)2013145
IRMINA M BRILLIANT MD
25 MEDICAL DRIVE
INJURY NY 12347
a. 2345678901 b.

NUCC Instruction Manual available at: www.nucc.org

APPROVED OMB-0938-0999 FORM CMS-1500 (08/05)

1500

HEALTH INSURANCE CLAIM FORM

APPROVED BY NATIONAL UNIFORM CLAIM COMMITTEE 08/05

☐☐ PICA / PICA ☐☐

CARRIER

1. MEDICARE [X] (Medicare #) MEDICAID ☐ (Medicaid #) TRICARE CHAMPUS ☐ (Sponsor's SSN) CHAMPVA ☐ (Member ID#) GROUP HEALTH PLAN ☐ (SSN or ID) FECA BLK LUNG ☐ (SSN) OTHER [X] (ID)	1a. INSURED'S I.D. NUMBER (For Program in Item 1) **888441234A**
2. PATIENT'S NAME (Last Name, First Name, Middle Initial) **BERRY, EMMA**	3. PATIENT'S BIRTH DATE **03 08 1905** SEX M☐ F[X]	4. INSURED'S NAME (Last Name, First Name, Middle Initial)
5. PATIENT'S ADDRESS (No., Street) **15 GOLDEN AGE ROAD**	6. PATIENT'S RELATIONSHIP TO INSURED Self☐ Spouse☐ Child☐ Other☐	7. INSURED'S ADDRESS (No., Street)
CITY **ANYWHERE** STATE **NY**	8. PATIENT STATUS Single [X] Married☐ Other☐	CITY STATE
ZIP CODE **12345-1234** TELEPHONE **(101)1117700**	Employed☐ Full-Time Student☐ Part-Time Student☐	ZIP CODE TELEPHONE ( )
9. OTHER INSURED'S NAME **SAME**	10. IS PATIENT'S CONDITION RELATED TO:	11. INSURED'S POLICY GROUP OR FECA NUMBER **NONE**
a. OTHER INSURED'S POLICY OR GROUP NUMBER **MEDIGAP 995432992**	a. EMPLOYMENT? YES☐ NO[X]	a. INSURED'S DATE OF BIRTH SEX M☐ F☐
b. OTHER INSURED'S DATE OF BIRTH **03 08 1905** SEX M☐ F[X]	b. AUTO ACCIDENT? YES☐ NO[X] PLACE (State)	b. EMPLOYER'S NAME OR SCHOOL NAME
c. EMPLOYER'S NAME OR SCHOOL NAME	c. OTHER ACCIDENT? YES☐ NO[X]	c. INSURANCE PLAN NAME OR PROGRAM NAME
d. INSURANCE PLAN NAME OR PROGRAM NAME **9876543212**	10d. RESERVED FOR LOCAL USE	d. IS THERE ANOTHER HEALTH BENEFIT PLAN? YES☐ NO☐ If yes, return to and complete item 9 a-d.

READ BACK OF FORM BEFORE COMPLETING & SIGNING THIS FORM.

12. PATIENT'S OR AUTHORIZED PERSON'S SIGNATURE SIGNED **SIGNATURE ON FILE** DATE _____

13. INSURED'S OR AUTHORIZED PERSON'S SIGNATURE SIGNED **SIGNATURE ON FILE**

14. DATE OF CURRENT: **03 02 YYYY** ILLNESS/INJURY/PREGNANCY	15. IF PATIENT HAS HAD SAME OR SIMILAR ILLNESS GIVE FIRST DATE	16. DATES PATIENT UNABLE TO WORK FROM TO
17. NAME OF REFERRING PROVIDER OR OTHER SOURCE	17a. 17b. NPI	18. HOSPITALIZATION DATES FROM **03 01 YYYY** TO **03 03 YYYY**
19. RESERVED FOR LOCAL USE		20. OUTSIDE LAB? YES☐ NO[X] $ CHARGES
21. DIAGNOSIS OR NATURE OF ILLNESS OR INJURY 1. **290.0** 2. **782.3** 3. ___ 4. ___		22. MEDICAID RESUBMISSION CODE ORIGINAL REF. NO.
		23. PRIOR AUTHORIZATION NUMBER

24.A DATE(S) OF SERVICE From / To	B. PLACE OF SERVICE	C. EMG	D. PROCEDURES CPT/HCPCS / MODIFIER	E. DIAGNOSIS POINTER	F. $ CHARGES	G. DAYS OR UNITS	H. EPSDT	I. ID QUAL	J. RENDERING PROVIDER ID. #
1 **03 02 YYYY**	31		99308	1	45 00	1		NPI	
2								NPI	
3								NPI	
4								NPI	
5								NPI	
6								NPI	

25. FEDERAL TAX I.D. NUMBER **111234632** SSN☐ EIN[X]	26. PATIENT'S ACCOUNT NO. **1-9**	27. ACCEPT ASSIGNMENT? YES[X] NO☐
28. TOTAL CHARGE $ **45 00**	29. AMOUNT PAID $	30. BALANCE DUE $
31. SIGNATURE OF PHYSICIAN OR SUPPLIER **ARNOLD J YOUNGLOVE MD** SIGNED DATE **MMDDYYYY**	32. SERVICE FACILITY LOCATION INFORMATION **GOOD LIFE SNF 200 GOLDEN AGE ROAD ANYWHERE NY 12345** a. **2234567890** b.	33. BILLING PROVIDER INFO & PH # **(101)2027754** **ARNOLD J YOUNGLOVE 21 PROVIDER ST INJURY NY 12347** a. **0123456789** b.

NUCC Instruction Manual available at: www.nucc.org

APPROVED OMB-0938-0999 FORM CMS-1500 (08/05)

1500

HEALTH INSURANCE CLAIM FORM

APPROVED BY NATIONAL UNIFORM CLAIM COMMITTEE 08/05

☐☐ PICA | PICA ☐☐

| 1. MEDICARE ☐ (Medicare #) | MEDICAID ☐ (Medicaid #) | TRICARE CHAMPUS ☐ (Sponsor's SSN) | CHAMPVA ☐ (Member ID#) | GROUP HEALTH PLAN ☐ (SSN or ID) | FECA BLK LUNG ☐ (SSN) | OTHER [X] (ID) | 1a. INSURED'S I.D. NUMBER (For Program in Item 1) 5626598 |

| 2. PATIENT'S NAME (Last Name, First Name, Middle Initial) CARTRIGHT, PETER | 3. PATIENT'S BIRTH DATE MM DD YY 12 24 1935 SEX M [X] F ☐ | 4. INSURED'S NAME (Last Name, First Name, Middle Initial) CARTRIGHT, PETER |

| 5. PATIENT'S ADDRESS (No., Street) 250 HILL STREET | 6. PATIENT'S RELATIONSHIP TO INSURED Self [X] Spouse ☐ Child ☐ Other ☐ | 7. INSURED'S ADDRESS (No., Street) 250 HILL STREET |

| CITY ANYWHERE | STATE NY | 8. PATIENT STATUS Single [X] Married ☐ Other ☐ | CITY ANYWHERE | STATE NY |

| ZIP CODE 12345-1234 | TELEPHONE (Include Area Code) (101)5557843 | Employed ☐ Full-Time Student ☐ Part-Time Student ☐ | ZIP CODE 12345-1234 | TELEPHONE (Include Area Code) (101)5557843 |

| 9. OTHER INSURED'S NAME (Last Name, First Name, Middle Initial) CARTRIGHT, PETER | 10. IS PATIENT'S CONDITION RELATED TO: | 11. INSURED'S POLICY GROUP OR FECA NUMBER |

| a. OTHER INSURED'S POLICY OR GROUP NUMBER | a. EMPLOYMENT? (Current or Previous) YES ☐ [X] NO | a. INSURED'S DATE OF BIRTH MM DD YY 12 24 1935 SEX M [X] F ☐ |

| b. OTHER INSURED'S DATE OF BIRTH MM DD YY SEX M ☐ F ☐ | b. AUTO ACCIDENT? YES ☐ [X] NO PLACE (State) | b. EMPLOYER'S NAME OR SCHOOL NAME |

| c. EMPLOYER'S NAME OR SCHOOL NAME | c. OTHER ACCIDENT? YES ☐ [X] NO | c. INSURANCE PLAN NAME OR PROGRAM NAME BCBS |

| d. INSURANCE PLAN NAME OR PROGRAM NAME | 10d. RESERVED FOR LOCAL USE | d. IS THERE ANOTHER HEALTH BENEFIT PLAN? YES ☐ NO ☐ If yes, return to and complete item 9 a-d. |

READ BACK OF FORM BEFORE COMPLETING & SIGNING THIS FORM.

12. PATIENT'S OR AUTHORIZED PERSON'S SIGNATURE I authorize the release of any medical or other information necessary to process this claim. I also request payment of government benefits either to myself or to the party who accepts assignment below.

SIGNED SIGNATURE ON FILE DATE

13. INSURED'S OR AUTHORIZED PERSON'S SIGNATURE I authorize payment of medical benefits to the undersigned physcian or supplier for services described below.

SIGNED

| 14. DATE OF CURRENT: MM DD YY 04 15 YYYY ILLNESS (First symptom) OR INJURY (Accident) OR PREGNANCY (LMP) | 15. IF PATIENT HAS HAD SAME OR SIMILAR ILLNESS. GIVE FIRST DATE MM DD YY | 16. DATES PATIENT UNABLE TO WORK IN CURRENT OCCUPATION MM DD YY TO MM DD YY FROM |

| 17. NAME OF REFERRING PROVIDER OR OTHER SOURCE | 17a. 17b. NPI | 18. HOSPITALIZATION DATES RELATED TO CURRENT SERVICES MM DD YY TO MM DD YY FROM |

| 19. RESERVED FOR LOCAL USE | 20. OUTSIDE LAB? YES ☐ [X] NO $ CHARGES |

21. DIAGNOSIS OR NATURE OF ILLNESS OR INJURY (Relate Items 1, 2, 3 or 4 to Item 24E by Line)

1. 250 . 00   3. ⌐____

2. ____   4. ____

| 22. MEDICAID RESUBMISSION CODE ORIGINAL REF. NO. |
| 23. PRIOR AUTHORIZATION NUMBER |

24. A. DATE(S) OF SERVICE From MM DD YY	To MM DD YY	B. PLACE OF SERVICE	C. EMG	D. PROCEDURES, SERVICES, OR SUPPLIES (Explain Unusual Circumstances) CPT/HCPCS MODIFIER	E. DIAGNOSIS POINTER	F. $ CHARGES	G. DAYS OR UNITS	H. EPSDT Family Plan	I. ID. QUAL.	J. RENDERING PROVIDER ID. #
1	04 15 YYYY		11		99212	1	50 00	1		NPI	
2										NPI	
3										NPI	
4										NPI	
5										NPI	
6										NPI	

| 25. FEDERAL TAX I.D. NUMBER SSN EIN 111982342 [X] | 26. PATIENT'S ACCOUNT NO. 1-10P | 27. ACCEPT ASSIGNMENT? (For govt. claims, see back) [X] YES ☐ NO | 28. TOTAL CHARGE $ 50 00 | 29. AMOUNT PAID $ | 30. BALANCE DUE $ |

| 31. SIGNATURE OF PHYSICIAN OR SUPPLIER INCLUDING DEGREES OR CREDENTIALS (I certify that the statements on the reverse apply to this bill and are made a part thereof.) ANGELA DILALIO MD SIGNED DATE MMDDYYYY | 32. SERVICE FACILITY LOCATION INFORMATION a. NPI b. | 33. BILLING PROVIDER INFO & PH # (101)2014321 ANGELA DILALIO MD 99 PROVIDER DR INJURY NY 12347 a. 4567890123 |

NUCC Instruction Manual available at: www.nucc.org

APPROVED OMB-0938-0999 FORM CMS-1500 (08/05)

1500	

HEALTH INSURANCE CLAIM FORM

APPROVED BY NATIONAL UNIFORM CLAIM COMMITTEE 08/05

1. MEDICARE	MEDICAID	TRICARE CHAMPUS	CHAMPVA	GROUP HEALTH PLAN	FECA BLK LUNG	OTHER	1a. INSURED'S I.D. NUMBER	(For Program in Item 1)
[X] (Medicare #)	(Medicaid #)	(Sponsor's SSN)	(Member ID#)	(SSN or ID)	(SSN)	[X] (ID)	235689569A	

2. PATIENT'S NAME (Last Name, First Name, Middle Initial)	3. PATIENT'S BIRTH DATE / SEX	4. INSURED'S NAME (Last Name, First Name, Middle Initial)
CARTRIGHT, PETER	12 24 1935 M[X] F	SAME

5. PATIENT'S ADDRESS (No., Street)	6. PATIENT'S RELATIONSHIP TO INSURED	7. INSURED'S ADDRESS (No., Street)
250 HILL STREET	Self [X] Spouse Child Other	SAME
CITY: ANYWHERE STATE: NY	8. PATIENT STATUS Single [X] Married Other	CITY STATE
ZIP CODE: 12345-1234 TELEPHONE: (101) 5557843	Employed Full-Time Student Part-Time Student	ZIP CODE TELEPHONE ( )

9. OTHER INSURED'S NAME (Last Name, First Name, Middle Initial)	10. IS PATIENT'S CONDITION RELATED TO:	11. INSURED'S POLICY GROUP OR FECA NUMBER
		5626598
a. OTHER INSURED'S POLICY OR GROUP NUMBER	a. EMPLOYMENT? (Current or Previous) YES [X] NO	a. INSURED'S DATE OF BIRTH 12 24 1935 SEX M[X] F
b. OTHER INSURED'S DATE OF BIRTH M F	b. AUTO ACCIDENT? PLACE (State) YES [X] NO	b. EMPLOYER'S NAME OR SCHOOL NAME
c. EMPLOYER'S NAME OR SCHOOL NAME	c. OTHER ACCIDENT? YES [X] NO	c. INSURANCE PLAN NAME OR PROGRAM NAME BCBS
d. INSURANCE PLAN NAME OR PROGRAM NAME	10d. RESERVED FOR LOCAL USE	d. IS THERE ANOTHER HEALTH BENEFIT PLAN? YES NO If yes, return to and complete item 9 a-d.

READ BACK OF FORM BEFORE COMPLETING & SIGNING THIS FORM.

12. PATIENT'S OR AUTHORIZED PERSON'S SIGNATURE I authorize the release of any medical or other information necessary to process this claim. I also request payment of government benefits either to myself or to the party who accepts assignment below.

SIGNED **SIGNATURE ON FILE**   DATE

13. INSURED'S OR AUTHORIZED PERSON'S SIGNATURE I authorize payment of medical benefits to the undersigned physician or supplier for services described below.

SIGNED

14. DATE OF CURRENT: ILLNESS (First symptom) OR INJURY (Accident) OR PREGNANCY (LMP) 04 15 YYYY	15. IF PATIENT HAS HAD SAME OR SIMILAR ILLNESS, GIVE FIRST DATE MM DD YY	16. DATES PATIENT UNABLE TO WORK IN CURRENT OCCUPATION FROM TO
17. NAME OF REFERRING PROVIDER OR OTHER SOURCE	17a. 17b. NPI	18. HOSPITALIZATION DATES RELATED TO CURRENT SERVICES FROM TO
19. RESERVED FOR LOCAL USE		20. OUTSIDE LAB? YES [X] NO $ CHARGES

21. DIAGNOSIS OR NATURE OF ILLNESS OR INJURY (Relate Items 1, 2, 3 or 4 to Item 24E by Line)

1. 250.00
2. ___
3. ___
4. ___

22. MEDICAID RESUBMISSION CODE ORIGINAL REF. NO.
23. PRIOR AUTHORIZATION NUMBER

24. A. DATE(S) OF SERVICE From / To MM DD YY	B. PLACE OF SERVICE	C. EMG	D. PROCEDURES, SERVICES, OR SUPPLIES (Explain Unusual Circumstances) CPT/HCPCS / MODIFIER	E. DIAGNOSIS POINTER	F. $ CHARGES	G. DAYS OR UNITS	H. EPSDT Family Plan	I. ID. QUAL.	J. RENDERING PROVIDER ID. #
1	04 15 YYYY	11		99212	1	50 00	1		NPI	
2									NPI	
3									NPI	
4									NPI	
5									NPI	
6									NPI	

25. FEDERAL TAX I.D. NUMBER SSN EIN	26. PATIENT'S ACCOUNT NO.	27. ACCEPT ASSIGNMENT? (For govt. claims, see back)	28. TOTAL CHARGE	29. AMOUNT PAID	30. BALANCE DUE
111982342 [X]	1-10S	[X] YES NO	$ 50 00	$	$

31. SIGNATURE OF PHYSICIAN OR SUPPLIER INCLUDING DEGREES OR CREDENTIALS (I certify that the statements on the reverse apply to this bill and are made a part thereof.) ANGELA DILALIO MD SIGNED DATE MMDDYYYY	32. SERVICE FACILITY LOCATION INFORMATION ANGELA DILALIO MD 99 PROVIDER DR INJURY NY 12347 a. 4567890123 b.	33. BILLING PROVIDER INFO & PH # (101) 2014321 ANGELA DILALIO MD 99 PROVIDER DR INJURY NY 12347 a. 4567890123 b.

NUCC Instruction Manual available at: www.nucc.org

APPROVED OMB-0938-0999 FORM CMS-1500 (08/05)

1500

HEALTH INSURANCE CLAIM FORM

APPROVED BY NATIONAL UNIFORM CLAIM COMMITTEE 08/05

| | PICA | | | | | | PICA | |

1. MEDICARE ☐ *(Medicare #)* MEDICAID ☐ *(Medicaid #)* TRICARE CHAMPUS ☐ *(Sponsor's SSN)* CHAMPVA ☐ *(Member ID#)* GROUP HEALTH PLAN ☐ *(SSN or ID)* FECA BLK LUNG ☐ *(SSN)* OTHER ☒ *(ID)*

1a. INSURED'S I.D. NUMBER (For Program in Item 1)
XYZ332999009

2. PATIENT'S NAME (Last Name, First Name, Middle Initial)
CARTWHEEL, FRED

3. PATIENT'S BIRTH DATE MM DD YY **SEX**
01 03 1930 M ☒ F ☐

4. INSURED'S NAME (Last Name, First Name, Middle Initial)
CARTWHEEL, FRED

5. PATIENT'S ADDRESS (No., Street)
RED WAGON RD

6. PATIENT'S RELATIONSHIP TO INSURED
Self ☒ Spouse ☐ Child ☐ Other ☐

7. INSURED'S ADDRESS (No., Street)
RED WAGON RD

CITY NOWHERE **STATE** NY

8. PATIENT STATUS
Single ☐ Married ☒ Other ☐

CITY NOWHERE **STATE** NY

ZIP CODE 12346-1234 **TELEPHONE** (Include Area Code) (101)1135567

Employed ☒ Full-Time Student ☐ Part-Time Student ☐

ZIP CODE 12346-1234 **TELEPHONE** (Include Area Code) (101)1135567

9. OTHER INSURED'S NAME (Last Name, First Name, Middle Initial)
CARTWHEEL, FRED

10. IS PATIENT'S CONDITION RELATED TO:

11. INSURED'S POLICY GROUP OR FECA NUMBER
201

a. OTHER INSURED'S POLICY OR GROUP NUMBER
332999999A

a. EMPLOYMENT? (Current or Previous)
YES ☐ NO ☒

a. INSURED'S DATE OF BIRTH MM DD YY **SEX**
01 03 1930 M ☒ F ☐

b. OTHER INSURED'S DATE OF BIRTH MM DD YY **SEX**
01 03 1930 M ☒ F ☐

b. AUTO ACCIDENT? PLACE (State)
YES ☐ NO ☒

b. EMPLOYER'S NAME OR SCHOOL NAME
WORLD UNIVERSITY

c. EMPLOYER'S NAME OR SCHOOL NAME
WORLD UNIVERSITY

c. OTHER ACCIDENT?
YES ☐ NO ☒

c. INSURANCE PLAN NAME OR PROGRAM NAME
METLIFE

d. INSURANCE PLAN NAME OR PROGRAM NAME
MEDICARE

10d. RESERVED FOR LOCAL USE

d. IS THERE ANOTHER HEALTH BENEFIT PLAN?
☒ YES ☐ NO *If yes,* return to and complete item 9 a-d.

READ BACK OF FORM BEFORE COMPLETING & SIGNING THIS FORM.
12. PATIENT'S OR AUTHORIZED PERSON'S SIGNATURE I authorize the release of any medical or other information necessary to process this claim. I also request payment of government benefits either to myself or to the party who accepts assignment below.

SIGNED SIGNATURE ON FILE DATE

13. INSURED'S OR AUTHORIZED PERSON'S SIGNATURE I authorize payment of medical benefits to the undersigned physician or supplier for services described below.

SIGNED SIGNATURE ON FILE

14. DATE OF CURRENT: MM DD YY ILLNESS (First symptom) OR INJURY (Accident) OR PREGNANCY (LMP)
03 12 YYYY

15. IF PATIENT HAS HAD SAME OR SIMILAR ILLNESS. GIVE FIRST DATE MM DD YY

16. DATES PATIENT UNABLE TO WORK IN CURRENT OCCUPATION MM DD YY
FROM TO

17. NAME OF REFERRING PROVIDER OR OTHER SOURCE
17a.
17b. NPI

18. HOSPITALIZATION DATES RELATED TO CURRENT SERVICES MM DD YY
FROM 03 14 YYYY TO 03 17 YYYY

19. RESERVED FOR LOCAL USE

20. OUTSIDE LAB? $ CHARGES
YES ☐ NO ☒

21. DIAGNOSIS OR NATURE OF ILLNESS OR INJURY (Relate Items 1, 2, 3 or 4 to Item 24E by Line)
1. 401.0
2. ___ . ___
3. ___ . ___
4. ___ . ___

22. MEDICAID RESUBMISSION CODE ORIGINAL REF. NO.

23. PRIOR AUTHORIZATION NUMBER

24. A DATE(S) OF SERVICE From MM DD YY	To MM DD YY	B. PLACE OF SERVICE	C. EMG	D. PROCEDURES, SERVICES, OR SUPPLIES (Explain Unusual Circumstances) CPT/HCPCS MODIFIER	E. DIAGNOSIS POINTER	F. $ CHARGES	G. DAYS OR UNITS	H. EPSDT Family Plan	I. ID. QUAL.	J. RENDERING PROVIDER ID. #
1	03 14 YYYY		21		99223	1	165 00	1		NPI	
2	03 15 YYYY	03 16 YYYY	21		99232	1	190 00	2		NPI	
3	03 17 YYYY		21		99238	1	55 00	1		NPI	
4										NPI	
5										NPI	
6										NPI	

25. FEDERAL TAX I.D. NUMBER SSN EIN
111982342 ☒

26. PATIENT'S ACCOUNT NO.
1-11P

27. ACCEPT ASSIGNMENT? (For govt. claims, see back)
☒ YES ☐ NO

28. TOTAL CHARGE
$ 410 00

29. AMOUNT PAID
$

30. BALANCE DUE
$ 410 00

31. SIGNATURE OF PHYSICIAN OR SUPPLIER INCLUDING DEGREES OR CREDENTIALS (I certify that the statements on the reverse apply to this bill and are made a part thereof.)
ANGELA DILALIO MD
SIGNED DATE MMDDYYYY

32. SERVICE FACILITY LOCATION INFORMATION
GOODMEDICINE HOSPITAL
1 PROVIDER ST
ANYWHERE NY 12345
a. 1123456789 b.

33. BILLING PROVIDER INFO & PH # (101)2014321
ANGELA DILALIO MD
99 PROVIDER DR
INJURY NY 12347
a. 4567890123 b.

NUCC Instruction Manual available at: www.nucc.org

APPROVED OMB-0938-0999 FORM CMS-1500 (08/05)

1500

HEALTH INSURANCE CLAIM FORM

APPROVED BY NATIONAL UNIFORM CLAIM COMMITTEE 08/05

	PICA									PICA	

1. MEDICARE	MEDICAID	TRICARE CHAMPUS	CHAMPVA	GROUP HEALTH PLAN	FECA BLK LUNG	OTHER	1a. INSURED'S I.D. NUMBER (For Program in Item 1)
X (Medicare #)	(Medicaid #)	(Sponsor's SSN)	(Member ID#)	(SSN or ID)	(SSN)	X (ID)	332999999A

2. PATIENT'S NAME (Last Name, First Name, Middle Initial)	3. PATIENT'S BIRTH DATE / SEX	4. INSURED'S NAME (Last Name, First Name, Middle Initial)
CARTWHEEL, FRED	MM 01 DD 03 YY 1930 M X F	SAME

5. PATIENT'S ADDRESS (No., Street)	6. PATIENT'S RELATIONSHIP TO INSURED	7. INSURED'S ADDRESS (No., Street)
RED WAGON RD	Self X Spouse Child Other	SAME

CITY	STATE	8. PATIENT STATUS	CITY	STATE
NOWHERE	NY	Single Married X Other		

ZIP CODE	TELEPHONE (Include Area Code)		ZIP CODE	TELEPHONE (Include Area Code)
12346-1234	(101)1135567	Employed X Full-Time Student Part-Time Student		( )

9. OTHER INSURED'S NAME (Last Name, First Name, Middle Initial)	10. IS PATIENT'S CONDITION RELATED TO:	11. INSURED'S POLICY GROUP OR FECA NUMBER
		XYZ332999009

a. OTHER INSURED'S POLICY OR GROUP NUMBER	a. EMPLOYMENT? (Current or Previous) YES X NO	a. INSURED'S DATE OF BIRTH MM 01 DD 03 YY 1930 / SEX M X F

b. OTHER INSURED'S DATE OF BIRTH MM DD YY / SEX M F	b. AUTO ACCIDENT? PLACE (State) YES X NO	b. EMPLOYER'S NAME OR SCHOOL NAME WORLD UNIVERSITY

c. EMPLOYER'S NAME OR SCHOOL NAME	c. OTHER ACCIDENT? YES X NO	c. INSURANCE PLAN NAME OR PROGRAM NAME METLIFE

d. INSURANCE PLAN NAME OR PROGRAM NAME	10d. RESERVED FOR LOCAL USE	d. IS THERE ANOTHER HEALTH BENEFIT PLAN? YES NO *If yes,* return to and complete item 9 a-d.

READ BACK OF FORM BEFORE COMPLETING & SIGNING THIS FORM.

12. PATIENT'S OR AUTHORIZED PERSON'S SIGNATURE I authorize the release of any medical or other information necessary to process this claim. I also request payment of government benefits either to myself or to the party who accepts assignment below.

SIGNED **SIGNATURE ON FILE**   DATE

13. INSURED'S OR AUTHORIZED PERSON'S SIGNATURE I authorize payment of medical benefits to the undersigned physcian or supplier for services described below.

SIGNED

14. DATE OF CURRENT: MM 03 DD 12 YY YYYY ◄ ILLNESS (First symptom) OR INJURY (Accident) OR PREGNANCY (LMP)	15. IF PATIENT HAS HAD SAME OR SIMILAR ILLNESS. GIVE FIRST DATE MM DD YY	16. DATES PATIENT UNABLE TO WORK IN CURRENT OCCUPATION MM DD YY MM DD YY FROM TO

17. NAME OF REFERRING PROVIDER OR OTHER SOURCE	17a.	18. HOSPITALIZATION DATES RELATED TO CURRENT SERVICES
	17b. NPI	MM 03 DD 14 YY YYYY MM 03 DD 17 YY YYYY FROM TO

19. RESERVED FOR LOCAL USE	20. OUTSIDE LAB? YES X NO $ CHARGES

21. DIAGNOSIS OR NATURE OF ILLNESS OR INJURY (Relate Items 1, 2, 3 or 4 to Item 24E by Line)	22. MEDICAID RESUBMISSION CODE ORIGINAL REF. NO.
1. 401.0 3.	
2. 4.	23. PRIOR AUTHORIZATION NUMBER

24. A. DATE(S) OF SERVICE From MM DD YY To MM DD YY	B. PLACE OF SERVICE	C. EMG	D. PROCEDURES, SERVICES, OR SUPPLIES (Explain Unusual Circumstances) CPT/HCPCS MODIFIER	E. DIAGNOSIS POINTER	F. $ CHARGES	G. DAYS OR UNITS	H. EPSDT Family Plan	I. ID. QUAL.	J. RENDERING PROVIDER ID. #
1	03 14 YYYY	21		99223	1	165 00	1		NPI	
2	03 15 YYYY 03 16 YYYY	21		99232	1	190 00	2		NPI	
3	03 17 YYYY	21		99238	1	55 00	1		NPI	
4									NPI	
5									NPI	
6									NPI	

25. FEDERAL TAX I.D. NUMBER SSN EIN	26. PATIENT'S ACCOUNT NO.	27. ACCEPT ASSIGNMENT? (For govt. claims, see back)	28. TOTAL CHARGE	29. AMOUNT PAID	30. BALANCE DUE
111982342 X	1-11S	X YES NO	$ 410 00	$	$

31. SIGNATURE OF PHYSICIAN OR SUPPLIER INCLUDING DEGREES OR CREDENTIALS (I certify that the statements on the reverse apply to this bill and are made a part thereof.)	32. SERVICE FACILITY LOCATION INFORMATION	33. BILLING PROVIDER INFO & PH # (101)2014321
ANGELA DILALIO MD	GOODMEDICINE HOSPITAL 1 PROVIDER ST ANYWHERE NY 12345	ANGELA DILALIO MD 99 PROVIDER DR INJURY NY 12347
SIGNED DATE MMDDYYYY	a. 1123456789 b.	a. 4567890123 b.

NUCC Instruction Manual available at: www.nucc.org

APPROVED OMB-0938-0999 FORM CMS-1500 (08/05)

1500

HEALTH INSURANCE CLAIM FORM

APPROVED BY NATIONAL UNIFORM CLAIM COMMITTEE 08/05

CARRIER

		PICA							PICA		

1. MEDICARE	MEDICAID	TRICARE CHAMPUS	CHAMPVA	GROUP HEALTH PLAN	FECA BLK LUNG	OTHER	1a. INSURED'S I.D. NUMBER (For Program in Item 1)
[X] (Medicare #)	[X] (Medicaid #)	(Sponsor's SSN)	(Member ID#)	(SSN or ID)	(SSN)	(ID)	101278769W

2. PATIENT'S NAME (Last Name, First Name, Middle Initial)	3. PATIENT'S BIRTH DATE		SEX	4. INSURED'S NAME (Last Name, First Name, Middle Initial)
MAKEBETTER, GERALDINE, T	MM 06 DD 20 YY 1945	M	F [X]	

5. PATIENT'S ADDRESS (No., Street)
7866A MEMORY LANE

6. PATIENT'S RELATIONSHIP TO INSURED
Self [ ] Spouse [ ] Child [ ] Other [ ]

7. INSURED'S ADDRESS (No., Street)

CITY	STATE	8. PATIENT STATUS	CITY	STATE
INJURY	NY	Single [X] Married [ ] Other [ ]		

ZIP CODE	TELEPHONE (Include Area Code)		ZIP CODE	TELEPHONE (Include Area Code)
12347-1234	(101)1119855	Employed [ ] Full-Time Student [ ] Part-Time Student [ ]		( )

9. OTHER INSURED'S NAME (Last Name, First Name, Middle Initial)

10. IS PATIENT'S CONDITION RELATED TO:

11. INSURED'S POLICY GROUP OR FECA NUMBER
NONE

a. OTHER INSURED'S POLICY OR GROUP NUMBER

a. EMPLOYMENT? (Current or Previous)
YES [ ] NO [X]

a. INSURED'S DATE OF BIRTH
MM DD YY   SEX
M [ ] F [ ]

b. OTHER INSURED'S DATE OF BIRTH
MM DD YY   SEX
M [ ] F [ ]

b. AUTO ACCIDENT?   PLACE (State)
YES [ ] NO [X]

b. EMPLOYER'S NAME OR SCHOOL NAME

c. EMPLOYER'S NAME OR SCHOOL NAME

c. OTHER ACCIDENT?
YES [ ] NO [X]

c. INSURANCE PLAN NAME OR PROGRAM NAME

d. INSURANCE PLAN NAME OR PROGRAM NAME

10d. RESERVED FOR LOCAL USE
MCD 1198555W

d. IS THERE ANOTHER HEALTH BENEFIT PLAN?
YES [ ] NO [ ] **If yes,** return to and complete item 9 a-d.

READ BACK OF FORM BEFORE COMPLETING & SIGNING THIS FORM.

12. PATIENT'S OR AUTHORIZED PERSON'S SIGNATURE I authorize the release of any medical or other information necessary to process this claim. I also request payment of government benefits either to myself or to the party who accepts assignment below.

SIGNED __SIGNATURE ON FILE__   DATE

13. INSURED'S OR AUTHORIZED PERSON'S SIGNATURE I authorize payment of medical benefits to the undersigned physician or supplier for services described below.

SIGNED

PATIENT AND INSURED INFORMATION

14. DATE OF CURRENT: MM DD YY 03 03 YYYY	ILLNESS (First symptom) OR INJURY (Accident) OR PREGNANCY (LMP)	15. IF PATIENT HAS HAD SAME OR SIMILAR ILLNESS, GIVE FIRST DATE MM DD YY	16. DATES PATIENT UNABLE TO WORK IN CURRENT OCCUPATION MM DD YY FROM TO MM DD YY

17. NAME OF REFERRING PROVIDER OR OTHER SOURCE

17a.
17b. NPI

18. HOSPITALIZATION DATES RELATED TO CURRENT SERVICES
MM DD YY FROM   TO   MM DD YY

19. RESERVED FOR LOCAL USE

20. OUTSIDE LAB? $ CHARGES
YES [ ] NO [X]

21. DIAGNOSIS OR NATURE OF ILLNESS OR INJURY (Relate Items 1, 2, 3 or 4 to Item 24E by Line)

1. V70 0   3.
2. 595 9   4.

22. MEDICAID RESUBMISSION CODE   ORIGINAL REF. NO.

23. PRIOR AUTHORIZATION NUMBER

24. A. DATE(S) OF SERVICE From To MM DD YY MM DD YY	B. PLACE OF SERVICE	C. EMG	D. PROCEDURES, SERVICES, OR SUPPLIES (Explain Unusual Circumstances) CPT/HCPCS MODIFIER	E. DIAGNOSIS POINTER	F. $ CHARGES	G. DAYS OR UNITS	H. EPSDT Family Plan	I. ID. QUAL.	J. RENDERING PROVIDER ID. #
1	03 03 YYYY	11		99396		1	75 00	1		NPI	
2	03 03 YYYY	11		99212	25	2	40 00	1		NPI	
3	03 03 YYYY	11		81000		2	8 00	1		NPI	
4	03 03 YYYY	11		82270		1	8 00	1		NPI	
5	03 03 YYYY	11		85025		1	40 00	1		NPI	
6	03 03 YYYY	11		99420		1	25 00	1		NPI	

25. FEDERAL TAX I.D. NUMBER SSN EIN	26. PATIENT'S ACCOUNT NO.	27. ACCEPT ASSIGNMENT? (For govt. claims, see back)	28. TOTAL CHARGE	29. AMOUNT PAID	30. BALANCE DUE
111234632 [X]	1-12	[X] YES [ ] NO	$ 196 00	$	$

31. SIGNATURE OF PHYSICIAN OR SUPPLIER INCLUDING DEGREES OR CREDENTIALS
(I certify that the statements on the reverse apply to this bill and are made a part thereof.)

ARNOLD J YOUNGLOVE MD
SIGNED   DATE MMDDYYYY

32. SERVICE FACILITY LOCATION INFORMATION
ARNOLD J YOUNGLOVE MD
21 PROVIDER ST
INJURY NY 12347
a. 0123456789   b.

33. BILLING PROVIDER INFO & PH # (101)2027754
ARNOLD J YOUNGLOVE MD
21 PROVIDER ST
INJURY NY 12347
a. 0123456789   b.

PHYSICIAN OR SUPPLIER INFORMATION

NUCC Instruction Manual available at: www.nucc.org

APPROVED OMB-0938-0999 FORM CMS-1500 (08/05)

1500

HEALTH INSURANCE CLAIM FORM

APPROVED BY NATIONAL UNIFORM CLAIM COMMITTEE 08/05

| | PICA | | | | | | | | | PICA | |

| 1. MEDICARE | MEDICAID | TRICARE CHAMPUS | CHAMPVA | GROUP HEALTH PLAN | FECA BLK LUNG | OTHER | 1a. INSURED'S I.D. NUMBER (For Program in Item 1) |
| (Medicare #) | [X] (Medicaid #) | (Sponsor's SSN) | (Member ID#) | (SSN or ID) | (SSN) | (ID) | 119850B |

2. PATIENT'S NAME (Last Name, First Name, Middle Initial)
FILBERT, FIONA, J

3. PATIENT'S BIRTH DATE   SEX
MM 03 DD 08 YY 1977   M [ ] F [X]

4. INSURED'S NAME (Last Name, First Name, Middle Initial)

5. PATIENT'S ADDRESS (No., Street)
1 BUTTERNUT STREET

6. PATIENT'S RELATIONSHIP TO INSURED
Self [ ] Spouse [ ] Child [ ] Other [ ]

7. INSURED'S ADDRESS (No., Street)

CITY: ANYWHERE   STATE: NY

8. PATIENT STATUS
Single [ ] Married [ ] Other [ ]

CITY   STATE

ZIP CODE: 12345-1234   TELEPHONE (Include Area Code): (101) 7918645

Employed [ ] Full-Time Student [ ] Part-Time Student [ ]

ZIP CODE   TELEPHONE (Include Area Code): ( )

9. OTHER INSURED'S NAME (Last Name, First Name, Middle Initial)

10. IS PATIENT'S CONDITION RELATED TO:

11. INSURED'S POLICY GROUP OR FECA NUMBER

a. OTHER INSURED'S POLICY OR GROUP NUMBER

a. EMPLOYMENT? (Current or Previous)
YES [ ] NO [X]

a. INSURED'S DATE OF BIRTH MM DD YY   SEX M [ ] F [ ]

b. OTHER INSURED'S DATE OF BIRTH MM DD YY   SEX M [ ] F [ ]

b. AUTO ACCIDENT?   PLACE (State)
YES [ ] NO [X]

b. EMPLOYER'S NAME OR SCHOOL NAME

c. EMPLOYER'S NAME OR SCHOOL NAME

c. OTHER ACCIDENT?
YES [ ] NO [X]

c. INSURANCE PLAN NAME OR PROGRAM NAME

d. INSURANCE PLAN NAME OR PROGRAM NAME

10d. RESERVED FOR LOCAL USE

d. IS THERE ANOTHER HEALTH BENEFIT PLAN?
YES [ ] NO [ ] If yes, return to and complete item 9 a-d.

READ BACK OF FORM BEFORE COMPLETING & SIGNING THIS FORM.
12. PATIENT'S OR AUTHORIZED PERSON'S SIGNATURE I authorize the release of any medical or other information necessary to process this claim. I also request payment of government benefits either to myself or to the party who accepts assignment below.

SIGNED _____   DATE _____

13. INSURED'S OR AUTHORIZED PERSON'S SIGNATURE I authorize payment of medical benefits to the undersigned physician or supplier for services described below.

SIGNED _____

14. DATE OF CURRENT: MM DD YY   ILLNESS (First symptom) OR INJURY (Accident) OR PREGNANCY (LMP)

15. IF PATIENT HAS HAD SAME OR SIMILAR ILLNESS, GIVE FIRST DATE MM DD YY

16. DATES PATIENT UNABLE TO WORK IN CURRENT OCCUPATION
FROM MM DD YY   TO MM DD YY

17. NAME OF REFERRING PROVIDER OR OTHER SOURCE
ARNOLD J YOUNGLOVE MD

17a.
17b. NPI 0123456789

18. HOSPITALIZATION DATES RELATED TO CURRENT SERVICES
FROM 03 10 YYYY   TO 03 10 YYYY

19. RESERVED FOR LOCAL USE

20. OUTSIDE LAB? $ CHARGES
YES [ ] NO [X]

21. DIAGNOSIS OR NATURE OF ILLNESS OR INJURY (Relate Items 1, 2, 3 or 4 to Item 24E by Line)
1. 217
2. ____
3. ____
4. ____

22. MEDICAID RESUBMISSION CODE   ORIGINAL REF. NO.

23. PRIOR AUTHORIZATION NUMBER

24. A DATE(S) OF SERVICE From MM DD YY	To MM DD YY	B. PLACE OF SERVICE	C. EMG	D. PROCEDURES, SERVICES, OR SUPPLIES (Explain Unusual Circumstances) CPT/HCPCS	MODIFIER	E. DIAGNOSIS POINTER	F. $ CHARGES	G. DAYS OR UNITS	H. EPSDT Family Plan	I. ID. QUAL.	J. RENDERING PROVIDER ID. #
1	03 10 YYYY		22		19120	LT	1	975 00	1		NPI	
2											NPI	
3											NPI	
4											NPI	
5											NPI	
6											NPI	

25. FEDERAL TAX I.D. NUMBER   SSN EIN
111397992   [X]

26. PATIENT'S ACCOUNT NO.
1-13

27. ACCEPT ASSIGNMENT? (For govt. claims, see back)
[X] YES [ ] NO

28. TOTAL CHARGE
$ 975 00

29. AMOUNT PAID
$

30. BALANCE DUE
$

31. SIGNATURE OF PHYSICIAN OR SUPPLIER INCLUDING DEGREES OR CREDENTIALS (I certify that the statements on the reverse apply to this bill and are made a part thereof.)
SEJAL RAJA MD
SIGNED   DATE MMDDYYYY

32. SERVICE FACILITY LOCATION INFORMATION
GOODMEDICINE HOSPITAL
1 PROVIDER STREET
ANYWHERE NY 12345
a. 1123456789   b.

33. BILLING PROVIDER INFO & PH # (101) 2022923
SEJAL RAJA MD
1 MEDICAL DRIVE
INJURY NY 12347
a. 7890123456   b.

NUCC Instruction Manual available at: www.nucc.org

APPROVED OMB-0938-0999 FORM CMS-1500 (08/05)

1500

HEALTH INSURANCE CLAIM FORM

APPROVED BY NATIONAL UNIFORM CLAIM COMMITTEE 08/05

| | PICA | | | | | | | | PICA | |

1. MEDICARE (Medicare #) MEDICAID (Medicaid #) TRICARE CHAMPUS **[X]** (Sponsor's SSN) CHAMPVA (Member ID#) GROUP HEALTH PLAN (SSN or ID) FECA BLK LUNG (SSN) OTHER (ID)

1a. INSURED'S I.D. NUMBER (For Program in Item 1)
071269845

2. PATIENT'S NAME (Last Name, First Name, Middle Initial)
WILLOWTREE, GREGORY

3. PATIENT'S BIRTH DATE MM 12 DD 12 YY 1942 **SEX** M **[X]** F

4. INSURED'S NAME (Last Name, First Name, Middle Initial)
WILLOWTREE, GREGORY

5. PATIENT'S ADDRESS (No., Street)
150 TREE LANE

6. PATIENT'S RELATIONSHIP TO INSURED
Self **[X]** Spouse Child Other

7. INSURED'S ADDRESS (No., Street)
150 TREE LANE

CITY NOWHERE STATE NY

8. PATIENT STATUS
Single **[X]** Married Other
Employed Full-Time Student Part-Time Student

CITY NOWHERE STATE NY

ZIP CODE 12346-1234 TELEPHONE (Include Area Code) (101)5552356

ZIP CODE 12346-1234 TELEPHONE (Include Area Code) (101)5552356

9. OTHER INSURED'S NAME (Last Name, First Name, Middle Initial)

10. IS PATIENT'S CONDITION RELATED TO:

11. INSURED'S POLICY GROUP OR FECA NUMBER

a. OTHER INSURED'S POLICY OR GROUP NUMBER

a. EMPLOYMENT? (Current or Previous) YES **[X]** NO

a. INSURED'S DATE OF BIRTH MM DD YY SEX M F

b. OTHER INSURED'S DATE OF BIRTH MM DD YY SEX M F

b. AUTO ACCIDENT? PLACE (State) YES **[X]** NO

b. EMPLOYER'S NAME OR SCHOOL NAME

c. EMPLOYER'S NAME OR SCHOOL NAME

c. OTHER ACCIDENT? YES **[X]** NO

c. INSURANCE PLAN NAME OR PROGRAM NAME

d. INSURANCE PLAN NAME OR PROGRAM NAME

10d. RESERVED FOR LOCAL USE

d. IS THERE ANOTHER HEALTH BENEFIT PLAN? YES **[X]** NO *If yes,* return to and complete item 9 a-d.

READ BACK OF FORM BEFORE COMPLETING & SIGNING THIS FORM.
12. PATIENT'S OR AUTHORIZED PERSON'S SIGNATURE I authorize the release of any medical or other information necessary to process this claim. I also request payment of government benefits either to myself or to the party who accepts assignment below.

SIGNED SIGNATURE ON FILE DATE

13. INSURED'S OR AUTHORIZED PERSON'S SIGNATURE I authorize payment of medical benefits to the undersigned physcian or supplier for services described below.

SIGNED SIGNATURE ON FILE

14. DATE OF CURRENT: MM 03 DD 19 YY YYYY ILLNESS (First symptom) OR INJURY (Accident) OR PREGNANCY (LMP)

15. IF PATIENT HAS HAD SAME OR SIMILAR ILLNESS. GIVE FIRST DATE MM DD YY

16. DATES PATIENT UNABLE TO WORK IN CURRENT OCCUPATION FROM MM DD YY TO MM DD YY

17. NAME OF REFERRING PROVIDER OR OTHER SOURCE
17a.
17b. NPI

18. HOSPITALIZATION DATES RELATED TO CURRENT SERVICES FROM MM 03 DD 19 YY YYYY TO MM 03 DD 19 YY YYYY

19. RESERVED FOR LOCAL USE

20. OUTSIDE LAB? YES **[X]** NO $ CHARGES

21. DIAGNOSIS OR NATURE OF ILLNESS OR INJURY (Relate Items 1, 2, 3 or 4 to Item 24E by Line)
1. 836.0
2. 727.83
3.
4.

22. MEDICAID RESUBMISSION CODE ORIGINAL REF. NO.

23. PRIOR AUTHORIZATION NUMBER

24. A. DATE(S) OF SERVICE From MM DD YY	To MM DD YY	B. PLACE OF SERVICE	C. EMG	D. PROCEDURES, SERVICES, OR SUPPLIES (Explain Unusual Circumstances) CPT/HCPCS	MODIFIER	E. DIAGNOSIS POINTER	F. $ CHARGES	G. DAYS OR UNITS	H. EPSDT Family Plan	I. ID. QUAL.	J. RENDERING PROVIDER ID. #
1	0319YYYY		22		29881	RT	1	2000 00	1		NPI	
2											NPI	
3											NPI	
4											NPI	
5											NPI	
6											NPI	

25. FEDERAL TAX I.D. NUMBER SSN EIN **[X]**
111982342

26. PATIENT'S ACCOUNT NO.
1-14

27. ACCEPT ASSIGNMENT? (For govt. claims, see back) **[X]** YES NO

28. TOTAL CHARGE $ 2000 00

29. AMOUNT PAID $

30. BALANCE DUE $ 2000 00

31. SIGNATURE OF PHYSICIAN OR SUPPLIER INCLUDING DEGREES OR CREDENTIALS (I certify that the statements on the reverse apply to this bill and are made a part thereof.)

ANGELA DILALIO MD
SIGNED DATE MMDDYYYY

32. SERVICE FACILITY LOCATION INFORMATION
GOODMEDICINE HOSPITAL
1 PROVIDER ST
ANYWHERE NY 12345
a. 1123456789 b.

33. BILLING PROVIDER INFO & PH # (101)2014321
ANGELA DILALIO MD
99 PROVIDER DR
INJURY NY 12347
a. 4567890123 b.

NUCC Instruction Manual available at: www.nucc.org

APPROVED OMB-0938-0999 FORM CMS-1500 (08/05)

| 1500 |
| HEALTH INSURANCE CLAIM FORM |

APPROVED BY NATIONAL UNIFORM CLAIM COMMITTEE 08/05

☐☐ PICA | | PICA ☐☐

| 1. MEDICARE   MEDICAID   TRICARE CHAMPUS   CHAMPVA   GROUP HEALTH PLAN   FECA BLK LUNG   OTHER | 1a. INSURED'S I.D. NUMBER (For Program in Item 1) |
| (Medicare #)   (Medicaid #) X (Sponsor's SSN)   (Member ID#)   (SSN or ID)   (SSN)   (ID) | 103236666 |

| 2. PATIENT'S NAME (Last Name, First Name, Middle Initial) | 3. PATIENT'S BIRTH DATE   SEX | 4. INSURED'S NAME (Last Name, First Name, Middle Initial) |
| PATTY, AGNES | MM 09 DD 03 YY 1947 M☐ F X | PATTY, GERRY |

5. PATIENT'S ADDRESS (No., Street)	6. PATIENT'S RELATIONSHIP TO INSURED	7. INSURED'S ADDRESS (No., Street)
1 PATTY CAKE DRIVE	Self☐ Spouse X Child☐ Other☐	1 PATTY CAKE DRIVE
CITY NOWHERE	STATE NY	8. PATIENT STATUS Single☐ Married X Other☐	CITY NOWHERE	STATE NY
ZIP CODE 12346-1234 TELEPHONE (Include Area Code) (101)1122701	Employed☐ Full-Time Student☐ Part-Time Student☐	ZIP CODE 12346-1234 TELEPHONE (Include Area Code) (101)1122701

9. OTHER INSURED'S NAME (Last Name, First Name, Middle Initial)	10. IS PATIENT'S CONDITION RELATED TO:	11. INSURED'S POLICY GROUP OR FECA NUMBER
a. OTHER INSURED'S POLICY OR GROUP NUMBER	a. EMPLOYMENT? (Current or Previous) YES☐ X NO	a. INSURED'S DATE OF BIRTH MM DD YY SEX M☐ F☐
b. OTHER INSURED'S DATE OF BIRTH MM DD YY SEX M☐ F☐	b. AUTO ACCIDENT? PLACE (State) YES☐ X NO	b. EMPLOYER'S NAME OR SCHOOL NAME
c. EMPLOYER'S NAME OR SCHOOL NAME	c. OTHER ACCIDENT? YES☐ X NO	c. INSURANCE PLAN NAME OR PROGRAM NAME
d. INSURANCE PLAN NAME OR PROGRAM NAME	10d. RESERVED FOR LOCAL USE	d. IS THERE ANOTHER HEALTH BENEFIT PLAN? YES☐ X NO If yes, return to and complete item 9 a-d.

READ BACK OF FORM BEFORE COMPLETING & SIGNING THIS FORM.

| 12. PATIENT'S OR AUTHORIZED PERSON'S SIGNATURE I authorize the release of any medical or other information necessary to process this claim. I also request payment of government benefits either to myself or to the party who accepts assignment below. | 13. INSURED'S OR AUTHORIZED PERSON'S SIGNATURE I authorize payment of medical benefits to the undersigned physician or supplier for services described below. |
| SIGNED SIGNATURE ON FILE   DATE | SIGNED SIGNATURE ON FILE |

14. DATE OF CURRENT: MM DD YY ILLNESS (First symptom) OR INJURY (Accident) OR PREGNANCY (LMP) 02 10 YYYY	15. IF PATIENT HAS HAD SAME OR SIMILAR ILLNESS, GIVE FIRST DATE MM DD YY	16. DATES PATIENT UNABLE TO WORK IN CURRENT OCCUPATION MM DD YY MM DD YY FROM TO
17. NAME OF REFERRING PROVIDER OR OTHER SOURCE	17a. 17b. NPI	18. HOSPITALIZATION DATES RELATED TO CURRENT SERVICES MM DD YY MM DD YY FROM TO
19. RESERVED FOR LOCAL USE		20. OUTSIDE LAB? $ CHARGES YES☐ X NO

21. DIAGNOSIS OR NATURE OF ILLNESS OR INJURY (Relate Items 1, 2, 3 or 4 to Item 24E by Line)	22. MEDICAID RESUBMISSION CODE ORIGINAL REF. NO.
1. 427.9 3.	23. PRIOR AUTHORIZATION NUMBER
2. 784.7 4.	

24. A DATE(S) OF SERVICE	B. PLACE OF SERVICE	C. EMG	D. PROCEDURES, SERVICES, OR SUPPLIES (Explain Unusual Circumstances)	E. DIAGNOSIS POINTER	F. $ CHARGES	G. DAYS OR UNITS	H. EPSDT Family Plan	I. ID. QUAL.	J. RENDERING PROVIDER ID. #
From MM DD YY To MM DD YY			CPT/HCPCS MODIFIER						
03 01 YYYY		11		99203		1	100 00	1		NPI	
03 01 YYYY		11		30901		2	65 00	1		NPI	
03 01 YYYY		11		93000		1	50 00	1		NPI	
										NPI	
										NPI	
										NPI	

| 25. FEDERAL TAX I.D. NUMBER   SSN EIN | 26. PATIENT'S ACCOUNT NO. | 27. ACCEPT ASSIGNMENT? (For govt. claims, see back) | 28. TOTAL CHARGE | 29. AMOUNT PAID | 30. BALANCE DUE |
| 117654312   X | 1-15 | X YES   NO☐ | $ 215 00 | $ | $ 180 00 |

| 31. SIGNATURE OF PHYSICIAN OR SUPPLIER INCLUDING DEGREES OR CREDENTIALS (I certify that the statements on the reverse apply to this bill and are made a part thereof.) IRMINA M BRILLIANT MD SIGNED   DATE MMDDYYYY | 32. SERVICE FACILITY LOCATION INFORMATION   a. NPI   b. | 33. BILLING PROVIDER INFO & PH # (101)2013145 IRMINA M BRILLIANT MD 25 MEDICAL DRIVE INJURY NY 12347 a. 2345678901   b. |

NUCC Instruction Manual available at: www.nucc.org | APPROVED OMB-0938-0999 FORM CMS-1500 (08/05)

1500

HEALTH INSURANCE CLAIM FORM

APPROVED BY NATIONAL UNIFORM CLAIM COMMITTEE 08/05

| | | PICA | | | | | | PICA | | |

1. MEDICARE (Medicare #) | **MEDICAID** (Medicaid #) | **TRICARE CHAMPUS** (Sponsor's SSN) [X] | **CHAMPVA** (Member ID#) | **GROUP HEALTH PLAN** (SSN or ID) | **FECA BLK LUNG** (SSN) | **OTHER** (ID) | **1a. INSURED'S I.D. NUMBER** (For Program in Item 1): 562356989

2. PATIENT'S NAME (Last Name, First Name, Middle Initial)
LEWIS, TERRY

3. PATIENT'S BIRTH DATE 05 05 1986 **SEX** M [X] F

4. INSURED'S NAME (Last Name, First Name, Middle Initial)
LEWIS, TERRY

5. PATIENT'S ADDRESS (No., Street)
9 RANDOLPH ROAD

6. PATIENT'S RELATIONSHIP TO INSURED
Self [X] Spouse Child Other

7. INSURED'S ADDRESS (No., Street)
9 RANDOLPH ROAD

CITY ANYWHERE **STATE** NY

8. PATIENT STATUS
Single [X] Married Other
Employed [X] Full-Time Student Part-Time Student

CITY ANYWHERE **STATE** NY

ZIP CODE 12345-1234 **TELEPHONE (Include Area Code)** (101) 5555169

ZIP CODE 12345-1234 **TELEPHONE (Include Area Code)** (101) 5555169

9. OTHER INSURED'S NAME (Last Name, First Name, Middle Initial)

10. IS PATIENT'S CONDITION RELATED TO:

11. INSURED'S POLICY GROUP OR FECA NUMBER

a. OTHER INSURED'S POLICY OR GROUP NUMBER

a. EMPLOYMENT? (Current or Previous) YES NO [X]

a. INSURED'S DATE OF BIRTH MM DD YY **SEX** M F

b. OTHER INSURED'S DATE OF BIRTH MM DD YY **SEX** M F

b. AUTO ACCIDENT? YES NO [X] **PLACE (State)**

b. EMPLOYER'S NAME OR SCHOOL NAME

c. EMPLOYER'S NAME OR SCHOOL NAME

c. OTHER ACCIDENT? YES NO [X]

c. INSURANCE PLAN NAME OR PROGRAM NAME

d. INSURANCE PLAN NAME OR PROGRAM NAME

10d. RESERVED FOR LOCAL USE

d. IS THERE ANOTHER HEALTH BENEFIT PLAN? YES NO [X] *If yes,* return to and complete item 9 a-d.

READ BACK OF FORM BEFORE COMPLETING & SIGNING THIS FORM.

12. PATIENT'S OR AUTHORIZED PERSON'S SIGNATURE I authorize the release of any medical or other information necessary to process this claim. I also request payment of government benefits either to myself or to the party who accepts assignment below.

SIGNED SIGNATURE ON FILE DATE

13. INSURED'S OR AUTHORIZED PERSON'S SIGNATURE I authorize payment of medical benefits to the undersigned physcian or supplier for services described below.

SIGNED SIGNATURE ON FILE

14. DATE OF CURRENT: ILLNESS (First symptom) OR INJURY (Accident) OR PREGNANCY (LMP) 06 19 YYYY

15. IF PATIENT HAS HAD SAME OR SIMILAR ILLNESS. GIVE FIRST DATE MM DD YY

16. DATES PATIENT UNABLE TO WORK IN CURRENT OCCUPATION FROM MM DD YY TO MM DD YY

17. NAME OF REFERRING PROVIDER OR OTHER SOURCE
17a.
17b. NPI

18. HOSPITALIZATION DATES RELATED TO CURRENT SERVICES FROM MM DD YY TO MM DD YY

19. RESERVED FOR LOCAL USE

20. OUTSIDE LAB? YES NO [X] **$ CHARGES**

21. DIAGNOSIS OR NATURE OF ILLNESS OR INJURY (Relate Items 1, 2, 3 or 4 to Item 24E by Line)
1. 300 00
2.
3.
4.

22. MEDICAID RESUBMISSION CODE **ORIGINAL REF. NO.**

23. PRIOR AUTHORIZATION NUMBER

24. A. DATE(S) OF SERVICE From MM DD YY	To MM DD YY	B. PLACE OF SERVICE	C. EMG	D. PROCEDURES, SERVICES, OR SUPPLIES (Explain Unusual Circumstances) CPT/HCPCS	MODIFIER	E. DIAGNOSIS POINTER	F. $ CHARGES	G. DAYS OR UNITS	H. EPSDT Family Plan	I. ID. QUAL.	J. RENDERING PROVIDER ID. #
1	0619YYYY		11		99212		1	35 00	1		NPI	
2											NPI	
3											NPI	
4											NPI	
5											NPI	
6											NPI	

25. FEDERAL TAX I.D. NUMBER 111982342 SSN EIN [X]

26. PATIENT'S ACCOUNT NO. 1-16

27. ACCEPT ASSIGNMENT? (For govt. claims, see back) [X] YES NO

28. TOTAL CHARGE $ 35 00

29. AMOUNT PAID $

30. BALANCE DUE $ 35 00

31. SIGNATURE OF PHYSICIAN OR SUPPLIER INCLUDING DEGREES OR CREDENTIALS (I certify that the statements on the reverse apply to this bill and are made a part thereof.)

ANGELA DILALIO MD
SIGNED DATE MMDDYYYY

32. SERVICE FACILITY LOCATION INFORMATION
a. NPI b.

33. BILLING PROVIDER INFO & PH # (101) 2014321
ANGELA DILALIO MD
99 PROVIDER DR
INJURY NY 12347
a. 4567890123 b.

NUCC Instruction Manual available at: www.nucc.org

APPROVED OMB-0938-0999 FORM CMS-1500 (08/05)

1500

HEALTH INSURANCE CLAIM FORM

APPROVED BY NATIONAL UNIFORM CLAIM COMMITTEE 08/05

| | PICA | | | | | | PICA | |

1. MEDICARE	MEDICAID	TRICARE CHAMPUS	CHAMPVA	GROUP HEALTH PLAN	FECA BLK LUNG	OTHER	1a. INSURED'S I.D. NUMBER (For Program in Item 1)
(Medicare #)	(Medicaid #)	(Sponsor's SSN)	(Member ID#)	(SSN or ID)	(SSN)	[X] (ID)	562156

2. PATIENT'S NAME (Last Name, First Name, Middle Initial)	3. PATIENT'S BIRTH DATE / SEX	4. INSURED'S NAME (Last Name, First Name, Middle Initial)
PARKER, MARY	06 06 1975 M☐ F[X]	PARKER, MARY

5. PATIENT'S ADDRESS (No., Street)	6. PATIENT'S RELATIONSHIP TO INSURED	7. INSURED'S ADDRESS (No., Street)
15 MAIN ST	Self [X] Spouse☐ Child☐ Other☐	15 MAIN ST

CITY	STATE	8. PATIENT STATUS	CITY	STATE
ANYWHERE	NY	Single☐ Married [X] Other☐	ANYWHERE	NY

ZIP CODE	TELEPHONE (Include Area Code)		ZIP CODE	TELEPHONE (Include Area Code)
12345-1234	(101)5555658	Employed [X] Full-Time Student☐ Part-Time Student☐	12345-1234	(101)5555658

9. OTHER INSURED'S NAME (Last Name, First Name, Middle Initial)	10. IS PATIENT'S CONDITION RELATED TO:	11. INSURED'S POLICY GROUP OR FECA NUMBER
PARKER, MARK		

a. OTHER INSURED'S POLICY OR GROUP NUMBER	a. EMPLOYMENT? (Current or Previous)	a. INSURED'S DATE OF BIRTH / SEX
23562598	YES☐ [X] NO	06 06 1975 M☐ F[X]

b. OTHER INSURED'S DATE OF BIRTH / SEX	b. AUTO ACCIDENT? PLACE (State)	b. EMPLOYER'S NAME OR SCHOOL NAME
04 30 1970 M[X] F☐	YES☐ [X] NO	WORLD UNIVERSITY

c. EMPLOYER'S NAME OR SCHOOL NAME	c. OTHER ACCIDENT?	c. INSURANCE PLAN NAME OR PROGRAM NAME
US NAVY	YES☐ [X] NO	AETNA

d. INSURANCE PLAN NAME OR PROGRAM NAME	10d. RESERVED FOR LOCAL USE	d. IS THERE ANOTHER HEALTH BENEFIT PLAN?
TRICARE		[X] YES ☐ NO If yes, return to and complete item 9 a-d.

READ BACK OF FORM BEFORE COMPLETING & SIGNING THIS FORM.

12. PATIENT'S OR AUTHORIZED PERSON'S SIGNATURE I authorize the release of any medical or other information necessary to process this claim. I also request payment of government benefits either to myself or to the party who accepts assignment below.

SIGNED SIGNATURE ON FILE DATE

13. INSURED'S OR AUTHORIZED PERSON'S SIGNATURE I authorize payment of medical benefits to the undersigned physician or supplier for services described below.

SIGNED SIGNATURE ON FILE

14. DATE OF CURRENT: ILLNESS (First symptom) OR INJURY (Accident) OR PREGNANCY (LMP)	15. IF PATIENT HAS HAD SAME OR SIMILAR ILLNESS. GIVE FIRST DATE	16. DATES PATIENT UNABLE TO WORK IN CURRENT OCCUPATION
06 19 YYYY		FROM TO

17. NAME OF REFERRING PROVIDER OR OTHER SOURCE	17a.	18. HOSPITALIZATION DATES RELATED TO CURRENT SERVICES
	17b. NPI	FROM TO

19. RESERVED FOR LOCAL USE	20. OUTSIDE LAB? $ CHARGES
	YES☐ [X] NO

21. DIAGNOSIS OR NATURE OF ILLNESS OR INJURY (Relate Items 1, 2, 3 or 4 to Item 24E by Line)	22. MEDICAID RESUBMISSION CODE / ORIGINAL REF. NO.
1. 493.90 3.	
2. 4.	23. PRIOR AUTHORIZATION NUMBER

24. A DATE(S) OF SERVICE From / To	B. PLACE OF SERVICE	C. EMG	D. PROCEDURES, SERVICES, OR SUPPLIES (Explain Unusual Circumstances) CPT/HCPCS MODIFIER	E. DIAGNOSIS POINTER	F. $ CHARGES	G. DAYS OR UNITS	H. EPSDT Family Plan	I. ID. QUAL.	J. RENDERING PROVIDER ID. #
1	06 19 YYYY	11		99212	1	35 00	1		NPI	
2									NPI	
3									NPI	
4									NPI	
5									NPI	
6									NPI	

25. FEDERAL TAX I.D. NUMBER SSN EIN	26. PATIENT'S ACCOUNT NO.	27. ACCEPT ASSIGNMENT? (For govt. claims, see back)	28. TOTAL CHARGE	29. AMOUNT PAID	30. BALANCE DUE
111982342 [X]	1-17P	[X] YES ☐ NO	$ 35 00	$	$ 35 00

31. SIGNATURE OF PHYSICIAN OR SUPPLIER INCLUDING DEGREES OR CREDENTIALS (I certify that the statements on the reverse apply to this bill and are made a part thereof.)	32. SERVICE FACILITY LOCATION INFORMATION	33. BILLING PROVIDER INFO & PH # (101)2014321
ANGELA DILALIO MD		ANGELA DILALIO MD 99 PROVIDER DR INJURY NY 12347
SIGNED DATE MMDDYYYY	a. NPI b.	a. 4567890123 b.

1500

HEALTH INSURANCE CLAIM FORM

APPROVED BY NATIONAL UNIFORM CLAIM COMMITTEE 08/05

| | | PICA | | | | | | | PICA | | |

| 1. MEDICARE (Medicare #) | MEDICAID (Medicaid #) | TRICARE CHAMPUS [X] (Sponsor's SSN) | CHAMPVA (Member ID#) | GROUP HEALTH PLAN (SSN or ID) | FECA BLK LUNG (SSN) | OTHER (ID) | 1a. INSURED'S I.D. NUMBER (For Program in Item 1) 23562598 |

| 2. PATIENT'S NAME (Last Name, First Name, Middle Initial) PARKER, MARY | 3. PATIENT'S BIRTH DATE MM DD YY 06 06 1975 SEX M[ ] F[X] | 4. INSURED'S NAME (Last Name, First Name, Middle Initial) PARKER, MARK |

| 5. PATIENT'S ADDRESS (No., Street) 15 MAIN ST | 6. PATIENT'S RELATIONSHIP TO INSURED Self[ ] Spouse[X] Child[ ] Other[ ] | 7. INSURED'S ADDRESS (No., Street) USS EISENHOWER |

| CITY ANYWHERE STATE NY | 8. PATIENT STATUS Single[ ] Married[X] Other[ ] | CITY FPO AE STATE |

| ZIP CODE 12345-1234 TELEPHONE (Include Area Code) (101)5555658 | Employed[X] Full-Time Student[ ] Part-Time Student[ ] | ZIP CODE 11600-3982 TELEPHONE (Include Area Code) ( ) |

| 9. OTHER INSURED'S NAME (Last Name, First Name, Middle Initial) PARKER, MARY | 10. IS PATIENT'S CONDITION RELATED TO: | 11. INSURED'S POLICY GROUP OR FECA NUMBER |

| a. OTHER INSURED'S POLICY OR GROUP NUMBER 562156 | a. EMPLOYMENT? (Current or Previous) YES[ ] NO[X] | a. INSURED'S DATE OF BIRTH MM DD YY 04 30 1970 SEX M[X] F[ ] |

| b. OTHER INSURED'S DATE OF BIRTH MM DD YY 06 06 1975 SEX M[ ] F[X] | b. AUTO ACCIDENT? PLACE (State) YES[ ] NO[X] | b. EMPLOYER'S NAME OR SCHOOL NAME US NAVY |

| c. EMPLOYER'S NAME OR SCHOOL NAME WORLD UNIVERSITY | c. OTHER ACCIDENT? YES[ ] NO[X] | c. INSURANCE PLAN NAME OR PROGRAM NAME TRICARE |

| d. INSURANCE PLAN NAME OR PROGRAM NAME AETNA | 10d. RESERVED FOR LOCAL USE | d. IS THERE ANOTHER HEALTH BENEFIT PLAN? YES[X] NO[ ] If yes, return to and complete item 9 a-d. |

READ BACK OF FORM BEFORE COMPLETING & SIGNING THIS FORM.

12. PATIENT'S OR AUTHORIZED PERSON'S SIGNATURE I authorize the release of any medical or other information necessary to process this claim. I also request payment of government benefits either to myself or to the party who accepts assignment below.

SIGNED SIGNATURE ON FILE DATE

13. INSURED'S OR AUTHORIZED PERSON'S SIGNATURE I authorize payment of medical benefits to the undersigned physcian or supplier for services described below.

SIGNED SIGNATURE ON FILE

| 14. DATE OF CURRENT: MM DD YY 06 19 YYYY ILLNESS (First symptom) OR INJURY (Accident) OR PREGNANCY (LMP) | 15. IF PATIENT HAS HAD SAME OR SIMILAR ILLNESS, GIVE FIRST DATE MM DD YY | 16. DATES PATIENT UNABLE TO WORK IN CURRENT OCCUPATION MM DD YY MM DD YY FROM TO |

| 17. NAME OF REFERRING PROVIDER OR OTHER SOURCE | 17a. 17b. NPI | 18. HOSPITALIZATION DATES RELATED TO CURRENT SERVICES MM DD YY MM DD YY FROM TO |

| 19. RESERVED FOR LOCAL USE | | 20. OUTSIDE LAB? YES[ ] NO[X] $ CHARGES |

| 21. DIAGNOSIS OR NATURE OF ILLNESS OR INJURY (Relate Items 1, 2, 3 or 4 to Item 24E by Line) 1. 493.90 3. 2. 4. | 22. MEDICAID RESUBMISSION CODE ORIGINAL REF. NO. 23. PRIOR AUTHORIZATION NUMBER |

24. A. DATE(S) OF SERVICE From MM DD YY To MM DD YY	B. PLACE OF SERVICE	C. EMG	D. PROCEDURES, SERVICES, OR SUPPLIES (Explain Unusual Circumstances) CPT/HCPCS MODIFIER	E. DIAGNOSIS POINTER	F. $ CHARGES	G. DAYS OR UNITS	H. EPSDT Family Plan	I. ID. QUAL.	J. RENDERING PROVIDER ID. #
1	0619YYYY	11		99212	1	35 00	1		NPI	
2									NPI	
3									NPI	
4									NPI	
5									NPI	
6									NPI	

| 25. FEDERAL TAX I.D. NUMBER SSN EIN 111982342 [X] | 26. PATIENT'S ACCOUNT NO. 1-17S | 27. ACCEPT ASSIGNMENT? (For govt. claims, see back) YES[X] NO[ ] | 28. TOTAL CHARGE $ 35 00 | 29. AMOUNT PAID $ | 30. BALANCE DUE $ 35 00 |

| 31. SIGNATURE OF PHYSICIAN OR SUPPLIER INCLUDING DEGREES OR CREDENTIALS (I certify that the statements on the reverse apply to this bill and are made a part thereof.) ANGELA DILALIO MD SIGNED DATE MMDDYYYY | 32. SERVICE FACILITY LOCATION INFORMATION a. NPI b. | 33. BILLING PROVIDER INFO & PH # (101)2014321 ANGELA DILALIO MD 99 PROVIDER DR INJURY NY 12347 a. 4567890123 b. |

NUCC Instruction Manual available at: www.nucc.org

APPROVED OMB-0938-0999 FORM CMS-1500 (08/05)

1500

HEALTH INSURANCE CLAIM FORM

APPROVED BY NATIONAL UNIFORM CLAIM COMMITTEE 08/05

	PICA													PICA		

1. MEDICARE	MEDICAID	TRICARE CHAMPUS	CHAMPVA	GROUP HEALTH PLAN	FECA BLK LUNG	OTHER	1a. INSURED'S I.D. NUMBER (For Program in Item 1)
(Medicare #)	(Medicaid #)	(Sponsor's SSN)	(Member ID#)	X (SSN or ID)	(SSN)	(ID)	235568956

2. PATIENT'S NAME (Last Name, First Name, Middle Initial)	3. PATIENT'S BIRTH DATE	SEX	4. INSURED'S NAME (Last Name, First Name, Middle Initial)
MILLION, IONA, J	MM 01 DD 01 YY 1970	M F X	ANYWHERE GOLF COURSE

5. PATIENT'S ADDRESS (No., Street)	6. PATIENT'S RELATIONSHIP TO INSURED	7. INSURED'S ADDRESS (No., Street)
100A PASTURES CT	Self Spouse Child Other X	RTE 20

CITY	STATE	8. PATIENT STATUS	CITY	STATE
ANYWHERE	NY	Single Married Other	GOLF	NY

ZIP CODE	TELEPHONE (Include Area Code)		ZIP CODE	TELEPHONE (Include Area Code)
12345-1234	(101)7590839	Employed X Full-Time Student Part-Time Student	12348	( )

9. OTHER INSURED'S NAME (Last Name, First Name, Middle Initial)	10. IS PATIENT'S CONDITION RELATED TO:	11. INSURED'S POLICY GROUP OR FECA NUMBER
		10173

a. OTHER INSURED'S POLICY OR GROUP NUMBER	a. EMPLOYMENT? (Current or Previous) X YES NO	a. INSURED'S DATE OF BIRTH MM DD YY SEX M F

b. OTHER INSURED'S DATE OF BIRTH MM DD YY SEX M F	b. AUTO ACCIDENT? PLACE (State) YES X NO	b. EMPLOYER'S NAME OR SCHOOL NAME ANYWHERE GOLF COURSE

c. EMPLOYER'S NAME OR SCHOOL NAME	c. OTHER ACCIDENT? YES X NO	c. INSURANCE PLAN NAME OR PROGRAM NAME HIGH RISK INSURANCE

d. INSURANCE PLAN NAME OR PROGRAM NAME	10d. RESERVED FOR LOCAL USE	d. IS THERE ANOTHER HEALTH BENEFIT PLAN? YES NO *If yes*, return to and complete item 9 a-d.

READ BACK OF FORM BEFORE COMPLETING & SIGNING THIS FORM.

12. PATIENT'S OR AUTHORIZED PERSON'S SIGNATURE I authorize the release of any medical or other information necessary to process this claim. I also request payment of government benefits either to myself or to the party who accepts assignment below.

SIGNED _____ DATE _____

13. INSURED'S OR AUTHORIZED PERSON'S SIGNATURE I authorize payment of medical benefits to the undersigned physican or supplier for services described below.

SIGNED _____

14. DATE OF CURRENT: MM 09 DD 08 YY YYYY ILLNESS (First symptom) OR INJURY (Accident) OR PREGNANCY (LMP)	15. IF PATIENT HAS HAD SAME OR SIMILAR ILLNESS, GIVE FIRST DATE MM DD YY	16. DATES PATIENT UNABLE TO WORK IN CURRENT OCCUPATION MM DD YY FROM 03 10 YYYY TO 03 31 YYYY

17. NAME OF REFERRING PROVIDER OR OTHER SOURCE	17a.	18. HOSPITALIZATION DATES RELATED TO CURRENT SERVICES MM DD YY MM DD YY FROM 03 10 YYYY TO 03 10 YYYY
	17b. NPI	

19. RESERVED FOR LOCAL USE	20. OUTSIDE LAB? YES X NO $ CHARGES

21. DIAGNOSIS OR NATURE OF ILLNESS OR INJURY (Relate Items 1, 2, 3 or 4 to Item 24E by Line)

1. V54 01
2. V45 89
3. 719 47
4. 905 4

22. MEDICAID RESUBMISSION CODE ORIGINAL REF. NO.
23. PRIOR AUTHORIZATION NUMBER

24. A DATE(S) OF SERVICE From MM DD YY To MM DD YY	B. PLACE OF SERVICE	C. EMG	D. PROCEDURES, SERVICES, OR SUPPLIES (Explain Unusual Circumstances) CPT/HCPCS MODIFIER	E. DIAGNOSIS POINTER	F. $ CHARGES	G. DAYS OR UNITS	H. EPSDT Family Plan	I. ID. QUAL.	J. RENDERING PROVIDER ID. #
1 03 10 YYYY	22		20680 LT	1	650 00	1		NPI	
2								NPI	
3								NPI	
4								NPI	
5								NPI	
6								NPI	

25. FEDERAL TAX I.D. NUMBER SSN EIN	26. PATIENT'S ACCOUNT NO.	27. ACCEPT ASSIGNMENT? (For govt. claims, see back)	28. TOTAL CHARGE	29. AMOUNT PAID	30. BALANCE DUE
111982342 X	1-18	X YES NO	$ 650 00	$	$

31. SIGNATURE OF PHYSICIAN OR SUPPLIER INCLUDING DEGREES OR CREDENTIALS (I certify that the statements on the reverse apply to this bill and are made a part thereof.) ANGELA DILALIO MD SIGNED DATE MMDDYYYY	32. SERVICE FACILITY LOCATION INFORMATION GOODMEDICINE HOSPITAL 1 PROVIDER ST ANYWHERE NY 12345 a. 1123456789 b.	33. BILLING PROVIDER INFO & PH # (101)2014321 ANGELA DILALIO MD 99 PROVIDER DR INJURY NY 12347 a. 4567890123 b.

NUCC Instruction Manual available at: www.nucc.org

APPROVED OMB-0938-0999 FORM CMS-1500 (08/05)

1500

HEALTH INSURANCE CLAIM FORM

APPROVED BY NATIONAL UNIFORM CLAIM COMMITTEE 08/05

☐☐☐ PICA | PICA ☐☐☐

1. MEDICARE (Medicare #) ☐ MEDICAID (Medicaid #) ☐ TRICARE CHAMPUS (Sponsor's SSN) ☐ CHAMPVA (Member ID#) ☐ GROUP HEALTH PLAN (SSN or ID) ☒ FECA BLK LUNG (SSN) ☐ OTHER (ID) ☐	1a. INSURED'S I.D. NUMBER (For Program in Item 1)
	356898459

2. PATIENT'S NAME (Last Name, First Name, Middle Initial)	3. PATIENT'S BIRTH DATE MM 06 DD 20 YY 1972 SEX M ☒ F ☐	4. INSURED'S NAME (Last Name, First Name, Middle Initial)
SCOPE, MIKE, R		BIO LABS

5. PATIENT'S ADDRESS (No., Street)	6. PATIENT'S RELATIONSHIP TO INSURED	7. INSURED'S ADDRESS (No., Street)
5 SPRUCE ST	Self ☐ Spouse ☐ Child ☐ Other ☒	10 LABORATORY CT

CITY NOWHERE	STATE NY	8. PATIENT STATUS Single ☐ Married ☐ Other ☐	CITY NOWHERE	STATE NY

ZIP CODE 12346-1234	TELEPHONE (Include Area Code) (101)1135567	Employed ☒ Full-Time Student ☐ Part-Time Student ☐	ZIP CODE 12346	TELEPHONE (Include Area Code) ( )

9. OTHER INSURED'S NAME (Last Name, First Name, Middle Initial)	10. IS PATIENT'S CONDITION RELATED TO:	11. INSURED'S POLICY GROUP OR FECA NUMBER 10199
a. OTHER INSURED'S POLICY OR GROUP NUMBER	a. EMPLOYMENT? (Current or Previous) YES ☐ NO ☒	a. INSURED'S DATE OF BIRTH MM DD YY SEX M ☐ F ☐
b. OTHER INSURED'S DATE OF BIRTH MM DD YY SEX M ☐ F ☐	b. AUTO ACCIDENT? PLACE (State) YES ☐ NO ☒	b. EMPLOYER'S NAME OR SCHOOL NAME BIO LABS
c. EMPLOYER'S NAME OR SCHOOL NAME	c. OTHER ACCIDENT? YES ☐ NO ☒	c. INSURANCE PLAN NAME OR PROGRAM NAME HIGH RISK INSURANCE
d. INSURANCE PLAN NAME OR PROGRAM NAME	10d. RESERVED FOR LOCAL USE	d. IS THERE ANOTHER HEALTH BENEFIT PLAN? YES ☐ NO ☐ If yes, return to and complete item 9 a-d.

READ BACK OF FORM BEFORE COMPLETING & SIGNING THIS FORM.

12. PATIENT'S OR AUTHORIZED PERSON'S SIGNATURE I authorize the release of any medical or other information necessary to process this claim. I also request payment of government benefits either to myself or to the party who accepts assignment below.

SIGNED _____ DATE _____

13. INSURED'S OR AUTHORIZED PERSON'S SIGNATURE I authorize payment of medical benefits to the undersigned physican or supplier for services described below.

SIGNED _____

14. DATE OF CURRENT: MM 03 DD 12 YY YYYY ILLNESS (First symptom) OR INJURY (Accident) OR PREGNANCY (LMP)	15. IF PATIENT HAS HAD SAME OR SIMILAR ILLNESS. GIVE FIRST DATE MM DD YY	16. DATES PATIENT UNABLE TO WORK IN CURRENT OCCUPATION MM DD YY MM DD YY FROM TO
17. NAME OF REFERRING PROVIDER OR OTHER SOURCE	17a. 17b. NPI	18. HOSPITALIZATION DATES RELATED TO CURRENT SERVICES MM DD YY MM DD YY FROM TO
19. RESERVED FOR LOCAL USE		20. OUTSIDE LAB? YES ☐ NO ☒ $ CHARGES

21. DIAGNOSIS OR NATURE OF ILLNESS OR INJURY (Relate Items 1, 2, 3 or 4 to Item 24E by Line)

1. 847 0   3. _____
2. 847 2   4. _____

22. MEDICAID RESUBMISSION CODE	ORIGINAL REF. NO.
23. PRIOR AUTHORIZATION NUMBER	

24. A. DATE(S) OF SERVICE From MM DD YY To MM DD YY	B. PLACE OF SERVICE	C. EMG	D. PROCEDURES, SERVICES, OR SUPPLIES (Explain Unusual Circumstances) CPT/HCPCS MODIFIER	E. DIAGNOSIS POINTER	F. $ CHARGES	G. DAYS OR UNITS	H. EPSDT Family Plan	I. ID. QUAL.	J. RENDERING PROVIDER ID. #
1	03 20 YYYY	11		99212	1	26 00	1		NPI	
2									NPI	
3									NPI	
4									NPI	
5									NPI	
6									NPI	

25. FEDERAL TAX I.D. NUMBER SSN EIN 111982342 ☒	26. PATIENT'S ACCOUNT NO. 1-19	27. ACCEPT ASSIGNMENT? (For govt. claims, see back) ☒ YES ☐ NO	28. TOTAL CHARGE $ 26 00	29. AMOUNT PAID $	30. BALANCE DUE $

31. SIGNATURE OF PHYSICIAN OR SUPPLIER INCLUDING DEGREES OR CREDENTIALS (I certify that the statements on the reverse apply to this bill and are made a part thereof.) ANGELA DILALIO MD SIGNED DATE MMDDYYYY	32. SERVICE FACILITY LOCATION INFORMATION a. NPI b.	33. BILLING PROVIDER INFO & PH # (101)2014321 ANGELA DILALIO MD 99 PROVIDER DR INJURY NY 12347 a. 4567890123 b. NPI

NUCC Instruction Manual available at: www.nucc.org   APPROVED OMB-0938-0999 FORM CMS-1500 (08/05)

1500

HEALTH INSURANCE CLAIM FORM

APPROVED BY NATIONAL UNIFORM CLAIM COMMITTEE 08/05

| | PICA | | | | | | PICA | |

| 1. MEDICARE (Medicare #) | MEDICAID (Medicaid #) | TRICARE CHAMPUS (Sponsor's SSN) | CHAMPVA (Member ID#) | GROUP HEALTH PLAN (SSN or ID) [X] | FECA BLK LUNG (SSN) | OTHER (ID) | 1a. INSURED'S I.D. NUMBER (For Program in Item 1) 467909560 |

| 2. PATIENT'S NAME (Last Name, First Name, Middle Initial) GALLO, JIM | 3. PATIENT'S BIRTH DATE MM 05 DD 02 YY 1975 SEX M [X] F | 4. INSURED'S NAME (Last Name, First Name, Middle Initial) WORLD UNIVERSITY |

| 5. PATIENT'S ADDRESS (No., Street) 115 GLENN ST | 6. PATIENT'S RELATIONSHIP TO INSURED Self [ ] Spouse [ ] Child [ ] Other [X] | 7. INSURED'S ADDRESS (No., Street) COLLEGE DRIVE |

| CITY ANYWHERE | STATE NY | 8. PATIENT STATUS Single [ ] Married [ ] Other [ ] | CITY ANYWHERE | STATE NY |

| ZIP CODE 12345-1234 | TELEPHONE (Include Area Code) (101)5558457 | Employed [X] Full-Time Student [ ] Part-Time Student [ ] | ZIP CODE 12345 | TELEPHONE (Include Area Code) ( ) |

| 9. OTHER INSURED'S NAME (Last Name, First Name, Middle Initial) | 10. IS PATIENT'S CONDITION RELATED TO: | 11. INSURED'S POLICY GROUP OR FECA NUMBER 10225 |

| a. OTHER INSURED'S POLICY OR GROUP NUMBER | a. EMPLOYMENT? (Current or Previous) YES [ ] NO [X] | a. INSURED'S DATE OF BIRTH MM DD YY SEX M [ ] F [ ] |

| b. OTHER INSURED'S DATE OF BIRTH MM DD YY SEX M [ ] F [ ] | b. AUTO ACCIDENT? YES [ ] NO [X] PLACE (State) | b. EMPLOYER'S NAME OR SCHOOL NAME WORLD UNIVERSITY |

| c. EMPLOYER'S NAME OR SCHOOL NAME | c. OTHER ACCIDENT? YES [ ] NO [X] | c. INSURANCE PLAN NAME OR PROGRAM NAME HIGH RISK INSURANCE |

| d. INSURANCE PLAN NAME OR PROGRAM NAME | 10d. RESERVED FOR LOCAL USE | d. IS THERE ANOTHER HEALTH BENEFIT PLAN? YES [ ] NO [ ] **If yes,** return to and complete item 9 a-d. |

READ BACK OF FORM BEFORE COMPLETING & SIGNING THIS FORM.

12. PATIENT'S OR AUTHORIZED PERSON'S SIGNATURE I authorize the release of any medical or other information necessary to process this claim. I also request payment of government benefits either to myself or to the party who accepts assignment below.

SIGNED _____ DATE _____

13. INSURED'S OR AUTHORIZED PERSON'S SIGNATURE I authorize payment of medical benefits to the undersigned physcian or supplier for services described below.

SIGNED _____

| 14. DATE OF CURRENT: MM 02 DD 15 YY YYYY ILLNESS (First symptom) OR INJURY (Accident) OR PREGNANCY (LMP) | 15. IF PATIENT HAS HAD SAME OR SIMILAR ILLNESS. GIVE FIRST DATE MM DD YY | 16. DATES PATIENT UNABLE TO WORK IN CURRENT OCCUPATION MM DD YY MM DD YY FROM 02 15 YYYY TO 02 20 YYYY |

| 17. NAME OF REFERRING PROVIDER OR OTHER SOURCE | 17a. 17b. NPI | 18. HOSPITALIZATION DATES RELATED TO CURRENT SERVICES MM DD YY MM DD YY FROM TO |

| 19. RESERVED FOR LOCAL USE | 20. OUTSIDE LAB? YES [ ] NO [X] $ CHARGES |

21. DIAGNOSIS OR NATURE OF ILLNESS OR INJURY (Relate Items 1, 2, 3 or 4 to Item 24E by Line)

1. 724.8
2. _____
3. _____
4. _____

| 22. MEDICAID RESUBMISSION CODE ORIGINAL REF. NO. |
| 23. PRIOR AUTHORIZATION NUMBER |

24. A DATE(S) OF SERVICE From MM DD YY To MM DD YY	B. PLACE OF SERVICE	C. EMG	D. PROCEDURES, SERVICES, OR SUPPLIES (Explain Unusual Circumstances) CPT/HCPCS MODIFIER	E. DIAGNOSIS POINTER	F. $ CHARGES	G. DAYS OR UNITS	H. EPSDT Family Plan	I. ID. QUAL.	J. RENDERING PROVIDER ID. #
1	02 15 YYYY	11		99212	1	35 00	1		NPI	
2									NPI	
3									NPI	
4									NPI	
5									NPI	
6									NPI	

| 25. FEDERAL TAX I.D. NUMBER 111982342 SSN [ ] EIN [X] | 26. PATIENT'S ACCOUNT NO. 1-20 | 27. ACCEPT ASSIGNMENT? (For govt. claims, see back) [X] YES [ ] NO | 28. TOTAL CHARGE $ 35 00 | 29. AMOUNT PAID $ | 30. BALANCE DUE $ |

| 31. SIGNATURE OF PHYSICIAN OR SUPPLIER INCLUDING DEGREES OR CREDENTIALS (I certify that the statements on the reverse apply to this bill and are made a part thereof.) ANGELA DILALIO MD SIGNED DATE MMDDYYYY | 32. SERVICE FACILITY LOCATION INFORMATION a. NPI b. | 33. BILLING PROVIDER INFO & PH # (101)2014321 ANGELA DILALIO MD 99 PROVIDER DR INJURY NY 12347 a. 4567890123 b. |

NUCC Instruction Manual available at: www.nucc.org

APPROVED OMB-0938-0999 FORM CMS-1500 (08/05)

CPT copyright 2007 American Medical Association. All rights reserved.

APPENDIX II   Completed Claims for Case Studies: Set Two

1500

HEALTH INSURANCE CLAIM FORM

APPROVED BY NATIONAL UNIFORM CLAIM COMMITTEE 08/05

PICA | PICA

1. MEDICARE (Medicare #) MEDICAID (Medicaid #) TRICARE CHAMPUS (Sponsor's SSN) CHAMPVA (Member ID#) GROUP HEALTH PLAN (SSN or ID) FECA BLK LUNG (SSN) OTHER X (ID)	1a. INSURED'S I.D. NUMBER (For Program in Item 1)
	222304040

2. PATIENT'S NAME (Last Name, First Name, Middle Initial)	3. PATIENT'S BIRTH DATE / SEX	4. INSURED'S NAME (Last Name, First Name, Middle Initial)
RAUL, JOSE, X	01 01 1968 M X F	RAUL, JOSE, X

5. PATIENT'S ADDRESS (No., Street)	6. PATIENT'S RELATIONSHIP TO INSURED	7. INSURED'S ADDRESS (No., Street)
10 MAIN STREET	Self X Spouse Child Other	10 MAIN STREET
CITY ANYWHERE STATE NY	8. PATIENT STATUS Single X Married Other	CITY ANYWHERE STATE NY
ZIP CODE 12345-1234 TELEPHONE (101)1115454	Employed X Full-Time Student Part-Time Student	ZIP CODE 12345-1234 TELEPHONE (101)1115454

9. OTHER INSURED'S NAME (Last Name, First Name, Middle Initial)	10. IS PATIENT'S CONDITION RELATED TO:	11. INSURED'S POLICY GROUP OR FECA NUMBER
		MD1
a. OTHER INSURED'S POLICY OR GROUP NUMBER	a. EMPLOYMENT? (Current or Previous) YES NO X	a. INSURED'S DATE OF BIRTH 01 01 1968 SEX M X F
b. OTHER INSURED'S DATE OF BIRTH SEX M F	b. AUTO ACCIDENT? PLACE (State) YES NO X	b. EMPLOYER'S NAME OR SCHOOL NAME ANYWHERE TELEPHONE CO
c. EMPLOYER'S NAME OR SCHOOL NAME	c. OTHER ACCIDENT? YES NO X	c. INSURANCE PLAN NAME OR PROGRAM NAME BELL ATLANTIC
d. INSURANCE PLAN NAME OR PROGRAM NAME	10d. RESERVED FOR LOCAL USE	d. IS THERE ANOTHER HEALTH BENEFIT PLAN? YES NO X If yes, return to and complete item 9 a-d.

READ BACK OF FORM BEFORE COMPLETING & SIGNING THIS FORM.

12. PATIENT'S OR AUTHORIZED PERSON'S SIGNATURE I authorize the release of any medical or other information necessary to process this claim. I also request payment of government benefits either to myself or to the party who accepts assignment below.

SIGNED SIGNATURE ON FILE DATE

13. INSURED'S OR AUTHORIZED PERSON'S SIGNATURE I authorize payment of medical benefits to the undersigned physican or supplier for services described below.

SIGNED SIGNATURE ON FILE

14. DATE OF CURRENT: ILLNESS (First symptom) OR INJURY (Accident) OR PREGNANCY (LMP) 06 20 YYYY	15. IF PATIENT HAS HAD SAME OR SIMILAR ILLNESS. GIVE FIRST DATE MM DD YY	16. DATES PATIENT UNABLE TO WORK IN CURRENT OCCUPATION FROM TO
17. NAME OF REFERRING PROVIDER OR OTHER SOURCE IM GOODDOC MD	17a. 17b. NPI 5678901234	18. HOSPITALIZATION DATES RELATED TO CURRENT SERVICES FROM TO
19. RESERVED FOR LOCAL USE		20. OUTSIDE LAB? YES NO X $ CHARGES

21. DIAGNOSIS OR NATURE OF ILLNESS OR INJURY (Relate Items 1, 2, 3 or 4 to Item 24E by Line)

1. 789 35   3.
2. 569 3   4.

22. MEDICAID RESUBMISSION CODE ORIGINAL REF. NO.

23. PRIOR AUTHORIZATION NUMBER

24. A DATE(S) OF SERVICE From MM DD YY To MM DD YY	B. PLACE OF SERVICE	C. EMG	D. PROCEDURES, SERVICES, OR SUPPLIES (Explain Unusual Circumstances) CPT/HCPCS MODIFIER	E. DIAGNOSIS POINTER	F. $ CHARGES	G. DAYS OR UNITS	H. EPSDT Family Plan	I. ID. QUAL.	J. RENDERING PROVIDER ID. #
1	06 20 YYYY	11		99243	1	100 00	1		NPI	3456789012
2									NPI	
3									NPI	
4									NPI	
5									NPI	
6									NPI	

25. FEDERAL TAX I.D. NUMBER SSN EIN	26. PATIENT'S ACCOUNT NO.	27. ACCEPT ASSIGNMENT? (For govt. claims, see back)	28. TOTAL CHARGE	29. AMOUNT PAID	30. BALANCE DUE
221234567 X	2-1	X YES NO	$ 100 00	$	$ 100 00

31. SIGNATURE OF PHYSICIAN OR SUPPLIER INCLUDING DEGREES OR CREDENTIALS (I certify that the statements on the reverse apply to this bill and are made a part thereof.) HENRY C CARDIAC MD SIGNED DATE MMDDYYYY	32. SERVICE FACILITY LOCATION INFORMATION a. NPI b.	33. BILLING PROVIDER INFO & PH # (101)1112222 GOODMEDICINE CLINIC 1 PROVIDER STREET ANYWHERE NY 12345 a. 3345678901 b.

NUCC Instruction Manual available at: www.nucc.org

APPROVED OMB-0938-0999 FORM CMS-1500 (08/05)

1500

HEALTH INSURANCE CLAIM FORM

APPROVED BY NATIONAL UNIFORM CLAIM COMMITTEE 08/05

| | PICA | | | | | | | | PICA | |

1. MEDICARE (Medicare #)	MEDICAID (Medicaid #)	TRICARE CHAMPUS (Sponsor's SSN)	CHAMPVA (Member ID#)	GROUP HEALTH PLAN (SSN or ID)	FECA BLK LUNG (SSN)	OTHER [X] (ID)	1a. INSURED'S I.D. NUMBER (For Program in Item 1)

1a. INSURED'S I.D. NUMBER (For Program in Item 1)
877345567

2. PATIENT'S NAME (Last Name, First Name, Middle Initial)
MOUTAINE, KAY

3. PATIENT'S BIRTH DATE   SEX
MM **06** DD **01** YY **1955**   M☐ F [X]

4. INSURED'S NAME (Last Name, First Name, Middle Initial)
MOUTAINE, CHARLES, W

5. PATIENT'S ADDRESS (No., Street)
634 GOODVIEW AVENUE

6. PATIENT'S RELATIONSHIP TO INSURED
Self☐ Spouse [X] Child☐ Other☐

7. INSURED'S ADDRESS (No., Street)
634 GOODVIEW AVENUE

CITY **ANYWHERE**   STATE **NY**

8. PATIENT STATUS
Single☐ Married [X] Other☐

CITY **ANYWHERE**   STATE **NY**

ZIP CODE **12345-1234**   TELEPHONE (Include Area Code) **(101)1151234**

Employed [X] Full-Time Student☐ Part-Time Student☐

ZIP CODE **12345-1234**   TELEPHONE (Include Area Code) **(101)1151234**

9. OTHER INSURED'S NAME (Last Name, First Name, Middle Initial)

10. IS PATIENT'S CONDITION RELATED TO:

11. INSURED'S POLICY GROUP OR FECA NUMBER
V143

a. OTHER INSURED'S POLICY OR GROUP NUMBER

a. EMPLOYMENT? (Current or Previous)
YES☐ [X] NO

a. INSURED'S DATE OF BIRTH
MM **03** DD **04** YY **1952**   M [X] F☐   SEX

b. OTHER INSURED'S DATE OF BIRTH
MM DD YY   SEX   M☐ F☐

b. AUTO ACCIDENT?   PLACE (State)
YES☐ [X] NO

b. EMPLOYER'S NAME OR SCHOOL NAME
GENERAL ELECTRIC

c. EMPLOYER'S NAME OR SCHOOL NAME

c. OTHER ACCIDENT?
YES☐ [X] NO

c. INSURANCE PLAN NAME OR PROGRAM NAME
CONNECTICUT GENERAL

d. INSURANCE PLAN NAME OR PROGRAM NAME

10d. RESERVED FOR LOCAL USE

d. IS THERE ANOTHER HEALTH BENEFIT PLAN?
YES☐ [X] NO   *If yes,* return to and complete item 9 a-d.

READ BACK OF FORM BEFORE COMPLETING & SIGNING THIS FORM.

12. PATIENT'S OR AUTHORIZED PERSON'S SIGNATURE I authorize the release of any medical or other information necessary to process this claim. I also request payment of government benefits either to myself or to the party who accepts assignment below.

SIGNED **SIGNATURE ON FILE**   DATE

13. INSURED'S OR AUTHORIZED PERSON'S SIGNATURE I authorize payment of medical benefits to the undersigned physcian or supplier for services described below.

SIGNED **SIGNATURE ON FILE**

14. DATE OF CURRENT: ILLNESS (First symptom) OR INJURY (Accident) OR PREGNANCY (LMP)
MM **06** DD **20** YY **YYYY**

15. IF PATIENT HAS HAD SAME OR SIMILAR ILLNESS, GIVE FIRST DATE MM DD YY

16. DATES PATIENT UNABLE TO WORK IN CURRENT OCCUPATION
FROM MM DD YY   TO MM DD YY

17. NAME OF REFERRING PROVIDER OR OTHER SOURCE

17a.
17b. NPI

18. HOSPITALIZATION DATES RELATED TO CURRENT SERVICES
FROM MM DD YY   TO MM DD YY

19. RESERVED FOR LOCAL USE

20. OUTSIDE LAB? $ CHARGES
YES☐ [X] NO

21. DIAGNOSIS OR NATURE OF ILLNESS OR INJURY (Relate Items 1, 2, 3 or 4 to Item 24E by Line)

1. **345.40**
2. **346.90**
3. **493.90**
4. **477.9**

22. MEDICAID RESUBMISSION CODE   ORIGINAL REF. NO.

23. PRIOR AUTHORIZATION NUMBER

24. A. DATE(S) OF SERVICE From / To MM DD YY	B. PLACE OF SERVICE	C. EMG	D. PROCEDURES, SERVICES, OR SUPPLIES (Explain Unusual Circumstances) CPT/HCPCS / MODIFIER	E. DIAGNOSIS POINTER	F. $ CHARGES	G. DAYS OR UNITS	H. EPSDT Family Plan	I. ID. QUAL.	J. RENDERING PROVIDER ID. #
1	**06 20 YYYY**	**11**		**99203**	**1**	**75 00**	**1**		NPI	**3456789012**
2									NPI	
3									NPI	
4									NPI	
5									NPI	
6									NPI	

25. FEDERAL TAX I.D. NUMBER   SSN EIN
221234567   [X]

26. PATIENT'S ACCOUNT NO.
2-2

27. ACCEPT ASSIGNMENT? (For govt. claims, see back)
[X] YES NO☐

28. TOTAL CHARGE
$ **75 00**

29. AMOUNT PAID
$

30. BALANCE DUE
$ **75 00**

31. SIGNATURE OF PHYSICIAN OR SUPPLIER INCLUDING DEGREES OR CREDENTIALS (I certify that the statements on the reverse apply to this bill and are made a part thereof.)

HENRY C CARDIAC MD
SIGNED   DATE **MMDDYYYY**

32. SERVICE FACILITY LOCATION INFORMATION

a. NPI   b.

33. BILLING PROVIDER INFO & PH # **(101)1112222**
GOODMEDICINE CLINIC
1 PROVIDER STREET
ANYWHERE NY 12345
a. **3345678901**   b.

NUCC Instruction Manual available at: www.nucc.org

APPROVED OMB-0938-0999 FORM CMS-1500 (08/05)

CARRIER

PATIENT AND INSURED INFORMATION

PHYSICIAN OR SUPPLIER INFORMATION

[1500]

HEALTH INSURANCE CLAIM FORM

APPROVED BY NATIONAL UNIFORM CLAIM COMMITTEE 08/05

| | PICA | | | | | | | | PICA | | |

1. MEDICARE (Medicare #) **MEDICAID** (Medicaid #) **TRICARE CHAMPUS** (Sponsor's SSN) **CHAMPVA** (Member ID#) **GROUP HEALTH PLAN** (SSN or ID) **FECA BLK LUNG** (SSN) **OTHER** [X] (ID)

1a. INSURED'S I.D. NUMBER (For Program in Item 1)
333669999

2. PATIENT'S NAME (Last Name, First Name, Middle Initial)
PING, CHANG, L

3. PATIENT'S BIRTH DATE MM DD YY
01 06 1945 **SEX** M [X] F

4. INSURED'S NAME (Last Name, First Name, Middle Initial)
PING, SONG

5. PATIENT'S ADDRESS (No., Street)
100 CHRISTA ST

6. PATIENT'S RELATIONSHIP TO INSURED
Self Spouse [X] Child Other

7. INSURED'S ADDRESS (No., Street)
100 CHRISTA ST

CITY INJURY **STATE** NY

8. PATIENT STATUS
Single Married [X] Other

CITY INJURY **STATE** NY

ZIP CODE 12347-1234 **TELEPHONE (Include Area Code)** (101)1114545

Employed [X] Full-Time Student Part-Time Student

ZIP CODE 12347-1234 **TELEPHONE (Include Area Code)** (101)1114545

9. OTHER INSURED'S NAME (Last Name, First Name, Middle Initial)

10. IS PATIENT'S CONDITION RELATED TO:

11. INSURED'S POLICY GROUP OR FECA NUMBER
93939

a. OTHER INSURED'S POLICY OR GROUP NUMBER

a. EMPLOYMENT? (Current or Previous)
YES [X] NO

a. INSURED'S DATE OF BIRTH MM DD YY
06 01 1942 **SEX** M F [X]

b. OTHER INSURED'S DATE OF BIRTH MM DD YY **SEX** M F

b. AUTO ACCIDENT? PLACE (State)
YES [X] NO

b. EMPLOYER'S NAME OR SCHOOL NAME
HUNAN INC

c. EMPLOYER'S NAME OR SCHOOL NAME
HUNAN INC

c. OTHER ACCIDENT?
YES [X] NO

c. INSURANCE PLAN NAME OR PROGRAM NAME
CONNECTICUT GENERAL

d. INSURANCE PLAN NAME OR PROGRAM NAME

10d. RESERVED FOR LOCAL USE

d. IS THERE ANOTHER HEALTH BENEFIT PLAN?
YES [X] NO **If yes,** return to and complete item 9 a-d.

READ BACK OF FORM BEFORE COMPLETING & SIGNING THIS FORM.
12. PATIENT'S OR AUTHORIZED PERSON'S SIGNATURE I authorize the release of any medical or other information necessary to process this claim. I also request payment of government benefits either to myself or to the party who accepts assignment below.

SIGNED SIGNATURE ON FILE DATE

13. INSURED'S OR AUTHORIZED PERSON'S SIGNATURE I authorize payment of medical benefits to the undersigned physican or supplier for services described below.

SIGNED SIGNATURE ON FILE

14. DATE OF CURRENT: MM DD YY
06 14 YYYY
ILLNESS (First symptom) OR INJURY (Accident) OR PREGNANCY (LMP)

15. IF PATIENT HAS HAD SAME OR SIMILAR ILLNESS. GIVE FIRST DATE MM DD YY

16. DATES PATIENT UNABLE TO WORK IN CURRENT OCCUPATION MM DD YY MM DD YY
FROM TO

17. NAME OF REFERRING PROVIDER OR OTHER SOURCE
17a.
17b. NPI

18. HOSPITALIZATION DATES RELATED TO CURRENT SERVICES MM DD YY MM DD YY
FROM 06 16 YYYY TO 06 20 YYYY

19. RESERVED FOR LOCAL USE

20. OUTSIDE LAB?
YES [X] NO **$ CHARGES**

21. DIAGNOSIS OR NATURE OF ILLNESS OR INJURY (Relate Items 1, 2, 3 or 4 to Item 24E by Line)
1. 153 3
2.
3.
4.

22. MEDICAID RESUBMISSION CODE ORIGINAL REF. NO.

23. PRIOR AUTHORIZATION NUMBER

24. A DATE(S) OF SERVICE From MM DD YY	To MM DD YY	B. PLACE OF SERVICE	C. EMG	D. PROCEDURES, SERVICES, OR SUPPLIES (Explain Unusual Circumstances) CPT/HCPCS	MODIFIER	E. DIAGNOSIS POINTER	F. $ CHARGES	G. DAYS OR UNITS	H. EPSDT Family Plan	I. ID. QUAL.	J. RENDERING PROVIDER ID. #
1	06 14 YYYY		11		99203	57	1	75 00	1		NPI	9012345678
2	06 16 YYYY		21		45110		1	800 00	1		NPI	9012345678
3											NPI	
4											NPI	
5											NPI	
6											NPI	

25. FEDERAL TAX I.D. NUMBER SSN EIN
331234567 [X]

26. PATIENT'S ACCOUNT NO.
2-3

27. ACCEPT ASSIGNMENT? (For govt. claims, see back)
[X] YES NO

28. TOTAL CHARGE
$ 875 00

29. AMOUNT PAID
$

30. BALANCE DUE
$ 875 00

31. SIGNATURE OF PHYSICIAN OR SUPPLIER INCLUDING DEGREES OR CREDENTIALS (I certify that the statements on the reverse apply to this bill and are made a part thereof.)
JANET B SURGEON MD
SIGNED DATE MMDDYYYY

32. SERVICE FACILITY LOCATION INFORMATION
GOODMEDICINE HOSPITAL
1 PROVIDER STREET
ANYWHERE NY 12345
a. 1123456789 b.

33. BILLING PROVIDER INFO & PH # (101)1112222
GOODMEDICINE CLINIC
1 PROVIDER STREET
ANYWHERE NY 12345
a. 3345678901 b.

NUCC Instruction Manual available at: www.nucc.org

APPROVED OMB-0938-0999 FORM CMS-1500 (08/05)

1500

HEALTH INSURANCE CLAIM FORM

APPROVED BY NATIONAL UNIFORM CLAIM COMMITTEE 08/05

| | PICA | | | | | | | | PICA | | |

1. MEDICARE	MEDICAID	TRICARE CHAMPUS	CHAMPVA	GROUP HEALTH PLAN	FECA BLK LUNG	OTHER	1a. INSURED'S I.D. NUMBER	(For Program in Item 1)
(Medicare #)	(Medicaid #)	(Sponsor's SSN)	(Member ID#)	(SSN or ID)	(SSN)	X (ID)	ZJW55544	

2. PATIENT'S NAME (Last Name, First Name, Middle Initial)	3. PATIENT'S BIRTH DATE MM DD YY	SEX	4. INSURED'S NAME (Last Name, First Name, Middle Initial)
RECALL, JOHN, J	06 03 1942	M X F	RECALL, JOHN, J

5. PATIENT'S ADDRESS (No., Street)	6. PATIENT'S RELATIONSHIP TO INSURED	7. INSURED'S ADDRESS (No., Street)
10 MEMORY LANE	Self X Spouse Child Other	10 MEMORY LANE

CITY	STATE	8. PATIENT STATUS	CITY	STATE
ANYWHERE	NY	Single X Married Other	ANYWHERE	NY

ZIP CODE	TELEPHONE (Include Area Code)		ZIP CODE	TELEPHONE (Include Area Code)
12345-1234	(101)1114444	Employed X Full-Time Student Part-Time Student	12345-1234	(101)1114444

9. OTHER INSURED'S NAME (Last Name, First Name, Middle Initial)	10. IS PATIENT'S CONDITION RELATED TO:	11. INSURED'S POLICY GROUP OR FECA NUMBER
		650

a. OTHER INSURED'S POLICY OR GROUP NUMBER	a. EMPLOYMENT? (Current or Previous)	a. INSURED'S DATE OF BIRTH MM DD YY	SEX
	YES X NO	06 03 1942	M X F

b. OTHER INSURED'S DATE OF BIRTH MM DD YY	SEX	b. AUTO ACCIDENT?	PLACE (State)	b. EMPLOYER'S NAME OR SCHOOL NAME
	M F	YES X NO		WILL SOLVE IT INC

c. EMPLOYER'S NAME OR SCHOOL NAME	c. OTHER ACCIDENT?	c. INSURANCE PLAN NAME OR PROGRAM NAME
	YES X NO	BCBS

d. INSURANCE PLAN NAME OR PROGRAM NAME	10d. RESERVED FOR LOCAL USE	d. IS THERE ANOTHER HEALTH BENEFIT PLAN?
		YES X NO **If yes,** return to and complete item 9 a-d.

READ BACK OF FORM BEFORE COMPLETING & SIGNING THIS FORM.

12. PATIENT'S OR AUTHORIZED PERSON'S SIGNATURE I authorize the release of any medical or other information necessary to process this claim. I also request payment of government benefits either to myself or to the party who accepts assignment below.

SIGNED **SIGNATURE ON FILE**   DATE _____

13. INSURED'S OR AUTHORIZED PERSON'S SIGNATURE I authorize payment of medical benefits to the undersigned physician or supplier for services described below.

SIGNED _____

14. DATE OF CURRENT: MM DD YY ILLNESS (First symptom) OR INJURY (Accident) OR PREGNANCY (LMP)	15. IF PATIENT HAS HAD SAME OR SIMILAR ILLNESS. GIVE FIRST DATE MM DD YY	16. DATES PATIENT UNABLE TO WORK IN CURRENT OCCUPATION MM DD YY MM DD YY
06 18 YYYY		FROM TO

17. NAME OF REFERRING PROVIDER OR OTHER SOURCE	17a.		18. HOSPITALIZATION DATES RELATED TO CURRENT SERVICES MM DD YY MM DD YY
ARNOLD YOUNGLOVE MD	17b. NPI	0123456789	FROM 06 19 YYYY TO 06 19 YYYY

19. RESERVED FOR LOCAL USE	20. OUTSIDE LAB?	$ CHARGES
	YES X NO	

21. DIAGNOSIS OR NATURE OF ILLNESS OR INJURY (Relate Items 1, 2, 3 or 4 to Item 24E by Line)

1. 574.10   3. 414.00
2. 250.00   4. V45.81

22. MEDICAID RESUBMISSION CODE	ORIGINAL REF. NO.

23. PRIOR AUTHORIZATION NUMBER

24. A. DATE(S) OF SERVICE From To MM DD YY MM DD YY	B. PLACE OF SERVICE	C. EMG	D. PROCEDURES, SERVICES, OR SUPPLIES (Explain Unusual Circumstances) CPT/HCPCS MODIFIER	E. DIAGNOSIS POINTER	F. $ CHARGES	G. DAYS OR UNITS	H. EPSDT Family Plan	I. ID. QUAL.	J. RENDERING PROVIDER ID. #
1	0618YYYY	11		99203 57	1	75 00	1		NPI	9012345678
2	0619YYYY	21		47600	1	1360 00	1		NPI	9012345678
3									NPI	
4									NPI	
5									NPI	
6									NPI	

25. FEDERAL TAX I.D. NUMBER	SSN EIN	26. PATIENT'S ACCOUNT NO.	27. ACCEPT ASSIGNMENT? (For govt. claims, see back)	28. TOTAL CHARGE	29. AMOUNT PAID	30. BALANCE DUE
331234567	X	2-4	X YES NO	$ 1435 00	$	$ 1435 00

31. SIGNATURE OF PHYSICIAN OR SUPPLIER INCLUDING DEGREES OR CREDENTIALS (I certify that the statements on the reverse apply to this bill and are made a part thereof.)	32. SERVICE FACILITY LOCATION INFORMATION	33. BILLING PROVIDER INFO & PH # (101)1112222
JANET B SURGEON MD	GOODMEDICINE HOSPITAL 1 PROVIDER STREET ANYWHERE NY 12345	GOODMEDICINE CLINIC 1 PROVIDER STREET ANYWHERE NY 12345
SIGNED DATE MMDDYYYY	a. 1123456789 b.	a. 3345678901 b.

APPROVED OMB-0938-0999 FORM CMS-1500 (08/05)

1500

HEALTH INSURANCE CLAIM FORM

APPROVED BY NATIONAL UNIFORM CLAIM COMMITTEE 08/05

| | PICA | | | | | PICA | | |

CARRIER

1. MEDICARE (Medicare #)	MEDICAID (Medicaid #)	TRICARE CHAMPUS (Sponsor's SSN)	CHAMPVA (Member ID#)	GROUP HEALTH PLAN (SSN or ID)	FECA BLK LUNG (SSN)	OTHER [X] (ID)	1a. INSURED'S I.D. NUMBER (For Program in Item 1)
							XWJ473655

2. PATIENT'S NAME (Last Name, First Name, Middle Initial)	3. PATIENT'S BIRTH DATE MM DD YY / SEX	4. INSURED'S NAME (Last Name, First Name, Middle Initial)
ISLANDER, PHILAMENA	11 21 1953 M[ ] F[X]	ISLANDER, RICHARD, T

5. PATIENT'S ADDRESS (No., Street)	6. PATIENT'S RELATIONSHIP TO INSURED	7. INSURED'S ADDRESS (No., Street)
129 HENRY COURT	Self[ ] Spouse[X] Child[ ] Other[ ]	129 HENRY COURT

CITY	STATE	8. PATIENT STATUS	CITY	STATE
ANYWHERE	NY	Single[ ] Married[X] Other[ ]	ANYWHERE	NY

ZIP CODE	TELEPHONE (Include Area Code)		ZIP CODE	TELEPHONE (Include Area Code)
12345-1234	(101)1117218	Employed[X] Full-Time Student[ ] Part-Time Student[ ]	12345-1234	(101)1117218

PATIENT AND INSURED INFORMATION

9. OTHER INSURED'S NAME (Last Name, First Name, Middle Initial)	10. IS PATIENT'S CONDITION RELATED TO:	11. INSURED'S POLICY GROUP OR FECA NUMBER
		101

a. OTHER INSURED'S POLICY OR GROUP NUMBER	a. EMPLOYMENT? (Current or Previous) YES[ ] NO[X]	a. INSURED'S DATE OF BIRTH MM DD YY / SEX
		02 11 1952 M[X] F[ ]

b. OTHER INSURED'S DATE OF BIRTH MM DD YY SEX M[ ] F[ ]	b. AUTO ACCIDENT? PLACE (State) YES[ ] NO[X]	b. EMPLOYER'S NAME OR SCHOOL NAME
		WONDERFUL PHOTOS

c. EMPLOYER'S NAME OR SCHOOL NAME	c. OTHER ACCIDENT? YES[ ] NO[X]	c. INSURANCE PLAN NAME OR PROGRAM NAME
		BCBS

d. INSURANCE PLAN NAME OR PROGRAM NAME	10d. RESERVED FOR LOCAL USE	d. IS THERE ANOTHER HEALTH BENEFIT PLAN? YES[ ] NO[X] **If yes,** return to and complete item 9 a-d.

READ BACK OF FORM BEFORE COMPLETING & SIGNING THIS FORM.

12. PATIENT'S OR AUTHORIZED PERSON'S SIGNATURE I authorize the release of any medical or other information necessary to process this claim. I also request payment of government benefits either to myself or to the party who accepts assignment below.

SIGNED **SIGNATURE ON FILE** DATE

13. INSURED'S OR AUTHORIZED PERSON'S SIGNATURE I authorize payment of medical benefits to the undersigned physcian or supplier for services described below.

SIGNED

14. DATE OF CURRENT: MM DD YY 06 20 YYYY ILLNESS (First symptom) OR INJURY (Accident) OR PREGNANCY (LMP)	15. IF PATIENT HAS HAD SAME OR SIMILAR ILLNESS. GIVE FIRST DATE MM DD YY	16. DATES PATIENT UNABLE TO WORK IN CURRENT OCCUPATION MM DD YY MM DD YY FROM TO

17. NAME OF REFERRING PROVIDER OR OTHER SOURCE	17a.	18. HOSPITALIZATION DATES RELATED TO CURRENT SERVICES MM DD YY MM DD YY
	17b. NPI	FROM TO

19. RESERVED FOR LOCAL USE	20. OUTSIDE LAB? YES[ ] NO[X] $ CHARGES

21. DIAGNOSIS OR NATURE OF ILLNESS OR INJURY (Relate Items 1, 2, 3 or 4 to Item 24E by Line)	22. MEDICAID RESUBMISSION CODE ORIGINAL REF. NO.
1. 565 . 0 3.	
2. 4.	23. PRIOR AUTHORIZATION NUMBER

PHYSICIAN OR SUPPLIER INFORMATION

24. A DATE(S) OF SERVICE From MM DD YY	To MM DD YY	B. PLACE OF SERVICE	C. EMG	D. PROCEDURES, SERVICES, OR SUPPLIES (Explain Unusual Circumstances) CPT/HCPCS / MODIFIER	E. DIAGNOSIS POINTER	F. $ CHARGES	G. DAYS OR UNITS	H. EPSDT Family Plan	I. ID. QUAL.	J. RENDERING PROVIDER ID. #
1	06 20 YYYY		11		46606	1	100 00	1		NPI	3456789012
2										NPI	
3										NPI	
4										NPI	
5										NPI	
6										NPI	

25. FEDERAL TAX I.D. NUMBER SSN EIN	26. PATIENT'S ACCOUNT NO.	27. ACCEPT ASSIGNMENT? (For govt. claims, see back)	28. TOTAL CHARGE	29. AMOUNT PAID	30. BALANCE DUE
221234567 [X]	2-5	YES[X] NO[ ]	$ 100 00	$	$

31. SIGNATURE OF PHYSICIAN OR SUPPLIER INCLUDING DEGREES OR CREDENTIALS (I certify that the statements on the reverse apply to this bill and are made a part thereof.)	32. SERVICE FACILITY LOCATION INFORMATION	33. BILLING PROVIDER INFO & PH # (101)1112222
HENRY C CARDIAC MD		GOODMEDICINE CLINIC
		1 PROVIDER STREET
		ANYWHERE NY 12345
SIGNED DATE MMDDYYYY	a. NPI b.	a. 3345678901 b.

APPROVED OMB-0938-0999 FORM CMS-1500 (08/05)

| 1500 |

HEALTH INSURANCE CLAIM FORM

APPROVED BY NATIONAL UNIFORM CLAIM COMMITTEE 08/05

| | PICA | | | | | PICA | |

1. MEDICARE [X] (Medicare #) MEDICAID [X] (Medicaid #) TRICARE CHAMPUS (Sponsor's SSN) CHAMPVA (Member ID#) GROUP HEALTH PLAN (SSN or ID) FECA BLK LUNG (SSN) OTHER (ID)

1a. INSURED'S I.D. NUMBER (For Program in Item 1)
777228888W

2. PATIENT'S NAME (Last Name, First Name, Middle Initial)
SUGAR, IMOGENE

3. PATIENT'S BIRTH DATE MM 03 DD 09 YY 1924 SEX M [ ] F [X]

4. INSURED'S NAME (Last Name, First Name, Middle Initial)

5. PATIENT'S ADDRESS (No., Street)
120 YOUNG STREET

6. PATIENT'S RELATIONSHIP TO INSURED
Self [ ] Spouse [ ] Child [ ] Other [ ]

7. INSURED'S ADDRESS (No., Street)

CITY INJURY STATE NY

8. PATIENT STATUS
Single [X] Married [ ] Other [ ]

CITY STATE

ZIP CODE 12347-1234 TELEPHONE (Include Area Code) (101)1118675

Employed [ ] Full-Time Student [ ] Part-Time Student [ ]

ZIP CODE TELEPHONE (Include Area Code) ( )

9. OTHER INSURED'S NAME (Last Name, First Name, Middle Initial)

10. IS PATIENT'S CONDITION RELATED TO:

11. INSURED'S POLICY GROUP OR FECA NUMBER
NONE

a. OTHER INSURED'S POLICY OR GROUP NUMBER

a. EMPLOYMENT? (Current or Previous)
YES [ ] NO [X]

a. INSURED'S DATE OF BIRTH MM DD YY SEX M [ ] F [ ]

b. OTHER INSURED'S DATE OF BIRTH MM DD YY SEX M [ ] F [ ]

b. AUTO ACCIDENT? PLACE (State)
YES [ ] NO [X]

b. EMPLOYER'S NAME OR SCHOOL NAME

c. EMPLOYER'S NAME OR SCHOOL NAME

c. OTHER ACCIDENT?
YES [ ] NO [X]

c. INSURANCE PLAN NAME OR PROGRAM NAME

d. INSURANCE PLAN NAME OR PROGRAM NAME

10d. RESERVED FOR LOCAL USE
MCD 1155773388

d. IS THERE ANOTHER HEALTH BENEFIT PLAN?
YES [ ] NO [ ] *If yes*, return to and complete item 9 a-d.

READ BACK OF FORM BEFORE COMPLETING & SIGNING THIS FORM.

12. PATIENT'S OR AUTHORIZED PERSON'S SIGNATURE I authorize the release of any medical or other information necessary to process this claim. I also request payment of government benefits either to myself or to the party who accepts assignment below.

SIGNED SIGNATURE ON FILE DATE

13. INSURED'S OR AUTHORIZED PERSON'S SIGNATURE I authorize payment of medical benefits to the undersigned physcian or supplier for services described below.

SIGNED

14. DATE OF CURRENT: MM 06 DD 20 YY YYYY ILLNESS (First symptom) OR INJURY (Accident) OR PREGNANCY (LMP)

15. IF PATIENT HAS HAD SAME OR SIMILAR ILLNESS. GIVE FIRST DATE MM DD YY

16. DATES PATIENT UNABLE TO WORK IN CURRENT OCCUPATION FROM MM DD YY TO MM DD YY

17. NAME OF REFERRING PROVIDER OR OTHER SOURCE

17a.
17b. NPI

18. HOSPITALIZATION DATES RELATED TO CURRENT SERVICES FROM MM DD YY TO MM DD YY

19. RESERVED FOR LOCAL USE

20. OUTSIDE LAB? YES [ ] NO [X] $ CHARGES

21. DIAGNOSIS OR NATURE OF ILLNESS OR INJURY (Relate Items 1, 2, 3 or 4 to Item 24E by Line)

1. 250.73
2. 443.9
3. V49.73
4.

22. MEDICAID RESUBMISSION CODE ORIGINAL REF. NO.

23. PRIOR AUTHORIZATION NUMBER

24. A DATE(S) OF SERVICE From / To MM DD YY MM DD YY	B. PLACE OF SERVICE	C. EMG	D. PROCEDURES, SERVICES, OR SUPPLIES (Explain Unusual Circumstances) CPT/HCPCS MODIFIER	E. DIAGNOSIS POINTER	F. $ CHARGES	G. DAYS OR UNITS	H. EPSDT Family Plan	I. ID. QUAL.	J. RENDERING PROVIDER ID. #
1	0620YYYY	12		99348	1	45 00	1		NPI	6789012345
2									NPI	
3									NPI	
4									NPI	
5									NPI	
6									NPI	

25. FEDERAL TAX I.D. NUMBER SSN EIN [X]
441234567

26. PATIENT'S ACCOUNT NO.
2-6

27. ACCEPT ASSIGNMENT? (For govt. claims, see back) YES [X] NO [ ]

28. TOTAL CHARGE $ 45 00

29. AMOUNT PAID $

30. BALANCE DUE $ 45 00

31. SIGNATURE OF PHYSICIAN OR SUPPLIER INCLUDING DEGREES OR CREDENTIALS (I certify that the statements on the reverse apply to this bill and are made a part thereof.)
NANCY J HEALER MD
SIGNED DATE MMDDYYYY

32. SERVICE FACILITY LOCATION INFORMATION
GOODMEDICINE CLINIC
1 PROVIDER STREET
ANYWHERE NY 12345
a. 3345678901 b.

33. BILLING PROVIDER INFO & PH # (101)1112222
GOODMEDICINE CLINIC
1 PROVIDER STREET
ANYWHERE NY 12345
a. 3345678901 b.

NUCC Instruction Manual available at: www.nucc.org

APPROVED OMB-0938-0999 FORM CMS-1500 (08/05)

| 1500 |

HEALTH INSURANCE CLAIM FORM
APPROVED BY NATIONAL UNIFORM CLAIM COMMITTEE 08/05

PICA | | | | | | | | PICA

1. MEDICARE	MEDICAID	TRICARE CHAMPUS	CHAMPVA	GROUP HEALTH PLAN	FECA BLK LUNG	OTHER	1a. INSURED'S I.D. NUMBER (For Program in Item 1)
X (Medicare #)	(Medicaid #)	(Sponsor's SSN)	(Member ID#)	(SSN or ID)	(SSN)	(ID)	101234591A

2. PATIENT'S NAME (Last Name, First Name, Middle Initial)	3. PATIENT'S BIRTH DATE MM DD YY	SEX	4. INSURED'S NAME (Last Name, First Name, Middle Initial)
GONZALES, ESAU	09 10 1933	M X F	

5. PATIENT'S ADDRESS (No., Street)	6. PATIENT'S RELATIONSHIP TO INSURED	7. INSURED'S ADDRESS (No., Street)
14 RIDLEY ST	Self Spouse Child Other	

CITY	STATE	8. PATIENT STATUS	CITY	STATE
NOWHERE	NY	Single X Married Other		

ZIP CODE	TELEPHONE (Include Area Code)		ZIP CODE	TELEPHONE (Include Area Code)
12346-1234	(101)1117689	Employed Full-Time Student Part-Time Student		( )

9. OTHER INSURED'S NAME (Last Name, First Name, Middle Initial)	10. IS PATIENT'S CONDITION RELATED TO:	11. INSURED'S POLICY GROUP OR FECA NUMBER
		NONE

a. OTHER INSURED'S POLICY OR GROUP NUMBER	a. EMPLOYMENT? (Current or Previous) YES X NO	a. INSURED'S DATE OF BIRTH MM DD YY SEX M F

b. OTHER INSURED'S DATE OF BIRTH MM DD YY SEX M F	b. AUTO ACCIDENT? PLACE (State) YES X NO	b. EMPLOYER'S NAME OR SCHOOL NAME

c. EMPLOYER'S NAME OR SCHOOL NAME	c. OTHER ACCIDENT? YES X NO	c. INSURANCE PLAN NAME OR PROGRAM NAME

d. INSURANCE PLAN NAME OR PROGRAM NAME	10d. RESERVED FOR LOCAL USE	d. IS THERE ANOTHER HEALTH BENEFIT PLAN? YES NO If yes, return to and complete item 9 a-d.

READ BACK OF FORM BEFORE COMPLETING & SIGNING THIS FORM.
12. PATIENT'S OR AUTHORIZED PERSON'S SIGNATURE I authorize the release of any medical or other information necessary to process this claim. I also request payment of government benefits either to myself or to the party who accepts assignment below.

SIGNED **SIGNATURE ON FILE** DATE

13. INSURED'S OR AUTHORIZED PERSON'S SIGNATURE I authorize payment of medical benefits to the undersigned physcian or supplier for services described below.

SIGNED

14. DATE OF CURRENT: MM DD YY ILLNESS (First symptom) OR INJURY (Accident) OR PREGNANCY (LMP)	15. IF PATIENT HAS HAD SAME OR SIMILAR ILLNESS, GIVE FIRST DATE MM DD YY	16. DATES PATIENT UNABLE TO WORK IN CURRENT OCCUPATION MM DD YY TO MM DD YY
0620YYYY		FROM TO

17. NAME OF REFERRING PROVIDER OR OTHER SOURCE	17a.	18. HOSPITALIZATION DATES RELATED TO CURRENT SERVICES
	17b. NPI	FROM MM DD YY TO MM DD YY

19. RESERVED FOR LOCAL USE	20. OUTSIDE LAB? $ CHARGES
	YES X NO

21. DIAGNOSIS OR NATURE OF ILLNESS OR INJURY (Relate Items 1, 2, 3 or 4 to Item 24E by Line)

1. 786.09   3. 272.4
2. 401.9   4. V45.81

22. MEDICAID RESUBMISSION CODE ORIGINAL REF. NO.
23. PRIOR AUTHORIZATION NUMBER

24. A. DATE(S) OF SERVICE From To MM DD YY MM DD YY	B. PLACE OF SERVICE	C. EMG	D. PROCEDURES, SERVICES, OR SUPPLIES (Explain Unusual Circumstances) CPT/HCPCS MODIFIER	E. DIAGNOSIS POINTER	F. $ CHARGES	G. DAYS OR UNITS	H. EPSDT Family Plan	I. ID. QUAL.	J. RENDERING PROVIDER ID. #
1	0620YYYY	11		99214		1	100 00	1		NPI	3456789012
2	0620YYYY	11		93000		1	65 00	1		NPI	3456789012
3										NPI	
4										NPI	
5										NPI	
6										NPI	

25. FEDERAL TAX I.D. NUMBER SSN EIN	26. PATIENT'S ACCOUNT NO.	27. ACCEPT ASSIGNMENT? (For govt. claims, see back)	28. TOTAL CHARGE	29. AMOUNT PAID	30. BALANCE DUE
221234567 X	2-7	X YES NO	$ 165 00	$	$

31. SIGNATURE OF PHYSICIAN OR SUPPLIER INCLUDING DEGREES OR CREDENTIALS (I certify that the statements on the reverse apply to this bill and are made a part thereof.)	32. SERVICE FACILITY LOCATION INFORMATION	33. BILLING PROVIDER INFO & PH # (101)1112222
HENRY C CARDIAC MD SIGNED DATE MMDDYYYY	GOODMEDICINE CLINIC 1 PROVIDER STREET ANYWHERE NY 12345 a. 3345678901 b.	GOODMEDICINE CLINIC 1 PROVIDER STREET ANYWHERE NY 12345 a. 3345678901 b.

NUCC Instruction Manual available at: www.nucc.org

APPROVED OMB-0938-0999 FORM CMS-1500 (08/05)

1500

HEALTH INSURANCE CLAIM FORM

APPROVED BY NATIONAL UNIFORM CLAIM COMMITTEE 08/05

| | PICA | | | | | | | | PICA | | |

1. MEDICARE	MEDICAID	TRICARE CHAMPUS	CHAMPVA	GROUP HEALTH PLAN	FECA BLK LUNG	OTHER	1a. INSURED'S I.D. NUMBER	(For Program in Item 1)
X (Medicare #)	(Medicaid #)	(Sponsor's SSN)	(Member ID#)	(SSN or ID)	(SSN)	X (ID)	071269645B	

2. PATIENT'S NAME (Last Name, First Name, Middle Initial)	3. PATIENT'S BIRTH DATE / SEX	4. INSURED'S NAME (Last Name, First Name, Middle Initial)
BUSH, MARY, B	04 01 1930 M / F X	

5. PATIENT'S ADDRESS (No., Street)	6. PATIENT'S RELATIONSHIP TO INSURED	7. INSURED'S ADDRESS (No., Street)
9910 WILLIAMS RD	Self Spouse Child Other	

CITY	STATE	8. PATIENT STATUS	CITY	STATE
NOWHERE	NY	Single X Married Other		

ZIP CODE	TELEPHONE (Include Area Code)		ZIP CODE	TELEPHONE (Include Area Code)
12346-1234	(101)1119922	Employed Full-Time Student Part-Time Student		( )

9. OTHER INSURED'S NAME (Last Name, First Name, Middle Initial)	10. IS PATIENT'S CONDITION RELATED TO:	11. INSURED'S POLICY GROUP OR FECA NUMBER
SAME		NONE

a. OTHER INSURED'S POLICY OR GROUP NUMBER	a. EMPLOYMENT? (Current or Previous)	a. INSURED'S DATE OF BIRTH / SEX
MEDIGAP ABC9876	YES X NO	M F

b. OTHER INSURED'S DATE OF BIRTH / SEX	b. AUTO ACCIDENT? PLACE (State)	b. EMPLOYER'S NAME OR SCHOOL NAME
04 01 1930 M F X	YES X NO	

c. EMPLOYER'S NAME OR SCHOOL NAME	c. OTHER ACCIDENT?	c. INSURANCE PLAN NAME OR PROGRAM NAME
	YES X NO	

d. INSURANCE PLAN NAME OR PROGRAM NAME	10d. RESERVED FOR LOCAL USE	d. IS THERE ANOTHER HEALTH BENEFIT PLAN?
9912345678		YES NO **If yes,** return to and complete item 9 a-d.

READ BACK OF FORM BEFORE COMPLETING & SIGNING THIS FORM.

12. PATIENT'S OR AUTHORIZED PERSON'S SIGNATURE I authorize the release of any medical or other information necessary to process this claim. I also request payment of government benefits either to myself or to the party who accepts assignment below.

SIGNED SIGNATURE ON FILE DATE _____

13. INSURED'S OR AUTHORIZED PERSON'S SIGNATURE I authorize payment of medical benefits to the undersigned physcian or supplier for services described below.

SIGNED SIGNATURE ON FILE

14. DATE OF CURRENT: ILLNESS (First symptom) OR INJURY (Accident) OR PREGNANCY (LMP)	15. IF PATIENT HAS HAD SAME OR SIMILAR ILLNESS. GIVE FIRST DATE MM DD YY	16. DATES PATIENT UNABLE TO WORK IN CURRENT OCCUPATION
06 20 YYYY		FROM MM DD YY TO MM DD YY

17. NAME OF REFERRING PROVIDER OR OTHER SOURCE	17a.	18. HOSPITALIZATION DATES RELATED TO CURRENT SERVICES
	17b. NPI	FROM MM DD YY TO MM DD YY

19. RESERVED FOR LOCAL USE	20. OUTSIDE LAB? $ CHARGES
	YES X NO

21. DIAGNOSIS OR NATURE OF ILLNESS OR INJURY (Relate Items 1, 2, 3 or 4 to Item 24E by Line)

1. 780.39   3. ___ . ___

2. ___ . ___   4. ___ . ___

22. MEDICAID RESUBMISSION CODE	ORIGINAL REF. NO.

23. PRIOR AUTHORIZATION NUMBER

24. A. DATE(S) OF SERVICE From MM DD YY	To MM DD YY	B. PLACE OF SERVICE	C. EMG	D. PROCEDURES, SERVICES, OR SUPPLIES (Explain Unusual Circumstances) CPT/HCPCS	MODIFIER	E. DIAGNOSIS POINTER	F. $ CHARGES	G. DAYS OR UNITS	H. EPSDT Family Plan	I. ID. QUAL.	J. RENDERING PROVIDER ID. #
1	06 20 YYYY		11		99214		1	100 00	1		NPI	6789012345
2											NPI	
3											NPI	
4											NPI	
5											NPI	
6											NPI	

25. FEDERAL TAX I.D. NUMBER	SSN EIN	26. PATIENT'S ACCOUNT NO.	27. ACCEPT ASSIGNMENT? (For govt. claims, see back)	28. TOTAL CHARGE	29. AMOUNT PAID	30. BALANCE DUE
441234567	X	2-8	X YES NO	$ 100 00	$	$

31. SIGNATURE OF PHYSICIAN OR SUPPLIER INCLUDING DEGREES OR CREDENTIALS (I certify that the statements on the reverse apply to this bill and are made a part thereof.)	32. SERVICE FACILITY LOCATION INFORMATION	33. BILLING PROVIDER INFO & PH # (101)1112222
NANCY J HEALER MD	GOODMEDICINE CLINC 1 PROVIDER STREET ANYWHERE NY 12345	GOODMEDICINE CLINIC 1 PROVIDER STREET ANYWHERE NY 12345
SIGNED DATE MMDDYYYY	a. 3345678901 b.	a. 3345678901 b.

NUCC Instruction Manual available at: www.nucc.org

APPROVED OMB-0938-0999 FORM CMS-1500 (08/05)

1500

HEALTH INSURANCE CLAIM FORM

APPROVED BY NATIONAL UNIFORM CLAIM COMMITTEE 08/05

| | PICA | | | | | | | | PICA | |

1. MEDICARE [X] (Medicare #) MEDICAID (Medicaid #) TRICARE CHAMPUS (Sponsor's SSN) CHAMPVA (Member ID#) GROUP HEALTH PLAN (SSN or ID) FECA BLK LUNG (SSN) OTHER (ID)

1a. INSURED'S I.D. NUMBER (For Program in Item 1): 001266811B

2. PATIENT'S NAME (Last Name, First Name, Middle Initial): CADILLAC, MARY, A

3. PATIENT'S BIRTH DATE: 04 30 1929 SEX: M F [X]

4. INSURED'S NAME (Last Name, First Name, Middle Initial):

5. PATIENT'S ADDRESS (No., Street): 500 CARR ST

6. PATIENT'S RELATIONSHIP TO INSURED: Self Spouse Child Other

7. INSURED'S ADDRESS (No., Street):

CITY: ANYWHERE STATE: NY

8. PATIENT STATUS: Single Married [X] Other Employed Full-Time Student Part-Time Student

CITY: STATE:

ZIP CODE: 12345-1234 TELEPHONE: (101) 2223333

ZIP CODE: TELEPHONE: ( )

9. OTHER INSURED'S NAME (Last Name, First Name, Middle Initial):

10. IS PATIENT'S CONDITION RELATED TO:

11. INSURED'S POLICY GROUP OR FECA NUMBER: NONE

a. OTHER INSURED'S POLICY OR GROUP NUMBER:

a. EMPLOYMENT? (Current or Previous): YES NO [X]

a. INSURED'S DATE OF BIRTH: MM DD YY SEX: M F

b. OTHER INSURED'S DATE OF BIRTH: MM DD YY SEX: M F

b. AUTO ACCIDENT?: YES NO [X] PLACE (State):

b. EMPLOYER'S NAME OR SCHOOL NAME:

c. EMPLOYER'S NAME OR SCHOOL NAME:

c. OTHER ACCIDENT?: YES NO [X]

c. INSURANCE PLAN NAME OR PROGRAM NAME:

d. INSURANCE PLAN NAME OR PROGRAM NAME:

10d. RESERVED FOR LOCAL USE:

d. IS THERE ANOTHER HEALTH BENEFIT PLAN?: YES NO If yes, return to and complete item 9 a-d.

12. PATIENT'S OR AUTHORIZED PERSON'S SIGNATURE: SIGNED SIGNATURE ON FILE DATE

13. INSURED'S OR AUTHORIZED PERSON'S SIGNATURE: SIGNED

14. DATE OF CURRENT: 06 20 YYYY ILLNESS (First symptom) OR INJURY (Accident) OR PREGNANCY (LMP)

15. IF PATIENT HAS HAD SAME OR SIMILAR ILLNESS GIVE FIRST DATE MM DD YY

16. DATES PATIENT UNABLE TO WORK IN CURRENT OCCUPATION: FROM TO

17. NAME OF REFERRING PROVIDER OR OTHER SOURCE: 17a. 17b. NPI

18. HOSPITALIZATION DATES RELATED TO CURRENT SERVICES: FROM 06 20 YYYY TO 06 20 YYYY

19. RESERVED FOR LOCAL USE:

20. OUTSIDE LAB?: YES NO [X] $ CHARGES

21. DIAGNOSIS OR NATURE OF ILLNESS OR INJURY: 1. 574 10 2. 573 8 3. 4.

22. MEDICAID RESUBMISSION CODE ORIGINAL REF. NO.

23. PRIOR AUTHORIZATION NUMBER

24.

A. DATE(S) OF SERVICE From / To	B. PLACE OF SERVICE	C. EMG	D. CPT/HCPCS	MODIFIER	E. DIAGNOSIS POINTER	F. $ CHARGES	G. DAYS OR UNITS	H. EPSDT	I. ID QUAL	J. RENDERING PROVIDER ID. #
06 20 YYYY	22		47563		1	1350 00	1		NPI	8901234567
06 20 YYYY	22		47001	51	1	100 00	1		NPI	8901234567
									NPI	
									NPI	
									NPI	
									NPI	

25. FEDERAL TAX I.D. NUMBER: 551234567 SSN EIN [X]

26. PATIENT'S ACCOUNT NO.: 2-9

27. ACCEPT ASSIGNMENT?: YES [X] NO

28. TOTAL CHARGE: $ 1450 00

29. AMOUNT PAID: $

30. BALANCE DUE: $

31. SIGNATURE OF PHYSICIAN OR SUPPLIER: TJ STITCHER MD SIGNED DATE MMDDYYYY

32. SERVICE FACILITY LOCATION INFORMATION: GOODMEDICINE HOSPITAL 1 PROVIDER ST ANYWHERE NY 12345 a. 1123456789 b.

33. BILLING PROVIDER INFO & PH # (101) 1112222: GOODMEDICINE CLINIC 1 PROVIDER STREET ANYWHERE NY 12345 a. 3345678901 b.

NUCC Instruction Manual available at: www.nucc.org

APPROVED OMB-0938-0999 FORM CMS-1500 (08/05)

1500

HEALTH INSURANCE CLAIM FORM

APPROVED BY NATIONAL UNIFORM CLAIM COMMITTEE 08/05

| | PICA | | | | | | | | | | | | | | | | PICA | |

1. MEDICARE	MEDICAID	TRICARE CHAMPUS	CHAMPVA	GROUP HEALTH PLAN	FECA BLK LUNG	OTHER	1a. INSURED'S I.D. NUMBER (For Program in Item 1)
X (Medicare #)	(Medicaid #)	(Sponsor's SSN)	(Member ID#)	(SSN or ID)	(SSN)	X (ID)	101101010A

2. PATIENT'S NAME (Last Name, First Name, Middle Initial)
HAMMERCLAW, JOHN, W

3. PATIENT'S BIRTH DATE   MM 05 DD 30 YY 1930   SEX M X F

4. INSURED'S NAME (Last Name, First Name, Middle Initial)

5. PATIENT'S ADDRESS (No., Street)
111 LUMBER ST

6. PATIENT'S RELATIONSHIP TO INSURED
Self   Spouse   Child   Other

7. INSURED'S ADDRESS (No., Street)

CITY **ANYWHERE**   STATE **NY**

8. PATIENT STATUS
Single X   Married   Other

CITY   STATE

ZIP CODE **12345-1234**   TELEPHONE (Include Area Code) **(101)1119191**

Employed   Full-Time Student   Part-Time Student

ZIP CODE   TELEPHONE (Include Area Code) ( )

9. OTHER INSURED'S NAME (Last Name, First Name, Middle Initial)
SAME

10. IS PATIENT'S CONDITION RELATED TO:

11. INSURED'S POLICY GROUP OR FECA NUMBER
NONE

a. OTHER INSURED'S POLICY OR GROUP NUMBER
MEDIGAP YXW10110

a. EMPLOYMENT? (Current or Previous)
YES   X NO

a. INSURED'S DATE OF BIRTH   MM DD YY   SEX M F

b. OTHER INSURED'S DATE OF BIRTH   MM 05 DD 30 YY 1930   SEX M X F

b. AUTO ACCIDENT?   PLACE (State)
YES   X NO

b. EMPLOYER'S NAME OR SCHOOL NAME

c. EMPLOYER'S NAME OR SCHOOL NAME

c. OTHER ACCIDENT?
YES   X NO

c. INSURANCE PLAN NAME OR PROGRAM NAME

d. INSURANCE PLAN NAME OR PROGRAM NAME
8812345678

10d. RESERVED FOR LOCAL USE

d. IS THERE ANOTHER HEALTH BENEFIT PLAN?
YES   NO   *If yes,* return to and complete item 9 a-d.

READ BACK OF FORM BEFORE COMPLETING & SIGNING THIS FORM.
12. PATIENT'S OR AUTHORIZED PERSON'S SIGNATURE I authorize the release of any medical or other information necessary to process this claim. I also request payment of government benefits either to myself or to the party who accepts assignment below.

SIGNED **SIGNATURE ON FILE**   DATE

13. INSURED'S OR AUTHORIZED PERSON'S SIGNATURE I authorize payment of medical benefits to the undersigned physician or supplier for services described below.

SIGNED

14. DATE OF CURRENT: MM 06 DD 20 YY YYYY   ◀ ILLNESS (First symptom) OR INJURY (Accident) OR PREGNANCY (LMP)

15. IF PATIENT HAS HAD SAME OR SIMILAR ILLNESS. GIVE FIRST DATE   MM DD YY

16. DATES PATIENT UNABLE TO WORK IN CURRENT OCCUPATION
FROM MM DD YY   TO MM DD YY

17. NAME OF REFERRING PROVIDER OR OTHER SOURCE
NANCY J HEALER MD

17a.
17b. NPI **6789012345**

18. HOSPITALIZATION DATES RELATED TO CURRENT SERVICES
FROM MM DD YY   TO MM DD YY

19. RESERVED FOR LOCAL USE

20. OUTSIDE LAB? $ CHARGES
YES   X NO

21. DIAGNOSIS OR NATURE OF ILLNESS OR INJURY (Relate Items 1, 2, 3 or 4 to Item 24E by Line)
1. **706 . 2**
2.
3.
4.

22. MEDICAID RESUBMISSION CODE   ORIGINAL REF. NO.

23. PRIOR AUTHORIZATION NUMBER

24. A DATE(S) OF SERVICE From MM DD YY To MM DD YY	B. PLACE OF SERVICE	C. EMG	D. PROCEDURES, SERVICES, OR SUPPLIES (Explain Unusual Circumstances) CPT/HCPCS MODIFIER	E. DIAGNOSIS POINTER	F. $ CHARGES	G. DAYS OR UNITS	H. EPSDT Family Plan	I. ID. QUAL.	J. RENDERING PROVIDER ID. #
1	0620YYYY	11		11406		1	360 00	1		NPI	8901234567
2	0620YYYY	11		11423 51		1	300 00	1		NPI	8901234567
3										NPI	
4										NPI	
5										NPI	
6										NPI	

25. FEDERAL TAX I.D. NUMBER   SSN EIN
551234567   X

26. PATIENT'S ACCOUNT NO.
2-10

27. ACCEPT ASSIGNMENT? (For govt. claims, see back)
X YES   NO

28. TOTAL CHARGE $ **660 00**

29. AMOUNT PAID $

30. BALANCE DUE $

31. SIGNATURE OF PHYSICIAN OR SUPPLIER INCLUDING DEGREES OR CREDENTIALS (I certify that the statements on the reverse apply to this bill and are made a part thereof.)
TJ STITCHER MD
SIGNED   DATE **MMDDYYYY**

32. SERVICE FACILITY LOCATION INFORMATION
**GOODMEDICINE CLINIC
1 PROVIDER STREET
ANYWHERE NY 12345**
a. **3345678901**   b.

33. BILLING PROVIDER INFO & PH # **(101)1112222**
**GOODMEDICINE CLINIC
1 PROVIDER STREET
ANYWHERE NY 12345**
a. **3345678901**   b.

NUCC Instruction Manual available at: www.nucc.org

APPROVED OMB-0938-0999 FORM CMS-1500 (08/05)

1500

HEALTH INSURANCE CLAIM FORM

APPROVED BY NATIONAL UNIFORM CLAIM COMMITTEE 08/05

☐☐ PICA   PICA ☐☐

| 1. MEDICARE ☐ (Medicare #) | MEDICAID ☒ (Medicaid #) | TRICARE CHAMPUS ☐ (Sponsor's SSN) | CHAMPVA ☐ (Member ID#) | GROUP HEALTH PLAN ☐ (SSN or ID) | FECA BLK LUNG ☐ (SSN) | OTHER ☐ (ID) | 1a. INSURED'S I.D. NUMBER (For Program in Item 1) 11347765 |

| 2. PATIENT'S NAME (Last Name, First Name, Middle Initial) FONTAINE, GERMANE | 3. PATIENT'S BIRTH DATE MM 05 DD 07 YY 1965 SEX M ☐ F ☒ | 4. INSURED'S NAME (Last Name, First Name, Middle Initial) |

| 5. PATIENT'S ADDRESS (No., Street) 132 CANAL ST | 6. PATIENT'S RELATIONSHIP TO INSURED Self ☐ Spouse ☐ Child ☐ Other ☐ | 7. INSURED'S ADDRESS (No., Street) |

| CITY INJURY | STATE NY | 8. PATIENT STATUS Single ☐ Married ☐ Other ☐ | CITY | STATE |

| ZIP CODE 12347-1234 | TELEPHONE (Include Area Code) (101)1119685 | Employed ☐ Full-Time Student ☐ Part-Time Student ☐ | ZIP CODE | TELEPHONE (Include Area Code) ( ) |

| 9. OTHER INSURED'S NAME (Last Name, First Name, Middle Initial) | 10. IS PATIENT'S CONDITION RELATED TO: | 11. INSURED'S POLICY GROUP OR FECA NUMBER |

| a. OTHER INSURED'S POLICY OR GROUP NUMBER | a. EMPLOYMENT? (Current or Previous) YES ☐ NO ☒ | a. INSURED'S DATE OF BIRTH MM DD YY SEX M ☐ F ☐ |

| b. OTHER INSURED'S DATE OF BIRTH MM DD YY SEX M ☐ F ☐ | b. AUTO ACCIDENT? PLACE (State) YES ☐ NO ☒ | b. EMPLOYER'S NAME OR SCHOOL NAME |

| c. EMPLOYER'S NAME OR SCHOOL NAME | c. OTHER ACCIDENT? YES ☐ NO ☒ | c. INSURANCE PLAN NAME OR PROGRAM NAME |

| d. INSURANCE PLAN NAME OR PROGRAM NAME | 10d. RESERVED FOR LOCAL USE | d. IS THERE ANOTHER HEALTH BENEFIT PLAN? YES ☐ NO ☐ If yes, return to and complete item 9 a-d. |

READ BACK OF FORM BEFORE COMPLETING & SIGNING THIS FORM.
12. PATIENT'S OR AUTHORIZED PERSON'S SIGNATURE I authorize the release of any medical or other information necessary to process this claim. I also request payment of government benefits either to myself or to the party who accepts assignment below.

SIGNED _____ DATE _____

13. INSURED'S OR AUTHORIZED PERSON'S SIGNATURE I authorize payment of medical benefits to the undersigned physcian or supplier for services described below.

SIGNED _____

| 14. DATE OF CURRENT: MM DD YY ILLNESS (First symptom) OR INJURY (Accident) OR PREGNANCY (LMP) | 15. IF PATIENT HAS HAD SAME OR SIMILAR ILLNESS, GIVE FIRST DATE MM DD YY | 16. DATES PATIENT UNABLE TO WORK IN CURRENT OCCUPATION MM DD YY MM DD YY FROM TO |

| 17. NAME OF REFERRING PROVIDER OR OTHER SOURCE | 17a. 17b. NPI | 18. HOSPITALIZATION DATES RELATED TO CURRENT SERVICES MM DD YY MM DD YY FROM TO |

| 19. RESERVED FOR LOCAL USE | 20. OUTSIDE LAB? YES ☐ NO ☒ $ CHARGES |

21. DIAGNOSIS OR NATURE OF ILLNESS OR INJURY (Relate Items 1, 2, 3 or 4 to Item 24E by Line)

1. 473.9   3. _____
2. 462   4. _____

| 22. MEDICAID RESUBMISSION CODE | ORIGINAL REF. NO. |
| 23. PRIOR AUTHORIZATION NUMBER |

24. A. DATE(S) OF SERVICE From MM DD YY To MM DD YY	B. PLACE OF SERVICE	C. EMG	D. PROCEDURES, SERVICES, OR SUPPLIES (Explain Unusual Circumstances) CPT/HCPCS	MODIFIER	E. DIAGNOSIS POINTER	F. $ CHARGES	G. DAYS OR UNITS	H. EPSDT Family Plan	I. ID. QUAL.	J. RENDERING PROVIDER ID. #
1	06 20 YYYY	11		99212		1	26 00	1		NPI	3456789012
2	06 20 YYYY	11		87430		1	12 00	1		NPI	3456789012
3										NPI	
4										NPI	
5										NPI	
6										NPI	

| 25. FEDERAL TAX I.D. NUMBER SSN EIN 221234567 ☒ | 26. PATIENT'S ACCOUNT NO. 2-11 | 27. ACCEPT ASSIGNMENT? (For govt. claims, see back) ☒ YES ☐ NO | 28. TOTAL CHARGE $ 38 00 | 29. AMOUNT PAID $ | 30. BALANCE DUE $ |

| 31. SIGNATURE OF PHYSICIAN OR SUPPLIER INCLUDING DEGREES OR CREDENTIALS (I certify that the statements on the reverse apply to this bill and are made a part thereof.) HENRY C CARDIAC MD SIGNED DATE MMDDYYYY | 32. SERVICE FACILITY LOCATION INFORMATION a. NPI b. | 33. BILLING PROVIDER INFO & PH # (101)1112222 GOODMEDICINE CLINIC 1 PROVIDER STREET ANYWHERE NY 12345 a. 3345678901 b. |

NUCC Instruction Manual available at: www.nucc.org   APPROVED OMB-0938-0999 FORM CMS-1500 (08/05)

1500

HEALTH INSURANCE CLAIM FORM

APPROVED BY NATIONAL UNIFORM CLAIM COMMITTEE 08/05

| | PICA | | | | | | | | | | PICA | |

1. MEDICARE	MEDICAID	TRICARE CHAMPUS	CHAMPVA	GROUP HEALTH PLAN	FECA BLK LUNG	OTHER	1a. INSURED'S I.D. NUMBER (For Program in Item 1)
(Medicare #)	[X] (Medicaid #)	(Sponsor's SSN)	(Member ID#)	(SSN or ID)	(SSN)	(ID)	1234567

2. PATIENT'S NAME (Last Name, First Name, Middle Initial)
APPLE, JAMES

3. PATIENT'S BIRTH DATE MM 11 DD 12 YY 1984   **SEX** M [X] F [ ]

4. INSURED'S NAME (Last Name, First Name, Middle Initial)

5. PATIENT'S ADDRESS (No., Street)
1 APPLEBLOSSOM COURT

6. PATIENT'S RELATIONSHIP TO INSURED
Self [ ] Spouse [ ] Child [ ] Other [ ]

7. INSURED'S ADDRESS (No., Street)

CITY HOMETOWN **STATE** NY

8. PATIENT STATUS
Single [ ] Married [ ] Other [ ]

CITY **STATE**

ZIP CODE 15123-1234 **TELEPHONE (Include Area Code)** (201)1112011

Employed [ ] Full-Time Student [ ] Part-Time Student [ ]

ZIP CODE **TELEPHONE (Include Area Code)** ( )

9. OTHER INSURED'S NAME (Last Name, First Name, Middle Initial)

10. IS PATIENT'S CONDITION RELATED TO:

11. INSURED'S POLICY GROUP OR FECA NUMBER

a. OTHER INSURED'S POLICY OR GROUP NUMBER

a. EMPLOYMENT? (Current or Previous)
YES [ ] [X] NO

a. INSURED'S DATE OF BIRTH MM DD YY **SEX** M [ ] F [ ]

b. OTHER INSURED'S DATE OF BIRTH MM DD YY **SEX** M [ ] F [ ]

b. AUTO ACCIDENT? PLACE (State)
YES [ ] [X] NO

b. EMPLOYER'S NAME OR SCHOOL NAME

c. EMPLOYER'S NAME OR SCHOOL NAME

c. OTHER ACCIDENT?
YES [ ] [X] NO

c. INSURANCE PLAN NAME OR PROGRAM NAME

d. INSURANCE PLAN NAME OR PROGRAM NAME

10d. RESERVED FOR LOCAL USE

d. IS THERE ANOTHER HEALTH BENEFIT PLAN?
YES [ ] NO [ ] *If yes*, return to and complete item 9 a-d.

READ BACK OF FORM BEFORE COMPLETING & SIGNING THIS FORM.
12. PATIENT'S OR AUTHORIZED PERSON'S SIGNATURE I authorize the release of any medical or other information necessary to process this claim. I also request payment of government benefits either to myself or to the party who accepts assignment below.

SIGNED _____ DATE _____

13. INSURED'S OR AUTHORIZED PERSON'S SIGNATURE I authorize payment of medical benefits to the undersigned physcian or supplier for services described below.

SIGNED _____

14. DATE OF CURRENT: MM DD YY ILLNESS (First symptom) OR INJURY (Accident) OR PREGNANCY (LMP)

15. IF PATIENT HAS HAD SAME OR SIMILAR ILLNESS. GIVE FIRST DATE MM DD YY

16. DATES PATIENT UNABLE TO WORK IN CURRENT OCCUPATION
MM DD YY FROM TO MM DD YY

17. NAME OF REFERRING PROVIDER OR OTHER SOURCE
17a.
17b. NPI

18. HOSPITALIZATION DATES RELATED TO CURRENT SERVICES
MM DD YY FROM 06 19 YYYY TO 06 20 YYYY

19. RESERVED FOR LOCAL USE

20. OUTSIDE LAB?
YES [ ] [X] NO $ CHARGES

21. DIAGNOSIS OR NATURE OF ILLNESS OR INJURY (Relate Items 1, 2, 3 or 4 to Item 24E by Line)
1. 540 . 9
2. ___ . ___
3. ___ . ___
4. ___ . ___

22. MEDICAID RESUBMISSION CODE ORIGINAL REF. NO.

23. PRIOR AUTHORIZATION NUMBER

24. A. DATE(S) OF SERVICE From MM DD YY To MM DD YY	B. PLACE OF SERVICE	C. EMG	D. PROCEDURES, SERVICES, OR SUPPLIES (Explain Unusual Circumstances) CPT/HCPCS MODIFIER	E. DIAGNOSIS POINTER	F. $ CHARGES	G. DAYS OR UNITS	H. EPSDT Family Plan	I. ID. QUAL.	J. RENDERING PROVIDER ID. #
1	0619YYYY		21	99223	1	165 00	1		NPI	3456789012
2									NPI	
3									NPI	
4									NPI	
5									NPI	
6									NPI	

25. FEDERAL TAX I.D. NUMBER 221234567 SSN [ ] EIN [X]

26. PATIENT'S ACCOUNT NO. 2-12A

27. ACCEPT ASSIGNMENT? (For govt. claims, see back)
[X] YES NO [ ]

28. TOTAL CHARGE $ 165 00

29. AMOUNT PAID $

30. BALANCE DUE $

31. SIGNATURE OF PHYSICIAN OR SUPPLIER INCLUDING DEGREES OR CREDENTIALS (I certify that the statements on the reverse apply to this bill and are made a part thereof.)
HENRY C CARDIAC MD
SIGNED DATE MMDDYYYY

32. SERVICE FACILITY LOCATION INFORMATION
GOODMEDICINE HOSPITAL
1 PROVIDER ST
ANYWHERE NY 12345
a. 1123456789 b.

33. BILLING PROVIDER INFO & PH # (101)1112222
GOODMEDICINE CLINIC
1 PROVIDER STREET
ANYWHERE NY 12345
a. 3345678901 b.

NUCC Instruction Manual available at: www.nucc.org

APPROVED OMB-0938-0999 FORM CMS-1500 (08/05)

1500

HEALTH INSURANCE CLAIM FORM

APPROVED BY NATIONAL UNIFORM CLAIM COMMITTEE 08/05

| | PICA | | | | | PICA | | |

1. MEDICARE ☐ (Medicare #) | MEDICAID ☒ (Medicaid #) | TRICARE CHAMPUS ☐ (Sponsor's SSN) | CHAMPVA ☐ (Member ID#) | GROUP HEALTH PLAN ☐ (SSN or ID) | FECA BLK LUNG ☐ (SSN) | OTHER ☐ (ID) | **1a. INSURED'S I.D. NUMBER** (For Program in Item 1)
1234567

2. PATIENT'S NAME (Last Name, First Name, Middle Initial)
APPLE, JAMES

3. PATIENT'S BIRTH DATE MM | DD | YY 11 | 12 | 1984 **SEX** M ☒ F ☐

4. INSURED'S NAME (Last Name, First Name, Middle Initial)

5. PATIENT'S ADDRESS (No., Street)
1 APPLEBLOSSOM COURT

6. PATIENT'S RELATIONSHIP TO INSURED
Self ☐ Spouse ☐ Child ☐ Other ☐

7. INSURED'S ADDRESS (No., Street)

CITY HOMETOWN **STATE** NY

8. PATIENT STATUS
Single ☐ Married ☐ Other ☐
Employed ☐ Full-Time Student ☐ Part-Time Student ☐

CITY **STATE**

ZIP CODE 15123-1234 **TELEPHONE** (Include Area Code) (201)1112011

ZIP CODE **TELEPHONE** (Include Area Code) ( )

9. OTHER INSURED'S NAME (Last Name, First Name, Middle Initial)

10. IS PATIENT'S CONDITION RELATED TO:

11. INSURED'S POLICY GROUP OR FECA NUMBER

a. OTHER INSURED'S POLICY OR GROUP NUMBER

a. EMPLOYMENT? (Current or Previous)
YES ☐ NO ☒

a. INSURED'S DATE OF BIRTH MM | DD | YY **SEX** M ☐ F ☐

b. OTHER INSURED'S DATE OF BIRTH MM | DD | YY **SEX** M ☐ F ☐

b. AUTO ACCIDENT? PLACE (State)
YES ☐ NO ☒

b. EMPLOYER'S NAME OR SCHOOL NAME

c. EMPLOYER'S NAME OR SCHOOL NAME

c. OTHER ACCIDENT?
YES ☐ NO ☒

c. INSURANCE PLAN NAME OR PROGRAM NAME

d. INSURANCE PLAN NAME OR PROGRAM NAME

10d. RESERVED FOR LOCAL USE

d. IS THERE ANOTHER HEALTH BENEFIT PLAN?
YES ☐ NO ☐ **If yes,** return to and complete item 9 a-d.

READ BACK OF FORM BEFORE COMPLETING & SIGNING THIS FORM.
12. PATIENT'S OR AUTHORIZED PERSON'S SIGNATURE I authorize the release of any medical or other information necessary to process this claim. I also request payment of government benefits either to myself or to the party who accepts assignment below.

SIGNED _____ DATE _____

13. INSURED'S OR AUTHORIZED PERSON'S SIGNATURE I authorize payment of medical benefits to the undersigned physcian or supplier for services described below.

SIGNED _____

14. DATE OF CURRENT: MM | DD | YY 06 | 19 | YYYY ◄ ILLNESS (First symptom) OR INJURY (Accident) OR PREGNANCY (LMP)

15. IF PATIENT HAS HAD SAME OR SIMILAR ILLNESS, GIVE FIRST DATE MM | DD | YY

16. DATES PATIENT UNABLE TO WORK IN CURRENT OCCUPATION MM | DD | YY FROM TO MM | DD | YY

17. NAME OF REFERRING PROVIDER OR OTHER SOURCE
17a.
17b. NPI

18. HOSPITALIZATION DATES RELATED TO CURRENT SERVICES MM | DD | YY FROM 06 | 19 | YYYY TO 06 | 20 | YYYY

19. RESERVED FOR LOCAL USE

20. OUTSIDE LAB? YES ☐ NO ☒ **$ CHARGES**

21. DIAGNOSIS OR NATURE OF ILLNESS OR INJURY (Relate Items 1, 2, 3 or 4 to Item 24E by Line)
1. 540 . 9
2. ____ . ____
3. ____ . ____
4. ____ . ____

22. MEDICAID RESUBMISSION CODE ORIGINAL REF. NO.

23. PRIOR AUTHORIZATION NUMBER

24. A. DATE(S) OF SERVICE From MM DD YY	To MM DD YY	B. PLACE OF SERVICE	C. EMG	D. PROCEDURES, SERVICES, OR SUPPLIES (Explain Unusual Circumstances) CPT/HCPCS	MODIFIER	E. DIAGNOSIS POINTER	F. $ CHARGES	G. DAYS OR UNITS	H. EPSDT Family Plan	I. ID. QUAL.	J. RENDERING PROVIDER ID. #
1 06 19 YYYY		21		44970		1	1400 00	1		NPI	8901234567
2										NPI	
3										NPI	
4										NPI	
5										NPI	
6										NPI	

25. FEDERAL TAX I.D. NUMBER SSN ☐ EIN ☒
551234567

26. PATIENT'S ACCOUNT NO.
2-12B

27. ACCEPT ASSIGNMENT? (For govt. claims, see back)
YES ☒ NO ☐

28. TOTAL CHARGE $ 1400 00

29. AMOUNT PAID $

30. BALANCE DUE $

31. SIGNATURE OF PHYSICIAN OR SUPPLIER INCLUDING DEGREES OR CREDENTIALS (I certify that the statements on the reverse apply to this bill and are made a part thereof.)
TJ STITCHER MD
SIGNED _____ DATE MMDDYYYY

32. SERVICE FACILITY LOCATION INFORMATION
GOODMEDICINE HOSPITAL
1 PROVIDER ST
ANYWHERE NY 12345
a. 1123456789 b.

33. BILLING PROVIDER INFO & PH # (101)1112222
GOODMEDICINE CLINIC
1 PROVIDER STREET
ANYWHERE NY 12345
a. 3345678901 b.

NUCC Instruction Manual available at: www.nucc.org

APPROVED OMB-0938-0999 FORM CMS-1500 (08/05)

Side margin: CARRIER | PATIENT AND INSURED INFORMATION | PHYSICIAN OR SUPPLIER INFORMATION

1500

HEALTH INSURANCE CLAIM FORM
APPROVED BY NATIONAL UNIFORM CLAIM COMMITTEE 08/05

☐☐ PICA | PICA ☐☐

| 1. MEDICARE (Medicare #) | MEDICAID (Medicaid #) | TRICARE CHAMPUS [X] (Sponsor's SSN) | CHAMPVA (Member ID#) | GROUP HEALTH PLAN (SSN or ID) | FECA BLK LUNG (SSN) | OTHER (ID) | 1a. INSURED'S I.D. NUMBER (For Program in Item 1) 123445555 |

2. PATIENT'S NAME (Last Name, First Name, Middle Initial)
BANANA, STANLEY, N

3. PATIENT'S BIRTH DATE MM 11 DD 11 YY 1956 SEX M [X] F ☐

4. INSURED'S NAME (Last Name, First Name, Middle Initial)
BANANA, STANLEY, N

5. PATIENT'S ADDRESS (No., Street)
1 BARRACK ST

6. PATIENT'S RELATIONSHIP TO INSURED
Self [X] Spouse ☐ Child ☐ Other ☐

7. INSURED'S ADDRESS (No., Street)
1 BARRACK ST

CITY ANYWHERE STATE NY

8. PATIENT STATUS
Single [X] Married ☐ Other ☐
Employed [X] Full-Time Student ☐ Part-Time Student ☐

CITY ANYWHERE STATE NY

ZIP CODE 12345-1234 TELEPHONE (Include Area Code) (101)1117676

ZIP CODE 12345-1234 TELEPHONE (Include Area Code) (101)1117676

9. OTHER INSURED'S NAME (Last Name, First Name, Middle Initial)

10. IS PATIENT'S CONDITION RELATED TO:

11. INSURED'S POLICY GROUP OR FECA NUMBER

a. OTHER INSURED'S POLICY OR GROUP NUMBER

a. EMPLOYMENT? (Current or Previous) ☐ YES [X] NO

a. INSURED'S DATE OF BIRTH MM DD YY SEX M ☐ F ☐

b. OTHER INSURED'S DATE OF BIRTH MM DD YY SEX M ☐ F ☐

b. AUTO ACCIDENT? PLACE (State) ☐ YES [X] NO

b. EMPLOYER'S NAME OR SCHOOL NAME

c. EMPLOYER'S NAME OR SCHOOL NAME

c. OTHER ACCIDENT? ☐ YES [X] NO

c. INSURANCE PLAN NAME OR PROGRAM NAME

d. INSURANCE PLAN NAME OR PROGRAM NAME

10d. RESERVED FOR LOCAL USE

d. IS THERE ANOTHER HEALTH BENEFIT PLAN? ☐ YES [X] NO If yes, return to and complete item 9 a-d.

READ BACK OF FORM BEFORE COMPLETING & SIGNING THIS FORM.
12. PATIENT'S OR AUTHORIZED PERSON'S SIGNATURE I authorize the release of any medical or other information necessary to process this claim. I also request payment of government benefits either to myself or to the party who accepts assignment below.

SIGNED SIGNATURE ON FILE DATE

13. INSURED'S OR AUTHORIZED PERSON'S SIGNATURE I authorize payment of medical benefits to the undersigned physician or supplier for services described below.

SIGNED SIGNATURE ON FILE

14. DATE OF CURRENT: MM 06 DD 20 YY YYYY ILLNESS (First symptom) OR INJURY (Accident) OR PREGNANCY (LMP)

15. IF PATIENT HAS HAD SAME OR SIMILAR ILLNESS. GIVE FIRST DATE MM DD YY

16. DATES PATIENT UNABLE TO WORK IN CURRENT OCCUPATION
FROM MM DD YY TO MM DD YY

17. NAME OF REFERRING PROVIDER OR OTHER SOURCE
NANCY J HEALER MD

17a.
17b. NPI 6789012345

18. HOSPITALIZATION DATES RELATED TO CURRENT SERVICES
FROM MM 06 DD 20 YY YYYY TO MM 06 DD 20 YY YYYY

19. RESERVED FOR LOCAL USE

20. OUTSIDE LAB? ☐ YES [X] NO $ CHARGES

21. DIAGNOSIS OR NATURE OF ILLNESS OR INJURY (Relate Items 1, 2, 3 or 4 to Item 24E by Line)
1. 565 0
2.
3.
4.

22. MEDICAID RESUBMISSION CODE ORIGINAL REF. NO.

23. PRIOR AUTHORIZATION NUMBER

24. A DATE(S) OF SERVICE		B. PLACE OF SERVICE	C. EMG	D. PROCEDURES, SERVICES, OR SUPPLIES (Explain Unusual Circumstances)		E. DIAGNOSIS POINTER	F. $ CHARGES	G. DAYS OR UNITS	H. EPSDT Family Plan	I. ID. QUAL.	J. RENDERING PROVIDER ID. #
From MM DD YY	To MM DD YY			CPT/HCPCS	MODIFIER						
1 06 20 YYYY		22		45330		1	600 00	1		NPI	9012345678
2										NPI	
3										NPI	
4										NPI	
5										NPI	
6										NPI	

25. FEDERAL TAX I.D. NUMBER SSN EIN
331234567 [X]

26. PATIENT'S ACCOUNT NO.
2-13

27. ACCEPT ASSIGNMENT? (For govt. claims, see back) [X] YES ☐ NO

28. TOTAL CHARGE $ 600 00

29. AMOUNT PAID $

30. BALANCE DUE $ 600 00

31. SIGNATURE OF PHYSICIAN OR SUPPLIER INCLUDING DEGREES OR CREDENTIALS (I certify that the statements on the reverse apply to this bill and are made a part thereof.)
JANET B SURGEON MD
SIGNED DATE MMDDYYYY

32. SERVICE FACILITY LOCATION INFORMATION
GOODMEDICINE HOSPITAL
1 PROVIDER ST
ANYWHERE NY 12345
a. 1123456789 b.

33. BILLING PROVIDER INFO & PH # (101)1112222
GOODMEDICINE CLINIC
1 PROVIDER ST
ANYWHERE NY 12345
a. 3345678901 b.

NUCC Instruction Manual available at: www.nucc.org

APPROVED OMB-0938-0999 FORM CMS-1500 (08/05)

1500

HEALTH INSURANCE CLAIM FORM
APPROVED BY NATIONAL UNIFORM CLAIM COMMITTEE 08/05

☐☐ PICA

<table>
<tr><td colspan="6">1. MEDICARE   MEDICAID   TRICARE CHAMPUS   CHAMPVA   GROUP HEALTH PLAN   FECA BLK LUNG   OTHER</td><td colspan="2">1a. INSURED'S I.D. NUMBER   (For Program in Item 1)</td></tr>
<tr><td>(Medicare #)</td><td>(Medicaid #)</td><td>[X] (Sponsor's SSN)</td><td>(Member ID#)</td><td>(SSN or ID)</td><td>(SSN)   (ID)</td><td colspan="2">012346543</td></tr>
</table>

2. PATIENT'S NAME (Last Name, First Name, Middle Initial)	3. PATIENT'S BIRTH DATE / SEX	4. INSURED'S NAME (Last Name, First Name, Middle Initial)
KAROT, REGINALD, T	10 01 1936 M[X] F☐	KAROT, REGINALD, T
5. PATIENT'S ADDRESS (No., Street)	6. PATIENT'S RELATIONSHIP TO INSURED	7. INSURED'S ADDRESS (No., Street)
15 CARING ST	Self [X] Spouse☐ Child☐ Other☐	15 CARING ST
CITY ANYWHERE STATE NY	8. PATIENT STATUS Single☐ Married [X] Other☐	CITY ANYWHERE STATE NY
ZIP CODE 12345-1234 TELEPHONE (101)2220022	Employed [X] Full-Time Student☐ Part-Time Student☐	ZIP CODE 12345-1234 TELEPHONE (101)2220022

9. OTHER INSURED'S NAME (Last Name, First Name, Middle Initial)	10. IS PATIENT'S CONDITION RELATED TO:	11. INSURED'S POLICY GROUP OR FECA NUMBER
KAROT, LOUISE		
a. OTHER INSURED'S POLICY OR GROUP NUMBER 22222222A ASD1	a. EMPLOYMENT? (Current or Previous) YES☐ [X] NO	a. INSURED'S DATE OF BIRTH SEX M☐ F☐
b. OTHER INSURED'S DATE OF BIRTH 10 11 1936 SEX M☐ F[X]	b. AUTO ACCIDENT? PLACE (State) YES☐ [X] NO	b. EMPLOYER'S NAME OR SCHOOL NAME
c. EMPLOYER'S NAME OR SCHOOL NAME ANYWHERE SCHOOL DISTRICT	c. OTHER ACCIDENT? YES☐ [X] NO	c. INSURANCE PLAN NAME OR PROGRAM NAME
d. INSURANCE PLAN NAME OR PROGRAM NAME METROPOLITAN	10d. RESERVED FOR LOCAL USE	d. IS THERE ANOTHER HEALTH BENEFIT PLAN? [X] YES ☐ NO If yes, return to and complete item 9 a-d.

READ BACK OF FORM BEFORE COMPLETING & SIGNING THIS FORM.

12. PATIENT'S OR AUTHORIZED PERSON'S SIGNATURE I authorize the release of any medical or other information necessary to process this claim. I also request payment of government benefits either to myself or to the party who accepts assignment below.	13. INSURED'S OR AUTHORIZED PERSON'S SIGNATURE I authorize payment of medical benefits to the undersigned physcian or supplier for services described below.
SIGNED SIGNATURE ON FILE DATE	SIGNED SIGNATURE ON FILE

14. DATE OF CURRENT: 06 20 YYYY ◄ ILLNESS (First symptom) OR INJURY (Accident) OR PREGNANCY (LMP)	15. IF PATIENT HAS HAD SAME OR SIMILAR ILLNESS, GIVE FIRST DATE MM DD YY	16. DATES PATIENT UNABLE TO WORK IN CURRENT OCCUPATION FROM TO
17. NAME OF REFERRING PROVIDER OR OTHER SOURCE NANCY J HEALER MD	17a. 17b. NPI 6789012345	18. HOSPITALIZATION DATES RELATED TO CURRENT SERVICES FROM TO
19. RESERVED FOR LOCAL USE		20. OUTSIDE LAB? YES☐ [X] NO $ CHARGES
21. DIAGNOSIS OR NATURE OF ILLNESS OR INJURY (Relate Items 1, 2, 3 or 4 to Item 24E by Line) 1. 550.92 3. 2. 4.		22. MEDICAID RESUBMISSION CODE ORIGINAL REF. NO.
		23. PRIOR AUTHORIZATION NUMBER

24. A. DATE(S) OF SERVICE From — To	B. PLACE OF SERVICE	C. EMG	D. PROCEDURES, SERVICES, OR SUPPLIES CPT/HCPCS	MODIFIER	E. DIAGNOSIS POINTER	F. $ CHARGES	G. DAYS OR UNITS	H. EPSDT Family Plan	I. ID. QUAL.	J. RENDERING PROVIDER ID. #
1 06 20 YYYY	11		99203	57	1	75 00	1		NPI	9012345678
2									NPI	
3									NPI	
4									NPI	
5									NPI	
6									NPI	

25. FEDERAL TAX I.D. NUMBER SSN EIN 331234567 [X]	26. PATIENT'S ACCOUNT NO. 2-14S	27. ACCEPT ASSIGNMENT? [X] YES ☐ NO	28. TOTAL CHARGE $ 75 00	29. AMOUNT PAID $	30. BALANCE DUE $ 75 00
31. SIGNATURE OF PHYSICIAN OR SUPPLIER INCLUDING DEGREES OR CREDENTIALS (I certify that the statements on the reverse apply to this bill and are made a part thereof.) JANET B SURGEON MD SIGNED DATE MMDDYYYY	32. SERVICE FACILITY LOCATION INFORMATION a. NPI b.		33. BILLING PROVIDER INFO & PH # (101)1112222 GOODMEDICINE CLINIC 1 PROVIDER STREET ANYWHERE NY 12345 a. 3345678901 b.		

NUCC Instruction Manual available at: www.nucc.org   APPROVED OMB-0938-0999 FORM CMS-1500 (08/05)

1500

HEALTH INSURANCE CLAIM FORM

APPROVED BY NATIONAL UNIFORM CLAIM COMMITTEE 08/05

| | PICA | | | | | | | | PICA | |

1. MEDICARE	MEDICAID	TRICARE CHAMPUS	CHAMPVA	GROUP HEALTH PLAN	FECA BLK LUNG	OTHER	1a. INSURED'S I.D. NUMBER	(For Program in Item 1)
(Medicare #)	(Medicaid #)	(Sponsor's SSN)	(Member ID#)	(SSN or ID) X	(SSN)	(ID)	321458765	

2. PATIENT'S NAME (Last Name, First Name, Middle Initial)	3. PATIENT'S BIRTH DATE	SEX	4. INSURED'S NAME (Last Name, First Name, Middle Initial)
BUTCHER, JAMES, L	02 29 1977 M X	F	PIGLET MEAT PACKERS

5. PATIENT'S ADDRESS (No., Street)	6. PATIENT'S RELATIONSHIP TO INSURED	7. INSURED'S ADDRESS (No., Street)
14 PIGSFEET RD	Self Spouse Child Other X	100 REYNOLDS WAY

CITY	STATE	8. PATIENT STATUS	CITY	STATE
ANYWHERE	NY	Single Married Other	ANYWHERE	NY

ZIP CODE	TELEPHONE (Include Area Code)		ZIP CODE	TELEPHONE (Include Area Code)
12345-1234	(101) 3334567	Employed X Full-Time Student Part-Time Student	12345	( )

9. OTHER INSURED'S NAME (Last Name, First Name, Middle Initial)	10. IS PATIENT'S CONDITION RELATED TO:	11. INSURED'S POLICY GROUP OR FECA NUMBER
		987123

a. OTHER INSURED'S POLICY OR GROUP NUMBER	a. EMPLOYMENT? (Current or Previous) X YES NO	a. INSURED'S DATE OF BIRTH MM DD YY SEX M F

b. OTHER INSURED'S DATE OF BIRTH MM DD YY SEX M F	b. AUTO ACCIDENT? PLACE (State) YES X NO	b. EMPLOYER'S NAME OR SCHOOL NAME PIGLET MEAT PACKERS

c. EMPLOYER'S NAME OR SCHOOL NAME	c. OTHER ACCIDENT? YES X NO	c. INSURANCE PLAN NAME OR PROGRAM NAME WORKERS COMP FUND

d. INSURANCE PLAN NAME OR PROGRAM NAME	10d. RESERVED FOR LOCAL USE	d. IS THERE ANOTHER HEALTH BENEFIT PLAN? YES NO If yes, return to and complete item 9 a-d.

READ BACK OF FORM BEFORE COMPLETING & SIGNING THIS FORM.
12. PATIENT'S OR AUTHORIZED PERSON'S SIGNATURE I authorize the release of any medical or other information necessary to process this claim. I also request payment of government benefits either to myself or to the party who accepts assignment below.

SIGNED _____ DATE _____

13. INSURED'S OR AUTHORIZED PERSON'S SIGNATURE I authorize payment of medical benefits to the undersigned physician or supplier for services described below.

SIGNED _____

14. DATE OF CURRENT: MM DD YY 06 19 YYYY ILLNESS (First symptom) OR INJURY (Accident) OR PREGNANCY (LMP)	15. IF PATIENT HAS HAD SAME OR SIMILAR ILLNESS, GIVE FIRST DATE MM DD YY	16. DATES PATIENT UNABLE TO WORK IN CURRENT OCCUPATION MM DD YY MM DD YY FROM 06 19 YYYY TO 08 18 YYYY

17. NAME OF REFERRING PROVIDER OR OTHER SOURCE	17a. 17b. NPI	18. HOSPITALIZATION DATES RELATED TO CURRENT SERVICES MM DD YY MM DD YY FROM 06 19 YYYY TO 06 19 YYYY

19. RESERVED FOR LOCAL USE	20. OUTSIDE LAB? YES X NO $ CHARGES

21. DIAGNOSIS OR NATURE OF ILLNESS OR INJURY (Relate Items 1, 2, 3 or 4 to Item 24E by Line)

1. 883 2
2. E9202
3.
4.

22. MEDICAID RESUBMISSION CODE ORIGINAL REF. NO.

23. PRIOR AUTHORIZATION NUMBER

24. A. DATE(S) OF SERVICE From MM DD YY To MM DD YY	B. PLACE OF SERVICE	C. EMG	D. PROCEDURES, SERVICES, OR SUPPLIES (Explain Unusual Circumstances) CPT/HCPCS MODIFIER	E. DIAGNOSIS POINTER	F. $ CHARGES	G. DAYS OR UNITS	H. EPSDT Family Plan	I. ID. QUAL.	J. RENDERING PROVIDER ID. #
1	06 19 YYYY		23		26410 LT	1	1400 00	1		NPI	8901234567
2										NPI	
3										NPI	
4										NPI	
5										NPI	
6										NPI	

25. FEDERAL TAX I.D. NUMBER SSN EIN	26. PATIENT'S ACCOUNT NO.	27. ACCEPT ASSIGNMENT? (For govt. claims, see back)	28. TOTAL CHARGE	29. AMOUNT PAID	30. BALANCE DUE
551234567 X	2-15	X YES NO	$ 1400 00	$	$

31. SIGNATURE OF PHYSICIAN OR SUPPLIER INCLUDING DEGREES OR CREDENTIALS (I certify that the statements on the reverse apply to this bill and are made a part thereof.) TJ STITCHER MD SIGNED DATE MMDDYYYY	32. SERVICE FACILITY LOCATION INFORMATION GOODMEDICINE HOSPITAL 1 PROVIDER ST ANYWHERE NY 12345 a. 1123456789 b.	33. BILLING PROVIDER INFO & PH # (101) 1112222 GOODMEDICINE CLINIC 1 PROVIDER STREET ANYWHERE NY 12345 a. 3345678901 b.

NUCC Instruction Manual available at: www.nucc.org

APPROVED OMB-0938-0999 FORM CMS-1500 (08/05)

1500

HEALTH INSURANCE CLAIM FORM

APPROVED BY NATIONAL UNIFORM CLAIM COMMITTEE 08/05

| | PICA | | | | | | | | | | PICA | | |

1. MEDICARE	MEDICAID	TRICARE CHAMPUS	CHAMPVA	GROUP HEALTH PLAN	FECA BLK LUNG	OTHER	1a. INSURED'S I.D. NUMBER	(For Program in Item 1)
(Medicare #)	(Medicaid #)	(Sponsor's SSN)	(Member ID#)	(SSN or ID) X	(SSN)	(ID)	112102121	

2. PATIENT'S NAME (Last Name, First Name, Middle Initial)	3. PATIENT'S BIRTH DATE	SEX	4. INSURED'S NAME (Last Name, First Name, Middle Initial)
HURTS, DAVID, J	02 28 1955	M X F	UC PAINTERS

5. PATIENT'S ADDRESS (No., Street)	6. PATIENT'S RELATIONSHIP TO INSURED	7. INSURED'S ADDRESS (No., Street)
4321 NOWHERE ST	Self Spouse Child Other X	1 CIRCLE DR

CITY	STATE	8. PATIENT STATUS	CITY	STATE
ANYWHERE	NY	Single Married Other	ANYWHERE	NY

ZIP CODE	TELEPHONE (Include Area Code)		ZIP CODE	TELEPHONE (Include Area Code)
12345-1234	(101)3141414	Employed X Full-Time Student Part-Time Student	12345	( )

9. OTHER INSURED'S NAME (Last Name, First Name, Middle Initial)	10. IS PATIENT'S CONDITION RELATED TO:	11. INSURED'S POLICY GROUP OR FECA NUMBER
		123987

a. OTHER INSURED'S POLICY OR GROUP NUMBER	a. EMPLOYMENT? (Current or Previous) X YES NO	a. INSURED'S DATE OF BIRTH MM DD YY	SEX M F

b. OTHER INSURED'S DATE OF BIRTH MM DD YY SEX M F	b. AUTO ACCIDENT? PLACE (State) YES X NO	b. EMPLOYER'S NAME OR SCHOOL NAME UC PAINTERS

c. EMPLOYER'S NAME OR SCHOOL NAME	c. OTHER ACCIDENT? YES X NO	c. INSURANCE PLAN NAME OR PROGRAM NAME INDUSTRIAL INDEMNITY CO

d. INSURANCE PLAN NAME OR PROGRAM NAME	10d. RESERVED FOR LOCAL USE	d. IS THERE ANOTHER HEALTH BENEFIT PLAN? YES NO *If yes,* return to and complete item 9 a-d.

READ BACK OF FORM BEFORE COMPLETING & SIGNING THIS FORM.

12. PATIENT'S OR AUTHORIZED PERSON'S SIGNATURE I authorize the release of any medical or other information necessary to process this claim. I also request payment of government benefits either to myself or to the party who accepts assignment below.

SIGNED SOF   DATE

13. INSURED'S OR AUTHORIZED PERSON'S SIGNATURE I authorize payment of medical benefits to the undersigned physcian or supplier for services described below.

SIGNED SOF

14. DATE OF CURRENT: MM DD YY 06 20 YYYY ILLNESS (First symptom) OR INJURY (Accident) OR PREGNANCY (LMP)	15. IF PATIENT HAS HAD SAME OR SIMILAR ILLNESS. GIVE FIRST DATE MM DD YY	16. DATES PATIENT UNABLE TO WORK IN CURRENT OCCUPATION MM DD YY MM DD YY FROM 06 20 YYYY TO 08 08 YYYY

17. NAME OF REFERRING PROVIDER OR OTHER SOURCE	17a.	18. HOSPITALIZATION DATES RELATED TO CURRENT SERVICES MM DD YY MM DD YY
	17b. NPI	FROM TO

19. RESERVED FOR LOCAL USE	20. OUTSIDE LAB? $ CHARGES YES X NO

21. DIAGNOSIS OR NATURE OF ILLNESS OR INJURY (Relate Items 1, 2, 3 or 4 to Item 24E by Line)

1. 813.41
2. 873.44
3. E8810
4. E8493

22. MEDICAID RESUBMISSION CODE	ORIGINAL REF. NO.

23. PRIOR AUTHORIZATION NUMBER

24. A. DATE(S) OF SERVICE				B. PLACE OF SERVICE	C. EMG	D. PROCEDURES, SERVICES, OR SUPPLIES (Explain Unusual Circumstances) CPT/HCPCS	MODIFIER	E. DIAGNOSIS POINTER	F. $ CHARGES	G. DAYS OR UNITS	H. EPSDT Family Plan	I. ID. QUAL.	J. RENDERING PROVIDER ID. #
From MM DD YY		To MM DD YY											
1	06 20 YYYY			11		25605	LT	1	300 00	1		NPI	1234567890
2	06 20 YYYY			11		73090	LT	1	80 00	1		NPI	1234567890
3	06 20 YYYY			11		12011		2	80 00	1		NPI	1234567890
4												NPI	
5												NPI	
6												NPI	

25. FEDERAL TAX I.D. NUMBER SSN EIN	26. PATIENT'S ACCOUNT NO.	27. ACCEPT ASSIGNMENT? (For govt. claims, see back)	28. TOTAL CHARGE	29. AMOUNT PAID	30. BALANCE DUE
661234567 X	2-16	X YES NO	$ 460 00	$	$

31. SIGNATURE OF PHYSICIAN OR SUPPLIER INCLUDING DEGREES OR CREDENTIALS (I certify that the statements on the reverse apply to this bill and are made a part thereof.) GAIL R BONES MD SIGNED DATE MMDDYYYY	32. SERVICE FACILITY LOCATION INFORMATION a. NPI b.	33. BILLING PROVIDER INFO & PH # (101)1112222 GOODMEDICINE CLINIC 1 PROVIDER STREET ANYWHERE NY 12345 a. 3345678901 b.

NUCC Instruction Manual available at: www.nucc.org

APPROVED OMB-0938-0999 FORM CMS-1500 (08/05)

1500

HEALTH INSURANCE CLAIM FORM

APPROVED BY NATIONAL UNIFORM CLAIM COMMITTEE 08/05

PICA ☐☐ | | PICA ☐☐

CARRIER

| 1. MEDICARE (Medicare #) ☐ | MEDICAID (Medicaid #) ☐ | TRICARE CHAMPUS (Sponsor's SSN) [X] | CHAMPVA (Member ID#) ☐ | GROUP HEALTH PLAN (SSN or ID) ☐ | FECA BLK LUNG (SSN) ☐ | OTHER (ID) ☐ | 1a. INSURED'S I.D. NUMBER (For Program in Item 1) 235236594 |

| 2. PATIENT'S NAME (Last Name, First Name, Middle Initial) SMITH, PETER, M | 3. PATIENT'S BIRTH DATE MM 02 DD 20 YY 1965 SEX M [X] F ☐ | 4. INSURED'S NAME (Last Name, First Name, Middle Initial) SMITH, PETER, M |

| 5. PATIENT'S ADDRESS (No., Street) 1000 MAIN ST APT B | 6. PATIENT'S RELATIONSHIP TO INSURED Self [X] Spouse ☐ Child ☐ Other ☐ | 7. INSURED'S ADDRESS (No., Street) 1000 MAIN ST APT B |

| CITY ANYWHERE | STATE NY | 8. PATIENT STATUS Single ☐ Married [X] Other ☐ | CITY ANYWHERE | STATE NY |

| ZIP CODE 12345-1234 | TELEPHONE (Include Area Code) (101)5629654 | Employed [X] Full-Time Student ☐ Part-Time Student ☐ | ZIP CODE 12345-1234 | TELEPHONE (Include Area Code) (101)5629654 |

| 9. OTHER INSURED'S NAME (Last Name, First Name, Middle Initial) | 10. IS PATIENT'S CONDITION RELATED TO: | 11. INSURED'S POLICY GROUP OR FECA NUMBER |

| a. OTHER INSURED'S POLICY OR GROUP NUMBER | a. EMPLOYMENT? (Current or Previous) YES ☐ [X] NO | a. INSURED'S DATE OF BIRTH MM DD YY SEX M ☐ F ☐ |

| b. OTHER INSURED'S DATE OF BIRTH MM DD YY SEX M ☐ F ☐ | b. AUTO ACCIDENT? PLACE (State) YES ☐ [X] NO | b. EMPLOYER'S NAME OR SCHOOL NAME |

| c. EMPLOYER'S NAME OR SCHOOL NAME | c. OTHER ACCIDENT? YES ☐ [X] NO | c. INSURANCE PLAN NAME OR PROGRAM NAME |

| d. INSURANCE PLAN NAME OR PROGRAM NAME | 10d. RESERVED FOR LOCAL USE | d. IS THERE ANOTHER HEALTH BENEFIT PLAN? YES ☐ [X] NO **If yes,** return to and complete item 9 a-d. |

READ BACK OF FORM BEFORE COMPLETING & SIGNING THIS FORM.

12. PATIENT'S OR AUTHORIZED PERSON'S SIGNATURE I authorize the release of any medical or other information necessary to process this claim. I also request payment of government benefits either to myself or to the party who accepts assignment below.

SIGNED SIGNATURE ON FILE DATE

13. INSURED'S OR AUTHORIZED PERSON'S SIGNATURE I authorize payment of medical benefits to the undersigned physician or supplier for services described below.

SIGNED SIGNATURE ON FILE

PATIENT AND INSURED INFORMATION

| 14. DATE OF CURRENT: MM 06 DD 20 YY YYYY ILLNESS (First symptom) OR INJURY (Accident) OR PREGNANCY (LMP) | 15. IF PATIENT HAS HAD SAME OR SIMILAR ILLNESS. GIVE FIRST DATE MM DD YY | 16. DATES PATIENT UNABLE TO WORK IN CURRENT OCCUPATION MM DD YY MM DD YY FROM TO |

| 17. NAME OF REFERRING PROVIDER OR OTHER SOURCE | 17a. / 17b. NPI | 18. HOSPITALIZATION DATES RELATED TO CURRENT SERVICES MM DD YY MM DD YY FROM TO |

| 19. RESERVED FOR LOCAL USE | 20. OUTSIDE LAB? YES ☐ [X] NO $ CHARGES |

21. DIAGNOSIS OR NATURE OF ILLNESS OR INJURY (Relate Items 1, 2, 3 or 4 to Item 24E by Line)

1. 998 . 59   3. E8798

2. V45 . 89   4.

| 22. MEDICAID RESUBMISSION CODE ORIGINAL REF. NO. |
| 23. PRIOR AUTHORIZATION NUMBER |

24. A. DATE(S) OF SERVICE		B. PLACE OF SERVICE	C. EMG	D. PROCEDURES, SERVICES, OR SUPPLIES (Explain Unusual Circumstances)		E. DIAGNOSIS POINTER	F. $ CHARGES	G. DAYS OR UNITS	H. EPSDT Family Plan	I. ID. QUAL.	J. RENDERING PROVIDER ID. #
From MM DD YY	To MM DD YY			CPT/HCPCS	MODIFIER						
1	06 20 YYYY		11		99214		1	100 00	1		NPI	9012345678
2											NPI	
3											NPI	
4											NPI	
5											NPI	
6											NPI	

PHYSICIAN OR SUPPLIER INFORMATION

| 25. FEDERAL TAX I.D. NUMBER SSN EIN 331234567 [X] | 26. PATIENT'S ACCOUNT NO. 2-17 | 27. ACCEPT ASSIGNMENT? (For govt. claims, see back) [X] YES ☐ NO | 28. TOTAL CHARGE $ 100 00 | 29. AMOUNT PAID $ | 30. BALANCE DUE $ 100 00 |

| 31. SIGNATURE OF PHYSICIAN OR SUPPLIER INCLUDING DEGREES OR CREDENTIALS (I certify that the statements on the reverse apply to this bill and are made a part thereof.) SIGNED JANET B SURGEON MD DATE MMDDYYYY | 32. SERVICE FACILITY LOCATION INFORMATION a. NPI b. | 33. BILLING PROVIDER INFO & PH # (101)1112222 GOODMEDICINE CLINIC 1 PROVIDER STREET ANYWHERE NY 12345 a. 3345678901 b. |

NUCC Instruction Manual available at: www.nucc.org

APPROVED OMB-0938-0999 FORM CMS-1500 (08/05)

1500

HEALTH INSURANCE CLAIM FORM

APPROVED BY NATIONAL UNIFORM CLAIM COMMITTEE 08/05

| | PICA | | | | | | | | PICA | |

1. MEDICARE	MEDICAID	TRICARE CHAMPUS	CHAMPVA	GROUP HEALTH PLAN	FECA BLK LUNG	OTHER	1a. INSURED'S I.D. NUMBER (For Program in Item 1)
(Medicare #)	(Medicaid #) [X]	(Sponsor's SSN)	(Member ID#)	(SSN or ID)	(SSN)	(ID)	232589571

2. PATIENT'S NAME (Last Name, First Name, Middle Initial)
MARTIN, MARY, A

3. PATIENT'S BIRTH DATE: MM 10 DD 05 YY 1955 SEX M F [X]

4. INSURED'S NAME (Last Name, First Name, Middle Initial)
MARTIN, MARY, A

5. PATIENT'S ADDRESS (No., Street)
5005 SOUTH AVE

6. PATIENT'S RELATIONSHIP TO INSURED
Self [X] Spouse Child Other

7. INSURED'S ADDRESS (No., Street)
5005 SOUTH AVE

CITY: ANYWHERE   STATE: NY

8. PATIENT STATUS
Single [X] Married Other
Employed [X] Full-Time Student Part-Time Student

CITY: ANYWHERE   STATE: NY

ZIP CODE: 12345-1234   TELEPHONE (Include Area Code) (101)1117676

ZIP CODE: 12345-1234   TELEPHONE (Include Area Code) (101)1117676

9. OTHER INSURED'S NAME (Last Name, First Name, Middle Initial)

10. IS PATIENT'S CONDITION RELATED TO:

11. INSURED'S POLICY GROUP OR FECA NUMBER

a. OTHER INSURED'S POLICY OR GROUP NUMBER

a. EMPLOYMENT? (Current or Previous)
 YES [X] NO

a. INSURED'S DATE OF BIRTH MM DD YY   SEX M F

b. OTHER INSURED'S DATE OF BIRTH MM DD YY SEX M F

b. AUTO ACCIDENT?   PLACE (State)
 YES [X] NO

b. EMPLOYER'S NAME OR SCHOOL NAME

c. EMPLOYER'S NAME OR SCHOOL NAME

c. OTHER ACCIDENT?
 YES [X] NO

c. INSURANCE PLAN NAME OR PROGRAM NAME

d. INSURANCE PLAN NAME OR PROGRAM NAME

10d. RESERVED FOR LOCAL USE

d. IS THERE ANOTHER HEALTH BENEFIT PLAN?
 YES [X] NO   If yes, return to and complete item 9 a-d.

READ BACK OF FORM BEFORE COMPLETING & SIGNING THIS FORM.
12. PATIENT'S OR AUTHORIZED PERSON'S SIGNATURE I authorize the release of any medical or other information necessary to process this claim. I also request payment of government benefits either to myself or to the party who accepts assignment below.

SIGNED SIGNATURE ON FILE   DATE

13. INSURED'S OR AUTHORIZED PERSON'S SIGNATURE I authorize payment of medical benefits to the undersigned physician or supplier for services described below.

SIGNED SIGNATURE ON FILE

14. DATE OF CURRENT: MM 06 DD 20 YY YYYY ILLNESS (First symptom) OR INJURY (Accident) OR PREGNANCY (LMP)

15. IF PATIENT HAS HAD SAME OR SIMILAR ILLNESS. GIVE FIRST DATE MM DD YY

16. DATES PATIENT UNABLE TO WORK IN CURRENT OCCUPATION
FROM MM DD YY TO MM DD YY

17. NAME OF REFERRING PROVIDER OR OTHER SOURCE
17a.
17b. NPI

18. HOSPITALIZATION DATES RELATED TO CURRENT SERVICES
FROM MM 06 DD 20 YY YYYY TO MM 06 DD 20 YY YYYY

19. RESERVED FOR LOCAL USE

20. OUTSIDE LAB? YES [X] NO $ CHARGES

21. DIAGNOSIS OR NATURE OF ILLNESS OR INJURY (Relate Items 1, 2, 3 or 4 to Item 24E by Line)
1. 626 2
2.
3.
4.

22. MEDICAID RESUBMISSION CODE   ORIGINAL REF. NO.

23. PRIOR AUTHORIZATION NUMBER

24. A. DATE(S) OF SERVICE From MM DD YY	To MM DD YY	B. PLACE OF SERVICE	C. EMG	D. PROCEDURES, SERVICES, OR SUPPLIES (Explain Unusual Circumstances) CPT/HCPCS	MODIFIER	E. DIAGNOSIS POINTER	F. $ CHARGES	G. DAYS OR UNITS	H. EPSDT Family Plan	I. ID. QUAL.	J. RENDERING PROVIDER ID. #
1	06 20 YYYY		22		58563		1	950 00	1		NPI	9012345678
2											NPI	
3											NPI	
4											NPI	
5											NPI	
6											NPI	

25. FEDERAL TAX I.D. NUMBER   SSN EIN
331234567   [X]

26. PATIENT'S ACCOUNT NO.
2-18

27. ACCEPT ASSIGNMENT? (For govt. claims, see back)
[X] YES NO

28. TOTAL CHARGE $ 950 00

29. AMOUNT PAID $

30. BALANCE DUE $ 950 00

31. SIGNATURE OF PHYSICIAN OR SUPPLIER INCLUDING DEGREES OR CREDENTIALS (I certify that the statements on the reverse apply to this bill and are made a part thereof.)
JANET B SURGEON MD
SIGNED   DATE MMDDYYYY

32. SERVICE FACILITY LOCATION INFORMATION
GOODMEDICINE HOSPITAL
1 PROVIDER ST
ANYWHERE NY 12345
a. 1123456789 b.

33. BILLING PROVIDER INFO & PH # (101)1112222
GOODMEDICINE CLINIC
1 PROVIDER STREET
ANYWHERE NY 12345
a. 3345678901 b.

NUCC Instruction Manual available at: www.nucc.org

APPROVED OMB-0938-0999 FORM CMS-1500 (08/05)

CARRIER →

1500

HEALTH INSURANCE CLAIM FORM

APPROVED BY NATIONAL UNIFORM CLAIM COMMITTEE 08/05

| | PICA | | | | | | PICA | | |

1. MEDICARE [X] (Medicare #) **MEDICAID** [X] (Medicaid #) **TRICARE CHAMPUS** (Sponsor's SSN) **CHAMPVA** (Member ID#) **GROUP HEALTH PLAN** (SSN or ID) **FECA BLK LUNG** (SSN) **OTHER** (ID)

1a. INSURED'S I.D. NUMBER (For Program in Item 1)
53231589A

2. PATIENT'S NAME (Last Name, First Name, Middle Initial)
SANTOS, CINDY

3. PATIENT'S BIRTH DATE MM 04 DD 29 YY 1935 **SEX** M [ ] F [X]

4. INSURED'S NAME (Last Name, First Name, Middle Initial)

5. PATIENT'S ADDRESS (No., Street)
3902 MAIN ST

6. PATIENT'S RELATIONSHIP TO INSURED
Self [ ] Spouse [ ] Child [ ] Other [ ]

7. INSURED'S ADDRESS (No., Street)

CITY ANYWHERE **STATE** NY

8. PATIENT STATUS
Single [X] Married [ ] Other [ ]

CITY **STATE**

ZIP CODE 12345-1234 **TELEPHONE (Include Area Code)** (101) 1115128

Employed [ ] Full-Time Student [ ] Part-Time Student [ ]

ZIP CODE **TELEPHONE (Include Area Code)** ( )

9. OTHER INSURED'S NAME (Last Name, First Name, Middle Initial)

10. IS PATIENT'S CONDITION RELATED TO:

11. INSURED'S POLICY GROUP OR FECA NUMBER
NONE

a. OTHER INSURED'S POLICY OR GROUP NUMBER

a. EMPLOYMENT? (Current or Previous)
YES [ ] NO [X]

a. INSURED'S DATE OF BIRTH MM DD YY **SEX** M [ ] F [ ]

b. OTHER INSURED'S DATE OF BIRTH MM DD YY **SEX** M [ ] F [ ]

b. AUTO ACCIDENT? PLACE (State)
YES [ ] NO [X]

b. EMPLOYER'S NAME OR SCHOOL NAME

c. EMPLOYER'S NAME OR SCHOOL NAME

c. OTHER ACCIDENT?
YES [ ] NO [X]

c. INSURANCE PLAN NAME OR PROGRAM NAME

d. INSURANCE PLAN NAME OR PROGRAM NAME

10d. RESERVED FOR LOCAL USE
MCD 231562584

d. IS THERE ANOTHER HEALTH BENEFIT PLAN?
YES [ ] NO [ ] If yes, return to and complete item 9 a-d.

READ BACK OF FORM BEFORE COMPLETING & SIGNING THIS FORM.
12. PATIENT'S OR AUTHORIZED PERSON'S SIGNATURE I authorize the release of any medical or other information necessary to process this claim. I also request payment of government benefits either to myself or to the party who accepts assignment below.

SIGNED **SIGNATURE ON FILE** DATE

13. INSURED'S OR AUTHORIZED PERSON'S SIGNATURE I authorize payment of medical benefits to the undersigned physician or supplier for services described below.

SIGNED

14. DATE OF CURRENT: MM 06 DD 20 YY YYYY ◄ ILLNESS (First symptom) OR INJURY (Accident) OR PREGNANCY (LMP)

15. IF PATIENT HAS HAD SAME OR SIMILAR ILLNESS. GIVE FIRST DATE MM DD YY

16. DATES PATIENT UNABLE TO WORK IN CURRENT OCCUPATION MM DD YY FROM TO MM DD YY

17. NAME OF REFERRING PROVIDER OR OTHER SOURCE
17a.
17b. NPI

18. HOSPITALIZATION DATES RELATED TO CURRENT SERVICES MM DD YY FROM TO MM DD YY

19. RESERVED FOR LOCAL USE

20. OUTSIDE LAB? $ CHARGES
YES [ ] NO [X]

21. DIAGNOSIS OR NATURE OF ILLNESS OR INJURY (Relate Items 1, 2, 3 or 4 to Item 24E by Line)
1. 401 9
3.
2.
4.

22. MEDICAID RESUBMISSION CODE ORIGINAL REF. NO.

23. PRIOR AUTHORIZATION NUMBER

24. A. DATE(S) OF SERVICE From MM DD YY To MM DD YY	B. PLACE OF SERVICE	C. EMG	D. PROCEDURES, SERVICES, OR SUPPLIES (Explain Unusual Circumstances) CPT/HCPCS	MODIFIER	E. DIAGNOSIS POINTER	F. $ CHARGES	G. DAYS OR UNITS	H. EPSDT Family Plan	I. ID. QUAL.	J. RENDERING PROVIDER ID. #
1	06 20 YYYY	11		99212		1	50 00	1		NPI	6789012345
2										NPI	
3										NPI	
4										NPI	
5										NPI	
6										NPI	

25. FEDERAL TAX I.D. NUMBER 441234567 SSN [ ] EIN [X]

26. PATIENT'S ACCOUNT NO. 2-19

27. ACCEPT ASSIGNMENT? (For govt. claims, see back) [X] YES [ ] NO

28. TOTAL CHARGE $ 50 00

29. AMOUNT PAID $

30. BALANCE DUE $

31. SIGNATURE OF PHYSICIAN OR SUPPLIER INCLUDING DEGREES OR CREDENTIALS (I certify that the statements on the reverse apply to this bill and are made a part thereof.)
NANCY J HEALER MD
SIGNED DATE MMDDYYYY

32. SERVICE FACILITY LOCATION INFORMATION
GOODMEDICINE CLINIC
1 PROVIDER STREET
ANYWHERE NY 12345
a. 3345678901 b.

33. BILLING PROVIDER INFO & PH # (101) 1112222
GOODMEDICINE CLINIC
1 PROVIDER STREET
ANYWHERE NY 12345
a. 3345678901 b.

NUCC Instruction Manual available at: www.nucc.org

APPROVED OMB-0938-0999 FORM CMS-1500 (08/05)

PATIENT AND INSURED INFORMATION

PHYSICIAN OR SUPPLIER INFORMATION

1500

HEALTH INSURANCE CLAIM FORM
APPROVED BY NATIONAL UNIFORM CLAIM COMMITTEE 08/05

☐☐ PICA | PICA ☐☐

1. MEDICARE ☐ (Medicare #) MEDICAID ☐ (Medicaid #) TRICARE CHAMPUS ☐ (Sponsor's SSN) CHAMPVA ☐ (Member ID#) GROUP HEALTH PLAN ☐ (SSN or ID) FECA BLK LUNG ☐ (SSN) OTHER ☒ (ID)	1a. INSURED'S I.D. NUMBER (For Program in Item 1) ABC123456

2. PATIENT'S NAME (Last Name, First Name, Middle Initial)
TOBIAS, LANA

3. PATIENT'S BIRTH DATE
MM 12 DD 15 YY 1967 M☐ SEX F☒

4. INSURED'S NAME (Last Name, First Name, Middle Initial)
TOBIAS, CASEY

5. PATIENT'S ADDRESS (No., Street)
3920 HILL ST

6. PATIENT'S RELATIONSHIP TO INSURED
Self ☐ Spouse ☒ Child ☐ Other ☐

7. INSURED'S ADDRESS (No., Street)
3920 HILL ST

CITY **ANYWHERE** STATE **NY**

8. PATIENT STATUS
Single ☐ Married ☒ Other ☐

CITY **ANYWHERE** STATE **NY**

ZIP CODE **12345-1234** TELEPHONE (Include Area Code) **(101)5551235**

Employed ☐ Full-Time Student ☐ Part-Time Student ☐

ZIP CODE **12345-1234** TELEPHONE (Include Area Code) **(101)5551235**

9. OTHER INSURED'S NAME (Last Name, First Name, Middle Initial)

10. IS PATIENT'S CONDITION RELATED TO:

11. INSURED'S POLICY GROUP OR FECA NUMBER
AB103

a. OTHER INSURED'S POLICY OR GROUP NUMBER

a. EMPLOYMENT? (Current or Previous)
YES ☐ NO ☒

a. INSURED'S DATE OF BIRTH
MM 05 DD 05 YY 1965 M☒ SEX F☐

b. OTHER INSURED'S DATE OF BIRTH
MM DD YY SEX M☐ F☐

b. AUTO ACCIDENT? PLACE (State)
YES ☐ NO ☒

b. EMPLOYER'S NAME OR SCHOOL NAME
STATE UNIVERSITY

c. EMPLOYER'S NAME OR SCHOOL NAME

c. OTHER ACCIDENT?
YES ☐ NO ☒

c. INSURANCE PLAN NAME OR PROGRAM NAME
BCBS

d. INSURANCE PLAN NAME OR PROGRAM NAME

10d. RESERVED FOR LOCAL USE

d. IS THERE ANOTHER HEALTH BENEFIT PLAN?
YES ☐ NO ☒ *If yes,* return to and complete item 9 a-d.

READ BACK OF FORM BEFORE COMPLETING & SIGNING THIS FORM.
12. PATIENT'S OR AUTHORIZED PERSON'S SIGNATURE I authorize the release of any medical or other information necessary to process this claim. I also request payment of government benefits either to myself or to the party who accepts assignment below.

SIGNED **SIGNATURE ON FILE** DATE

13. INSURED'S OR AUTHORIZED PERSON'S SIGNATURE I authorize payment of medical benefits to the undersigned physcian or supplier for services described below.

SIGNED

14. DATE OF CURRENT:
MM 06 DD 20 YY YYYY ◄ ILLNESS (First symptom) OR INJURY (Accident) OR PREGNANCY (LMP)

15. IF PATIENT HAS HAD SAME OR SIMILAR ILLNESS. GIVE FIRST DATE MM DD YY

16. DATES PATIENT UNABLE TO WORK IN CURRENT OCCUPATION
MM DD YY FROM TO MM DD YY

17. NAME OF REFERRING PROVIDER OR OTHER SOURCE

17a.
17b. NPI

18. HOSPITALIZATION DATES RELATED TO CURRENT SERVICES
MM DD YY FROM TO MM DD YY

19. RESERVED FOR LOCAL USE

20. OUTSIDE LAB? $ CHARGES
YES ☐ NO ☒

21. DIAGNOSIS OR NATURE OF ILLNESS OR INJURY (Relate Items 1, 2, 3 or 4 to Item 24E by Line)
1. 719 . 45
2. ___ . ___
3. ___ . ___
4. ___ . ___

22. MEDICAID RESUBMISSION
CODE ORIGINAL REF. NO.

23. PRIOR AUTHORIZATION NUMBER

24. A. DATE(S) OF SERVICE From MM DD YY	To MM DD YY	B. PLACE OF SERVICE	C. EMG	D. PROCEDURES, SERVICES, OR SUPPLIES (Explain Unusual Circumstances) CPT/HCPCS	MODIFIER	E. DIAGNOSIS POINTER	F. $ CHARGES	G. DAYS OR UNITS	H. EPSDT Family Plan	I. ID. QUAL.	J. RENDERING PROVIDER ID. #
1 06 20 YYYY		11		99212		1	50 00	1		NPI	8901234567
2										NPI	
3										NPI	
4										NPI	
5										NPI	
6										NPI	

25. FEDERAL TAX I.D. NUMBER **551234567** SSN ☐ EIN ☒

26. PATIENT'S ACCOUNT NO. **2-20**

27. ACCEPT ASSIGNMENT? (For govt. claims, see back) YES ☒ NO ☐

28. TOTAL CHARGE $ **50 00**

29. AMOUNT PAID $

30. BALANCE DUE $

31. SIGNATURE OF PHYSICIAN OR SUPPLIER INCLUDING DEGREES OR CREDENTIALS (I certify that the statements on the reverse apply to this bill and are made a part thereof.)
TJ STITCHER MD
SIGNED DATE **MMDDYYYY**

32. SERVICE FACILITY LOCATION INFORMATION

a. NPI b.

33. BILLING PROVIDER INFO & PH # **(101)1112222**
GOODMEDICINE CLINIC
1 PROVIDER STREET
ANYWHERE NY 12345
a. **3345678901** b.

NUCC Instruction Manual available at: www.nucc.org

APPROVED OMB-0938-0999 FORM CMS-1500 (08/05)

SECTION V Instructor's Materials

FINAL EXAMINATION CASE STUDIES
Final Examination Case Study 1

GOODMEDICINE CLINIC
1 Provider Street ■ Anywhere NY 12345 ■ (607) 587-2222
NPI: 3345678901

Case Study

PROVIDER: NANCY J. HEALER, M.D.　　　**EIN: 44-1234567**　　　**NPI: 6789012345**

PATIENT INFORMATION:		INSURANCE INFORMATION:	
Name:	Molly Smith	Patient Number:	Final 1
Address:	3559 Jericho Hill	Place of Service:	Office
City:	College Town	Primary Insurance Plan:	Empire Plan
State:	NY	Primary Insurance Plan ID #:	123456789
Zip Code:	14802	Group #:	1234
Telephone:	(607) 587-5555	Primary Policyholder:	Molly Smith
Gender:	Female	Policyholder Date of Birth:	01-03-1964
Date of Birth:	01-03-1964	Relationship to Patient:	Self
Occupation:	Professor	Secondary Insurance Plan:	
Employer:	Local College	Secondary Insurance Plan ID #:	
Spouse's Employer:	Local Factory	Secondary Policyholder:	
Spouse's Date of Birth:	12-05-1960		

Patient Status　　[X] Married　　　[ ] Divorced　　　[ ] Single　　　[ ] Student　　　[ ] Other

---

DIAGNOSIS INFORMATION

Diagnosis	Code	Diagnosis	Code
1. Annual physical examination	V70.0	5.	
2.		6.	
3.		7.	
4.		8.	

PROCEDURE INFORMATION

Description of Procedure or Service	Date	Code	Charge
1. Annual physical examination, established patient	07-20-YYYY	99395	$45.00
2.			
3.			
4.			
5.			

SPECIAL NOTES:

Patient paid $8 copayment.

Final Examination Case Study 2

GOODMEDICINE CLINIC

1 Provider Street ■ Anywhere NY 12345 ■ (607) 587-2222

NPI: 3345678901

Case Study

PROVIDER: HENRY C. CARDIAC, M.D.

EIN: 22-1234567
NPI: 3456789012

PATIENT INFORMATION:

Name:	Joe Brown
Address:	Route A1A
City:	Coastal Town
State:	NY
Zip Code:	14802
Telephone:	(101) 111-1325
Gender:	Male
Date of Birth:	02-08-1930
Occupation:	
Employer:	
Spouse's Employer:	

INSURANCE INFORMATION:

Patient Number:	Final 2
Place of Service:	Office
Primary Insurance Plan:	Medicare
Primary Insurance Plan ID #:	215353265B
Group #:	
Primary Policyholder:	Joe Brown
Policyholder Date of Birth:	02-08-1930
Relationship to Patient:	Self
Secondary Insurance Plan:	
Secondary Insurance Plan ID #:	
Secondary Policyholder:	

Patient Status ☐ Married   ☐ Divorced   ☒ Single   ☐ Student   ☐ Other

DIAGNOSIS INFORMATION

Diagnosis	Code	Diagnosis	Code
1. Hypertension	401.9	5.	
2. Emphysema	492.8	6.	
3.		7.	
4.		8.	

PROCEDURE INFORMATION

Description of Procedure or Service	Date	Code	Charge
1. Office visit, level IV, established patient	07-20-YYYY	99214	$35.00
2.			
3.			
4.			
5.			

SPECIAL NOTES:

Chest x-ray ordered for 7/25/YYYY. Return visit scheduled for 10/20/YYYY

Final Examination Case Study 3

GOODMEDICINE CLINIC

1 Provider Street ■ Anywhere NY 12345 ■ (607) 587-2222

NPI: 3345678901

Case Study

PROVIDER: NANCY J. HEALER, M.D.   EIN: 44-1234567   NPI: 6789012345

PATIENT INFORMATION:

Name:	Michael Patrick
Address:	939 Main St
City:	Hornell
State:	NY
Zip Code:	14843
Telephone:	(607) 324-5555
Gender:	Male
Date of Birth:	05-14-1957
Occupation:	Laborer
Employer:	Light Factory
Spouse's Employer:	

INSURANCE INFORMATION:

Patient Number:	Final 3
Place of Service:	Inpatient Hospital
Primary Insurance Plan:	BlueCross
Primary Insurance Plan ID #:	AJC67858
Group #:	980
Primary Policyholder:	Michael Patrick
Policyholder Date of Birth:	05-14-1957
Relationship to Patient:	Self
Secondary Insurance Plan:	
Secondary Insurance Plan ID #:	
Secondary Policyholder:	

Patient Status   ☒ Married   ☐ Divorced   ☐ Single   ☐ Student   ☐ Other

DIAGNOSIS INFORMATION

Diagnosis	Code	Diagnosis	Code
1. Uncontrolled Type I diabetes mellitus	250.03	5.	
2.		6.	
3.		7.	
4.		8.	

PROCEDURE INFORMATION

Description of Procedure or Service	Date	Code	Charge
1. Initial hospital care, level II	05-01-YYYY	99222	$55.00
2. Subsequent hospital care, level II	05-02-YYYY	99232	$45.00
3. Subsequent hospital care, level II	05-03-YYYY	99232	$45.00
4. Discharge day management, 30 minutes	05-04-YYYY	99238	$35.00
5.			

SPECIAL NOTES: Inpatient care provided at Goodmedicine Hospital, 1 Provider Street, Anywhere NY 12345. (NPI: 1123456789).
    Follow-up in office on 05/11/YYYY.

Final Examination Case Study 4

GOODMEDICINE CLINIC

1 Provider Street ■ Anywhere NY 12345 ■ (607) 587-2222

NPI: 3345678901

Case Study

PROVIDER: HENRY C. CARDIAC, M.D.   EIN: 22-1234567   NPI: 3456789012

PATIENT INFORMATION:

Name:	Eric Brown
Address:	512 Sheridan Drive
City:	Wellsville
State:	NY
Zip Code:	14895
Telephone:	(716) 593-0000
Gender:	Male
Date of Birth:	08-02-1994
Occupation:	
Employer:	
Spouse's Employer:	

INSURANCE INFORMATION:

Patient Number:	Final 4
Place of Service:	Office
Primary Insurance Plan:	Medicaid
Primary Insurance Plan ID #:	2356417
Group #:	
Primary Policyholder:	Eric Brown
Policyholder Date of Birth:	08-02-1994
Relationship to Patient:	Self
Secondary Insurance Plan:	
Secondary Insurance Plan ID #:	
Secondary Policyholder:	

Patient Status   ☐ Married   ☐ Divorced   ☒ Single   ☐ Student   ☐ Other

---

DIAGNOSIS INFORMATION

Diagnosis	Code	Diagnosis	Code
1. Flu	487.1	5.	
2.		6.	
3.		7.	
4.		8.	

PROCEDURE INFORMATION

Description of Procedure or Service	Date	Code	Charge
1. Office visit, level II, established patient	07-20-YYYY	99212	$30.00
2.			
3.			
4.			
5.			

SPECIAL NOTES:

Final Examination Case Study 5

GOODMEDICINE CLINIC

1 Provider Street ■ Anywhere NY 12345 ■ (607) 587-2222

NPI: 3345678901

Case Study

PROVIDER: HENRY C. CARDIAC, M.D.   EIN: 22-1234567   NPI: 3456789012

PATIENT INFORMATION:

Name:	Alicia Damrath
Address:	562 Maple Drive, Apt 5
City:	Anywhere
State:	NY
Zip Code:	11111
Telephone:	(101) 111-2123
Gender:	Female
Date of Birth:	06-30-1968
Occupation:	Instructor
Employer:	Community College
Spouse's Employer:	US Navy

INSURANCE INFORMATION:

Patient Number:	Final 5
Place of Service:	Office
Primary Insurance Plan:	TRICARE
Primary Insurance Plan ID #:	235623265
Group #:	
Primary Policyholder:	Philip Damrath (Colonel)
Policyholder Date of Birth:	05-30-1965
Relationship to Patient:	Spouse
Secondary Insurance Plan:	
Secondary Insurance Plan ID #:	
Secondary Policyholder:	

Patient Status   ☒ Married   ☐ Divorced   ☐ Single   ☐ Student   ☐ Other

---

DIAGNOSIS INFORMATION

Diagnosis	Code	Diagnosis	Code
1. Pregnancy	V22.1	5.	
2.		6.	
3.		7.	
4.		8.	

PROCEDURE INFORMATION

Description of Procedure or Service	Date	Code	Charge
1. Office visit, level III, new patient	08-15-YYYY	99203	$45.00
2.			
3.			
4.			
5.			

SPECIAL NOTES:

Patient stated LMP was 07-01-YYYY. Urine specimen taken for pregnancy test and done by hospital lab was positive.

Final Examination Case Study 6

GOODMEDICINE CLINIC

1 Provider Street ■ Anywhere NY 12345 ■ (607) 587-2222
NPI: 3345678901

Case Study

PROVIDER: NANCY J. HEALER, M.D.   EIN: 44-1234567   NPI: 6789012345

PATIENT INFORMATION:		INSURANCE INFORMATION:	
Name:	Deb Gilmore	Patient Number:	Final 6
Address:	5628 Route 244	Place of Service:	Office
City:	Belmont	Primary Insurance Plan:	Travelers WC
State:	NY	Primary Insurance Plan ID #:	
Zip Code:	11111	Group #:	
Telephone:	(607) 587-0000	Primary Policyholder:	Community College
Gender:	Female	Policyholder Date of Birth:	
Date of Birth:	03-01-1958	Relationship to Patient:	Employer
Occupation:	Professor	Address:	5 Main St
Employer:	Community College		Belmont NY, 11111
Spouse's Employer:			(607) 587-1111

Patient Status	☒ Married	☐ Divorced	☐ Single	☐ Student	☐ Other

DIAGNOSIS INFORMATION

Diagnosis	Code	Diagnosis	Code
1. Muscle spasms, upper back	728.85	5.	
2.		6.	
3.		7.	
4.		8.	

PROCEDURE INFORMATION

Description of Procedure or Service	Date	Code	Charge
1. Office visit, level III, new patient	08-25-YYYY	99203	$45.00
2.			
3.			
4.			
5.			

SPECIAL NOTES:

Workers' Compensation Claim #: 56298

Patient's SSN is 456-78-9123

ANSWER KEYS TO FINAL EXAMINATION CASE STUDIES
Final Exam 1 Empire Plan

[1500]

HEALTH INSURANCE CLAIM FORM

APPROVED BY NATIONAL UNIFORM CLAIM COMMITTE 08/05

| | PICA | | | | | | | | PICA | | |

1. MEDICARE (Medicare #) · MEDICAID (Medicaid #) · TRICARE CHAMPUS (Sponsor's SSN) · CHAMPVA (Member ID#) · GROUP HEALTH PLAN (SSN or ID) · FECA BLK LUNG (SSN) · OTHER [X] (ID)

1a. INSURED'S I.D. NUMBER (For Program in Item 1)
123456789

2. PATIENT'S NAME (Last Name, First Name, Middle Initial)
SMITH, MOLLY

3. PATIENT'S BIRTH DATE MM 01 DD 03 YY 1964   **SEX** M □   F [X]

4. INSURED'S NAME (Last Name, First Name, Middle Initial)
SMITH, MOLLY

5. PATIENT'S ADDRESS (No., Street)
3559 JERICHO HILL

6. PATIENT'S RELATIONSHIP TO INSURED
Self [X] Spouse □ Child □ Other □

7. INSURED'S ADDRESS (No., Street)
3559 JERICHO HILL

CITY COLLEGE TOWN   **STATE** NY

8. PATIENT STATUS
Single □ Married [X] Other □

CITY COLLEGE TOWN   **STATE** NY

ZIP CODE 14802   **TELEPHONE** (Include Area Code) (607) 5875555

Employed [X] Full-Time Student □ Part-Time Student □

ZIP CODE 14802   **TELEPHONE** (Include Area Code) (607) 5875555

9. OTHER INSURED'S NAME (Last Name, First Name, Middle Initial)

10. IS PATIENT'S CONDITION RELATED TO:

11. INSURED'S POLICY GROUP OR FECA NUMBER
1234

a. OTHER INSURED'S POLICY OR GROUP NUMBER

a. EMPLOYMENT? (Current or Previous)
□ YES [X] NO

a. INSURED'S DATE OF BIRTH MM 01 DD 03 YY 1964   **SEX** M □ F [X]

b. OTHER INSURED'S DATE OF BIRTH MM DD YY   **SEX** M □ F □

b. AUTO ACCIDENT?   PLACE (State)
□ YES [X] NO

b. EMPLOYER'S NAME OR SCHOOL NAME
LOCAL COLLEGE

c. EMPLOYER'S NAME OR SCHOOL NAME

c. OTHER ACCIDENT?
□ YES [X] NO

c. INSURANCE PLAN NAME OR PROGRAM NAME
EMPIRE PLAN

d. INSURANCE PLAN NAME OR PROGRAM NAME

10d. RESERVED FOR LOCAL USE

d. IS THERE ANOTHER HEALTH BENEFIT PLAN?
□ YES [X] NO *If yes,* return to and complete item 9 a-d.

READ BACK OF FORM BEFORE COMPLETING & SIGNING THIS FORM.

12. PATIENT'S OR AUTHORIZED PERSON'S SIGNATURE I authorize the release of any medical or other information necessary to process this claim. I also request payment of government benefits either to myself or to the party who accepts assignment below.
SIGNED SIGNATURE ON FILE   DATE

13. INSURED'S OR AUTHORIZED PERSON'S SIGNATURE I authorize payment of medical benefits to the undersigned physician or supplier for services described below.
SIGNED SIGNATURE ON FILE

14. DATE OF CURRENT: MM 07 DD 20 YY YYYY ILLNESS (First symptom) OR INJURY (Accident) OR PREGNANCY (LMP)

15. IF PATIENT HAS HAD SAME OR SIMILAR ILLNESS. GIVE FIRST DATE MM DD YY

16. DATES PATIENT UNABLE TO WORK IN CURRENT OCCUPATION
FROM MM DD YY   TO MM DD YY

17. NAME OF REFERRING PROVIDER OR OTHER SOURCE
17a.
17b. NPI

18. HOSPITALIZATION DATES RELATED TO CURRENT SERVICES
FROM MM DD YY   TO MM DD YY

19. RESERVED FOR LOCAL USE

20. OUTSIDE LAB? □ YES [X] NO   **$ CHARGES**

21. DIAGNOSIS OR NATURE OF ILLNESS OR INJURY (Relate Items 1, 2, 3 or 4 to Item 24E by Line)
1. V70 0
2.
3.
4.

22. MEDICAID RESUBMISSION CODE   ORIGINAL REF. NO.

23. PRIOR AUTHORIZATION NUMBER

24. A DATE(S) OF SERVICE From MM DD YY	To MM DD YY	B. PLACE OF SERVICE	C. EMG	D. PROCEDURES, SERVICES, OR SUPPLIES (Explain Unusual Circumstances) CPT/HCPCS MODIFER	E. DIAGNOSIS POINTER	F. $ CHARGES	G. DAYS OR UNITS	H. EPSDT Family Plan	I. ID. QUAL.	J. RENDERING PROVIDER ID. #
1	0720YYYY		11		99395	1	45 00	1		NPI	6789012345
2										NPI	
3										NPI	
4										NPI	
5										NPI	
6										NPI	

25. FEDERAL TAX I.D. NUMBER SSN EIN
441234567 [X]

26. PATIENT'S ACCOUNT NO.
FINAL 1

27. ACCEPT ASSIGNMENT? (For govt. claims, see back)
[X] YES □ NO

28. TOTAL CHARGE
$ 45 00

29. AMOUNT PAID
$ 8 00

30. BALANCE DUE
$ 37 00

31. SIGNATURE OF PHYSICIAN OR SUPPLIER INCLUDING DEGREES OR CREDENTIALS (I certify that the statements on the reverse apply to this bill and are made a part thereof.)
NANCY J HEALER MD
SIGNED   DATE MMDDYYYY

32. SERVICE FACILITY LOCATION INFORMATION
a. NPI   b.

33. BILLING PROVIDER INFO & PH # (607)5872222
GOODMEDICINE CLINIC
1 PROVIDER STREET
ANYWHERE NY 12345
a.3345678901 b.

APPROVED OMB-0938-0999 FORM CMS-1500 (08/05)

Final Exam 2 Medicare

[1500]

HEALTH INSURANCE CLAIM FORM

APPROVED BY NATIONAL UNIFORM CLAIM COMMITTE 08/05

							CARRIER

☐☐ PICA   PICA ☐☐

1. MEDICARE	MEDICAID	TRICARE CHAMPUS	CHAMPVA	GROUP HEALTH PLAN	FECA BLK LUNG	OTHER	1a. INSURED'S I.D. NUMBER (For Program in Item 1)
[X] (Medicare #)	☐ (Medicaid #)	☐ (Sponsor's SSN)	☐ (Member ID#)	☐ (SSN or ID)	☐ (SSN)	☐ (ID)	215353265B

2. PATIENT'S NAME (Last Name, First Name, Middle Initial)	3. PATIENT'S BIRTH DATE	SEX	4. INSURED'S NAME (Last Name, First Name, Middle Initial)
BROWN, JOE	MM 02 DD 08 YY 1930	M [X] F ☐	

5. PATIENT'S ADDRESS (No., Street)	6. PATIENT'S RELATIONSHIP TO INSURED	7. INSURED'S ADDRESS (No., Street)
ROUTE A1A	Self ☐ Spouse ☐ Child ☐ Other ☐	

CITY	STATE	8. PATIENT STATUS	CITY	STATE
COASTAL TOWN	NY	Single [X] Married ☐ Other ☐		

ZIP CODE	TELEPHONE (Include Area Code)		ZIP CODE	TELEPHONE (Include Area Code)
14802	(101) 1111325	Employed ☐ Full-Time Student ☐ Part-Time Student ☐		( )

9. OTHER INSURED'S NAME (Last Name, First Name, Middle Initial)	10. IS PATIENT'S CONDITION RELATED TO:	11. INSURED'S POLICY GROUP OR FECA NUMBER
		NONE

a. OTHER INSURED'S POLICY OR GROUP NUMBER	a. EMPLOYMENT? (Current or Previous) ☐ YES [X] NO	a. INSURED'S DATE OF BIRTH MM DD YY	SEX M ☐ F ☐

b. OTHER INSURED'S DATE OF BIRTH MM DD YY SEX M ☐ F ☐	b. AUTO ACCIDENT? PLACE (State) ☐ YES [X] NO	b. EMPLOYER'S NAME OR SCHOOL NAME

c. EMPLOYER'S NAME OR SCHOOL NAME	c. OTHER ACCIDENT? ☐ YES [X] NO	c. INSURANCE PLAN NAME OR PROGRAM NAME

d. INSURANCE PLAN NAME OR PROGRAM NAME	10d. RESERVED FOR LOCAL USE	d. IS THERE ANOTHER HEALTH BENEFIT PLAN? ☐ YES ☐ NO *If yes,* return to and complete item 9 a-d.

READ BACK OF FORM BEFORE COMPLETING & SIGNING THIS FORM.

12. PATIENT'S OR AUTHORIZED PERSON'S SIGNATURE I authorize the release of any medical or other information necessary to process this claim. I also request payment of government benefits either to myself or to the party who accepts assignment below.

SIGNED __SIGNATURE ON FILE__   DATE _____

13. INSURED'S OR AUTHORIZED PERSON'S SIGNATURE I authorize payment of medical benefits to the undersigned physcian or supplier for services described below.

SIGNED _____

14. DATE OF CURRENT: MM 07 DD 20 YY YYYY ◄ ILLNESS (First symptom) OR INJURY (Accident) OR PREGNANCY (LMP)	15. IF PATIENT HAS HAD SAME OR SIMILAR ILLNESS, GIVE FIRST DATE MM DD YY	16. DATES PATIENT UNABLE TO WORK IN CURRENT OCCUPATION FROM MM DD YY TO MM DD YY

17. NAME OF REFERRING PROVIDER OR OTHER SOURCE	17a.	18. HOSPITALIZATION DATES RELATED TO CURRENT SERVICES FROM MM DD YY TO MM DD YY
	17b. NPI	

19. RESERVED FOR LOCAL USE	20. OUTSIDE LAB? ☐ YES [X] NO	$ CHARGES

21. DIAGNOSIS OR NATURE OF ILLNESS OR INJURY (Relate Items 1, 2, 3 or 4 to Item 24E by Line)

1. |401 . 9   3. |___ . ___

2. |492 . 8   4. |___ . ___

22. MEDICAID RESUBMISSION CODE	ORIGINAL REF. NO.

23. PRIOR AUTHORIZATION NUMBER

24. A DATE(S) OF SERVICE From MM DD YY To MM DD YY	B. PLACE OF SERVICE	C. EMG	D. PROCEDURES, SERVICES, OR SUPPLIES (Explain Unusual Circumstances) CPT/HCPCS MODIFER	E. DIAGNOSIS POINTER	F. $ CHARGES	G. DAYS OR UNITS	H. EPSDT Family Plan	I. ID. QUAL.	J. RENDERING PROVIDER ID. #
1	0720YYYY	11		99214	1	35 00	1		NPI	3456789012
2									NPI	
3									NPI	
4									NPI	
5									NPI	
6									NPI	

25. FEDERAL TAX I.D. NUMBER SSN EIN	26. PATIENT'S ACCOUNT NO.	27. ACCEPT ASSIGNMENT? (For govt. claims, see back)	28. TOTAL CHARGE	29. AMOUNT PAID	30. BALANCE DUE
221234567 [X]	FINAL 2	[X] YES ☐ NO	$ 35 00	$	$

31. SIGNATURE OF PHYSICIAN OR SUPPLIER INCLUDING DEGREES OR CREDENTIALS (I certify that the statements on the reverse apply to this bill and are made a part thereof.)	32. SERVICE FACILITY LOCATION INFORMATION	33. BILLING PROVIDER INFO & PH # (607) 5872222
HENRY C CARDIAC MD	a. NPI b.	GOODMEDICINE CLINIC 1 PROVIDER STREET ANYWHERE NY 12345
SIGNED DATE MMDDYYYY		a. 3345678901 b. NPI

APPROVED OMB-0938-0999 FORM CMS-1500 (08/05)

PATIENT AND INSURED INFORMATION

PHYSICIAN OR SUPPLIER INFORMATION

Final Exam 3 Blue Cross

1500

HEALTH INSURANCE CLAIM FORM

APPROVED BY NATIONAL UNIFORM CLAIM COMMITTE 08/05

| | PICA | | | | | | | PICA | | |

1. MEDICARE	MEDICAID	TRICARE CHAMPUS	CHAMPVA	GROUP HEALTH PLAN	FECA BLK LUNG	OTHER	1a. INSURED'S I.D. NUMBER	(For Program in Item 1)
(Medicare #)	(Medicaid #)	(Sponsor's SSN)	(Member ID#)	(SSN or ID)	(SSN)	X (ID)	AJC67858	

2. PATIENT'S NAME (Last Name, First Name, Middle Initial)
PATRICK, MICHAEL

3. PATIENT'S BIRTH DATE MM DD YY
05 14 1957 **SEX** M X F

4. INSURED'S NAME (Last Name, First Name, Middle Initial)
PATRICK, MICHAEL

5. PATIENT'S ADDRESS (No., Street)
939 MAIN ST

6. PATIENT'S RELATIONSHIP TO INSURED
Self X Spouse Child Other

7. INSURED'S ADDRESS (No., Street)
939 MAIN ST

CITY HORNELL **STATE** NY

8. PATIENT STATUS
Single Married X Other

CITY HORNELL **STATE** NY

ZIP CODE 14843 **TELEPHONE** (Include Area Code) (607) 3245555

Employed Full-Time Student Part-Time Student

ZIP CODE 14802 **TELEPHONE** (Include Area Code) (607) 3245555

9. OTHER INSURED'S NAME (Last Name, First Name, Middle Initial)

10. IS PATIENT'S CONDITION RELATED TO:

11. INSURED'S POLICY GROUP OR FECA NUMBER
1234

a. OTHER INSURED'S POLICY OR GROUP NUMBER

a. EMPLOYMENT? (Current or Previous)
YES X NO

a. INSURED'S DATE OF BIRTH MM DD YY
05 14 1957 **SEX** M X F

b. OTHER INSURED'S DATE OF BIRTH MM DD YY **SEX** M F

b. AUTO ACCIDENT? PLACE (State)
YES X NO

b. EMPLOYER'S NAME OR SCHOOL NAME
LIGHT FACTORY

c. EMPLOYER'S NAME OR SCHOOL NAME

c. OTHER ACCIDENT?
YES X NO

c. INSURANCE PLAN NAME OR PROGRAM NAME
BLUECROSS

d. INSURANCE PLAN NAME OR PROGRAM NAME

10d. RESERVED FOR LOCAL USE

d. IS THERE ANOTHER HEALTH BENEFIT PLAN?
YES X NO *If yes,* return to and complete item 9 a-d.

READ BACK OF FORM BEFORE COMPLETING & SIGNING THIS FORM.
12. PATIENT'S OR AUTHORIZED PERSON'S SIGNATURE I authorize the release of any medical or other information necessary to process this claim. I also request payment of government benefits either to myself or to the party who accepts assignment below.

SIGNED SIGNATURE ON FILE DATE

13. INSURED'S OR AUTHORIZED PERSON'S SIGNATURE I authorize payment of medical benefits to the undersigned physcian or supplier for services described below.

SIGNED SIGNATURE ON FILE

14. DATE OF CURRENT: MM DD YY
05 01 YYYY
ILLNESS (First symptom) OR INJURY (Accident) OR PREGNANCY (LMP)

15. IF PATIENT HAS HAD SAME OR SIMILAR ILLNESS. GIVE FIRST DATE MM DD YY

16. DATES PATIENT UNABLE TO WORK IN CURRENT OCCUPATION
MM DD YY MM DD YY
FROM TO

17. NAME OF REFERRING PROVIDER OR OTHER SOURCE

17a.
17b. NPI

18. HOSPITALIZATION DATES RELATED TO CURRENT SERVICES
MM DD YY MM DD YY
FROM 05 01 YYYY TO 05 04 YYYY

19. RESERVED FOR LOCAL USE

20. OUTSIDE LAB? $ CHARGES
YES X NO

21. DIAGNOSIS OR NATURE OF ILLNESS OR INJURY (Relate Items 1, 2, 3 or 4 to Item 24E by Line)

1. 250.03
2.
3.
4.

22. MEDICAID RESUBMISSION CODE ORIGINAL REF. NO.

23. PRIOR AUTHORIZATION NUMBER

24. A DATE(S) OF SERVICE From MM DD YY	To MM DD YY	B. PLACE OF SERVICE	C. EMG	D. PROCEDURES, SERVICES, OR SUPPLIES (Explain Unusual Circumstances) CPT/HCPCS	MODIFER	E. DIAGNOSIS POINTER	F. $ CHARGES	G. DAYS OR UNITS	H. EPSDT Family Plan	I. ID. QUAL.	J. RENDERING PROVIDER ID. #
1	05 01 YYYY		21		99222		1	55 00	1		NPI	6789012345
2	05 02 YYYY	05 03 YYYY	21		99232		1	90 00	2		NPI	6789012345
3	05 04 YYYY		21		99238		1	35 00	1		NPI	6789012345
4											NPI	
5											NPI	
6											NPI	

25. FEDERAL TAX I.D. NUMBER SSN EIN
441234567 X

26. PATIENT'S ACCOUNT NO.
FINAL 3

27. ACCEPT ASSIGNMENT? (For govt. claims, see back)
X YES NO

28. TOTAL CHARGE
$ 180 00

29. AMOUNT PAID
$

30. BALANCE DUE
$

31. SIGNATURE OF PHYSICIAN OR SUPPLIER INCLUDING DEGREES OR CREDENTIALS (I certify that the statements on the reverse apply to this bill and are made a part thereof.)

SIGNED NANCY J HEALER MD DATE MMDDYYYY

32. SERVICE FACILITY LOCATION INFORMATION
GOODMEDICINE CLINIC
1 PROVIDER STREET
ANYWHERE NY 12345
a1123456789 b

33. BILLING PROVIDER INFO & PH # (607)5872222
GOODMEDICINE CLINIC
1 PROVIDER STREET
ANYWHERE NY 12345
a3345678901 b

NUCC Instruction Manual available at: www.nucc.org

APPROVED OMB-0938-0999 FORM CMS-1500 (08/05)

Final Exam 4 Medicaid

1500

HEALTH INSURANCE CLAIM FORM

APPROVED BY NATIONAL UNIFORM CLAIM COMMITTE 08/05

							PICA					PICA	

1. MEDICARE ☐ (Medicare #)   MEDICAID ☒ (Medicaid #)   TRICARE CHAMPUS ☐ (Sponsor's SSN)   CHAMPVA ☐ (Member ID#)   GROUP HEALTH PLAN ☐ (SSN or ID)   FECA BLK LUNG ☐ (SSN)   OTHER ☐ (ID)

1a. INSURED'S I.D. NUMBER (For Program in Item 1)
2356417

2. PATIENT'S NAME (Last Name, First Name, Middle Initial)
BROWN, ERIC

3. PATIENT'S BIRTH DATE   MM 08 DD 02 YY 1994   SEX M ☒ F ☐

4. INSURED'S NAME (Last Name, First Name, Middle Initial)

5. PATIENT'S ADDRESS (No., Street)
512 SHERIDAN DRIVE

6. PATIENT'S RELATIONSHIP TO INSURED
Self ☐ Spouse ☐ Child ☐ Other ☐

7. INSURED'S ADDRESS (No., Street)

CITY WELLSVILLE   STATE NY

8. PATIENT STATUS
Single ☒ Married ☐ Other ☐
Employed ☐ Full-Time Student ☐ Part-Time Student ☐

CITY   STATE

ZIP CODE 14895   TELEPHONE (Include Area Code) (716) 5930000

ZIP CODE   TELEPHONE (Include Area Code) ( )

9. OTHER INSURED'S NAME (Last Name, First Name, Middle Initial)

10. IS PATIENT'S CONDITION RELATED TO:

11. INSURED'S POLICY GROUP OR FECA NUMBER

a. OTHER INSURED'S POLICY OR GROUP NUMBER

a. EMPLOYMENT? (Current or Previous) YES ☐ NO ☒

a. INSURED'S DATE OF BIRTH MM DD YY   SEX M ☐ F ☐

b. OTHER INSURED'S DATE OF BIRTH MM DD YY   SEX M ☐ F ☐

b. AUTO ACCIDENT? PLACE (State) YES ☐ NO ☒

b. EMPLOYER'S NAME OR SCHOOL NAME

c. EMPLOYER'S NAME OR SCHOOL NAME

c. OTHER ACCIDENT? YES ☐ NO ☒

c. INSURANCE PLAN NAME OR PROGRAM NAME

d. INSURANCE PLAN NAME OR PROGRAM NAME

10d. RESERVED FOR LOCAL USE

d. IS THERE ANOTHER HEALTH BENEFIT PLAN? YES ☐ NO ☐ *If yes,* return to and complete item 9 a-d.

READ BACK OF FORM BEFORE COMPLETING & SIGNING THIS FORM.

12. PATIENT'S OR AUTHORIZED PERSON'S SIGNATURE I authorize the release of any medical or other information necessary to process this claim. I also request payment of government benefits either to myself or to the party who accepts assignment below.

SIGNED SIGNATURE ON FILE   DATE

13. INSURED'S OR AUTHORIZED PERSON'S SIGNATURE I authorize payment of medical benefits to the undersigned physcian or supplier for services described below.

SIGNED

14. DATE OF CURRENT: MM DD YY ◄ ILLNESS (First symptom) OR INJURY (Accident) OR PREGNANCY (LMP)

15. IF PATIENT HAS HAD SAME OR SIMILAR ILLNESS, GIVE FIRST DATE MM DD YY

16. DATES PATIENT UNABLE TO WORK IN CURRENT OCCUPATION FROM MM DD YY TO MM DD YY

17. NAME OF REFERRING PROVIDER OR OTHER SOURCE
17a.
17b. NPI

18. HOSPITALIZATION DATES RELATED TO CURRENT SERVICES FROM MM DD YY TO MM DD YY

19. RESERVED FOR LOCAL USE

20. OUTSIDE LAB? YES ☐ NO ☒ $ CHARGES

21. DIAGNOSIS OR NATURE OF ILLNESS OR INJURY (Relate Items 1, 2, 3 or 4 to Item 24E by Line)
1. 487 1
2.
3.
4.

22. MEDICAID RESUBMISSION CODE   ORIGINAL REF. NO.

23. PRIOR AUTHORIZATION NUMBER

24. A	DATE(S) OF SERVICE		B. PLACE OF SERVICE	C. EMG	D. PROCEDURES, SERVICES, OR SUPPLIES (Explain Unusual Circumstances)		E. DIAGNOSIS POINTER	F. $ CHARGES	G. DAYS OR UNITS	H. EPSDT Family Plan	I. ID. QUAL.	J. RENDERING PROVIDER ID. #
	From MM DD YY	To MM DD YY			CPT/HCPCS	MODIFER						
1	0720YYYY		11		99212		1	30 00	1		NPI	3456789012
2											NPI	
3											NPI	
4											NPI	
5											NPI	
6											NPI	

25. FEDERAL TAX I.D. NUMBER   SSN ☐ EIN ☒
221234567

26. PATIENT'S ACCOUNT NO.
FINAL 4

27. ACCEPT ASSIGNMENT? (For govt. claims, see back) YES ☒ NO ☐

28. TOTAL CHARGE $ 30 00

29. AMOUNT PAID $

30. BALANCE DUE $

31. SIGNATURE OF PHYSICIAN OR SUPPLIER INCLUDING DEGREES OR CREDENTIALS (I certify that the statements on the reverse apply to this bill and are made a part thereof.)
HENRY C CARDIAC MD
SIGNED   DATE MMDDYYYY

32. SERVICE FACILITY LOCATION INFORMATION
a. NPI   b.

33. BILLING PROVIDER INFO & PH # (607) 5872222
GOODMEDICINE CLINIC
1 PROVIDER STREET
ANYWHERE NY 12345
a. 3345678901   b.

NUCC Instruction Manual available at: www.nucc.org

APPROVED OMB-0938-0999 FORM CMS-1500 (08/05)

Final Exam 5 TRICARE

[1500]

HEALTH INSURANCE CLAIM FORM

APPROVED BY NATIONAL UNIFORM CLAIM COMMITTE 08/05

| | PICA | | | | | | | | PICA | |

1. MEDICARE (Medicare #)   **MEDICAID** (Medicaid #)   **TRICARE CHAMPUS** [X] (Sponsor's SSN)   **CHAMPVA** (Member ID#)   **GROUP HEALTH PLAN** (SSN or ID)   **FECA BLK LUNG** (SSN)   **OTHER** (ID)

1a. INSURED'S I.D. NUMBER (For Program in Item 1)
235623265

2. PATIENT'S NAME (Last Name, First Name, Middle Initial)
DAMRATH, ALICIA

3. PATIENT'S BIRTH DATE MM 06 DD 03 YY 1968   **SEX** M [X] F

4. INSURED'S NAME (Last Name, First Name, Middle Initial)
DAMRATH, PHILIP

5. PATIENT'S ADDRESS (No., Street)
562 MAPLE DRIVE APT 5

6. PATIENT'S RELATIONSHIP TO INSURED
Self   Spouse [X]   Child   Other

7. INSURED'S ADDRESS (No., Street)
562 MAPLE DRIVE APT 5

CITY ANYWHERE   **STATE** NY

8. PATIENT STATUS Single   Married [X]   Other

CITY ANYWHERE   **STATE** NY

ZIP CODE 11111   **TELEPHONE (Include Area Code)** (101) 1112123

Employed [X]   Full-Time Student   Part-Time Student

ZIP CODE 11111   **TELEPHONE (Include Area Code)** (101) 1112123

9. OTHER INSURED'S NAME (Last Name, First Name, Middle Initial)

10. IS PATIENT'S CONDITION RELATED TO:

11. INSURED'S POLICY GROUP OR FECA NUMBER

a. OTHER INSURED'S POLICY OR GROUP NUMBER

a. EMPLOYMENT? (Current or Previous) YES [X] NO

a. INSURED'S DATE OF BIRTH MM DD YY   **SEX** M F

b. OTHER INSURED'S DATE OF BIRTH MM DD YY   **SEX** M F

b. AUTO ACCIDENT? YES [X] NO   **PLACE (State)**

b. EMPLOYER'S NAME OR SCHOOL NAME

c. EMPLOYER'S NAME OR SCHOOL NAME

c. OTHER ACCIDENT? YES [X] NO

c. INSURANCE PLAN NAME OR PROGRAM NAME

d. INSURANCE PLAN NAME OR PROGRAM NAME

10d. RESERVED FOR LOCAL USE

d. IS THERE ANOTHER HEALTH BENEFIT PLAN? YES [X] NO   *If yes,* return to and complete item 9 a-d.

READ BACK OF FORM BEFORE COMPLETING & SIGNING THIS FORM.
12. PATIENT'S OR AUTHORIZED PERSON'S SIGNATURE I authorize the release of any medical or other information necessary to process this claim. I also request payment of government benefits either to myself or to the party who accepts assignment below.

SIGNED   SIGNATURE ON FILE   DATE

13. INSURED'S OR AUTHORIZED PERSON'S SIGNATURE I authorize payment of medical benefits to the undersigned physician or supplier for services described below.

SIGNED   SIGNATURE ON FILE

14. DATE OF CURRENT: MM 07 DD 01 YY YYYY   ILLNESS (First symptom) OR INJURY (Accident) OR PREGNANCY (LMP)

15. IF PATIENT HAS HAD SAME OR SIMILAR ILLNESS, GIVE FIRST DATE MM DD YY

16. DATES PATIENT UNABLE TO WORK IN CURRENT OCCUPATION FROM MM DD YY TO MM DD YY

17. NAME OF REFERRING PROVIDER OR OTHER SOURCE
17a.
17b. NPI

18. HOSPITALIZATION DATES RELATED TO CURRENT SERVICES FROM MM DD YY TO MM DD YY

19. RESERVED FOR LOCAL USE

20. OUTSIDE LAB? YES [X] NO   **$ CHARGES**

21. DIAGNOSIS OR NATURE OF ILLNESS OR INJURY (Relate Items 1, 2, 3 or 4 to Item 24E by Line)
1. V22.1
2.
3.
4.

22. MEDICAID RESUBMISSION CODE   ORIGINAL REF. NO.

23. PRIOR AUTHORIZATION NUMBER

24. A DATE(S) OF SERVICE From MM DD YY	To MM DD YY	B. PLACE OF SERVICE	C. EMG	D. PROCEDURES, SERVICES, OR SUPPLIES (Explain Unusual Circumstances) CPT/HCPCS	MODIFIER	E. DIAGNOSIS POINTER	F. $ CHARGES	G. DAYS OR UNITS	H. EPSDT Family Plan	I. ID. QUAL.	J. RENDERING PROVIDER ID. #
1	0815YYYY		11		99203		1	45 00	1		NPI	3456789012
2											NPI	
3											NPI	
4											NPI	
5											NPI	
6											NPI	

25. FEDERAL TAX I.D. NUMBER 221234567   **SSN EIN** [X]

26. PATIENT'S ACCOUNT NO. FINAL 5

27. ACCEPT ASSIGNMENT? (For govt. claims, see back) [X] YES   NO

28. TOTAL CHARGE $ 45 00

29. AMOUNT PAID $

30. BALANCE DUE $ 45 00

31. SIGNATURE OF PHYSICIAN OR SUPPLIER INCLUDING DEGREES OR CREDENTIALS (I certify that the statements on the reverse apply to this bill and are made a part thereof.)

SIGNED HENRY C CARDIAC MD   DATE MMDDYYYY

32. SERVICE FACILITY LOCATION INFORMATION
a. NPI   b.

33. BILLING PROVIDER INFO & PH # (607) 5872222
GOODMEDICINE CLINIC
1 PROVIDER STREET
ANYWHERE NY 12345
a. 3345678901   b.

NUCC Instruction Manual available at: www.nucc.org

APPROVED OMB-0938-0999 FORM CMS-1500 (08/05)

Final Exam 6 Traveler's Workers' Compensation

[1500]

HEALTH INSURANCE CLAIM FORM

APPROVED BY NATIONAL UNIFORM CLAIM COMMITTE 08/05

| | PICA | | | | | | | | PICA | | |

1. MEDICARE	MEDICAID	TRICARE CHAMPUS	CHAMPVA	GROUP HEALTH PLAN	FECA BLK LUNG	OTHER	1a. INSURED'S I.D. NUMBER (For Program in Item 1)
(Medicare #)	(Medicaid #)	(Sponsor's SSN)	(Member ID#)	(SSN or ID) [X]	(SSN)	(ID)	456789123

2. PATIENT'S NAME (Last Name, First Name, Middle Initial)	3. PATIENT'S BIRTH DATE SEX	4. INSURED'S NAME (Last Name, First Name, Middle Initial)
GILMORE, DEB	MM 03 DD 01 YY 1958 M [ ] F [X]	COMMUNITY COLLEGE

5. PATIENT'S ADDRESS (No., Street)	6. PATIENT'S RELATIONSHIP TO INSURED	7. INSURED'S ADDRESS (No., Street)
5628 ROUTE 244	Self [ ] Spouse [ ] Child [ ] Other [X]	5 MAIN ST

CITY	STATE	8. PATIENT STATUS	CITY	STATE
BELMONT	NY	Single [ ] Married [ ] Other [ ]	BELMONT	NY

ZIP CODE	TELEPHONE (Include Area Code)		ZIP CODE	TELEPHONE (Include Area Code)
11111	(607) 5870000	Employed [X] Full-Time Student [ ] Part-Time Student [ ]	11111	(607) 5871111

9. OTHER INSURED'S NAME (Last Name, First Name, Middle Initial)	10. IS PATIENT'S CONDITION RELATED TO:	11. INSURED'S POLICY GROUP OR FECA NUMBER
		56298

a. OTHER INSURED'S POLICY OR GROUP NUMBER	a. EMPLOYMENT? (Current or Previous) [X] YES [ ] NO	a. INSURED'S DATE OF BIRTH MM DD YY SEX M [ ] F [ ]

b. OTHER INSURED'S DATE OF BIRTH MM DD YY SEX M [ ] F [ ]	b. AUTO ACCIDENT? PLACE (State) [ ] YES [X] NO	b. EMPLOYER'S NAME OR SCHOOL NAME COMMUNITY COLLEGE

c. EMPLOYER'S NAME OR SCHOOL NAME	c. OTHER ACCIDENT? [ ] YES [X] NO	c. INSURANCE PLAN NAME OR PROGRAM NAME TRAVELERS WC

d. INSURANCE PLAN NAME OR PROGRAM NAME	10d. RESERVED FOR LOCAL USE	d. IS THERE ANOTHER HEALTH BENEFIT PLAN? [ ] YES [ ] NO **If yes,** return to and complete item 9 a-d.

READ BACK OF FORM BEFORE COMPLETING & SIGNING THIS FORM.

12. PATIENT'S OR AUTHORIZED PERSON'S SIGNATURE I authorize the release of any medical or other information necessary to process this claim. I also request payment of government benefits either to myself or to the party who accepts assignment below.

SIGNED _____ DATE _____

13. INSURED'S OR AUTHORIZED PERSON'S SIGNATURE I authorize payment of medical benefits to the undersigned physician or supplier for services described below.

SIGNED _____

14. DATE OF CURRENT: MM DD YY 08 25 YYYY	ILLNESS (First symptom) OR INJURY (Accident) OR PREGNANCY (LMP)	15. IF PATIENT HAS HAD SAME OR SIMILAR ILLNESS. GIVE FIRST DATE MM DD YY	16. DATES PATIENT UNABLE TO WORK IN CURRENT OCCUPATION MM DD YY FROM TO MM DD YY

17. NAME OF REFERRING PROVIDER OR OTHER SOURCE	17a.	18. HOSPITALIZATION DATES RELATED TO CURRENT SERVICES MM DD YY FROM TO MM DD YY
	17b. NPI	

19. RESERVED FOR LOCAL USE	20. OUTSIDE LAB? [ ] YES [X] NO $ CHARGES

21. DIAGNOSIS OR NATURE OF ILLNESS OR INJURY (Relate Items 1, 2, 3 or 4 to Item 24E by Line)

1. 728 . 85   3. ___ . ___

2. ___ . ___   4. ___ . ___

22. MEDICAID RESUBMISSION CODE ORIGINAL REF. NO.
23. PRIOR AUTHORIZATION NUMBER

24. A. DATE(S) OF SERVICE From To MM DD YY MM DD YY	B. PLACE OF SERVICE	C. EMG	D. PROCEDURES, SERVICES, OR SUPPLIES (Explain Unusual Circumstances) CPT/HCPCS	MODIFER	E. DIAGNOSIS POINTER	F. $ CHARGES	G. DAYS OR UNITS	H. EPSDT Family Plan	I. ID. QUAL.	J. RENDERING PROVIDER ID. #
1	08 25 YYYY	11		99203		1	45 00	1		NPI	6789012345
2										NPI	
3										NPI	
4										NPI	
5										NPI	
6										NPI	

25. FEDERAL TAX I.D. NUMBER SSN EIN	26. PATIENT'S ACCOUNT NO.	27. ACCEPT ASSIGNMENT? (For govt. claims, see back)	28. TOTAL CHARGE	29. AMOUNT PAID	30. BALANCE DUE
441234567 [X]	FINAL 6	[X] YES [ ] NO	$ 45 00	$	$

31. SIGNATURE OF PHYSICIAN OR SUPPLIER INCLUDING DEGREES OR CREDENTIALS (I certify that the statements on the reverse apply to this bill and are made a part thereof.) NANCY J HEALER MD SIGNED DATE MMDDYYYY	32. SERVICE FACILITY LOCATION INFORMATION a. NPI b.	33. BILLING PROVIDER INFO & PH # (607) 5872222 GOODMEDICINE CLINIC 1 PROVIDER STREET ANYWHERE NY 12345 a. 3345678901 b.

NUCC Instruction Manual available at: www.nucc.org

APPROVED OMB-0938-0999 FORM CMS-1500 (08/05)

BLANK CMS-1500 CLAIM

1500

HEALTH INSURANCE CLAIM FORM

APPROVED BY NATIONAL UNIFORM CLAIM COMMITTE 08/05

| | PICA |

| PICA | | |

| 1. MEDICARE MEDICAID TRICARE CHAMPUS CHAMPVA GROUP HEALTH PLAN FECA BLK LUNG OTHER | 1a. INSURED'S I.D. NUMBER   (For Program in Item 1) |
| (Medicare #) (Medicaid #) (Sponsor's SSN) (Member ID#) (SSN or ID) (SSN) (ID) | |

2. PATIENT'S NAME (Last Name, First Name, Middle Initial)

3. PATIENT'S BIRTH DATE MM DD YY   SEX   M   F

4. INSURED'S NAME (Last Name, First Name, Middle Initial)

5. PATIENT'S ADDRESS (No., Street)

6. PATIENT'S RELATIONSHIP TO INSURED   Self   Spouse   Child   Other

7. INSURED'S ADDRESS (No., Street)

CITY   STATE

8. PATIENT STATUS   Single   Married   Other

CITY   STATE

ZIP CODE   TELEPHONE (Include Area Code) (   )

Employed   Full-Time Student   Part-Time Student

ZIP CODE   TELEPHONE (Include Area Code) (   )

9. OTHER INSURED'S NAME (Last Name, First Name, Middle Initial)

10. IS PATIENT'S CONDITION RELATED TO:

11. INSURED'S POLICY GROUP OR FECA NUMBER

a. OTHER INSURED'S POLICY OR GROUP NUMBER

a. EMPLOYMENT? (Current or Previous)   YES   NO

a. INSURED'S DATE OF BIRTH MM DD YY   SEX   M   F

b. OTHER INSURED'S DATE OF BIRTH MM DD YY   SEX   M   F

b. AUTO ACCIDENT?   PLACE (State)   YES   NO

b. EMPLOYER'S NAME OR SCHOOL NAME

c. EMPLOYER'S NAME OR SCHOOL NAME

c. OTHER ACCIDENT?   YES   NO

c. INSURANCE PLAN NAME OR PROGRAM NAME

d. INSURANCE PLAN NAME OR PROGRAM NAME

10d. RESERVED FOR LOCAL USE

d. IS THERE ANOTHER HEALTH BENEFIT PLAN?   YES   NO   *If yes,* return to and complete item 9 a-d.

READ BACK OF FORM BEFORE COMPLETING & SIGNING THIS FORM.

12. PATIENT'S OR AUTHORIZED PERSON'S SIGNATURE I authorize the release of any medical or other information necessary to process this claim. I also request payment of government benefits either to myself or to the party who accepts assignment below.

SIGNED _____ DATE _____

13. INSURED'S OR AUTHORIZED PERSON'S SIGNATURE I authorize payment of medical benefits to the undersigned physcian or supplier for services described below.

SIGNED _____

14. DATE OF CURRENT: MM DD YY   ILLNESS (First symptom) OR INJURY (Accident) OR PREGNANCY (LMP)

15. IF PATIENT HAS HAD SAME OR SIMILAR ILLNESS, GIVE FIRST DATE MM DD YY

16. DATES PATIENT UNABLE TO WORK IN CURRENT OCCUPATION MM DD YY FROM TO MM DD YY

17. NAME OF REFERRING PROVIDER OR OTHER SOURCE

17a.

17b. NPI

18. HOSPITALIZATION DATES RELATED TO CURRENT SERVICES MM DD YY FROM TO MM DD YY

19. RESERVED FOR LOCAL USE

20. OUTSIDE LAB?   YES   NO $ CHARGES

21. DIAGNOSIS OR NATURE OF ILLNESS OR INJURY (Relate Items 1, 2, 3 or 4 to Item 24E by Line)

1. _____ . _____

2. _____ . _____

3. _____ . _____

4. _____ . _____

22. MEDICAID RESUBMISSION CODE   ORIGINAL REF. NO.

23. PRIOR AUTHORIZATION NUMBER

24. A DATE(S) OF SERVICE			B. PLACE OF SERVICE	C. EMG	D. PROCEDURES, SERVICES, OR SUPPLIES (Explain Unusual Circumstances)		E. DIAGNOSIS POINTER	F. $ CHARGES	G. DAYS OR UNITS	H. EPSDT Family Plan	I. ID. QUAL.	J. RENDERING PROVIDER ID. #
From		To			CPT/HCPCS	MODIFER						
MM DD YY	MM DD YY											
1											NPI	
2											NPI	
3											NPI	
4											NPI	
5											NPI	
6											NPI	

25. FEDERAL TAX I.D. NUMBER   SSN EIN

26. PATIENT'S ACCOUNT NO.

27. ACCEPT ASSIGNMENT? (For govt. claims, see back)   YES   NO

28. TOTAL CHARGE $

29. AMOUNT PAID $

30. BALANCE DUE $

31. SIGNATURE OF PHYSICIAN OR SUPPLIER INCLUDING DEGREES OR CREDENTIALS (I certify that the statements on the reverse apply to this bill and are made a part thereof.)

SIGNED _____ DATE _____

32. SERVICE FACILITY LOCATION INFORMATION

a. NPI b.

33. BILLING PROVIDER INFO & PH # (   )

a. NPI b.

NUCC Instruction Manual available at: www.nucc.org

APPROVED OMB-0938-0999 FORM CMS-1500 (08/05)

Side labels: CARRIER — PATIENT AND INSURED INFORMATION — PHYSICIAN OR SUPPLIER INFORMATION

BLANK CASE STUDY FOR CUSTOMIZING TESTS

GOODMEDICINE CLINIC

1 Provider Street ■ Anywhere NY 12345 ■ (607) 587-2222
NPI: 3345678901

Case Study

PROVIDER: EIN: NPI:

PATIENT INFORMATION:

Name:

Address:

City:

State:

Zip Code:

Telephone:

Gender:

Date of Birth:

Occupation:

Employer:

Spouse's Employer:

INSURANCE INFORMATION:

Patient Number:

Place of Service:

Primary Insurance Plan:

Primary Insurance Plan ID #:

Group #:

Primary Policyholder:

Policyholder Date of Birth:

Relationship to Patient:

Secondary Insurance Plan:

Secondary Insurance Plan ID #:

Secondary Policyholder:

Patient Status   ☐ Married   ☐ Divorced   ☐ Single   ☐ Student   ☐ Other

DIAGNOSIS INFORMATION

Diagnosis	Code	Diagnosis	Code
1.		5.	
2.		6.	
3.		7.	
4.		8.	

PROCEDURE INFORMATION

Description of Procedure or Service	Date	Code	Charge
1.			
2.			
3.			
4.			
5.			

SPECIAL NOTES:

BLANK PATIENT RECORD FOR CUSTOMIZING TESTS

GOODMEDICINE CLINIC

1 Provider Street ■ Anywhere NY 12345 ■ (607) 587-2222

Patient Record

PROVIDER:

OFFICE VISIT

S:

O:

A:

P:

INPATIENT HOSPITALIZATION   Admission   Discharge:

PART 2: Instructor's Manual to Accompany the WORKBOOK

SECTION VI Answer Keys to Workbook Chapter Assignments

ANSWER KEY FOR WORKBOOK CASE STUDIES: ICD-9-CM CODES AND CPT/HCPCS CODES

This answer key is provided for your convenience in checking the CMS-1500 claims prepared for the case studies in Chapters 12 through 17. However, if you do not want your students to determine the codes, you can provide the codes for the appropriate case studies. This will allow the students to concentrate on completing the CMS-1500 claims accurately.

The ICD-9-CM codes reported in columns 1 through 4 of the following table represent the diagnoses for each case (reported in Block 24, #1 through #4, of the CMS-1500 claim). CPT codes in the remaining columns are listed in the order that they are to be reported on lines 1 through 6 of Block 24D of the CMS-1500 claim. (To justify medical necessity, link the diagnosis reference number with CPT code in Block 24E of the CMS-1500 claim.)

> **NOTE**: If a case requires the submission of multiple CMS-1500 claims, the case number contains a P (primary) and S (secondary) (e.g., 12-c-P, 12-c-S).

CASE NO.	ICD-9-CM CODES				CPT/HCPCS CODES				
12-a	784.0	786.2			99212				
12-b	466.0	034.0			99242	86403			
12-c-P	786.52	786.59			99213	93000			
12-c-S	786.52	786.59			99213	93000			
13-a	783.21	783.5	783.6		99204	81001			
13-b	346.01				99211				
13-c	372.10	692.9			99211				
13-d	372.10	372.50			99241				
13-e-P	728.85				99212				
13-e-S	728.85				99212				
14-a	611.72	611.71	V16.3		99212				
14-b	611.72	611.71	V16.3		99242				
14-c	569.3	787.91	783.21		99224	99233	99232	99238	
14-d	562.13				99254	99263			
14-e	401.0	780.2			99204	93000	36415		
14-f	485	786.3	599.7		99204	71020	81001		
14-g	695.3				99243				
15-a	626.2	626.4			99213				
15-b	626.2	626.4			99243				
15-c	719.07				99213				
15-d	826.0				99242	73660	28490		
15-e	V30.00				99431	99436	99432		
16-a	461.1	784.1			99202				

(continues)

(continued)

CASE NO.	ICD-9-CM CODES				CPT/HCPCS CODES				
16-b	575.11				99214				
16-c	575.11				47562				
16-d	787.1				99211				
16-e	780.6	780.79	783.0	783.21	99223	99233	99232	99232	
17-a	814.00	E884.2			99204				
17-b	802.0				99203				

CHAPTER 1   Health Insurance Specialist Career

ASSIGNMENT 1.1   Interview of a Professional

The student will submit a three-page, double-spaced, word-processed report on an interview of a professional; the paper should be in paragraph form (not written in a question/answer format). Each paragraph should include a minimum of three complete sentences, containing no typographical or grammatical errors. The last paragraph of the paper should summarize the student's reaction to the interview and whether the student would be interested in having this professional's position (along with why or why not). Also, the student should predict where she or he will be in 10 years (in terms of family, employment, and so on).

ASSIGNMENT 1.2   Ready, Set, Get a Job!

The student will submit a résumé and cover letter, using Figures 1-2 and 1-3 in the Workbook for guidance.

ASSIGNMENT 1.3   Journal Abstract

The student will submit a one-page, word-processed journal abstract, which should be evaluated to make sure it contains the following information:

- Name of article
- Name of author
- Name of journal
- Date of journal
- Journal article summary, in double-spaced paragraph format, that summarizes the article's content (and does not include the student's opinion about the content of the article)

ASSIGNMENT 1.4   Professional Discussion Forums (Listservs)

The student will go to the **list.nih.gov** Web site, and click on "What Is Listserv?" to learn about online discussion forums (listservs). The student will also select a professional discussion forum from Table 1-2 in the Workbook and follow its membership instructions. If this assignment is completed by a student outside of class, the instructor can require students to submit a summary of the experience (or, if teaching online, to post a discussion).

ASSIGNMENT 1.5 Learning About Professional Credentials

NOTE:

· Students will navigate each Web site to locate information needed to complete the table. This will help them learn how to locate information at professional association Web sites, which often requires using tool bars and pull-down menus.

· For AAPC credentials, individuals who hold two credentials must complete 48 CEUs per two-year cycle. Individuals with all three credentials (CPC, CPC-H, and CPC-P) must complete 60 CEUs per two-year cycle.

· For AHIMA credentials, individuals who hold multiple credentials must complete 30 CEUs per two-year cycle plus 10 CEUs for each additional credential, for a maximum 60 CEUs per two-year cycle.

American Academy of Professional Coders (AAPC) www.aapc.com					
Credential Abbreviation	**Meaning of Credential**	**Education Requirements**	**Experience Requirements**	**Exam Fee (member/ nonmember)**	**CEU Requirements**
CPC-A	Certified Professional Coder Apprentice	High school diploma or GED equivalent	AAPC membership, but has not met the two years of coding work experience required to take the CPC examination	$285	36 continuing education units (CEUs) every two years
CPC	Certified Professional Coder	High school diploma or GED equivalent	AAPC membership and two years of coding experience	$285	36 continuing education units (CEUs) every two years
CPC-H-A	Certified Professional Coder Hospital Apprentice	High school diploma or GED equivalent	AAPC membership, but has not met the two years of coding work experience required to take the CPC examination	$285	36 continuing education units (CEUs) every two years
CPC-H	Certified Professional Coder Hospital	High school diploma or GED equivalent	AAPC membership and two years of coding experience	$285	36 continuing education units (CEUs) every two years
CPC-P-A	Certified Professional Coder Payer Apprentice	High school diploma or GED equivalent	AAPC membership, but has not met the two years of coding work experience required to take the CPC examination	$285	36 continuing education units (CEUs) every two years
CPC-P	Certified Professional Coder Payer	High school diploma or GED equivalent	AAPC membership and two years of coding experience	$285	36 continuing education units (CEUs) every two years

American Health Information Management Association www.ahima.org					
Credential Abbreviation	**Meaning of Credential**	**Education Requirements**	**Experience Requirements**	**Exam Fee(member/ nonmember)**	**CEU Requirements**
CCA	Certified Coding Associate	High School Diploma or GED equivalent	Six months of coding experience or completion of an approved AHIMA coding certificate program	$195/$250	20 CEUs plus annual assessment, CEU cycle is two years
CCS	Certified Coding Specialist	High School Diploma or GED equivalent	Recommended three or more years of inpatient coding experience	$300/$385	20 CEUs plus annual assessment, CEU cycle is two years
CCS-P	Certified Coding Specialist - Physician-based	High School Diploma or GED equivalent	Recommended three or more years of inpatient coding experience	$300/$385	20 CEUs plus annual assessment, CEU cycle is two years

American Medical Billers Association www.ambanet.net					
Credential Abbreviation	**Meaning of Credential**	**Education Requirements**	**Experience Requirements**	**Exam Fee(member/ nonmember)**	**CEU Requirements**
CMRS	Certified Medical Reimbursement Specialist	High School Diploma or GED equivalent is recommended	Recommended experience in medical billing	$325	15 CEUs per year

ASSIGNMENT 1.6 Multiple Choice Review

1.	b	**11.**	b
2.	a	**12.**	d
3.	a	**13.**	c
4.	b	**14.**	c
5.	b	**15.**	d
6.	b	**16.**	b
7.	a	**17.**	c
8.	b	**18.**	a
9.	a	**19.**	b
10.	c	**20.**	c

CHAPTER 2 Introduction to Health Insurance

ASSIGNMENT 2.1 Health Insurance Coverage Statistics

1. Students will review Chapter 2 content about health insurance coverage statistics.

2a. Private insurance.

2b. There was an increase of 0.8 percent from 2002 to 2003.

> **NOTE:** 12.4% - 11.6% = -0.8%

2c. Military health care.

2d. The student may mention any two of the following:

- Increase in premium costs of employer-sponsored plans
- Increase in premium costs of private insurance plans
- Change in labor market; fewer individuals qualify for coverage
- Increase in poverty rate; more individuals qualify for Medicaid

2e. The student may mention any three of the following:

- No early preventive screening; disease not detected in early, more treatable stage
- No early intervention for disease; outcome not as favorable
- Patient may suffer from early death as health care risk factor screening may not be performed
- Increase in infection rate due to lack of treatment of infectious disease, passing the disease on to others and little or no education on infection control
- Injuries that are treatable may cause long-term problems with lack of medical care

3a. The percentage of the general population who had no break in health insurance coverage between the years 1996 to 1999.

3b. Women were more likely to have continuous health care coverage than men.

3c. The Hispanic population had the smallest percentage of individuals with continuous health insurance coverage.

3d. Each group is experiencing a slow, incremental increase year-to-year in the number of individuals who have continuous health insurance coverage.

4. Case Study: The student will create a pie chart in Microsoft Excel using the detailed instructions provided in the Workbook, which will look like the following image:

	A	B
1	Type of Health Insurance Coverage	Percentage of Patients Covered
2	HMO	45%
3	Medicaid	18%
4	Medicare	23%
5	Military	4%
6	Self-pay	10%

Percentage of Patients Covered by Health Insurance

- HMO
- Medicaid
- Medicare
- Military
- Self-pay

ASSIGNMENT 2.2 Major Developments in Health Insurance (Research Paper)

1. The student will complete the TILT tutorial and submit each TILT module quiz to the instructor's e-mail address.

2. The student will prepare an annotated bibliography that incorporates at least four of the following items:
   - Description of the content and/or focus of the article
   - Consideration of whether the article content is useful
   - Limitations of the article (e.g., outdated)
   - Audience for which the article is intended
   - Evaluation of any research methods used in the article
   - Author's background
   - Any conclusions the author(s) made about the topic
   - Student's reaction to the article

3. The student will review, sign, and submit the plagiarism policy (Figure 2-5 in the Workbook) to the instructor.

4. The student will submit a research paper (no more than five pages in length) that focuses on major developments in health insurance during a specific period of time. The paper will discuss the impact on health care quality, access, technology, reimbursement, and so on. The student will create a bibliography that cites a minimum of five references according to APA or MLA format, to be determined by the instructor.

ASSIGNMENT 2.3 COBRA Insurance

1. b
2. c
3. a
4. b
5. d

ASSIGNMENT 2.4 Multiple Choice Review

1. b   11. b
2. b   12. c
3. c   13. b
4. b   14. a
5. a   15. b
6. b   16. d
7. b   17. a
8. c   18. c
9. b   19. c
10. b   20. d

CHAPTER 3 Managed Health Care

ASSIGNMENT 3.1 National Committee for Quality Assurance (NCQA) Health Plan Report Card

The student will review the information on NCQA in Chapter 3 of the textbook and then go to the NCQA Web site to create a Health Plan Report Card. The student will also submit a one-page, double-spaced, word-processed document that summarizes the results of the report card generated. The following information should be included in the summary:

- Comparison of accreditation outcomes for the plans
- Number of health plans that earned an "excellent" rating
- Significance of an "excellent" rating

ASSIGNMENT 3.2 Managed Health Care Federal Legislation

The student will review Table 3-2, "Timeline for managed care federal legislation," in Chapter 3 of the textbook and select an act of legislation that the student believes most significantly influenced the growth of managed care. (More than one piece of legislation can be selected.) The student will conduct a literature search to locate at least 10 articles about the legislation selected and prepare a two- to three-page, double-spaced, word-processed document that summarizes the findings. The document should be organized as follows:

- The first paragraph should discuss the legislation the student selected as most significantly influencing the growth of managed care.
- The second and subsequent paragraphs should list reasons (from articles located via the literature search) that support the chosen legislation as being the most influential regarding the growth of managed care.
- The last paragraph will contain a conclusion about the growth of managed care as the result of the impact of the legislation that the student chose as being most influential.
- The student should include a bibliography of the 10 articles located during the literature search.

ASSIGNMENT 3.3 Joint Commission

The student will review the information on the Joint Commission in the textbook and then go to the Joint Commission Web site to complete their summary. The student will submit a one- to two-page summary, double-spaced, word-processed document that summarizes information on the Joint Commission. The following information should be included in the summary:

- Types of health care facilities that the Joint Commission accredits
- Types of certifications that the Joint Commission awards
- Define and discuss a sentinel event
- Discuss the Joint Commission's performance measurement initiatives

> **NOTE:** Students will navigate the Web site to locate information needed to complete the summary. This will help them learn how to locate information using the Internet and will require them to use tool bars and pull-down menus. Students will also gain the ability to use the Internet as a research tool.

ASSIGNMENT 3.4 HealthEast Care System

The student will review the information on HealthEast Care System in the textbook and then go to the HealthEast Web site to complete their summary. The student will submit a one to two-page, double-spaced, word-processed document that summarizes information on HealthEast. The following information should be included in the summary:

- Discussion/summary of HealthEast's privacy policy for payment purposes
- Summary and listing of the types of disease-focused programs offered by this IDS

- Discussion/summary of HealthEast's patient safety focus
- Discussion/summary of HealthEast's wellness program

NOTE: Students will navigate the Web site to locate information needed to complete the summary. This will help them learn how to locate information using the Internet and will require them to use tool bars and pull-down menus. Students will also gain the ability to use the Internet as a research tool.

ASSIGNMENT 3.5 CHIPA

1. Steps of the denial process include:
   - Consultation with medical director
   - Telephone peer review process (within 24 hours)
   - Verbal communication with patient and provider
   - Provider has right to appeal
2. Prospective reviews
3. Two to three days for inpatient stays and three to five days for partial inpatient admissions, and 10 to 14 for outpatient admissions.
4. Patients receive verbal information including authorization number, number of sessions authorized, and any plan limitations.
5. The patient has a DSM IV diagnosis that has been established by licensed provider. The patient also has an illness that has been determined to impair daily life activities, and the patient is motivated to get treatment.

ASSIGNMENT 3.6 Multiple Choice Review

1. b		**11.** d	
2. a		**12.** a	
3. c		**13.** b	
4. c		**14.** c	
5. d		**15.** d	
6. c		**16.** c	
7. b		**17.** b	
8. b		**18.** c	
9. d		**19.** d	
10. b		**20.** b	

CHAPTER 4   Development of an Insurance Claim

ASSIGNMENT 4.1 Payment of Claims: Encounter Form

1. TENDINITIS, 726.90
2. YES; ASSIGNMENT AND RELEASE
3. Block 14
4. Workers' Compensation
5. 99203, 99204, 99205
6. SERVICE PERFORMED
7. 99054—SERVICES SUN. & HOLIDAYS
8. REF. DR. & #
9. The diagnosis code does not correlate with the procedure performed; therefore, medical necessity is not proven. The health insurance specialist should consult with the provider to determine if either of the codes was selected in error and to obtain clarification.
10. Two: 93000, 93005

ASSIGNMENT 4.2 Payment of Claims: Remittance Advice

1. 235698, $905.00
2. $20.00
3. CPT code 99385 is for preventive care (e.g., annual physical exam), and the payer probably does not require patients to pay a coinsurance amount. Another reason is office staff might have forgotten to collect the coinsurance amount.
4. BAKE 1234567-01
5. $60.00
6. 454545544
7. 5
8. The $27.00 is the 20 percent coinsurance amount, based on the $135 billed amount.
9. $0.00
10. $65.00 (NET refers to the amount the provider billed the payer, or $65.00).
11. 05/08/YY
12. 46600
13. $420.00 (NET refers to the amount the provider billed the payer, or $420.00).
14. 11
15. $845.00
16. Amount provider billed payer
17. $190.00
18. $83.00
19. $0.00
20. BRIS396715-01
21. $75.00
22. 31055
23. 1-800-555-2468
24. $112.00
25. Place-of-service code
26. D.O. (Doctor of Osteopathy)
27. 05/22/YY
28. 05/31/YY

29. 2

30. $65.00

ASSIGNMENT 4.3 Payment of Claims: Explanation of Benefits

1. $40.25

2. $121.64

3. BLS 123456789

4. $40.25

5. $249.00

ASSIGNMENT 4.4 State Insurance Regulators

The student will review the information in the textbook on various terms used in the insurance industry (deductible, copay, etc.) and then go to the insurance information Web site to complete their summary. The student will submit a one- to two-page summary, double-spaced, word-processed document that summarizes information on a specific state insurance regulator. The information following may be included in the summary. There is a variety of information for each state site; students may provide different areas in their summary. All of the Web sites are different in format and in what is available on them.

- Mission statement
- Online services and publications
- Information on how to file a complaint
- Latest news
- Quality review activities

NOTE: Students will navigate the Web site to locate information needed to complete the summary. This will help them learn how to locate information using the Internet and will require them to use tool bars and pull-down menus. Students will also gain the ability to use the Internet as a research tool.

ASSIGNMENT 4.5 Multiple Choice Review

1.	c	**11.**	a
2.	d	**12.**	d
3.	c	**13.**	d
4.	a	**14.**	a
5.	c	**15.**	b
6.	b	**16.**	d
7.	a	**17.**	a
8.	b	**18.**	d
9.	d	**19.**	d
10.	c	**20.**	a

CHAPTER 5 Legal and Regulatory Issues

ASSIGNMENT 5.1 HIPAA: Student Confidentiality Statement

The student will review, complete, and sign the student confidentiality statement located in Figure 5-1 of the Workbook, and submit it to the instructor.

ASSIGNMENT 5.2 HIPAA: Preventing Health Care Fraud and Abuse

F   1. An insurance company agreed to pay the United States $87.3 million to settle health care fraud allegations that it and its predecessor companies violated the False Claims Act (FCA) with respect to claims submitted to the Office of Personnel Management (OPM). This represents the largest civil settlement involving the Federal Employees Health Benefits Program (FEHBP). (Permission to reuse in accordance with **www.cms.hhs.gov** Content Reuse and Linking policy.)

F   2. An actual state and county agreed to pay $73.3 million to resolve their civil liability under the FCA and Civil Monetary Penalties law for submitting claims for services provided to minors who were not Medicaid eligible. The settlement resolved allegations that the state and the county had fraudulently billed the federal health care program for services provided to minors when these jurisdictions had no basis for concluding that these individuals financially qualified for Medicaid services. (Permission to reuse in accordance with **www.cms.hhs.gov** Content Reuse and Linking policy.)

A   3. Providing unnecessary services (e.g., medical supplies) that the provider ordered in good faith is a form of health care abuse. Providers treat patients as they deem necessary, but Medicare (and other payers) do not always agree that the services are warranted (when compared to similar practices by the same type of provider). In this case, the provider did not intentionally overcharge or try to cheat the payer. (Permission to reuse granted by Stephen Barrett, M.D.)

F   4. An insurance company agreed to pay $76 million to settle allegations of misconduct (fraud) that occurred when the company served as a Medicare Part B carrier. The payer had submitted false information to CMS regarding the accuracy of and timeliness with which it handled those claims. In addition, the payer's former Medicare director was sentenced to 27 months in prison for conspiracy to falsify and conceal information from federal auditors. (Permission to reuse in accordance with **www.cms.hhs.gov** Content Reuse and Linking policy.)

A   5. Ordering a standard set of laboratory tests can be useful in some situations but not in others. The key question in judging whether a diagnostic test is necessary is whether the results will influence management of the patient. The provider felt he had documented medical necessity for each test. The payer disagreed and denied reimbursement (based on a comparison of testing practices of other similar providers). (Permission to reuse granted by Stephen Barrett, M.D.)

F   6. An insurance company paid $84 million to settle allegations of misconduct (fraud) after it was discovered that the company (1) breached its Medicare contract by failing to report errors identified in the quality assurance process; (2) concealed its true error rate by deleting claims selected for review by CMS and replacing them with claim files that would not significantly affect the error rate; and (3) allegedly hid documents, altered others, and falsified numerous reports. The company's Medicare carrier contract was terminated. (Permission to reuse in accordance with **www.cms.hhs.gov** Content Reuse and Linking policy.)

A   7. Diagnostic ultrasound procedures have many legitimate uses; however, ultrasonography is not appropriate for "diagnosing muscle spasm or inflammation" or for following the progress of patients treated for back pain. (Permission to reuse granted by Stephen Barrett, M.D.)

F   8. One of the nation's largest ambulance service providers agreed to pay the federal government $20 million to resolve its civil and administrative liability for false claims submitted to Medicare (fraud). The *qui tam* (lawsuit) action involved allegations that the ambulance subsidiary and certain of its predecessor companies had billed for medically unnecessary services, falsified certificates of medical necessity, and engaged in other improper billing practices. As part of the settlement, the ambulance service provider entered into a three-year corporate integrity agreement with the Department of Health and Human Services Office of Inspector General (HHS OIG). (Permission to reuse in accordance with **www.cms.hhs.gov** Content Reuse and Linking policy.)

__F__ 9. The consulting firm agreed to pay $9 million, plus interest, to the federal government to resolve allegations that the consultant had submitted false hospital cost reports (fraud) to the Medicare and Medicaid programs on behalf of client hospitals. The government alleged that the consulting firm knowingly made claims that were false, exaggerated, or ineligible for payment, and concealed errors from government auditors, thereby permitting the client hospitals to retain funds to which they were not entitled. The consulting firm also prepared "reserve" cost reports detailing nonallowable expenses and allocations contained in the filed cost reports and estimated the reimbursement impact in the event that these nonallowable expenses and allocations were detected on audit. (Permission to reuse in accordance with **www.cms.hhs.gov** Content Reuse and Linking policy.)

__A__ 10. A "spinal videofluoroscopy" procedure produces and records x-rays of the spinal joints to show the extent to which joint motion is restricted. Because physical examination procedures such as asking the patient to bend provide enough information to guide patient treatment, such testing is considered excessive and inappropriate. (Permission to reuse granted by Stephen Barrett, M.D.)

ASSIGNMENT 5.3 HIPAA: Privacy and Security Rules

__S__ 1. Defines authorized users of patient information to control access.

__S__ 2. Implements a tracking procedure to sign out records to authorized personnel.

__P__ 3. Establishes fines and penalties for misuse of protected health information.

__S__ 4. Limits record storage access to authorized users.

__P__ 5. Gives patients greater access to their own medical records and more control over how their personal health information is used.

__P__ 6. Creates national standards to protect individuals' medical records and other personal health information

__S__ 7. Requires that record storage areas be locked at all times.

__P__ 8. Addresses obligations that physicians, hospitals, and other health care providers have to obtain a patient's written consent and an authorization before using or disclosing PHI to carry out treatment, payment, or health care operations (TPO).

__P__ 9. Exempts psychotherapy notes from a patient's right to access to his or her own records.

__S__ 10. Requires the original medical record to remain in the facility at all times.

ASSIGNMENT 5.4 Covered Entities

1. What are the three types of covered entities specified in the HIPAA privacy rule? Health plans, health care clearinghouses, and health care providers that transmit electronic data

2. How many regions does the Office for Civil Rights divide the United States into to assign regional offices? Ten (10)

3. In what region are the states of Maryland and Virginia? Region III

4. In what city is the regional office of the OCR located in for the region VI? The city of Dallas

5. In addition to using the Web site, what other method can individuals use to find out more information about their privacy rights? Toll free phone number 1-866-627-7748

ASSIGNMENT 5.5 Multiple Choice Review

1. c		**11.** c
2. d		**12.** d
3. b		**13.** a
4. a		**14.** c
5. a		**15.** d
6. c		**16.** b
7. d		**17.** c
8. c		**18.** a
9. d		**19.** d
10. b		**20.** c

> **NOTE:** Students will navigate the Web site to locate information needed to complete the summary. This will help them learn how to locate information using the Internet and will require them to use tool bars and pull-down menus. Students will also gain the ability to use the Internet as a research tool.

CHAPTER 6 ICD-9-CM Coding

ASSIGNMENT 6.1 ICD-9-CM Index to Diseases

1. Acute <u>confusion</u>
2. Tension <u>headache</u>
3. Brain stem <u>infarction</u>
4. Allergic <u>bronchitis</u>
5. Bronchial <u>croup</u>
6. Newborn <u>anoxia</u>
7. Acute abdominal <u>cramp</u>
8. Insect <u>bite</u>
9. Radiation <u>sickness</u>
10. Car <u>sickness</u>

ASSIGNMENT 6.2 Basic Coding

1.	<u>053.9</u>	Herpes zoster
2.	<u>332.0</u>	Parkinson's disease
3.	<u>473.0</u>	Maxillary sinusitis
4.	<u>487.0</u>	Pneumonia with influenza
5.	<u>553.3</u>	Hiatal hernia
6.	<u>597.0</u>	Skene's gland abscess
7.	<u>692.4</u>	Skin eruption due to chemical product
8.	<u>695.9</u>	Infectional erythema
9.	<u>755.01</u>	Polydactyly of fingers
10.	<u>950.9</u>	Blindness due to injury

ASSIGNMENT 6.3 Multiple Coding

1.	<u>132.0; 373.6</u>	Parasitic infestation of eyelid due to pediculosis
2.	<u>055.0; 323.6</u>	Post-infectious encephalitis due to measles (20 years ago)
3.	<u>242.90; 337.1</u>	Peripheral neuropathy in hyperthyroidism
4.	<u>272.7; 330.2</u>	Cerebral degeneration due to Fabry's disease
5.	<u>359.2; 366.43</u>	Myotonic cataract due to Thomsen's disease
6.	<u>372.00; 372.10</u>	Acute and chronic conjunctivitis
7.	<u>272.5; 374.51</u>	Xanthelasma of the eyelid due to lipoprotein deficiency
8.	<u>385.31; 385.32</u>	Cholesteatoma, middle ear and attic
9.	<u>671.03; 454.2</u>	Varicose vein with inflammation and ulcer due to pregnancy, patient at 30 weeks
10.	<u>696.0; 696.2</u>	Psoriatic arthropathy and parapsoriasis

ASSIGNMENT 6.4 Combination Coding

1.	<u>250.10</u>	Diabetes with ketoacidosis
2.	<u>361.03</u>	Detached retina with giant tear
3.	<u>391.9</u>	Rheumatic fever with heart involvement
4.	<u>428.1</u>	Acute lung edema with heart disease
5.	<u>440.21</u>	Atherosclerosis of the extremities with intermittent claudication
6.	<u>491.22</u>	Emphysema with acute and chronic bronchitis
7.	<u>531.20</u>	Acute gastric ulcer with perforation and hemorrhage
8.	<u>562.11</u>	Diverticulosis with diverticulitis

9. <u>575.12</u>   Acute and chronic cholecystitis
10. <u>823.82</u>   Fractured fibula (closed) with tibia

ASSIGNMENT 6.5 Coding Hypertension

1. <u>401.1</u>   Hypertension, benign
2. <u>405.99; 239.6</u>   Hypertension due to brain tumor, unspecified
3. <u>404.01; 428.0</u>   Malignant hypertension with congestive heart failure
4. <u>760.0</u>   Newborn affected by maternal hypertension
5. <u>405.99</u>   Hypertensive disease due to pheochromocytoma
6. <u>459.10</u>   Chronic venous hypertension due to deep vein thrombosis
7. <u>401.0</u>   Malignant labile hypertension
8. <u>405.11</u>   Benign renovascular hypertension
9. <u>405.99</u>   Secondary hypertension due to Cushing's disease
10. <u>401.0</u>   Necrotizing hypertension

ASSIGNMENT 6.6 Coding Neoplasms

1. <u>146.0</u>   Carcinoma of the right palatine tonsil
2. <u>197.7</u>   Metastatic ovarian cancer to the liver
3. <u>151.9</u>   Stomach cancer
4. <u>214.8</u>   Lipoma of muscle of forearm
5. <u>170.7</u>   Osteosarcoma of the left femoral head
6. <u>237.70</u>   Neurofibromatosis
7. <u>201.20</u>   Hodgkin's sarcoma
8. <u>204.10</u>   Chronic lymphocytic leukemia
9. <u>200.02</u>   Intrathoracic reticulosarcoma
10. <u>154.8</u>   Adenocarcinoma of the rectum and anus

ASSIGNMENT 6.7 Assigning V Codes (Factors Influencing Health Status and Contact with Health Services)

1. <u>V65.41</u>   Exercise counseling
2. <u>V11.3</u>   Personal history of alcoholism
3. <u>V61.20</u>   Counseling for parent–child conflict
4. <u>V76.9</u>   Screening, cancer, unspecified
5. <u>V67.00</u>   Follow-up exam, postsurgery
6. <u>V70.0</u>   Health check, adult
7. <u>V20.2</u>   Routine child health check
8. <u>V52.2</u>   Fitting of artificial eye
9. <u>V04.81</u>   Flu shot
10. <u>V16.3</u>   Family history of breast cancer

ASSIGNMENT 6.8 Coding Burns, Fractures, and Late Effects

1. <u>943.29</u>   Second-degree burn, right upper arm and shoulder
2. <u>941.09</u>   Burns of the mouth, pharynx, and esophagus
3. <u>942.30</u>   Third-degree burn, trunk
4. <u>806.79</u>   Open fracture of coccyx with other spinal cord injury
5. <u>815.01</u>   Bennett's fracture, closed
6. <u>805.05</u>   Fifth cervical vertebra fracture, closed
7. <u>709.2; 906.7</u> Scarring due to third-degree burn of left arm
8. <u>438.20</u>   Hemiplegia due to old CVA

9. 959.2; 908.9   Flail arm due to car accident 10 years ago
10. 348.9; 326   Brain damage due to old cerebral abscess

ASSIGNMENT 6.9 Assigning E Codes (External Causes of Injury and Poisoning)

1. E963   Assault by hanging and strangulation
2. E930.0   Brain damage due to allergic reaction to penicillin
3. E958.5; E849.5   Self-inflicted injury by crashing of motor vehicle, highway
4. E928.1; E849.6   Exposure to noise at nightclub
5. E916; E849.2   Struck accidentally by falling rock at quarry
6. E906.0   Dog bite
7. E865.1; E849.6   Accidental poisoning from shellfish at restaurant
8. E871.0   Foreign object left in body during surgical operation
9. E881.0; E849.0   Fall from ladder at home
10. E922.2; E849.4   Accident caused by hunting rifle at rifle range

ASSIGNMENT 6.10 Coding Procedures

1. 70.12   Incision and drainage of pelvic abscess (female)
2. 13.19; 13.71   Cataract extraction with lens implant
3. 89.64   Insertion of Swan-Ganz catheter
4. 44.39   Jaboulay operation
5. 45.16   Esophagogastroduodenoscopy (EGD) with closed biopsy
6. 39.93   Replacement of arteriovenous shunt for renal dialysis
7. 20.01; 20.01   Insertion of bilateral myringotomy tubes
8. 98.51   Extracorporeal shock wave lithotripsy (ESWL) of staghorn calculus, left kidney
9. 72.51   Forceps delivery with partial breech extraction
10. 77.57   Repair of claw toe by tendon lengthening

ASSIGNMENT 6.11 Coding Patient Cases

1. PATIENT CASE #1

414.00   Coronary artery disease
278.00   Exogenous obesity
715.89   Degenerative joint disease involving multiple joints
V12.59   History of congestive heart failure
427.31   Atrial fibrillation
412   History of myocardial infarction

> **NOTE:** To assign the code for "History of myocardial infarction," the exclusion note below the code category of V12.5 directs you to code 412.

2. PATIENT CASE #2

781.2   Gait disorder
721.0   Cervical spondylosis
356.9   Peripheral neuropathy

3. **PATIENT CASE #3**

<u>272.4</u>	Hyperlipidemia
<u>414.00</u>	Coronary artery disease
<u>437.9</u>	Cerebrovascular disease
<u>530.81</u>	Esophageal reflux
<u>300.4</u>	Anxiety with depression

4. **PATIENT CASE #4**

<u>863.89</u>	Anal tear
<u>455.6</u>	Hemorrhoids

5. **PATIENT CASE #5**

<u>478.19</u>	Sinus pain
<u>719.45</u>	Right hip pain

ASSIGNMENT 6.12 ICD-9-CM Coding

1.	<u>112.4</u>	Pneumonia, Candidiasis of lung
2.	<u>115.95</u>	Histoplasmosis, Pneumonia NOS
3.	<u>480.8</u>	Pneumonia, viral NEC
4.	<u>280.9</u>	Anemia, iron deficiency, unspecified
5.	<u>381.6</u>	Otitis media, nonsuppurative with stenosis of the Eustachian Tube
6.	<u>401.1</u>	Hypertension, essential, benign
7.	<u>250.10</u>	Diabetes, with ketoacidosis, type II, not stated as uncontrolled
8.	<u>V77.91</u>	Hyperlipidemia, screening
9.	<u>789.07</u>	Abdominal pain, generalized
10.	<u>473.8</u>	Sinusitis, chronic, pansinusitis

NOTE: Students will need to navigate the encoder Web site using the terms provided in the exercise to locate the correct ICD-9-CM code. They also need to utilize the search text box on the Web site. The exercise is given in a manner to assist them in finding the code; for example, for Number 8 they should type in the term *hyperlipidemia* in the search text box on the site and then scroll down to the selection that says *screening for hyperlipidemia.*

ASSIGNMENT 6.13 Multiple Choice Review

1.	b	11.	a
2.	d	12.	c
3.	a	13.	b
4.	a	14.	b
5.	b	15.	c
6.	d	16.	c
7.	b	17.	a
8.	a	18.	b
9.	b	19.	b
10.	a	20.	a

CHAPTER 7 CPT Coding

ASSIGNMENT 7.1 CPT Index

1. Ankle <u>amputation</u>
2. Lower arm <u>biopsy</u>
3. <u>Artery</u> angioplasty
4. Bone marrow <u>aspiration</u>
5. Bladder <u>aspiration</u>
6. Bladder neck <u>resection</u>
7. Rib <u>resection</u>
8. Salivary duct <u>dilation</u>
9. Wrist <u>disarticulation</u>
10. <u>Drinking test</u> for glaucoma
11. <u>Dwyer procedure</u>
12. New patient <u>office</u> visit
13. <u>Well baby care</u>
14. <u>Wound repair</u> of pancreas
15. Inpatient hospital <u>discharge</u>

ASSIGNMENT 7.2 Evaluation and Management (E/M) Coding

1.	<u>99252</u>	Subsequent hospital care, expanded
2.	<u>99307</u>	Subsequent nursing facility care, problem focused
3.	<u>99201</u>	Initial office visit, problem focused
4.	<u>99218</u>	Initial observation care, detailed
5.	<u>99232</u>	New patient, inpatient consultation, detailed
6.	<u>99343</u>	Initial home visit, detailed
7.	<u>99350</u>	Follow-up home visit, comprehensive
8.	<u>99217</u>	Observation care discharge
9.	<u>99253</u>	Initial inpatient consult, detailed
10.	<u>99284</u>	Emergency Department (ED) visit, detailed

ASSIGNMENT 7.3 Anesthesia Coding

1.	<u>00560-P4</u>	Coronary angioplasty of two vessels; patient has severe coronary artery disease
2.	<u>00842-P2</u>	Amniocentesis; patient has petit mal epilepsy
3.	<u>00873-P2</u>	Extracorporeal shock wave lithotripsy; patient has controlled hypertension
4.	<u>00702-P3</u>	Percutaneous liver biopsy; patient has chronic alcoholism
5.	<u>01952-P1</u>	Debridement of third-degree burns of right arm, 6 percent body surface area; patient is two years old and otherwise healthy
6.	<u>01214-P2</u>	Total hip replacement, open procedure; patient has controlled diabetes mellitus
7.	<u>00454-P3</u>	Biopsy of clavicle; patient is postoperative mastectomy two years ago and is undergoing biopsy procedure for suspected metastatic bone cancer
8.	<u>01820-P1</u>	Hand cast application; patient is otherwise healthy
9.	<u>01464-P2</u>	Arthroscopic procedure of the ankle joint; patient has generalized arthritis
10.	<u>00864-P3</u>	Total cystectomy; patient has bladder cancer, which is localized

ASSIGNMENT 7.4 Surgery Coding

1.	<u>11403</u>	Excision, one-inch benign lesion, left leg
2.	<u>12002</u>	Simple repair of two-inch laceration on the right foot
3.	<u>12044</u>	Layer closure of three-inch stab wound of the neck
4.	<u>11622</u>	Excision, half-inch malignant lesion, left first finger
5.	<u>12035</u>	Intermediate repair of five-inch laceration of the right thigh
6.	<u>28505</u>	Open reduction with external fixation of fracture of great toe phalanx fracture
7.	<u>21320</u>	Closed reduction of nasal bone fracture with stabilization
8.	<u>29834</u>	Surgical elbow arthroscopy with removal of loose body
9.	<u>21198</u>	Segmental osteotomy of the mandible
10.	<u>26055</u>	Trigger finger release
11.	<u>31615</u>	Tracheobronchoscopy through existing tracheostomy incision
12.	<u>30450</u>	Secondary rhinoplasty with major reconstruction of nasal tip to correct results of an initial rhinoplasty done elsewhere
13.	<u>32661</u>	Surgical thoracoscopy with excision of pericardial tumor
14.	<u>32220</u>	Total pulmonary decortication
15.	<u>32540</u>	Extraplural enucleation of empyema
16.	<u>61697</u>	Direct repair of cerebral artery aneurysm
17.	<u>35556</u>	Femoral-popliteal bypass graft
18.	<u>33534</u>	Coronary artery bypass graft (using two arterial grafts)
19.	<u>75554</u>	Complete cardiac MRI with contrast
20.	<u>33217</u>	Insertion of dual-chamber pacemaker with electrodes
21.	<u>40701</u>	Complete cleft lip repair, primary bilateral, one-stage procedure
22.	<u>47610</u>	Laparoscopic cholecystectomy with exploration of the common duct
23.	<u>49250</u>	Umbilectomy
24.	<u>48152</u>	Pancreatectomy with Whipple procedure
25.	<u>49041</u>	Percutaneous drainage of subdiaphragmatic abscess
26.	<u>49500</u>	Inguinal hernia repair without hydrocelectomy; the patient is a 14-month-old male.
27.	<u>52240</u>	Cystourethroscopy with fulguration of large (6.5 cm) bladder tumor
28.	<u>50396</u>	Manometric studies through pyelostomy tube
29.	<u>50500</u>	Nephrorrhaphy of right kidney wound
30.	<u>51600</u>	Injection of contrast for voiding urethrocystography
31.	<u>54057</u>	Laser removal of three condylomata from penis
32.	<u>55705</u>	Incisional biopsy of the prostate
33.	<u>56440</u>	Marsupialization of Bartholin's gland cyst
34.	<u>58720</u>	Total bilateral salpingectomy and oophorectomy
35.	<u>59426</u>	Antepartum care, 10 visits
36.	<u>61154</u>	Burr holes with evacuation and drainage of subdural hematoma
37.	<u>62100</u>	Craniotomy for repair of cerebrospinal fluid leak and rhinorrhea
38.	<u>63003</u>	Thoracic laminectomy with exploration, two vertebrae
39.	<u>63615</u>	Stereotactic biopsy of spinal cord
40.	<u>64712</u>	Neuroplasty of the sciatic nerve
41.	<u>65093</u>	Evisceration of eye with implant
42.	<u>66761</u>	Laser iridectomy for glaucoma
43.	<u>68520</u>	Total dacryocystectomy
44.	<u>69210</u>	Removal of bilateral cerumen impaction
45.	<u>69930</u>	Successful cochlear implant

ASSIGNMENT 7.5 Radiology Coding

1. <u>70110</u>   Complete radiographic examination of the mandible
2. <u>74420</u>   Urography, retrograde
3. <u>74710</u>   Pelvimetry
4. <u>77073</u>   Orthoroentgenogram, scanogram
5. <u>71023</u>   Chest x-ray, two views, with fluoroscopy
6. <u>70150</u>   X-ray of the facial bones, four views
7. <u>74160</u>   CAT scan of the abdomen, with contrast
8. <u>78262</u>   Gastroesophageal reflux study
9. <u>72040</u>   X-ray of the cervical spine, two views
10. <u>74270</u>   Barium enema

ASSIGNMENT 7.6 Pathology and Laboratory Coding

1. <u>85041</u>   Red blood cell count
2. <u>82800</u>   Blood gases, pH only
3. <u>82955</u>   Glucose-6-phosphate dehydrogenase screen
4. <u>82960</u>   Glucose tolerance test, three specimens
5. <u>87210</u>   KOH prep
6. <u>86689</u>   HIV antibody and confirmatory test
7. <u>83718</u>   HDL cholesterol
8. <u>86403</u>   Rapid test for infection, screen, each antibody
9. <u>87530</u>   Herpes simplex virus, quantification
10. <u>81002</u>   Urine dip, nonautomated, without microscopy

ASSIGNMENT 7.7 Medicine Coding

1. <u>93530</u>   Right heart catheterization, for congenital cardiac anomalies
2. <u>99075</u>   Medical testimony
3. <u>99050</u>   Services requested between 10:00 p.m. and 8:00 a.m. in addition to basic service, normal office hours 9:00 a.m. to 6:00 p.m.
4. <u>97813</u>   Acupuncture, one or more needles, with electrical stimulation
5. <u>90880</u>   Hypnotherapy
6. <u>96101</u>   One hour of psychological testing by psychiatrist, with interpretation and report
7. <u>97542</u>   Wheelchair management/propulsion training, 15 minutes
8. <u>97124</u> $\times$ 3   Massage therapy, 45 minutes
9. <u>94640</u>   Nonpressurized inhalation treatment for acute airway obstruction
10. <u>99071</u>   Educational videotapes for the patient

ASSIGNMENT 7.8 Assigning CPT Modifiers

1. <u>55400-74</u>   Vasovasostomy discontinued after anesthesia due to heart arrhythmia, hospital outpatient
2. <u>99204-57</u>   Decision for surgery during initial office visit, comprehensive
3. <u>99213-24</u>   Expanded office visit for follow-up of mastectomy; new onset diabetes was discovered and treatment initiated
4. <u>47600-55</u>   Cholecystectomy, postoperative management only
5. <u>46221-73</u>   Hospital outpatient hemorrhoidectomy by simple ligature discontinued prior to anesthesia due to severe drop in blood pressure
6. <u>53210-54</u>   Total urethrectomy including cystotomy, female, surgical care only
7. <u>12002-53</u>   Simple repair of two-inch laceration of the right foot, discontinued due to near-syncope, physician's office

8. <u>42820</u>;

<u>17110-51</u>

Tonsillectomy and adenoidectomy, age 10, and laser wart removal from the patient's neck while in the operating room

9. <u>27405-76</u>   Repeat left medial collateral ligament repair, same surgeon

10. <u>28290-50</u>   At the patient's request, bilateral Silver procedures were performed for correction of bunion deformity

ASSIGNMENT 7.9 Coding Case Studies

1. **PATIENT CASE #1**

<u>99241</u>

Office consultation, new or established patient (problem-focused history and physical examination; straightforward medical decision making)

<u>85025</u>   CBC with differential

<u>70210</u>   Sinus x-ray

2. **PATIENT CASE #2**

<u>52000</u>   Cystoscopy

3. **PATIENT CASE #3**

<u>99213</u>

Office visit, established patient (expanded problem-focused history, medical decision making of low complexity)

<u>85018</u>   Hemoglobin

<u>80061</u>   Fasting lipid profile

4. **PATIENT CASE #4**

<u>99212</u>

Office visit, established patient (problem-focused examination, straightforward medical decision making)

5. **PATIENT CASE #5**

<u>11771</u>   Pilonidal cystectomy, cyst tract exploration and irrigation

ASSIGNMENT 7.10 CPT Code Verification

Health Record Number	Coding Statement	Code(s) Assigned	Coding Verification
25899	Office visit level 2	99213	**99212**
60159	Flexible diagnostic bronchoscopy	31624	**31622**
30121	Biopsy of the Oropharynx	42800	**42800**
11133	CT scan of the thoracic spine with contrast	72128	**72129**
45456	Hepatic panel	82040, 82247, 82248, 84075, 84155, 84460	**80076**
55667	Routine ECG tracing only	93000	**93005**
91912	Application of figure-of-eight cast	29049	**29049**
34343	Initial posterior nasal packing	30905	**30905**
555789	Extensive excision of a pilonidal cyst	11770	**11771**
12332	Fitting of bifocals	92340	**92341**

The student will also provide a double-spaced, word processed document that outlines analysis and recommendations of the above verification process. Seven out of the ten records reviewed were coded incorrectly (70 percent); three out of the ten records reviewed were coded correctly (30 percent). Recommendations that may be provided include:

- Coder education and training
- Specificity in coding
- Reading of complete code descriptor before assigning code(s)
- Review of CPT guidelines (e.g., using a panel code 80076 instead of separate codes)

Students may provide additional insight in how the coding could be improved based on the 10 records reviewed in the exercise.

ASSIGNMENT 7.11 Relative Value Units

For CPT code 99285, the non-facility RVUs for the following locations are:

- Philadelphia, Pennsylvania — $160.03
- Oklahoma — $142.60
- Arizona — $152.35
- Los Angeles, California — $160.58
- Nevada — $154.08
- District of Columbia (Maryland and Virginia suburbs) — $163.71
- New York (Manhattan) — $172.03

The highest payment amount is in Manhattan, New York; the lowest payment amount is in Oklahoma. The difference between these two locations is $29.43. The average amount of these seven locations is $157.92. The most obvious pattern is that the urban locations (District of Columbia, Manhattan, Philadelphia, and Los Angeles) have a higher payment amount than the nonurban locations of Nevada, Arizona, and Oklahoma. Also, when using the Internet search, those states are not broken down into subareas like Pennsylvania or California.

NOTE: Students will navigate the Web site to locate information needed for their analysis. This will help them learn how to locate information using the Internet and will require them to use tool bars and pull-down menus. Students will also gain the ability to use the Internet as a research tool.

ASSIGNMENT 7.12 Multiple Choice Review

1. d
2. a
3. d
4. b
5. d
6. b
7. c
8. d
9. a
10. b
11. b
12. c
13. a
14. b
15. b
16. b
17. c
18. c
19. b
20. a

CHAPTER 8 HCPCS Level II Coding

ASSIGNMENT 8.1 HCPCS Index

1. Breast <u>pump</u>
2. Cardiac output <u>assessment</u>
3. <u>Diasylate</u> solution
4. External defibrillator <u>electrode</u>
5. Fracture <u>orthosis</u>
6. Liquid <u>gas system</u>
7. Oral <u>antiemetic</u>
8. Pneumatic <u>nebulizer</u> administration set
9. Pneumococcal <u>vaccination administration</u>
10. <u>Wheelchair</u> shock absorber

ASSIGNMENT 8.2 HCPCS Level II Coding

Transport Services Including Ambulance (A0000–A0999)

1.	A0433	Advanced life support, Level 2
2.	A0225	Ambulance transport of newborn from rural hospital to a children's specialty hospital
3.	A0429	Patient received basic life support (BLS) during emergency transport via ambulance
4.	A0422	Patient received life-sustaining oxygen in ambulance during transport to hospital
5.	A0130	Wheelchair van transporting patient from assisted living facility to doctor's office

Medical and Surgical Supplies (A4000–A8999)

6.	A4208	Physician gave patient injection using a sterile 3 cc syringe with needle
7.	A4246	One pint of pHisoHex solution
8.	A4260	Contraception implant system (including implants and supplies)
9.	A4282	Replacement adapter for breast pump
10.	A4265	One pound of paraffin
11.	A4349	Male external catheter with adhesive coating
12.	A4338	Two-way indwelling Foley catheter
13.	A4367	Ostomy belt
14.	A4458	Reusable enema bag with tubing
15.	A4556	One pair of apnea monitor electrodes
16.	A4561	Rubber pessary
17.	A4625	Tracheostomy care kit for new tracheostomy
18.	A4670	Automatic blood pressure monitor
19.	A4774	Ammonia test strips for dialysis (50 count)
20.	A5501	Patient with diabetes was fitted with a pair of shoes custom-molded from casts of the patient's feet

Administrative, Miscellaneous, and Investigational (A9000–A9999)

21.	A9901	DME delivery and setup
22.	A9300	Exercise equipment

23. A9528	I-131 sodium iodide capsule as radiopharmaceutical diagnostic agent (1 millicurie)
24. A9700	Injectable contrast material for use in echocardiography, one study
25. A9500	One dose technetium Tc99m sestamibi

Enteral and Parenteral Therapy (B4000–B9999)

26. B4184	500 cc of 10 percent lipids parenteral nutrition solution
27. B4155	Enteral formula via feeding tube (100 calories/1 unit)
28. B9002	Enteral infusion pump with alarm
29. B4036	Gravity-fed enteral feeding supply kit (one day)
30. B4224 × 2	Parenteral nutrition administration kit (two days)

C Codes for Use Under the Hospital Outpatient Prospective Payment System (C1000–C9999)

31. C1717	Brachytherapy seed, high-dose rate iridium 192
32. C1764	Cardiac event recorder (implantable)
33. C9105	Injection of 1 ml of hepatitis B immunoglobulin
34. C8905	Patient underwent left breast MRI without contrast, followed by left breast MRI with contrast
35. C1752	Short-term hemodialysis catheter
36. C1722	Single-chamber implantable cardioverter-defibrillator

Durable Medical Equipment (E0100–E9999)

37. E0910	"Patient helper" trapeze bars (attached to bed)
38. E0455	Adult oxygen tent
39. E0202	Bilirubin light with photometer
40. E0590	Dispensing fee for DME nebulizer drug
41. E0135	Folding walker with adjustable height
42. E0730	Four-lead TENS unit
43. E0850	Free-standing cervical traction stand
44. E0303	Heavy-duty, extra-wide hospital bed with mattress to accommodate patient who weighs 460 pounds
45. E1520	Heparin infusion pump for hemodialysis
46. E0325	Jug urinal (male)
47. E0189	Lambswool sheepskin heel pad for decubitus prevention
48. E0760	Low-intensity ultrasound osteogenesis stimulator
49. E0275	Metal bed pan
50. E1902	Non-electronic communication board
51. E0112	Patient was fitted with a pair of underarm wooden crutches with pads, tips, and handgrips
52. E0235	Portable paraffin bath (unit)
53. E0160	Portable sitz bath
54. E0105	Quad cane with tips
55. E0244	Raised toilet seat
56. E2320	Remote joystick power wheelchair accessory including all electronics and fixed mounting hardware
57. E0159	Replacement brake attachment for wheeled walker
58. E0693	Ultraviolet light therapy six-foot panel, with bulbs, timer, and eye protection
59. E0255	Variable height hospital bed with mattress and side rails
60. E0971	Wheelchair anti-tipping device

Procedures/Professional Services (Temporary) (G0000–G9999)

61. G0306   Automated CBC (complete) with automated WBC differential count

62. G0315   End-stage renal disease (ESRD) services for 16-year-old patient, three physician visits per month

63. G9016   Individual smoking cessation counseling (10 minutes)

64. G0245   Initial E/M evaluation for patient with LOPS

65. G0252   PET imaging for initial diagnosis of breast cancer

Alcohol and/or Drug Abuse Treatment Services (H0001–H2037)

66. H0004 × 2   Behavioral health counseling and therapy, 30 minutes

67. H0035   Partial hospitalization for mental health crisis, 18 hours

68. H2013   Psychiatric health facility services (one day)

69. H0045   Respite care services, not in the home (*per diem*)

70. H2032 × 2   Thirty minutes of activity therapy

Temporary Durable Medical Equipment (K0000–K9999)

71. K0072 × 2   Complete front caster assembly for wheelchair with two semi-pneumatic tires

72. K0105   IV hanger (each)

73. K0038   Leg strap (for wheelchair)

74. K0012   Lightweight portable motorized wheelchair

75. K0603   Replacement alkaline battery, 1.5 volt, for patient-owned external infusion pump

Orthotic Procedures (L0000–L4999)

76. L0160   Cervical wire frame, semi-rigid, for occipital/mandibular support

77. L0220   Custom-fabricated thoracic rib belt

78. L0830   HALO procedure; cervical halo incorporated into Milwaukee orthosis

79. L3310   Neoprene heel and sole elevation lift (one inch)

80. L1960   Posterior solid ankle plastic AFO, custom fabricated

81. L3001   Spenco foot insert

Prosthetic Procedures (L5000–L9999)

82. L5150   Below-knee disarticulation prosthesis, molded socket, shin, with SACH foot

83. L7025   Electric hand, myoelectrically controlled, Otto Bock

84. L5000   Partial foot prosthesis, shoe insert with longitudinal arch, toe filler

85. L5595   Preparatory prosthesis for hip disarticulation-hemipelvectomy; pylon, no cover, solid ankle cushion heel foot, thermoplastic, molded to patient model

86. L8030   Silicone breast prosthesis

Medical Services (M0000–M0399)

87. M0064   Brief office visit to change prescription medication used for treating the patient's personality disorder

88. M0075   Cellular therapy

89. M0300   Chemical endarterectomy (IV chelation therapy)

90. M0301   Fabric wrapping of abdominal aneurysm

91. M0076   Prolotherapy

Pathology and Laboratory Services (P0000–P2999)

92.	P9612	Catheterization for collection of specimen (one patient)
93.	P2029	Congo red, blood
94.	P9019	Platelets, each unit
95.	P9010 × 2	Two units whole blood for transfusion

Q Codes: Temporary Codes (Q0000–Q9999)

96.	Q0083	Chemotherapy administration by push
97.	Q3031	Collagen skin test
98.	Q2002	Elliott's B solution injection, 1 ml
99.	G0010	Injection hepatitis B vaccination, pediatric dose
100.	Q0112	KOH preparation
101.	Q0113	Pinworm examination

Diagnostic Radiology Services (R0000–R5999)

102.	R0070	Portable x-ray service transportation to nursing home, one trip, one patient seen
103.	R0076	Transportation of portable ECG to nursing facility, one patient seen
104.	R0075 × 2	Transportation of portable x-ray service to patient's home, two patients seen (husband and wife)

Temporary National Codes (Non-Medicare) (S0000–S9999)

105.	S2142	Allogenic cord-blood-derived stem cell transplant
106.	S2202	Echosclerotherapy
107.	S3708	Gastrointestinal fat absorption study
108.	S0400	Global fee for extracorporeal shock wave lithotripsy (ESWL) treatment of kidney stone
109.	S2055	Harvesting of multivisceral organs from cadaver with preparation and maintenance of allografts
110.	S9439	Vaginal birth after Cesarean (VBAC) classes

National T Codes Established for State Medicaid Agencies (T1000–T9999)

111.	T1027	Family training and counseling for child development, 15 minutes
112.	T2101	Human breast milk processing, storage, and distribution
113.	T1502-TE	Intramuscular medication administration by home health LPN
114.	T1000 × 2	Private-duty nursing, 30 minutes
115.	T2035	Waiver for utility services to support medical equipment

Vision Services (V0000–V2999)

116.	V2208 × 2	Bifocal lenses, bilateral, 5.25 sphere, 2.12 cylinder
117.	V2025	Deluxe frame
118.	V2744 × 2	Photochromatic tint for two lenses
119.	V2785	Processing, preserving, and transporting corneal tissue
120.	V2626	Reduction of ocular prosthesis

Hearing Services (V5000–V5999)

121.	V5010	Assessment for hearing aid
122.	V5140	Binaural behind-the-ear hearing aid
123.	V5245	Digitally programmable monaural hearing aid, analog
124.	V5240	Dispensing fee, BICROS
125.	V5268	Telephone amplifier

ASSIGNMENT 8.3 Coding Drugs in HCPCS

1.	J0120	Tetracycline 250 mg injection
2.	J0690	Ancef 500 mg IV
3.	J0735	Clonidine HCl, 1 mg
4.	J0587	Botulinum toxin type B, 100 units
5.	J2271	Duramorph 100 mg SC
6.	J3301 × 2	Kenalog-40 20 mg
7.	J2995	Streptokinase 250,000 IU IV
8.	J2780	Ranitidine HCl injection, 25 mg
9.	J1817	NPH insulin 50 units via pump
10.	J1940	Lasix 10 mg IM

ASSIGNMENT 8.4 HCPCS Level II National Modifiers

_g_	**1.**	AH	a.	Left hand, thumb
_e_	**2.**	E4	b.	Technical component
_a_	**3.**	FA	c.	Four patients served
_f_	**4.**	NU	d.	Registered nurse (RN)
_h_	**5.**	RC	e.	Lower right eyelid
_j_	**6.**	SB	f.	New equipment
_i_	**7.**	TA	g.	Clinical psychologist
_b_	**8.**	TC	h.	Right coronary artery
_d_	**9.**	TD	i.	Left foot, great toe
_c_	**10.**	UQ	j.	Nurse midwife

ASSIGNMENT 8.5 Coding Case Studies

1. PATIENT CASE #1

J0456	Zithromax (azythromycin) 500 mg injection
R0070	Chest x-ray by mobile service; one patient seen. (The radiology company would bill for this service.)

2. PATIENT CASE #2

J1670	Injection, tetanus immune globulin, human, up to 250 mg
E0112	Wooden crutches

3. PATIENT CASE #3

G0206-GH	Diagnostic mammography, producing digital image, unilateral (converted from screening mammogram on the same day)

4. PATIENT CASE #4

Q0091	Screening Pap smear; obtaining, preparing, and conveyance of smear to laboratory
G0306	Complete CBC with differential (automated)

> **NOTE:** The thyroid panel and complete metabolic panel codes will be assigned from CPT.

5. **PATIENT CASE #5**

<u>V2624</u>   Polishing/resurfacing of ocular prosthesis

ASSIGNMENT 8.6 Coding Verification

Health Record Number	Coding Statement	Code Assigned	Coding Verification
585598	Azathioprine Oral 50 mg	J7501	**J7500**
111454	20 mg injection of methylprednisolone acetate	J1030	**J1020**
313258	Injection of digoxin 0.3 mg	J1160	**J1160**
899784	Zidovudine 10 mg injection	S0104	**J3485**
123456	Prochlorperazine, 10 mg injection	Q0164	**J0780**
778541	200 mg injection of fluconazole	J1450	**J1450**
549786	3 mg injection of hydromorphone	J1170	**J1170**
343437	2 mg injection of Urecholine	J0520 x 2	**J0520**
777845	6 mg injection of pegfilgrastim	J1141	**J2505**
233233	500 mg injection of cefazolin sodium	J0690	**J0690**

The student will also provide a double-spaced, word-processed document that outlines analysis and recommendations of the above verification process. Six out of the ten records reviewed were coding incorrectly (60 percent); four out of the ten records reviewed were coding correctly (40 percent). Recommendations that may be provided include:

- Coder education and training
- Specificity in coding

NOTE: Students will navigate the Web site to locate information needed for their analysis. This will help them learn how to locate information using the Internet and will require them to use tool bars and pull-down menus. Students will also gain the ability to use the Internet as a research tool.

- Reading of complete code descriptor before assigning code(s)
- Using Internet as tool for coding verification

Students may provide additional insight in how the coding could be improved based on the 10 records reviewed in the exercise.

ASSIGNMENT 8.7 Multiple Choice Review

1. c		**11.** b	
2. b		**12.** a	
3. c		**13.** b	
4. d		**14.** c	
5. b		**15.** a	
6. d		**16.** a	
7. b		**17.** b	
8. b		**18.** a	
9. d		**19.** c	
10. b		**20.** d	

CHAPTER 9 CMS Reimbursement Methodologies

ASSIGNMENT 9.1 Outpatient Prospective Payment System (OPPS)

1. $13

> **NOTE:** $65 × 20% = $13, which is less than the copayment of $15.

2. $15

> **NOTE:** $75 × 20% = $15, which is less than the copayment of $25.

3. $20

> **NOTE:** $122 × 20% = $24.40, which is more than the copayment of $20.

4. $16.20

> **NOTE:** $81 × 20% = $16.20, which is less than the copayment of $25.

5. $15

> **NOTE:** $78 × 20% is $15.60, which is more than the copayment of $15.

ASSIGNMENT 9.2 Diagnosis-Related Groups

Interpretation of Figure 9-1:

      a. DRG 524

      b. DRG 18

      c. DRG 13

      d. DRG 19

      e. DRG 16

Interpretation of Figure 9-2:

      a. DRG 543

      b. DRG 3

      c. DRG 1

      d. DRG 8

      e. DRG 531

ASSIGNMENT 9.3 Data Reports

1. For 2005, what CPT level I code is ranked number one in the amount of allowed charges and allowed services? **99213**

2. For 2005, what was the total allowed services for CPT code 99285? **7,097,240**

3. For 2005, what is the percentage of non E/M codes in the top 20 ranking?

30 percent (6/20 x 100 = 30 percent) The six non E/M codes in the top 20 are 66984, 78465, 88305, 97110, 92014, and 93307

> **NOTE:** A4253 is not a transport HCPCS code. That is the code for blood glucose reagent strips.

4. For 2005, what was the total allowed charges for HCPCS code A0425? **$711,606,130**

5. For 2005, what is the percentage of transport HCPCS codes in the top 20 ranking? **20 percent (4/20 x 100 = 20 percent) The transport codes in the top 20 are A0427, A0428, A0425, A0429.**

6. In his annual meeting, a CFO at a local hospital stated that for 2005, CMS paid $3.2 million for services in critical care units under CPT code 99291. Is this correct? **No, in 2005 the allowed charges for 99291 were $687,923,768. The amount the CFO stated of 3.2 million was for the allowed services.**

7. For 2005, what was the national allowed charge for a diagnostic flexible colonoscopy? **CPT code 45378 is for a diagnostic flexible colonoscopy. The total allowed charge for 2005 was $380,787,913.**

8. For 2005, what was the highest ranking CPT surgical code? **66984, which is for an Extracapsular Cataract Extraction (ECCE)**

9. For 2005, what HCPCS code(s) had an allowed charge of $21.9 million? **J0800 ($21,984,748) and J7502 ($21,990,530)**

10. For 2005, what is the radiology procedure code with the highest allowed charge amount? What is the yearly total allowed charge for this procedure code? What is this radiology procedure code for? **78465, for a national total of $1,129,055,555. This is the code for a single photon emission-computed tomography (SPECT) multiple studies.**

> **NOTE:** Students will navigate the Web site to locate information needed to complete the summary. This will help them learn how to locate information using the Internet and will require them to use tool bars and pull-down menus. Students will also gain the ability to use the Internet as a research tool.

ASSIGNMENT 9.4 CMS DRG Versus MS DRG

1. a. 1.1476
   b. 486, which is for pneumonia
   c. Principal diagnosis given by coder was 428.0, which is for congestive heart failure (CHF). MCC dx was 486.

2. a. 00238
   b. 541
   c. CMS v24 DRG is weighted higher, with a weight of 1.4100. The MS DRG is 0.9184.

3. a. CMS assigned DRG 00130 PERIPHERAL VASCULAR DISORDERS W CC

4. a. The higher DRG is the MS DRG at 2.8568, which is compared to the CMS DRG weight of 1.9022.
   b. The principal diagnosis assigned by the coder was 820.8, which is for the femur or hip fracture. The MCC diagnosis is 427.5, which is for the cardiac arrest.

5. a. 00197 for the cholecystectomy
   b. The CMS v24 DRG weight is higher (2.5518) than the MS DRG weight (2.0539).
   c. Yes, both DRGs are assigned with a CC.
   d. 154.2, which is the ICD-9-CM code for the anal sphincter cancer.

ASSIGNMENT 9.5 Multiple Choice Review

1. c	**6.** b	**11.** d	**16.** a
2. c	**7.** c	**12.** b	**17.** c
3. a	**8.** c	**13.** d	**18.** c
4. c	**9.** a	**14.** b	**19.** d
5. b	**10.** b	**15.** b	**20.** c

CHAPTER 10 Coding for Medical Necessity

ASSIGNMENT 10.1 Choosing the First-Listed Diagnosis

1. pain, left knee
2. gastroesophageal reflux disease
3. hypertension
4. sore throat
5. lipoma

ASSIGNMENT 10.2 Linking Diagnoses with Procedures/Services

e 1. allergy test
b 2. EKG
a 3. inhalation treatment
c 4. Pap smear
g 5. removal of ear wax
i 6. sigmoidoscopy
j 7. strep test
f 8. urinalysis
h 9. venipuncture
d 10. X-ray, radius and ulna

a. bronchial asthma
b. chest pain
c. family history, cervical cancer
d. fractured wrist
e. hay fever
f. hematuria
g. impacted cerumen
h. jaundice
i. rectal bleeding
j. sore throat

ASSIGNMENT 10.3 National Coverage Determinations

1. Apheresis (or pheresis or therapeutic pheresis) (CPT code 36512) is a medical procedure that uses specialized equipment to remove selected blood constituents (cells, leukocytes, plasma, or platelets) from whole blood. The remainder of the blood is retransfused into the person from whom the blood was taken. For purposes of Medicare coverage, *apheresis* is defined as an autologous procedure (e.g., blood is taken from the patient, processed, and returned to the patient as part of a continuous procedure) as distinguished from the procedure in which a patient donates blood preoperatively and is transfused with the donated blood at a later date. Medicare covers apheresis treatment for Guillain-Barré syndrome (ICD code 357.0).

2. Blood glucose chemistry levels (CPT code 82948) are often necessary for the management of patients with diabetes mellitus (ICD code 250.00), where hyperglycemia and hypoglycemia are often present.

3. Gastric bypass surgery (CPT code 43644) for severe obesity (ICD code 278.01) is covered under the program if it is medically appropriate for the individual to have such surgery and the surgery is to correct an illness that caused the obesity or was aggravated by the obesity, such as hypertension (ICD code 401.9) or uncontrolled diabetes mellitus (ICD code 250.02).

4. Medicare coverage of cardiac rehabilitation programs (HCPCS code S9472) is considered reasonable and necessary only for patients with a clear medical need, who are referred by their attending physician and have a documented diagnosis of acute myocardial infarction (ICD code 410.91) within the preceding 12 months.

5. A screening mammography, bilateral (CPT code 76092), is a radiologic procedure furnished to a woman without signs or symptoms of breast disease (ICD code V76.12), for the purpose of early detection of breast cancer, and includes a physician's interpretation of the results of the procedure. A screening mammography has limitations as it must be, at a minimum, a two-view exposure of each breast. For an asymptomatic woman over age 39, payment may be made for a screening mammography performed after at least 11 months have passed following the month in which the last screening mammography was performed.

ASSIGNMENT 10.4 Coding from Case Scenarios

CPT Codes	ICD-9-CM Codes
1. 99213, 57500	626.2, 626.4
2. 99241, 72114	722.52
3. 74280	562.11
4. 99214, 71020	496
5. 99285	789.34

ASSIGNMENT 10.5 Coding from SOAP Notes and Operative Reports

CPT Codes	ICD-9-CM Codes
1. 99202	789.06
2. 99212	531.30
3. 99203, 12001, 70250, 73060, 23605	850.11, 873.0, 812.03
4. 99212	455.4
5. 99202	788.42, 783.5, 783.21, 791.5
6. 65426-RT	372.40
7. 11423	214.1
8. 49560, 49568	533.20
9. 67311-RT, 67312-51-LT	378.24, 368.33
or 67133-50	
10. 26508	727.03

ASSIGNMENT 10.6 National Correct Coding Initiative (NCCI)

1. A 45-year-old male patient presents for outpatient surgery. The patient has subcutaneous cyst of his shoulder area. The surgeon performs an incision and drainage of this cyst. The physician notes on the operative note that another small cyst was also found and incised. The chart was coded with the following codes: 20000 and 10061. Based on NCCI edits, is this correct coding? Why or why not? **No, per NCCI edits, 10061 is a mutually exclusive for code 10061. This means that code 10061 is bundled into code 20000. Both 20000 and 10061 should not be reported together on the same claim.**

2. A 19-year-old female patient presents for surgery. The patient reported symptoms of vaginal bleeding with nausea and vomiting. Lab tests revealed the patient had an HCG level of 200,000 mIU/mL. Ultrasound confirmed that the patient has a hydatidiform mole. The patient consented to the removal of this mole. In the health record the following statement was documented: "induced abortion of hydatidiform mole with evacuation and curettage." Mary Spring, the coder for this physician, assigned the following codes: 59856 and 59870-51. Based on NCCI edit information, is this correct coding? Why or why not? **No, per NCCI edits, 59870 is a mutually exclusive for code 59856. This means that code 59856 is bundled into code 59870. Only code 59870 should be reported for this case.**

3. A 75-year-old patient presents on 04/02/YY for a keratoplasty with an extracapsular cataract extraction (ECCE) and a posterior lens implantation. The following codes are listed on the claim for this surgical event: 65755, 66984-51, and 66985-51. Based on NCCI edit information, is this correct coding? Why or why not? **No, per NCCI edits, 66984 is a mutually exclusive for code 65755. This means that code 65755 is bundled into code 66984. Code 66985 is bundled into 66984. This means code 66984 is part of code 66985. Only code 66984 should be reported for this ECCE.**

4. A patient has two electrodes implanted, percutaneous for neurostimulation of neuromuscular nerves for the right and left side of his body. The claim listed the following: 64565-50. Based on NCCI edit information, is this correct coding? Why or why not? **No, per the NCCI edits, code 64565 should not have a modifier attached. The code descriptor states "electrodes," which would cover multiple electrodes. Only report 64565.**

5. A 45-year-old patient presents for the first of two surgeries for a nerve pedicle transfer. The goal of this surgery is to treat the patient's facial paralysis. The physician documents a nerve grafting procedure in which 4.5 cm of nerve is taken from the patient's leg. This is the donor site. The nerve harvested from the leg is then transferred to the damaged site on the patient's face after the surgeon has access to the damaged facial nerve and has removed the injured portion. The codes reported on the claim are 64905 and 64898-51. Based on NCCI edit information, is this correct coding? Why or why not? **No, per NCCI edits, 64898 is a mutually exclusive for code 64905. This means that code 64898 is bundled into code 64905. Only code 64905 should be reported for this case. The grafting portion of this surgery is included in the transfer code.**

> **NOTE:** Students will navigate the Web site to locate information needed to answer the questions in this assignment. This will require them to use Web page links and to read, review, and interpret information from a table/spreadsheet. The NCCI edits are presented on a Microsoft Excel spreadsheet.

ASSIGNMENT 10.7 VistA-Office Electronic Health Record

1. What parties developed the VistA-Office EHR? **Centers for Medicare and Medicaid Services (CMS) and Veterans Health Administration (VHA).**

2. What four additional features were added to this Electronic Health Record to make it functional for a physician's office? **This electronic health record system includes interfaces for practice management and billing systems, ability to produce quality management (QM) reports, use of clinical reminders, and templates for OB/GYN and pediatric offices.**

3. This EHR has a report feature that allows for data to be presented. List three types of reports that this EHR can generate. **VistA-Office can produce the following report types per the Web site: clinical reports, health summary, dietetics profile and nutritional assessment, cumulative vitals, procedures, daily order summary report, outpatient prescription (Rx) profile, and order summary using a data range.**

> **NOTE:** Students are asked to list only three types of reports. There are a total of nine report types listed on the Web site.

4. Define and briefly explain the acronym DOQ-IT. **Doctor's Office Quality-Information Technology. This is the acronym used on the Web site for reminders that can be generated by the software for clinical areas, registration areas, and quality management issues.**

5. What is the goal of VistA-Office EHR? **In summary from the Web site, the goal of VistA-Office is to have a functional EHR that can be used by physicians to meet the needs of patients and the goal of U.S. adoption of digital technology in the health information arena.**

> **NOTE:** Students will be required to navigate the WorldVista Web site to research information needed to answer the questions listed in this assignment. This will help them continue to build skill in using the Internet as a research tool and using Web sites, which often requires using tool bars, pull-down menus, and Web page links.

ASSIGNMENT 10.8 Multiple Choice Review

1. c	**11.** a
2. a	**12.** d
3. c	**13.** b
4. c	**14.** d
5. a	**15.** a
6. c	**16.** d
7. b	**17.** a
8. c	**18.** b
9. d	**19.** d
10. d	**20.** d

CHAPTER 11 Essential CMS-1500 Claim Instructions

ASSIGNMENT 11.1 NPI and NPEES

1. What is the electronic file interchange (EFI)?

   The EFI is also known as the bulk enumeration. EFI is a process where a provider or group can have an organization apply for their NPI.

2. What five steps does CMS recommend for staff training related to the NPI?
   a. Focus on any new business processes or staff responsibilities that relate to the usage of an NPI
   b. Staff training on steps of a procedure to obtain another provider's NPI
   c. Who is responsible for maintaining NPI data with CMS
   d. Training on collection and validation of other providers or facility NPIs
   e. Policy on sharing of NPI with other providers for billing purposes

3. What day-to-day business processes and technology may be impacted by the NPI?
   a. Electronic Medical Records (EMR)
   b. E-prescribing
   c. Document Imaging
   d. Workflow processes
   e. HIPAA transaction standards

   > **NOTE:** The students may provide these items in any order.

4. What Web site can providers or office staff go to for the latest NPI information?
   www.cms.hhs.gov/NationalProvidentStand/02_WhatsNew.asp#TopOfPage

5. What is the grace period for NPI compliance?
   CMS has implemented a 12 month grace period after the May 23, 2008 deadline.

ASSIGNMENT 11.2 Medically Unlikely Edits (MUE) Project

1. How will CMS communicate information about MUE to providers?
   CMS will communicate through its Web site and listservs.

2. What program is MUE a part of?
   MUE is a part of the Medical Review process, which is a part of the Medicare Integrity Program.

3. What are the benefits of the medical review process for providers?
   a. Reduced payment error rate
   b. Reduced or decreased denials
   c. Feedback and education on all denied claims from CMS

   > **NOTE:** The students may provide these items in any order.

4. When were the first MUE edits implemented by CMS?
   January 2007 for anatomical edits and the typographical edits in April of 2007.

5. What legislation requires CMS to ensure that payment is made for medically necessary services?
   Social Security Act

ASSIGNMENT 11.3 Multiple Choice Review

1.	d	**11.**	c
2.	b	**12.**	a
3.	c	**13.**	a
4.	a	**14.**	d
5.	b	**15.**	a
6.	b	**16.**	a
7.	d	**17.**	c
8.	a	**18.**	a
9.	d	**19.**	b
10.	b	**20.**	d

CHAPTER 12 Commercial Insurance

ASSIGNMENT 12.1 Commercial Primary CMS-1500 Claims Completion

Case Study 12-a Northwest Health

Case Study 12-b Metropolitan

1500

HEALTH INSURANCE CLAIM FORM

APPROVED BY NATIONAL UNIFORM CLAIM COMMITTE 08/05

	PICA								PICA	

1. MEDICARE (Medicare #)   MEDICAID (Medicaid #)   TRICARE CHAMPUS (Sponsor's SSN)   CHAMPVA (Member ID#)   GROUP HEALTH PLAN (SSN or ID)   FECA BLK LUNG (SSN)   OTHER [X] (ID)

1a. INSURED'S I.D. NUMBER (For Program in Item 1)
212224545

2. PATIENT'S NAME (Last Name, First Name, Middle Initial)
BRANCH, BETHANY, L

3. PATIENT'S BIRTH DATE MM DD YY   SEX
05 03 1986   M [ ] F [X]

4. INSURED'S NAME (Last Name, First Name, Middle Initial)
BRANCH, JOHN, L

5. PATIENT'S ADDRESS (No., Street)
401 CARTVALLEY COURT

6. PATIENT'S RELATIONSHIP TO INSURED
Self [ ] Spouse [ ] Child [X] Other [ ]

7. INSURED'S ADDRESS (No., Street)
SAME

CITY
ANYWHERE

STATE
US

8. PATIENT STATUS
Single [X] Married [ ] Other [ ]

CITY

STATE

ZIP CODE
12345

TELEPHONE (Include Area Code)
(101) 3334466

Employed [ ] Full-Time Student [ ] Part-Time Student [X]

ZIP CODE

TELEPHONE (Include Area Code)
( )

9. OTHER INSURED'S NAME (Last Name, First Name, Middle Initial)

10. IS PATIENT'S CONDITION RELATED TO:

11. INSURED'S POLICY GROUP OR FECA NUMBER
GW292

a. OTHER INSURED'S POLICY OR GROUP NUMBER
315661111

a. EMPLOYMENT? (Current or Previous)
YES [ ] NO [X]

a. INSURED'S DATE OF BIRTH MM DD YY   SEX
10 10 1954   M [X] F [ ]

b. OTHER INSURED'S DATE OF BIRTH MM DD YY   SEX
09 01 1955   M [X] F [ ]

b. AUTO ACCIDENT?   PLACE (State)
YES [ ] NO [X]

b. EMPLOYER'S NAME OR SCHOOL NAME
GATEWAY COMPUTERS INC

c. EMPLOYER'S NAME OR SCHOOL NAME
GATEWAY COMPUTERS INC

c. OTHER ACCIDENT?
YES [ ] NO [X]

c. INSURANCE PLAN NAME OR PROGRAM NAME
METROPOLITAN

d. INSURANCE PLAN NAME OR PROGRAM NAME
METROPOLITAN

10d. RESERVED FOR LOCAL USE

d. IS THERE ANOTHER HEALTH BENEFIT PLAN?
[X] YES [ ] NO   If yes, return to and complete item 9 a-d.

READ BACK OF FORM BEFORE COMPLETING & SIGNING THIS FORM.

12. PATIENT'S OR AUTHORIZED PERSON'S SIGNATURE I authorize the release of any medical or other information necessary to process this claim. I also request payment of government benefits either to myself or to the party who accepts assignment below.

SIGNED   SIGNATURE ON FILE   DATE

13. INSURED'S OR AUTHORIZED PERSON'S SIGNATURE I authorize payment of medical benefits to the undersigned physcian or supplier for services described below.

SIGNED

14. DATE OF CURRENT: MM DD YY   ILLNESS (First symptom) OR INJURY (Accident) OR PREGNANCY (LMP)
12 04 YYYY

15. IF PATIENT HAS HAD SAME OR SIMILAR ILLNESS, GIVE FIRST DATE MM DD YY

16. DATES PATIENT UNABLE TO WORK IN CURRENT OCCUPATION MM DD YY
FROM   TO

17. NAME OF REFERRING PROVIDER OR OTHER SOURCE
JAMES R FELTBETTER MD

17a.
17b. NPI 7778878781

18. HOSPITALIZATION DATES RELATED TO CURRENT SERVICES MM DD YY
FROM   TO

19. RESERVED FOR LOCAL USE

20. OUTSIDE LAB? $ CHARGES
YES [ ] NO [X]

21. DIAGNOSIS OR NATURE OF ILLNESS OR INJURY (Relate Items 1, 2, 3 or 4 to Item 24E by Line)
1. 466 0
2. 034 0
3.
4.

22. MEDICAID RESUBMISSION CODE   ORIGINAL REF. NO.

23. PRIOR AUTHORIZATION NUMBER

24. A DATE(S) OF SERVICE From MM DD YY To MM DD YY	B. PLACE OF SERVICE	C. EMG	D. PROCEDURES, SERVICES, OR SUPPLIES (Explain Unusual Circumstances) CPT/HCPCS MODIFER	E. DIAGNOSIS POINTER	F. $ CHARGES	G. DAYS OR UNITS	H. EPSDT Family Plan	I. ID. QUAL.	J. RENDERING PROVIDER ID. #
1	1204YYYY	11		99242	1	75 00	1		NPI
2	1204YYYY	11		86403	1	12 00	1		NPI
3									NPI
4									NPI
5									NPI
6									NPI

25. FEDERAL TAX I.D. NUMBER   SSN EIN
111234562   [X]

26. PATIENT'S ACCOUNT NO.
12-B

27. ACCEPT ASSIGNMENT? (For govt. claims, see back)
[X] YES [ ] NO

28. TOTAL CHARGE
$ 87 00

29. AMOUNT PAID
$

30. BALANCE DUE
$ 87 00

31. SIGNATURE OF PHYSICIAN OR SUPPLIER INCLUDING DEGREES OR CREDENTIALS
(I certify that the statements on the reverse apply to this bill and are made a part thereof.)
DONALD L GIVINGS MD
SIGNED   DATE MMDDYYYY

32. SERVICE FACILITY LOCATION INFORMATION
DONALD L GIVINGS MD
11350 MEDICAL DRIVE
ANYWHERE US 12345
1234567890   b.

33. BILLING PROVIDER INFO & PH # (101)1115555
DONALD L GIVINGS MD
11350 MEDICAL DRIVE
ANYWHERE US 12345
a.1234567890   b.

NUCC Instruction Manual available at: www.nucc.org

APPROVED OMB-0938-0999 FORM CMS-1500 (08/05)

CARRIER · PATIENT AND INSURED INFORMATION · PHYSICIAN OR SUPPLIER INFORMATION

ASSIGNMENT 12.2 Commercial Secondary CMS-1500 Claims Completion

Case Study 12-c US Health-Primary

1500

HEALTH INSURANCE CLAIM FORM

APPROVED BY NATIONAL UNIFORM CLAIM COMMITTEE 08/05

| | PICA | | | | | | | | PICA | | |

Field	Value
1. MEDICARE (Medicare #) MEDICAID (Medicaid #) TRICARE CHAMPUS (Sponsor's SSN) CHAMPVA (Member ID#) GROUP HEALTH PLAN (SSN or ID) FECA BLK LUNG (SSN) OTHER [X] (ID)	1a. INSURED'S I.D. NUMBER (For Program in Item 1) C7489593
2. PATIENT'S NAME (Last Name, First Name, Middle Initial) REED, LAURIE, P	3. PATIENT'S BIRTH DATE 06 05 1964 SEX M F [X]	4. INSURED'S NAME (Last Name, First Name, Middle Initial) SAME
5. PATIENT'S ADDRESS (No., Street) 579 VACATION DRIVE	6. PATIENT'S RELATIONSHIP TO INSURED Self [X] Spouse Child Other	7. INSURED'S ADDRESS (No., Street) SAME
CITY ANYWHERE STATE US	8. PATIENT STATUS Single [X] Married Other	CITY STATE
ZIP CODE 12345 TELEPHONE (Include Area Code) (101) 3335555	Employed [X] Full-Time Student Part-Time Student	ZIP CODE TELEPHONE (Include Area Code) ( )
9. OTHER INSURED'S NAME (Last Name, First Name, Middle Initial) REED, LAURIE, P	10. IS PATIENT'S CONDITION RELATED TO:	11. INSURED'S POLICY GROUP OR FECA NUMBER TLC345
a. OTHER INSURED'S POLICY OR GROUP NUMBER 345679999	a. EMPLOYMENT? (Current or Previous) YES NO [X]	a. INSURED'S DATE OF BIRTH 06 05 1964 SEX M F [X]
b. OTHER INSURED'S DATE OF BIRTH 06 08 1964 SEX M F [X]	b. AUTO ACCIDENT? YES NO [X] PLACE (State)	b. EMPLOYER'S NAME OR SCHOOL NAME THE LEARNING CENTER
c. EMPLOYER'S NAME OR SCHOOL NAME THE LEARNING CENTER	c. OTHER ACCIDENT? YES NO [X]	c. INSURANCE PLAN NAME OR PROGRAM NAME US HEALTH
d. INSURANCE PLAN NAME OR PROGRAM NAME CIGNA	10d. RESERVED FOR LOCAL USE	d. IS THERE ANOTHER HEALTH BENEFIT PLAN? [X] YES NO If yes, return to and complete item 9 a-d.

READ BACK OF FORM BEFORE COMPLETING & SIGNING THIS FORM.

12. PATIENT'S OR AUTHORIZED PERSON'S SIGNATURE I authorize the release of any medical or other information necessary to process this claim. I also request payment of government benefits either to myself or to the party who accepts assignment below.

SIGNED **SIGNATURE ON FILE** DATE

13. INSURED'S OR AUTHORIZED PERSON'S SIGNATURE I authorize payment of medical benefits to the undersigned physcian or supplier for services described below.

SIGNED

Field	Value
14. DATE OF CURRENT: 10 28 YYYY ILLNESS (First symptom) OR INJURY (Accident) OR PREGNANCY (LMP)	15. IF PATIENT HAS HAD SAME OR SIMILAR ILLNESS, GIVE FIRST DATE MM DD YY	16. DATES PATIENT UNABLE TO WORK IN CURRENT OCCUPATION FROM MM DD YY TO MM DD YY
17. NAME OF REFERRING PROVIDER OR OTHER SOURCE	17a. 17b. NPI	18. HOSPITALIZATION DATES RELATED TO CURRENT SERVICES FROM MM DD YY TO MM DD YY
19. RESERVED FOR LOCAL USE		20. OUTSIDE LAB? YES [X] NO $ CHARGES
21. DIAGNOSIS OR NATURE OF ILLNESS OR INJURY (Relate Items 1, 2, 3 or 4 to Item 24E by Line) 1. 477 9 3. 2. 4.		22. MEDICAID RESUBMISSION CODE ORIGINAL REF. NO. 23. PRIOR AUTHORIZATION NUMBER

24. A DATE(S) OF SERVICE From MM DD YY To MM DD YY	B. PLACE OF SERVICE	C. EMG	D. PROCEDURES, SERVICES, OR SUPPLIES (Explain Unusual Circumstances) CPT/HCPCS MODIFER	E. DIAGNOSIS POINTER	F. $ CHARGES	G. DAYS OR UNITS	H. EPSDT Family Plan	I. ID. QUAL.	J. RENDERING PROVIDER ID. #
1 10 28 YYYY	11		99212	1	55 00			NPI	
2								NPI	
3								NPI	
4								NPI	
5								NPI	
6								NPI	

Field	Value
25. FEDERAL TAX I.D. NUMBER 111234562 SSN EIN [X]	26. PATIENT'S ACCOUNT NO. 12-C	27. ACCEPT ASSIGNMENT? (For govt. claims, see back) [X] YES NO	28. TOTAL CHARGE $ 55 00	29. AMOUNT PAID $	30. BALANCE DUE $ 55 00
31. SIGNATURE OF PHYSICIAN OR SUPPLIER INCLUDING DEGREES OR CREDENTIALS (I certify that the statements on the reverse apply to this bill and are made a part thereof.) DONALD L GIVINGS MD SIGNED DATE MMDDYYYY	32. SERVICE FACILITY LOCATION INFORMATION DONALD L GIVINGS MD 11350 MEDICAL DRIVE ANYWHERE US 12345 a. 1234567890 b.	33. BILLING PROVIDER INFO & PH # (101)1115555 DONALD L GIVINGS MD 11350 MEDICAL DRIVE ANYWHERE US 12345 a. 1234567890 b.

NUCC Instruction Manual available at: www.nucc.org

APPROVED OMB-0938-0999 FORM CMS-1500 (08/05)

Case Study 12-c CIGNA-Secondary

1500

HEALTH INSURANCE CLAIM FORM

APPROVED BY NATIONAL UNIFORM CLAIM COMMITTE 08/05

| | PICA | | | | | | | | PICA | |

1. MEDICARE (Medicare #) MEDICAID (Medicaid #) TRICARE CHAMPUS (Sponsor's SSN) CHAMPVA (Member ID#) GROUP HEALTH PLAN (SSN or ID) FECA BLK LUNG (SSN) OTHER [X] (ID)

1a. INSURED'S I.D. NUMBER (For Program in Item 1)
34579999

2. PATIENT'S NAME (Last Name, First Name, Middle Initial)
REED, LAURIE, P

3. PATIENT'S BIRTH DATE MM 06 DD 05 YY 1964 SEX M F [X]

4. INSURED'S NAME (Last Name, First Name, Middle Initial)
SAME

5. PATIENT'S ADDRESS (No., Street)
579 VACATION DRIVE

6. PATIENT'S RELATIONSHIP TO INSURED
Self [X] Spouse Child Other

7. INSURED'S ADDRESS (No., Street)
SAME

CITY
ANYWHERE
STATE
US

8. PATIENT STATUS
Single [X] Married Other

CITY
STATE

ZIP CODE
12345
TELEPHONE (Include Area Code)
(101) 3335555

Employed [X] Full-Time Student Part-Time Student

ZIP CODE
TELEPHONE (Include Area Code)
( )

9. OTHER INSURED'S NAME (Last Name, First Name, Middle Initial)
REED, LAURIE, P

10. IS PATIENT'S CONDITION RELATED TO:

11. INSURED'S POLICY GROUP OR FECA NUMBER

a. OTHER INSURED'S POLICY OR GROUP NUMBER
C748593

a. EMPLOYMENT? (Current or Previous)
YES NO [X]

a. INSURED'S DATE OF BIRTH MM 06 DD 05 YY 1964 SEX M F [X]

b. OTHER INSURED'S DATE OF BIRTH MM 06 DD 08 YY 1964 SEX M F [X]

b. AUTO ACCIDENT? PLACE (State)
YES NO [X]

b. EMPLOYER'S NAME OR SCHOOL NAME
THE LEARNING CENTER

c. EMPLOYER'S NAME OR SCHOOL NAME
THE LEARNING CENTER

c. OTHER ACCIDENT?
YES NO [X]

c. INSURANCE PLAN NAME OR PROGRAM NAME
CIGNA

d. INSURANCE PLAN NAME OR PROGRAM NAME
US HEALTH

10d. RESERVED FOR LOCAL USE

d. IS THERE ANOTHER HEALTH BENEFIT PLAN?
[X] YES NO *If yes,* return to and complete item 9 a-d.

READ BACK OF FORM BEFORE COMPLETING & SIGNING THIS FORM.
12. PATIENT'S OR AUTHORIZED PERSON'S SIGNATURE I authorize the release of any medical or other information necessary to process this claim. I also request payment of government benefits either to myself or to the party who accepts assignment below.

SIGNED SIGNATURE ON FILE DATE

13. INSURED'S OR AUTHORIZED PERSON'S SIGNATURE I authorize payment of medical benefits to the undersigned physcian or supplier for services described below.

SIGNED

14. DATE OF CURRENT: MM 10 DD 28 YY YYYY ILLNESS (First symptom) OR INJURY (Accident) OR PREGNANCY (LMP)

15. IF PATIENT HAS HAD SAME OR SIMILAR ILLNESS, GIVE FIRST DATE MM DD YY

16. DATES PATIENT UNABLE TO WORK IN CURRENT OCCUPATION FROM MM DD YY TO MM DD YY

17. NAME OF REFERRING PROVIDER OR OTHER SOURCE
17a.
17b. NPI

18. HOSPITALIZATION DATES RELATED TO CURRENT SERVICES FROM MM DD YY TO MM DD YY

19. RESERVED FOR LOCAL USE

20. OUTSIDE LAB? YES NO [X] $ CHARGES

21. DIAGNOSIS OR NATURE OF ILLNESS OR INJURY (Relate Items 1, 2, 3 or 4 to Item 24E by Line)
1. 477 .9
2.
3.
4.

22. MEDICAID RESUBMISSION CODE ORIGINAL REF. NO.

23. PRIOR AUTHORIZATION NUMBER

24. A DATE(S) OF SERVICE From MM DD YY To MM DD YY	B. PLACE OF SERVICE	C. EMG	D. PROCEDURES, SERVICES, OR SUPPLIES (Explain Unusual Circumstances) CPT/HCPCS MODIFER	E. DIAGNOSIS POINTER	F. $ CHARGES	G. DAYS OR UNITS	H. EPSDT Family Plan	I. ID. QUAL.	J. RENDERING PROVIDER ID. #
1 10 28 YYYY	11		99212	1	55 00			NPI	
2								NPI	
3								NPI	
4								NPI	
5								NPI	
6								NPI	

25. FEDERAL TAX I.D. NUMBER SSN EIN
111234562 [X]

26. PATIENT'S ACCOUNT NO.
12-C

27. ACCEPT ASSIGNMENT? (For govt. claims, see back)
[X] YES NO

28. TOTAL CHARGE
$ 55 00

29. AMOUNT PAID
$

30. BALANCE DUE
$ 55 00

31. SIGNATURE OF PHYSICIAN OR SUPPLIER INCLUDING DEGREES OR CREDENTIALS (I certify that the statements on the reverse apply to this bill and are made a part thereof.)
DONALD L GIVINGS MD
SIGNED DATE MMDDYYYY

32. SERVICE FACILITY LOCATION INFORMATION
DONALD L GIVINGS MD
11350 MEDICAL DRIVE
ANYWHERE US 12345
1234567890 b.

33. BILLING PROVIDER INFO & PH # (101)1115555
DONALD L GIVINGS MD
11350 MEDICAL DRIVE
ANYWHERE US 12345
a.1234567890 b.

NUCC Instruction Manual available at: www.nucc.org

APPROVED OMB-0938-0999 FORM CMS-1500 (08/05)

CPT copyright 2007 American Medical Association. All rights reserved.

ASSIGNMENT 12.3 Multiple Choice Review

1. c
2. b
3. a
4. a
5. c
6. b
7. d
8. a
9. c
10. b

11. d
12. a
13. b
14. c
15. a
16. d
17. d
18. a
19. c
20. b

CHAPTER 13 Blue Cross Blue Shield

ASSIGNMENT 13.1 BCBS Primary CMS-1500 Claims Completion

Case Study 13-a BCBS

| 1500 |

HEALTH INSURANCE CLAIM FORM

APPROVED BY NATIONAL UNIFORM CLAIM COMMITTEE 08/05

| | PICA | | | | | | | | PICA | | |

1. MEDICARE (Medicare #)	MEDICAID (Medicaid #)	TRICARE CHAMPUS (Sponsor's SSN)	CHAMPVA (Member ID#)	GROUP HEALTH PLAN (SSN or ID)	FECA BLK LUNG (SSN)	OTHER [X] (ID)	1a. INSURED'S I.D. NUMBER (For Program in Item 1) NXY678223434

2. PATIENT'S NAME (Last Name, First Name, Middle Initial) BOOKER, MONTY, L	3. PATIENT'S BIRTH DATE MM 12 DD 25 YY 1966 SEX M [X] F	4. INSURED'S NAME (Last Name, First Name, Middle Initial) SAME

5. PATIENT'S ADDRESS (No., Street) 47 SNOWFLAKE ROAD	6. PATIENT'S RELATIONSHIP TO INSURED Self [X] Spouse [ ] Child [ ] Other [ ]	7. INSURED'S ADDRESS (No., Street) SAME

CITY ANYWHERE	STATE US	8. PATIENT STATUS Single [ ] Married [X] Other [ ]	CITY	STATE

ZIP CODE 12345	TELEPHONE (Include Area Code) (101) 3355555	Employed [X] Full-Time Student [ ] Part-Time Student [ ]	ZIP CODE	TELEPHONE (Include Area Code) ( )

9. OTHER INSURED'S NAME (Last Name, First Name, Middle Initial)	10. IS PATIENT'S CONDITION RELATED TO:	11. INSURED'S POLICY GROUP OR FECA NUMBER 678

a. OTHER INSURED'S POLICY OR GROUP NUMBER	a. EMPLOYMENT? (Current or Previous) YES [ ] NO [X]	a. INSURED'S DATE OF BIRTH MM DD YY SEX M [ ] F [ ]

b. OTHER INSURED'S DATE OF BIRTH MM DD YY SEX M [ ] F [ ]	b. AUTO ACCIDENT? YES [ ] NO [X] PLACE (State)	b. EMPLOYER'S NAME OR SCHOOL NAME ATLANTA PUBLISHER

c. EMPLOYER'S NAME OR SCHOOL NAME	c. OTHER ACCIDENT? YES [ ] NO [X]	c. INSURANCE PLAN NAME OR PROGRAM NAME BCBS US

d. INSURANCE PLAN NAME OR PROGRAM NAME	10d. RESERVED FOR LOCAL USE	d. IS THERE ANOTHER HEALTH BENEFIT PLAN? YES [ ] NO [X] *If yes*, return to and complete item 9 a-d.

READ BACK OF FORM BEFORE COMPLETING & SIGNING THIS FORM.

12. PATIENT'S OR AUTHORIZED PERSON'S SIGNATURE I authorize the release of any medical or other information necessary to process this claim. I also request payment of government benefits either to myself or to the party who accepts assignment below.

SIGNED SIGNATURE ON FILE   DATE

13. INSURED'S OR AUTHORIZED PERSON'S SIGNATURE I authorize payment of medical benefits to the undersigned physcian or supplier for services described below.

SIGNED

14. DATE OF CURRENT: MM 01 DD 19 YY YYYY ILLNESS (First symptom) OR INJURY (Accident) OR PREGNANCY (LMP)	15. IF PATIENT HAS HAD SAME OR SIMILAR ILLNESS, GIVE FIRST DATE MM DD YY	16. DATES PATIENT UNABLE TO WORK IN CURRENT OCCUPATION FROM MM DD YY TO MM DD YY

17. NAME OF REFERRING PROVIDER OR OTHER SOURCE	17a. 17b. NPI	18. HOSPITALIZATION DATES RELATED TO CURRENT SERVICES FROM MM DD YY TO MM DD YY

19. RESERVED FOR LOCAL USE		20. OUTSIDE LAB? YES [ ] NO [X] $ CHARGES

21. DIAGNOSIS OR NATURE OF ILLNESS OR INJURY (Relate Items 1, 2, 3 or 4 to Item 24E by Line) 1. 783.21 3. 783.6 2. 783.5 4.	22. MEDICAID RESUBMISSION CODE ORIGINAL REF. NO. 23. PRIOR AUTHORIZATION NUMBER

24. A DATE(S) OF SERVICE From MM DD YY To MM DD YY	B. PLACE OF SERVICE	C. EMG	D. PROCEDURES, SERVICES, OR SUPPLIES (Explain Unusual Circumstances) CPT/HCPCS MODIFER	E. DIAGNOSIS POINTER	F. $ CHARGES	G. DAYS OR UNITS	H. EPSDT Family Plan	I. ID. QUAL.	J. RENDERING PROVIDER ID. #
1	01 19 YYYY	11		99204	1	100 00	1		NPI	
2	01 19 YYYY	11		81001	2	10 00	1		NPI	
3									NPI	
4									NPI	
5									NPI	
6									NPI	

25. FEDERAL TAX I.D. NUMBER 111234562 SSN [ ] EIN [X]	26. PATIENT'S ACCOUNT NO. 13-A	27. ACCEPT ASSIGNMENT? (For govt. claims, see back) [X] YES [ ] NO	28. TOTAL CHARGE $ 110 00	29. AMOUNT PAID $	30. BALANCE DUE $

31. SIGNATURE OF PHYSICIAN OR SUPPLIER INCLUDING DEGREES OR CREDENTIALS (I certify that the statements on the reverse apply to this bill and are made a part thereof.) DONALD L GIVINGS MD SIGNED DATE MMDDYYYY	32. SERVICE FACILITY LOCATION INFORMATION DONALD L GIVINGS MD 11350 MEDICAL DRIVE ANYWHERE US 12345 a.1234567890 b.	33. BILLING PROVIDER INFO & PH # (101)1115555 DONALD L GIVINGS MD 11350 MEDICAL DRIVE ANYWHERE US 12345 a.1234567890 b.

NUCC Instruction Manual available at: www.nucc.org

APPROVED OMB-0938-0999 FORM CMS-1500 (08/05)

Case Study 13-b BCBS

1500

HEALTH INSURANCE CLAIM FORM

APPROVED BY NATIONAL UNIFORM CLAIM COMMITTE 08/05

PICA | | | PICA | | |

1. MEDICARE (Medicare #)	MEDICAID (Medicaid #)	TRICARE CHAMPUS (Sponsor's SSN)	CHAMPVA (Member ID#)	GROUP HEALTH PLAN (SSN or ID)	FECA BLK LUNG (SSN)	OTHER [X] (ID)	1a. INSURED'S I.D. NUMBER (For Program in Item 1)
							XWG214556666

2. PATIENT'S NAME (Last Name, First Name, Middle Initial)	3. PATIENT'S BIRTH DATE MM DD YY SEX	4. INSURED'S NAME (Last Name, First Name, Middle Initial)
STRONG, ANITA, B	04 25 1959 M☐ F[X]	SAME

5. PATIENT'S ADDRESS (No., Street)	6. PATIENT'S RELATIONSHIP TO INSURED	7. INSURED'S ADDRESS (No., Street)
124 PROSPER WAY	Self [X] Spouse ☐ Child ☐ Other ☐	SAME

CITY	STATE	8. PATIENT STATUS	CITY	STATE
ANYWHERE	US	Single ☐ Married [X] Other ☐		

ZIP CODE	TELEPHONE (Include Area Code)		ZIP CODE	TELEPHONE (Include Area Code)
12345	(101) 3355555	Employed [X] Full-Time Student ☐ Part-Time Student ☐		( )

9. OTHER INSURED'S NAME (Last Name, First Name, Middle Initial)	10. IS PATIENT'S CONDITION RELATED TO:	11. INSURED'S POLICY GROUP OR FECA NUMBER
		1357

a. OTHER INSURED'S POLICY OR GROUP NUMBER	a. EMPLOYMENT? (Current or Previous) ☐ YES [X] NO	a. INSURED'S DATE OF BIRTH MM DD YY SEX M☐ F☐

b. OTHER INSURED'S DATE OF BIRTH MM DD YY SEX M☐ F☐	b. AUTO ACCIDENT? PLACE (State) ☐ YES [X] NO	b. EMPLOYER'S NAME OR SCHOOL NAME SELF

c. EMPLOYER'S NAME OR SCHOOL NAME	c. OTHER ACCIDENT? ☐ YES [X] NO	c. INSURANCE PLAN NAME OR PROGRAM NAME BCBS US

d. INSURANCE PLAN NAME OR PROGRAM NAME	10d. RESERVED FOR LOCAL USE	d. IS THERE ANOTHER HEALTH BENEFIT PLAN? ☐ YES [X] NO If yes, return to and complete item 9 a-d.

READ BACK OF FORM BEFORE COMPLETING & SIGNING THIS FORM.

12. PATIENT'S OR AUTHORIZED PERSON'S SIGNATURE I authorize the release of any medical or other information necessary to process this claim. I also request payment of government benefits either to myself or to the party who accepts assignment below.

SIGNED SIGNATURE ON FILE DATE _____

13. INSURED'S OR AUTHORIZED PERSON'S SIGNATURE I authorize payment of medical benefits to the undersigned physcian or supplier for services described below.

SIGNED _____

14. DATE OF CURRENT: MM DD YY ILLNESS (First symptom) OR INJURY (Accident) OR PREGNANCY (LMP) 11 07 YYYY	15. IF PATIENT HAS HAD SAME OR SIMILAR ILLNESS, GIVE FIRST DATE MM DD YY	16. DATES PATIENT UNABLE TO WORK IN CURRENT OCCUPATION MM DD YY MM DD YY FROM TO

17. NAME OF REFERRING PROVIDER OR OTHER SOURCE	17a.	18. HOSPITALIZATION DATES RELATED TO CURRENT SERVICES MM DD YY MM DD YY
	17b. NPI	FROM TO

19. RESERVED FOR LOCAL USE	20. OUTSIDE LAB? ☐ YES [X] NO $ CHARGES

21. DIAGNOSIS OR NATURE OF ILLNESS OR INJURY (Relate Items 1, 2, 3 or 4 to Item 24E by Line)	22. MEDICAID RESUBMISSION CODE ORIGINAL REF. NO.
1. 346 01 3. ⌐	
2. ⌐ 4. ⌐	23. PRIOR AUTHORIZATION NUMBER

24. A. DATE(S) OF SERVICE From To MM DD YY MM DD YY	B. PLACE OF SERVICE	C. EMG	D. PROCEDURES, SERVICES, OR SUPPLIES (Explain Unusual Circumstances) CPT/HCPCS MODIFER	E. DIAGNOSIS POINTER	F. $ CHARGES	G. DAYS OR UNITS	H. EPSDT Family Plan	I. ID. QUAL.	J. RENDERING PROVIDER ID. #
1 1107YYYY	11		99211	1	55 00	1		NPI	
2								NPI	
3								NPI	
4								NPI	
5								NPI	
6								NPI	

25. FEDERAL TAX I.D. NUMBER SSN EIN	26. PATIENT'S ACCOUNT NO.	27. ACCEPT ASSIGNMENT? (For govt. claims, see back)	28. TOTAL CHARGE	29. AMOUNT PAID	30. BALANCE DUE
111234562 [X]	13-B	[X] YES ☐ NO	$ 55 00	$	$

31. SIGNATURE OF PHYSICIAN OR SUPPLIER INCLUDING DEGREES OR CREDENTIALS (I certify that the statements on the reverse apply to this bill and are made a part thereof.) DONALD L GIVINGS MD SIGNED _____ DATE MMDDYYYY	32. SERVICE FACILITY LOCATION INFORMATION DONALD L GIVINGS MD 11350 MEDICAL DRIVE ANYWHERE US 12345 a. 1234567890 b.	33. BILLING PROVIDER INFO & PH # (101)1115555 DONALD L GIVINGS MD 11350 MEDICAL DRIVE ANYWHERE US 12345 a. 1234567890 b.

NUCC Instruction Manual available at: www.nucc.org

APPROVED OMB-0938-0999 FORM CMS-1500 (08/05)

Case Study 13-c BCBS POS-Primary

1500

HEALTH INSURANCE CLAIM FORM

APPROVED BY NATIONAL UNIFORM CLAIM COMMITTE 08/05

| | PICA | | | PICA | | |

1. MEDICARE (Medicare #) **MEDICAID** (Medicaid #) **TRICARE CHAMPUS** (Sponsor's SSN) **CHAMPVA** (Member ID#) **GROUP HEALTH PLAN** (SSN or ID) **FECA BLK LUNG** (SSN) **OTHER** [X] (ID)

1a. INSURED'S I.D. NUMBER (For Program in Item 1)
XWN212567972

2. PATIENT'S NAME (Last Name, First Name, Middle Initial)
LOVE, VIRGINIA, A

3. PATIENT'S BIRTH DATE MM DD YY
07 04 1962 **SEX** M [ ] F [X]

4. INSURED'S NAME (Last Name, First Name, Middle Initial)
LOVE, CHARLES, L

5. PATIENT'S ADDRESS (No., Street)
61 ISAIAH CIRCLE

6. PATIENT'S RELATIONSHIP TO INSURED
Self [ ] Spouse [X] Child [ ] Other [ ]

7. INSURED'S ADDRESS (No., Street)
SAME

CITY ANYWHERE **STATE** US

8. PATIENT STATUS
Single [ ] Married [X] Other [ ]

CITY **STATE**

ZIP CODE 12345 **TELEPHONE (Include Area Code)** (101) 3335555

Employed [X] Full-Time Student [ ] Part-Time Student [ ]

ZIP CODE **TELEPHONE (Include Area Code)** ( )

9. OTHER INSURED'S NAME (Last Name, First Name, Middle Initial)
LOVE, VIRGINIA, A

10. IS PATIENT'S CONDITION RELATED TO:

11. INSURED'S POLICY GROUP OR FECA NUMBER
123

a. OTHER INSURED'S POLICY OR GROUP NUMBER
111451111

a. EMPLOYMENT? (Current or Previous)
YES [ ] NO [X]

a. INSURED'S DATE OF BIRTH MM DD YY
10 06 60 **SEX** M [X] F [ ]

b. OTHER INSURED'S DATE OF BIRTH MM DD YY
07 04 1962 **SEX** M [ ] F [X]

b. AUTO ACCIDENT? PLACE (State)
YES [ ] NO [X]

b. EMPLOYER'S NAME OR SCHOOL NAME
IMPERIAL BAYLINERS

c. EMPLOYER'S NAME OR SCHOOL NAME
H & H DESIGNS

c. OTHER ACCIDENT?
YES [ ] NO [X]

c. INSURANCE PLAN NAME OR PROGRAM NAME
BCBS POS

d. INSURANCE PLAN NAME OR PROGRAM NAME
BCBS POS

10d. RESERVED FOR LOCAL USE

d. IS THERE ANOTHER HEALTH BENEFIT PLAN?
[X] YES [ ] NO *If yes, return to and complete item 9 a-d.*

READ BACK OF FORM BEFORE COMPLETING & SIGNING THIS FORM.
12. PATIENT'S OR AUTHORIZED PERSON'S SIGNATURE I authorize the release of any medical or other information necessary to process this claim. I also request payment of government benefits either to myself or to the party who accepts assignment below.

SIGNED SIGNATURE ON FILE DATE

13. INSURED'S OR AUTHORIZED PERSON'S SIGNATURE I authorize payment of medical benefits to the undersigned physcian or supplier for services described below.

SIGNED

14. DATE OF CURRENT: MM DD YY 07 03 YYYY ◄ ILLNESS (First symptom) OR INJURY (Accident) OR PREGNANCY (LMP)

15. IF PATIENT HAS HAD SAME OR SIMILAR ILLNESS, GIVE FIRST DATE MM DD YY

16. DATES PATIENT UNABLE TO WORK IN CURRENT OCCUPATION MM DD YY FROM TO

17. NAME OF REFERRING PROVIDER OR OTHER SOURCE
17a.
17b. NPI

18. HOSPITALIZATION DATES RELATED TO CURRENT SERVICES MM DD YY FROM TO

19. RESERVED FOR LOCAL USE

20. OUTSIDE LAB? $ CHARGES
YES [ ] NO [X]

21. DIAGNOSIS OR NATURE OF ILLNESS OR INJURY (Relate Items 1, 2, 3 or 4 to Item 24E by Line)
1. 372.10
2. 692.9
3.
4.

22. MEDICAID RESUBMISSION CODE ORIGINAL REF. NO.

23. PRIOR AUTHORIZATION NUMBER

24. A DATE(S) OF SERVICE From MM DD YY	To MM DD YY	B. PLACE OF SERVICE	C. EMG	D. PROCEDURES, SERVICES, OR SUPPLIES (Explain Unusual Circumstances) CPT/HCPCS	MODIFER	E. DIAGNOSIS POINTER	F. $ CHARGES	G. DAYS OR UNITS	H. EPSDT Family Plan	I. ID. QUAL.	J. RENDERING PROVIDER ID. #
1	0703YYYY		11		00212		12	55 00	1		NPI	
2											NPI	
3											NPI	
4											NPI	
5											NPI	
6											NPI	

25. FEDERAL TAX I.D. NUMBER SSN EIN
111234562 [X]

26. PATIENT'S ACCOUNT NO.
13-C

27. ACCEPT ASSIGNMENT? (For govt. claims, see back)
[X] YES [ ] NO

28. TOTAL CHARGE
$ 55 00

29. AMOUNT PAID
$

30. BALANCE DUE
$

31. SIGNATURE OF PHYSICIAN OR SUPPLIER INCLUDING DEGREES OR CREDENTIALS (I certify that the statements on the reverse apply to this bill and are made a part thereof.)
DONALD L GIVINGS MD
SIGNED DATE MMDDYYYY

32. SERVICE FACILITY LOCATION INFORMATION
DONALD L GIVINGS MD
11350 MEDICAL DRIVE
ANYWHERE US 12345
1234567890 b.

33. BILLING PROVIDER INFO & PH # (101)1115555
DONALD L GIVINGS MD
11350 MEDICAL DRIVE
ANYWHERE US 12345
a.1234567890 b.

CARRIER | PATIENT AND INSURED INFORMATION | PHYSICIAN OR SUPPLIER INFORMATION

NUCC Instruction Manual available at: www.nucc.org

APPROVED OMB-0938-0999 FORM CMS-1500 (08/05)

Case Study 13-c BCBS POS-Secondary

1500
HEALTH INSURANCE CLAIM FORM
APPROVED BY NATIONAL UNIFORM CLAIM COMMITTE 08/05

| | PICA | | | | | | | PICA | | |

| 1. MEDICARE | MEDICAID | TRICARE CHAMPUS | CHAMPVA | GROUP HEALTH PLAN | FECA BLK LUNG | OTHER | 1a. INSURED'S I.D. NUMBER | (For Program in Item 1) |

(Medicare #)　(Medicaid #)　(Sponsor's SSN)　(Member ID#)　(SSN or ID)　(SSN) [X] (ID)

2. PATIENT'S NAME (Last Name, First Name, Middle Initial)
LOVE, VIRGINIA, A

3. PATIENT'S BIRTH DATE
MM 07 DD 04 YY 1962　SEX M　F [X]

4. INSURED'S NAME (Last Name, First Name, Middle Initial)
LOVE, VIRGINIA, A

5. PATIENT'S ADDRESS (No., Street)
61 ISAIAH CIRCLE

6. PATIENT'S RELATIONSHIP TO INSURED
Self [X]　Spouse　Child　Other

7. INSURED'S ADDRESS (No., Street)
SAME

CITY
ANYWHERE　STATE US

8. PATIENT STATUS
Single　Married [X]　Other

CITY　STATE

ZIP CODE 12345　TELEPHONE (Include Area Code) (101) 3335555

Employed [X]　Full-Time Student　Part-Time Student

ZIP CODE　TELEPHONE (Include Area Code) ( )

9. OTHER INSURED'S NAME (Last Name, First Name, Middle Initial)
LOVE, CHARLES, L

10. IS PATIENT'S CONDITION RELATED TO:

11. INSURED'S POLICY GROUP OR FECA NUMBER

a. OTHER INSURED'S POLICY OR GROUP NUMBER
XWN212567972123

a. EMPLOYMENT? (Current or Previous)
YES　[X] NO

a. INSURED'S DATE OF BIRTH
MM 07 DD 04 YY 62　SEX M　F [X]

b. OTHER INSURED'S DATE OF BIRTH
MM 10 DD 06 YY 60　SEX M [X]　F

b. AUTO ACCIDENT?　PL
YES　[X] NO

b. EMPLOYER'S NAME OR SCHOOL NAME
H&H DESIGNS

c. EMPLOYER'S NAME OR SCHOOL NAME
IMPERIAL BAYLINERS

c. OTHER ACCIDENT?
YES　[X] NO

c. INSURANCE PLAN NAME OR PROGRAM NAME
BCBS US

d. INSURANCE PLAN NAME OR PROGRAM NAME
BCBS POS

10d. RESERVED FOR LOCAL USE

d. IS THERE ANOTHER HEALTH BENEFIT PLAN?
[X] YES　NO　If yes, return to and complete item 9 a-d.

READ BACK OF FORM BEFORE COMPLETING & SIGNING THIS FORM.
12. PATIENT'S OR AUTHORIZED PERSON'S SIGNATURE I authorize the release of any medical or other information necessary to process this claim. I also request payment of government benefits either to myself or to the party who accepts assignment below.

SIGNED　SIGNATURE ON FILE　DATE

13. INSURED'S OR AUTHORIZED PERSON'S SIGNATURE I authorize payment of medical benefits to the undersigned physician or supplier for services described below.

SIGNED

14. DATE OF CURRENT:
MM 07 DD 03 YY YYYY　ILLNESS (First symptom) OR INJURY (Accident) OR PREGNANCY (LMP)

15. IF PATIENT HAS HAD SAME OR SIMILAR ILLNESS. GIVE FIRST DATE MM DD YY

16. DATES PATIENT UNABLE TO WORK IN CURRENT OCCUPATION
MM DD YY　FROM　TO MM DD YY

17. NAME OF REFERRING PROVIDER OR OTHER SOURCE

17a.
17b. NPI

18. HOSPITALIZATION DATES RELATED TO CURRENT SERVICES
MM DD YY　FROM　TO MM DD YY

19. RESERVED FOR LOCAL USE

20. OUTSIDE LAB?
YES　[X] NO　$ CHARGES

21. DIAGNOSIS OR NATURE OF ILLNESS OR INJURY (Relate Items 1, 2, 3 or 4 to Item 24E by Line)
1. 372.10
2. 692.9
3.
4.

22. MEDICAID RESUBMISSION
CODE　ORIGINAL REF. NO.

23. PRIOR AUTHORIZATION NUMBER

24. A DATE(S) OF SERVICE From MM DD YY　To MM DD YY	B. PLACE OF SERVICE	C. EMG	D. PROCEDURES, SERVICES, OR SUPPLIES (Explain Unusual Circumstances) CPT/HCPCS　MODIFER	E. DIAGNOSIS POINTER	F. $ CHARGES	G. DAYS OR UNITS	H. EPSDT Family Plan	I. ID. QUAL.	J. RENDERING PROVIDER ID. #
1 0703YYYY	11		99212	12	55 00	1		NPI	
2								NPI	
3								NPI	
4								NPI	
5								NPI	
6								NPI	

25. FEDERAL TAX I.D. NUMBER　SSN EIN
111234562　[X]

26. PATIENT'S ACCOUNT NO.
13-C

27. ACCEPT ASSIGNMENT? (For govt. claims, see back)
[X] YES　NO

28. TOTAL CHARGE
$ 55 00

29. AMOUNT PAID
$

30. BALANCE DUE
$

31. SIGNATURE OF PHYSICIAN OR SUPPLIER INCLUDING DEGREES OR CREDENTIALS
(I certify that the statements on the reverse apply to this bill and are made a part thereof.)
DONALD L GIVINGS MD
SIGNED　DATE MMDDYYYY

32. SERVICE FACILITY LOCATION INFORMATION
DONALD L GIVINGS MD
11350 MEDICAL DRIVE
ANYWHERE US 12345
1234567890

33. BILLING PROVIDER INFO & PH # (101)1115555
DONALD L GIVINGS MD
11350 MEDICAL DRIVE
ANYWHERE US 12345
a1234567890

NUCC Instruction Manual available at: www.nucc.org

APPROVED OMB-0938-0999 FORM CMS-1500 (08/05)

Case Study 13-d BCBS POS-Primary

| 1500 |

HEALTH INSURANCE CLAIM FORM

APPROVED BY NATIONAL UNIFORM CLAIM COMMITTE 08/05

☐☐ PICA | | | | PICA ☐☐

| 1. MEDICARE ☐ (Medicare #) | MEDICAID ☐ (Medicaid #) | TRICARE CHAMPUS ☐ (Sponsor's SSN) | CHAMPVA ☐ (Member ID#) | GROUP HEALTH PLAN ☐ (SSN or ID) | FECA BLK LUNG ☐ (SSN) | OTHER ☒ (ID) | 1a. INSURED'S I.D. NUMBER (For Program in Item 1) XWN212567972 |

| 2. PATIENT'S NAME (Last Name, First Name, Middle Initial) LOVE, VIRGINIA, A | 3. PATIENT'S BIRTH DATE MM 07 DD 04 YY 1962 SEX M☐ F☒ | 4. INSURED'S NAME (Last Name, First Name, Middle Initial) LOVE, CHARLES, L |

| 5. PATIENT'S ADDRESS (No.. Street) 61 ISAIAH CIRCLE | 6. PATIENT'S RELATIONSHIP TO INSURED Self☐ Spouse☒ Child☐ Other☐ | 7. INSURED'S ADDRESS (No., Street) SAME |

| CITY ANYWHERE | STATE US | 8. PATIENT STATUS Single☐ Married☒ Other☐ | CITY | STATE |

| ZIP CODE 12345 | TELEPHONE (Include Area Code) (101) 3335555 | Employed☒ Full-Time Student☐ Part-Time Student☐ | ZIP CODE | TELEPHONE (Include Area Code) ( ) |

| 9. OTHER INSURED'S NAME (Last Name, First Name, Middle Initial) LOVE, VIRGINIA, A | 10. IS PATIENT'S CONDITION RELATED TO: | 11. INSURED'S POLICY GROUP OR FECA NUMBER 123 |

| a. OTHER INSURED'S POLICY OR GROUP NUMBER 111451111 | a. EMPLOYMENT? (Current or Previous) YES☐ NO☒ | a. INSURED'S DATE OF BIRTH MM 10 DD 06 YY 60 SEX M☒ F☐ |

| b. OTHER INSURED'S DATE OF BIRTH MM 07 DD 04 YY 1962 SEX M☐ F☒ | b. AUTO ACCIDENT? PLACE (State) YES☐ NO☒ | b. EMPLOYER'S NAME OR SCHOOL NAME IMPERIAL BAYLINERS |

| c. EMPLOYER'S NAME OR SCHOOL NAME H & H DESIGNS | c. OTHER ACCIDENT? YES☐ NO☒ | c. INSURANCE PLAN NAME OR PROGRAM NAME BCBS POS |

| d. INSURANCE PLAN NAME OR PROGRAM NAME BCBS POS | 10d. RESERVED FOR LOCAL USE | d. IS THERE ANOTHER HEALTH BENEFIT PLAN? YES☒ NO☐ If yes, return to and complete item 9 a-d. |

READ BACK OF FORM BEFORE COMPLETING & SIGNING THIS FORM.

12. PATIENT'S OR AUTHORIZED PERSON'S SIGNATURE I authorize the release of any medical or other information necessary to process this claim. I also request payment of government benefits either to myself or to the party who accepts assignment below.

SIGNED SIGNATURE ON FILE DATE

13. INSURED'S OR AUTHORIZED PERSON'S SIGNATURE I authorize payment of medical benefits to the undersigned physcian or supplier for services described below.

SIGNED

| 14. DATE OF CURRENT: MM 07 DD 03 YY YYYY ◄ ILLNESS (First symptom) OR INJURY (Accident) OR PREGNANCY (LMP) | 15. IF PATIENT HAS HAD SAME OR SIMILAR ILLNESS, GIVE FIRST DATE MM DD YY | 16. DATES PATIENT UNABLE TO WORK IN CURRENT OCCUPATION FROM MM DD YY TO MM DD YY |

| 17. NAME OF REFERRING PROVIDER OR OTHER SOURCE | 17a. 17b. NPI | 18. HOSPITALIZATION DATES RELATED TO CURRENT SERVICES FROM MM DD YY TO MM DD YY |

| 19. RESERVED FOR LOCAL USE | 20. OUTSIDE LAB? YES☐ NO☒ $ CHARGES |

| 21. DIAGNOSIS OR NATURE OF ILLNESS OR INJURY (Relate Items 1, 2, 3 or 4 to Item 24E by Line) 1. 372.10 2. 372.50 3. 4. | 22. MEDICAID RESUBMISSION CODE ORIGINAL REF. NO. 23. PRIOR AUTHORIZATION NUMBER |

24. A. DATE(S) OF SERVICE From MM DD YY To MM DD YY	B. PLACE OF SERVICE	C. EMG	D. PROCEDURES, SERVICES, OR SUPPLIES (Explain Unusual Circumstances) CPT/HCPCS MODIFER	E. DIAGNOSIS POINTER	F. $ CHARGES	G. DAYS OR UNITS	H. EPSDT Family Plan	I. ID. QUAL.	J. RENDERING PROVIDER ID. #
1	0703YYYY	11		99241	1	65 00	1		NPI	
2									NPI	
3									NPI	
4									NPI	
5									NPI	
6									NPI	

| 25. FEDERAL TAX I.D. NUMBER 116161612 SSN☐ EIN☒ | 26. PATIENT'S ACCOUNT NO. 13-D | 27. ACCEPT ASSIGNMENT? (For govt. claims, see back) YES☒ NO☐ | 28. TOTAL CHARGE $ 65 00 | 29. AMOUNT PAID $ | 30. BALANCE DUE $ |

| 31. SIGNATURE OF PHYSICIAN OR SUPPLIER INCLUDING DEGREES OR CREDENTIALS (I certify that the statements on the reverse apply to this bill and are made a part thereof.) IRIS A GLANCE MD SIGNED DATE MMDDYYYY | 32. SERVICE FACILITY LOCATION INFORMATION IRIS A GLANCE MD 66 GRANITE DRIVE ANYWHERE US 12345 6789137892 | 33. BILLING PROVIDER INFO & PH # (101)1115555 IRIS A GLANCE MD 66 GRANITE DRIVE ANYWHERE US 12345 6789137892 |

NUCC Instruction Manual available at: www.nucc.org

APPROVED OMB-0938-0999 FORM CMS-1500 (08/05)

Case Study 13-d BCBS POS-Secondary

1500

HEALTH INSURANCE CLAIM FORM

APPROVED BY NATIONAL UNIFORM CLAIM COMMITTE 08/05

| | PICA | | | | | | PICA | |

| 1. MEDICARE | MEDICAID | TRICARE CHAMPUS | CHAMPVA | GROUP HEALTH PLAN | FECA BLK LUNG | OTHER | 1a. INSURED'S I.D. NUMBER (For Program in Item 1) |
| (Medicare #) | (Medicaid #) | (Sponsor's SSN) | (Member ID#) | (SSN or ID) | (SSN) | X (ID) | 111451111 |

2. PATIENT'S NAME (Last Name, First Name, Middle Initial)
LOVE, VIRGINIA, A

3. PATIENT'S BIRTH DATE   MM 07 DD 04 YY 1962   **SEX** M F X

4. INSURED'S NAME (Last Name, First Name, Middle Initial)
LOVE, VIRGINIA, A

5. PATIENT'S ADDRESS (No., Street)
61 ISAIAH CIRCLE

6. PATIENT'S RELATIONSHIP TO INSURED
Self X Spouse Child Other

7. INSURED'S ADDRESS (No., Street)
SAME

CITY ANYWHERE   STATE US

8. PATIENT STATUS
Single Married X Other

CITY   STATE

ZIP CODE 12345   TELEPHONE (Include Area Code) (101) 3335555

Employed X Full-Time Student Part-Time Student

ZIP CODE   TELEPHONE (Include Area Code) ( )

9. OTHER INSURED'S NAME (Last Name, First Name, Middle Initial)
LOVE, CHARLES, L

10. IS PATIENT'S CONDITION RELATED TO:

11. INSURED'S POLICY GROUP OR FECA NUMBER

a. OTHER INSURED'S POLICY OR GROUP NUMBER
XWN212567972123

a. EMPLOYMENT? (Current or Previous)
YES X NO

a. INSURED'S DATE OF BIRTH MM 07 DD 04 YY 62   **SEX** M F X

b. OTHER INSURED'S DATE OF BIRTH MM 10 DD 06 YY 60   SEX M X F

b. AUTO ACCIDENT?   PL
YES X NO

b. EMPLOYER'S NAME OR SCHOOL NAME
H&H DESIGNS

c. EMPLOYER'S NAME OR SCHOOL NAME
IMPERIAL BAYLINERS

c. OTHER ACCIDENT?
YES X NO

c. INSURANCE PLAN NAME OR PROGRAM NAME
BCBS US

d. INSURANCE PLAN NAME OR PROGRAM NAME
BCBS POS

10d. RESERVED FOR LOCAL USE

d. IS THERE ANOTHER HEALTH BENEFIT PLAN?
X YES NO *If yes,* return to and complete item 9 a-d.

READ BACK OF FORM BEFORE COMPLETING & SIGNING THIS FORM.

12. PATIENT'S OR AUTHORIZED PERSON'S SIGNATURE I authorize the release of any medical or other information necessary to process this claim. I also request payment of government benefits either to myself or to the party who accepts assignment below.

SIGNED SIGNATURE ON FILE   DATE

13. INSURED'S OR AUTHORIZED PERSON'S SIGNATURE I authorize payment of medical benefits to the undersigned physcian or supplier for services described below.

SIGNED

14. DATE OF CURRENT: MM 07 DD 03 YY YYYY   ILLNESS (First symptom) OR INJURY (Accident) OR PREGNANCY (LMP)

15. IF PATIENT HAS HAD SAME OR SIMILAR ILLNESS, GIVE FIRST DATE MM DD YY

16. DATES PATIENT UNABLE TO WORK IN CURRENT OCCUPATION MM DD YY FROM   MM DD YY TO

17. NAME OF REFERRING PROVIDER OR OTHER SOURCE
DONALD L GIVINGS MD

17a.
17b. NPI 1234567890

18. HOSPITALIZATION DATES RELATED TO CURRENT SERVICES MM DD YY FROM   MM DD YY TO

19. RESERVED FOR LOCAL USE

20. OUTSIDE LAB? YES X NO $ CHARGES

21. DIAGNOSIS OR NATURE OF ILLNESS OR INJURY (Relate Items 1, 2, 3 or 4 to Item 24E by Line)

1. 372.10
2. 372.50
3.
4.

22. MEDICAID RESUBMISSION CODE   ORIGINAL REF. NO.

23. PRIOR AUTHORIZATION NUMBER

24. A DATE(S) OF SERVICE From MM DD YY To MM DD YY	B. PLACE OF SERVICE	C. EMG	D. PROCEDURES, SERVICES, OR SUPPLIES (Explain Unusual Circumstances) CPT/HCPCS MODIFER	E. DIAGNOSIS POINTER	F. $ CHARGES	G. DAYS OR UNITS	H. EPSDT Family Plan	I. ID. QUAL.	J. RENDERING PROVIDER ID. #
1	0703YYYY	11		99241	1	65 00	1		NPI	
2									NPI	
3									NPI	
4									NPI	
5									NPI	
6									NPI	

25. FEDERAL TAX I.D. NUMBER SSN EIN
116161612 X

26. PATIENT'S ACCOUNT NO.
13-D

27. ACCEPT ASSIGNMENT? (For govt. claims, see back)
X YES NO

28. TOTAL CHARGE
$ 65 00

29. AMOUNT PAID
$

30. BALANCE DUE
$

31. SIGNATURE OF PHYSICIAN OR SUPPLIER INCLUDING DEGREES OR CREDENTIALS (I certify that the statements on the reverse apply to this bill and are made a part thereof.)
IRIS A GLANCE MD
SIGNED   DATE MMDDYYYY

32. SERVICE FACILITY LOCATION INFORMATION
IRIS A GLANCE MD
66 GRANITE DRIVE
ANYWHERE US 12345
a. 6789137892 b.

33. BILLING PROVIDER INFO & PH # (101) 1115555
IRIS A GLANCE MD
66 GRANITE DRIVE
ANYWHERE US 12345
a. 6789137892 b.

NUCC Instruction Manual available at: www.nucc.org

APPROVED OMB-0938-0999 FORM CMS-1500 (08/05)

ASSIGNMENT 13.2 BCBS Secondary CMS-1500 Claims Completion

Case Study 13-e BCBS-US-Primary

<table>
<tr><td colspan="3">

1500

HEALTH INSURANCE CLAIM FORM

APPROVED BY NATIONAL UNIFORM CLAIM COMMITTEE 08/05

☐☐ PICA

1. MEDICARE ☐ (Medicare #)　MEDICAID ☐ (Medicaid #)　TRICARE CHAMPUS ☐ (Sponsor's SSN)　CHAMPVA ☐ (Member ID#)　GROUP HEALTH PLAN ☐ (SSN or ID)　FECA BLK LUNG ☐ (SSN)　OTHER ☒ (ID)　**1a. INSURED'S I.D. NUMBER** (For Program in Item 1)　FLX31399777

2. PATIENT'S NAME (Last Name, First Name, Middle Initial)　KUTTER, KEITH, S

3. PATIENT'S BIRTH DATE　MM 12　DD 01　YY 1955　SEX M ☒ F ☐

4. INSURED'S NAME (Last Name, First Name, Middle Initial)　SAME

5. PATIENT'S ADDRESS (No., Street)　22 PINEWOOD AVENUE

6. PATIENT'S RELATIONSHIP TO INSURED　Self ☒ Spouse ☐ Child ☐ Other ☐

7. INSURED'S ADDRESS (No., Street)　SAME

CITY　ANYWHERE　STATE US

8. PATIENT STATUS　Single ☐ Married ☒ Other ☐

CITY　STATE

ZIP CODE 12345　TELEPHONE (Include Area Code) (101) 3335555

Employed ☒ Full-Time Student ☐ Part-Time Student ☐

ZIP CODE　TELEPHONE (Include Area Code) ( )

9. OTHER INSURED'S NAME (Last Name, First Name, Middle Initial)　KUTTER, LINDA

10. IS PATIENT'S CONDITION RELATED TO:

11. INSURED'S POLICY GROUP OR FECA NUMBER　567

a. OTHER INSURED'S POLICY OR GROUP NUMBER　212446868

a. EMPLOYMENT? (Current or Previous) YES ☐ NO ☒

a. INSURED'S DATE OF BIRTH MM DD YY　SEX M ☐ F ☐

b. OTHER INSURED'S DATE OF BIRTH MM 05 DD 22 YY 1956　SEX M ☐ F ☒

b. AUTO ACCIDENT? YES ☐ NO ☒　PLACE (State) ☐

b. EMPLOYER'S NAME OR SCHOOL NAME　FIRST LEAGUE

c. EMPLOYER'S NAME OR SCHOOL NAME　ANDERSON MUSIC & SOUND

c. OTHER ACCIDENT? YES ☐ NO ☒

c. INSURANCE PLAN NAME OR PROGRAM NAME　BCBS US

d. INSURANCE PLAN NAME OR PROGRAM NAME　BCBS EMPIRE

10d. RESERVED FOR LOCAL USE

d. IS THERE ANOTHER HEALTH BENEFIT PLAN? ☒ YES ☐ NO *If yes*, return to and complete item 9 a-d.

READ BACK OF FORM BEFORE COMPLETING & SIGNING THIS FORM.

12. PATIENT'S OR AUTHORIZED PERSON'S SIGNATURE I authorize the release of any medical or other information necessary to process this claim. I also request payment of government benefits either to myself or to the party who accepts assignment below.

SIGNED **SIGNATURE ON FILE**　DATE

13. INSURED'S OR AUTHORIZED PERSON'S SIGNATURE I authorize payment of medical benefits to the undersigned physcian or supplier for services described below.

SIGNED

14. DATE OF CURRENT: MM 09 DD 03 YY YYYY ◄ ILLNESS (First symptom) OR INJURY (Accident) OR PREGNANCY (LMP)

15. IF PATIENT HAS HAD SAME OR SIMILAR ILLNESS. GIVE FIRST DATE MM DD YY

16. DATES PATIENT UNABLE TO WORK IN CURRENT OCCUPATION FROM MM DD YY TO MM DD YY

17. NAME OF REFERRING PROVIDER OR OTHER SOURCE

17a.
17b. NPI

18. HOSPITALIZATION DATES RELATED TO CURRENT SERVICES FROM MM DD YY TO MM DD YY

19. RESERVED FOR LOCAL USE

20. OUTSIDE LAB? ☐ YES ☒ NO　$ CHARGES

21. DIAGNOSIS OR NATURE OF ILLNESS OR INJURY (Relate Items 1, 2, 3 or 4 to Item 24E by Line)

1. 728 85　3.
2. 　4.

22. MEDICAID RESUBMISSION CODE　ORIGINAL REF. NO.

23. PRIOR AUTHORIZATION NUMBER

24. A DATE(S) OF SERVICE From MM DD YY	To MM DD YY	B. PLACE OF SERVICE	C. EMG	D. PROCEDURES, SERVICES, OR SUPPLIES (Explain Unusual Circumstances) CPT/HCPCS | MODIFER	E. DIAGNOSIS POINTER	F. $ CHARGES	G. DAYS OR UNITS	H. EPSDT Family Plan	I. ID. QUAL.	J. RENDERING PROVIDER ID. #
1　0903 YYYY		11		99212	1	65 00	1		NPI	
2									NPI	
3									NPI	
4									NPI	
5									NPI	
6									NPI	

25. FEDERAL TAX I.D. NUMBER 111234562　SSN ☐ EIN ☒

26. PATIENT'S ACCOUNT NO. 13-E

27. ACCEPT ASSIGNMENT? (For govt. claims, see back) ☒ YES ☐ NO

28. TOTAL CHARGE $ 65 00

29. AMOUNT PAID $

30. BALANCE DUE $

31. SIGNATURE OF PHYSICIAN OR SUPPLIER INCLUDING DEGREES OR CREDENTIALS (I certify that the statements on the reverse apply to this bill and are made a part thereof.)

DONALD L GIVINGS MD

SIGNED　DATE MMDDYYYY

32. SERVICE FACILITY LOCATION INFORMATION DONALD L GIVINGS MD 11350 MEDICAL DRIVE ANYWHERE US 12345
1234567890 ᵇ

33. BILLING PROVIDER INFO & PH # (101)1115555 DONALD L GIVINGS MD 11350 MEDICAL DRIVE ANYWHERE US 12345
ª1234567890 ᵇ

NUCC Instruction Manual available at: www.nucc.org

APPROVED OMB-0938-0999 FORM CMS-1500 (08/05)

</td></tr>
</table>

Case Study 13-e BCBS Empire-Secondary

1500

HEALTH INSURANCE CLAIM FORM
APPROVED BY NATIONAL UNIFORM CLAIM COMMITTE 08/05

PICA

1. MEDICARE MEDICAID TRICARE CHAMPUS CHAMPVA GROUP HEALTH PLAN FECA BLK LUNG OTHER	1a. INSURED'S I.D. NUMBER (For Program in Item 1)
☐ (Medicare #) ☐ (Medicaid #) ☐ (Sponsor's SSN) ☐ (Member ID#) ☐ (SSN or ID) ☐ (SSN) ☒ (ID)	212446868

2. PATIENT'S NAME (Last Name, First Name, Middle Initial)	3. PATIENT'S BIRTH DATE MM DD YY SEX	4. INSURED'S NAME (Last Name, First Name, Middle Initial)
KUTTER, KEITH, S	12 01 1955 M ☒ F ☐	KUTTER, LINDA

5. PATIENT'S ADDRESS (No., Street)	6. PATIENT'S RELATIONSHIP TO INSURED	7. INSURED'S ADDRESS (No., Street)
22 PINEWOOD AVENUE	Self ☐ Spouse ☒ Child ☐ Other ☐	SAME
CITY ANYWHERE STATE US	8. PATIENT STATUS Single ☐ Married ☒ Other ☐	CITY STATE
ZIP CODE 12345 TELEPHONE (Include Area Code) (101) 3335555	Employed ☒ Full-Time Student ☐ Part-Time Student ☐	ZIP CODE TELEPHONE (Include Area Code) ( )

9. OTHER INSURED'S NAME (Last Name, First Name, Middle Initial)	10. IS PATIENT'S CONDITION RELATED TO:	11. INSURED'S POLICY GROUP OR FECA NUMBER
KUTTER, KEITH, S		
a. OTHER INSURED'S POLICY OR GROUP NUMBER FLX313997777567	a. EMPLOYMENT? (Current or Previous) ☐ YES ☒ NO	a. INSURED'S DATE OF BIRTH MM DD YY SEX 05 22 1956 M ☐ F ☒
b. OTHER INSURED'S DATE OF BIRTH MM DD YY SEX 12 01 1955 M ☒ F ☐	b. AUTO ACCIDENT? PLACE (State) ☐ YES ☒ NO	b. EMPLOYER'S NAME OR SCHOOL NAME ANDERSON MUSIC & SOUND
c. EMPLOYER'S NAME OR SCHOOL NAME FIRST LEAGUE	c. OTHER ACCIDENT? ☐ YES ☒ NO	c. INSURANCE PLAN NAME OR PROGRAM NAME BCBS EMPIRE
d. INSURANCE PLAN NAME OR PROGRAM NAME BCBS US	10d. RESERVED FOR LOCAL USE	d. IS THERE ANOTHER HEALTH BENEFIT PLAN? ☒ YES ☐ NO If yes, return to and complete item 9 a-d.

READ BACK OF FORM BEFORE COMPLETING & SIGNING THIS FORM.
12. PATIENT'S OR AUTHORIZED PERSON'S SIGNATURE I authorize the release of any medical or other information necessary to process this claim. I also request payment of government benefits either to myself or to the party who accepts assignment below.

SIGNED SIGNATURE ON FILE DATE

13. INSURED'S OR AUTHORIZED PERSON'S SIGNATURE I authorize payment of medical benefits to the undersigned physcian or supplier for services described below.

SIGNED

14. DATE OF CURRENT: MM DD YY ILLNESS (First symptom) OR INJURY (Accident) OR PREGNANCY (LMP) 09 03 YYYY	15. IF PATIENT HAS HAD SAME OR SIMILAR ILLNESS, GIVE FIRST DATE MM DD YY	16. DATES PATIENT UNABLE TO WORK IN CURRENT OCCUPATION MM DD YY MM DD YY FROM TO
17. NAME OF REFERRING PROVIDER OR OTHER SOURCE	17a. 17b. NPI	18. HOSPITALIZATION DATES RELATED TO CURRENT SERVICES MM DD YY MM DD YY FROM TO
19. RESERVED FOR LOCAL USE		20. OUTSIDE LAB? $ CHARGES ☐ YES ☒ NO

21. DIAGNOSIS OR NATURE OF ILLNESS OR INJURY (Relate Items 1, 2, 3 or 4 to Item 24E by Line)	22. MEDICAID RESUBMISSION CODE ORIGINAL REF. NO.
1. 728 85 3.	
2. _____ 4. _____	23. PRIOR AUTHORIZATION NUMBER

24. A. DATE(S) OF SERVICE From To MM DD YY MM DD YY	B. PLACE OF SERVICE	C. EMG	D. PROCEDURES, SERVICES, OR SUPPLIES (Explain Unusual Circumstances) CPT/HCPCS MODIFER	E. DIAGNOSIS POINTER	F. $ CHARGES	G. DAYS OR UNITS	H. EPSDT Family Plan	I. ID. QUAL.	J. RENDERING PROVIDER ID. #
1 0903 YYYY	3		99212	1	65 00	1		NPI	
2								NPI	
3								NPI	
4								NPI	
5								NPI	
6								NPI	

25. FEDERAL TAX I.D. NUMBER SSN EIN 111234562 ☒	26. PATIENT'S ACCOUNT NO. 13-E	27. ACCEPT ASSIGNMENT? (For govt. claims, see back) ☒ YES ☐ NO	28. TOTAL CHARGE $ 65 00	29. AMOUNT PAID $	30. BALANCE DUE $
31. SIGNATURE OF PHYSICIAN OR SUPPLIER INCLUDING DEGREES OR CREDENTIALS (I certify that the statements on the reverse apply to this bill and are made a part thereof.) DONALD L GIVINGS MD SIGNED DATE MMDDYYYY	32. SERVICE FACILITY LOCATION INFORMATION DONALD L GIVINGS MD 11350 MEDICAL DRIVE ANYWHERE US 12345 1234567890		33. BILLING PROVIDER INFO & PH # (101)1115555 DONALD L GIVINGS MD 11350 MEDICAL DRIVE ANYWHERE US 12345 a1234567890		

APPROVED OMB-0938-0999 FORM CMS-1500 (08/05)

ASSIGNMENT 13.3 Multiple Choice Review

1. b
2. b
3. d
4. c
5. a
6. a
7. b
8. d
9. a
10. a

11. b
12. c
13. d
14. c
15. d
16. c
17. d
18. a
19. a
20. b

CHAPTER 14 Medicare

ASSIGNMENT 14.1 Medicare Primary CMS-1500 Claims Completion

Case Study 14-a Medicare

1500

HEALTH INSURANCE CLAIM FORM

APPROVED BY NATIONAL UNIFORM CLAIM COMMITTE 08/05

| | PICA | | | | | | | | PICA | | |

1. MEDICARE	MEDICAID	TRICARE CHAMPUS	CHAMPVA	GROUP HEALTH PLAN	FECA BLK LUNG	OTHER	1a. INSURED'S I.D. NUMBER (For Program in Item 1)
X (Medicare #)	(Medicaid #)	(Sponsor's SSN)	(Member ID#)	(SSN or ID)	(SSN)	(ID)	444223333A

2. PATIENT'S NAME (Last Name, First Name, Middle Initial)
WORTHINGTON, ALICE, E

3. PATIENT'S BIRTH DATE MM 02 DD 16 YY 1926 **SEX** M F X

4. INSURED'S NAME (Last Name, First Name, Middle Initial)

5. PATIENT'S ADDRESS (No., Street)
3301 SUNNY DAY DRIVE

6. PATIENT'S RELATIONSHIP TO INSURED
Self X Spouse Child Other

7. INSURED'S ADDRESS (No., Street)

CITY ANYWHERE **STATE** US

8. PATIENT STATUS
Single X Married Other
Employed Full-Time Student Part-Time Student

CITY **STATE**

ZIP CODE 12345 **TELEPHONE (Include Area Code)** (101) 3335555

ZIP CODE **TELEPHONE (Include Area Code)** ( )

9. OTHER INSURED'S NAME (Last Name, First Name, Middle Initial)

10. IS PATIENT'S CONDITION RELATED TO:

11. INSURED'S POLICY GROUP OR FECA NUMBER
NONE

a. OTHER INSURED'S POLICY OR GROUP NUMBER

a. EMPLOYMENT? (Current or Previous) YES X NO

a. INSURED'S DATE OF BIRTH MM DD YY **SEX** M F

b. OTHER INSURED'S DATE OF BIRTH MM DD YY **SEX** M F

b. AUTO ACCIDENT? PLACE (State) YES X NO

b. EMPLOYER'S NAME OR SCHOOL NAME

c. EMPLOYER'S NAME OR SCHOOL NAME

c. OTHER ACCIDENT? YES X NO

c. INSURANCE PLAN NAME OR PROGRAM NAME

d. INSURANCE PLAN NAME OR PROGRAM NAME

10d. RESERVED FOR LOCAL USE

d. IS THERE ANOTHER HEALTH BENEFIT PLAN? YES NO *If yes,* return to and complete item 9 a-d.

READ BACK OF FORM BEFORE COMPLETING & SIGNING THIS FORM.
12. PATIENT'S OR AUTHORIZED PERSON'S SIGNATURE I authorize the release of any medical or other information necessary to process this claim. I also request payment of government benefits either to myself or to the party who accepts assignment below.

SIGNED _____ DATE _____

13. INSURED'S OR AUTHORIZED PERSON'S SIGNATURE I authorize payment of medical benefits to the undersigned physcian or supplier for services described below.

SIGNED _____

14. DATE OF CURRENT: MM 07 DD 12 YY YYYY ILLNESS (First symptom) OR INJURY (Accident) OR PREGNANCY (LMP)

15. IF PATIENT HAS HAD SAME OR SIMILAR ILLNESS, GIVE FIRST DATE MM DD YY

16. DATES PATIENT UNABLE TO WORK IN CURRENT OCCUPATION FROM MM DD YY TO MM DD YY

17. NAME OF REFERRING PROVIDER OR OTHER SOURCE
17a.
17b. NPI 1234567890

18. HOSPITALIZATION DATES RELATED TO CURRENT SERVICES FROM MM DD YY TO MM DD YY

19. RESERVED FOR LOCAL USE

20. OUTSIDE LAB? YES X NO $ CHARGES

21. DIAGNOSIS OR NATURE OF ILLNESS OR INJURY (Relate Items 1, 2, 3 or 4 to Item 24E by Line)
1. 611.72
2. 611.71
3. V16.3
4.

22. MEDICAID RESUBMISSION CODE ORIGINAL REF. NO.

23. PRIOR AUTHORIZATION NUMBER

24. A. DATE(S) OF SERVICE From MM DD YY To MM DD YY	B. PLACE OF SERVICE	C. EMG	D. PROCEDURES, SERVICES, OR SUPPLIES (Explain Unusual Circumstances) CPT/HCPCS MODIFER	E. DIAGNOSIS POINTER	F. $ CHARGES	G. DAYS OR UNITS	H. EPSDT Family Plan	I. ID. QUAL.	J. RENDERING PROVIDER ID. #
1 07 12 YYYY	11		99212	12	65 00			NPI	
2								NPI	
3								NPI	
4								NPI	
5								NPI	
6								NPI	

25. FEDERAL TAX I.D. NUMBER SSN EIN
111234562 X

26. PATIENT'S ACCOUNT NO.
14-A

27. ACCEPT ASSIGNMENT? (For govt. claims, see back)
X YES NO

28. TOTAL CHARGE
$ 65 00

29. AMOUNT PAID
$

30. BALANCE DUE
$

31. SIGNATURE OF PHYSICIAN OR SUPPLIER INCLUDING DEGREES OR CREDENTIALS
(I certify that the statements on the reverse apply to this bill and are made a part thereof.)
DONALD L GIVINGS MD
SIGNED ___ DATE MMDDYYYY

32. SERVICE FACILITY LOCATION INFORMATION
DONALD L GIVINGS MD
11350 MEDICAL DRIVE
ANYWHERE US 12345
1234567890

33. BILLING PROVIDER INFO & PH # (101)1115555
DONALD L GIVINGS MD
11350 MEDICAL DRIVE
ANYWHERE US 12345
a 1234567890

NUCC Instruction Manual available at: www.nucc.org

APPROVED OMB-0938-0999 FORM CMS-1500 (08/05)

Case Study 14-b Medicare

1500

HEALTH INSURANCE CLAIM FORM

APPROVED BY NATIONAL UNIFORM CLAIM COMMITTE 08/05

CARRIER

PICA			PICA

1. MEDICARE	MEDICAID	TRICARE CHAMPUS	CHAMPVA	GROUP HEALTH PLAN	FECA BLK LUNG	OTHER	1a. INSURED'S I.D. NUMBER (For Program in Item 1)
[X] (Medicare #)	(Medicaid #)	(Sponsor's SSN)	(Member ID#)	(SSN or ID)	(SSN)	(ID)	444223333A

2. PATIENT'S NAME (Last Name, First Name, Middle Initial)
WORTHINGTON, ALICE, E

3. PATIENT'S BIRTH DATE MM DD YY 02 16 1926 SEX M [ ] F [X]

4. INSURED'S NAME (Last Name, First Name, Middle Initial)

5. PATIENT'S ADDRESS (No., Street)
3301 SUNNY DAY DRIVE

6. PATIENT'S RELATIONSHIP TO INSURED
Self [ ] Spouse [ ] Child [ ] Other [ ]

7. INSURED'S ADDRESS (No., Street)

CITY ANYWHERE   STATE US

8. PATIENT STATUS
Single [X] Married [ ] Other [ ]

CITY   STATE

ZIP CODE 12345   TELEPHONE (Include Area Code) (101) 3335555

Employed [ ] Full-Time Student [ ] Part-Time Student [ ]

ZIP CODE   TELEPHONE (Include Area Code) ( )

9. OTHER INSURED'S NAME (Last Name, First Name, Middle Initial)

10. IS PATIENT'S CONDITION RELATED TO:

11. INSURED'S POLICY GROUP OR FECA NUMBER
NONE

a. OTHER INSURED'S POLICY OR GROUP NUMBER

a. EMPLOYMENT? (Current or Previous) YES [ ] NO [X]

a. INSURED'S DATE OF BIRTH MM DD YY   SEX M [ ] F [ ]

b. OTHER INSURED'S DATE OF BIRTH MM DD YY SEX M [ ] F [ ]

b. AUTO ACCIDENT? YES [ ] NO [X] PLACE (State)

b. EMPLOYER'S NAME OR SCHOOL NAME

c. EMPLOYER'S NAME OR SCHOOL NAME

c. OTHER ACCIDENT? YES [ ] NO [X]

c. INSURANCE PLAN NAME OR PROGRAM NAME

d. INSURANCE PLAN NAME OR PROGRAM NAME

10d. RESERVED FOR LOCAL USE

d. IS THERE ANOTHER HEALTH BENEFIT PLAN?
YES [ ] NO [ ] If yes, return to and complete item 9 a-d.

READ BACK OF FORM BEFORE COMPLETING & SIGNING THIS FORM.
12. PATIENT'S OR AUTHORIZED PERSON'S SIGNATURE I authorize the release of any medical or other information necessary to process this claim. I also request payment of government benefits either to myself or to the party who accepts assignment below.

SIGNED SIGNATURE ON FILE   DATE

13. INSURED'S OR AUTHORIZED PERSON'S SIGNATURE I authorize payment of medical benefits to the undersigned physcian or supplier for services described below.

SIGNED

14. DATE OF CURRENT: MM DD YY 07 12 YYYY ILLNESS (First symptom) OR INJURY (Accident) OR PREGNANCY (LMP)

15. IF PATIENT HAS HAD SAME OR SIMILAR ILLNESS, GIVE FIRST DATE MM DD YY

16. DATES PATIENT UNABLE TO WORK IN CURRENT OCCUPATION FROM MM DD YY TO MM DD YY

17. NAME OF REFERRING PROVIDER OR OTHER SOURCE

17a.
17b. NPI 1234567890

18. HOSPITALIZATION DATES RELATED TO CURRENT SERVICES FROM MM DD YY TO MM DD YY

19. RESERVED FOR LOCAL USE

20. OUTSIDE LAB? YES [ ] NO [X] $ CHARGES

21. DIAGNOSIS OR NATURE OF ILLNESS OR INJURY (Relate Items 1, 2, 3 or 4 to Item 24E by Line)
1. 611.72
2. 611.71
3. V16.3
4.

22. MEDICAID RESUBMISSION CODE   ORIGINAL REF. NO.

23. PRIOR AUTHORIZATION NUMBER

24. A DATE(S) OF SERVICE From MM DD YY To MM DD YY	B. PLACE OF SERVICE	C. EMG	D. PROCEDURES, SERVICES, OR SUPPLIES (Explain Unusual Circumstances) CPT/HCPCS	MODIFER	E. DIAGNOSIS POINTER	F. $ CHARGES	G. DAYS OR UNITS	H. EPSDT Family Plan	I. ID. QUAL.	J. RENDERING PROVIDER ID. #
1	0715YYYY	11		99242		123	75 00	1		NPI	
2										NPI	
3										NPI	
4										NPI	
5										NPI	
6										NPI	

25. FEDERAL TAX I.D. NUMBER 111234562 SSN [ ] EIN [X]

26. PATIENT'S ACCOUNT NO. 14-B

27. ACCEPT ASSIGNMENT? (For govt. claims, see back) YES [X] NO [ ]

28. TOTAL CHARGE $ 75 00

29. AMOUNT PAID $

30. BALANCE DUE $

31. SIGNATURE OF PHYSICIAN OR SUPPLIER INCLUDING DEGREES OR CREDENTIALS (I certify that the statements on the reverse apply to this bill and are made a part thereof.)
JONATHAN B KUTTER MD
SIGNED   DATE MMDDYYYY

32. SERVICE FACILITY LOCATION INFORMATION
JONATHAN B KUTTER MD
339 WOODLAND PLACE
ANYWHERE US 12345
a. 234ABC5678 b.

33. BILLING PROVIDER INFO & PH # (101)1115555
JONATHAN B KUTTER MD
339 WOODLAND PLACE
ANYWHERE US 12345
a. 234ABC5678 b.

ASSIGNMENT 14.2 Medicare as Secondary Payer CMS-1500 Claims Completion

Case Study 14-c

[1500]

HEALTH INSURANCE CLAIM FORM

APPROVED BY NATIONAL UNIFORM CLAIM COMMITTE 08/05

| | PICA | | | | | | | | PICA | | |

1. MEDICARE	MEDICAID	TRICARE CHAMPUS	CHAMPVA	GROUP HEALTH PLAN	FECA BLK LUNG	OTHER	1a. INSURED'S I.D. NUMBER	(For Program in Item 1)
[X] (Medicare #)	(Medicaid #)	(Sponsor's SSN)	(Member ID#)	(SSN or ID)	(SSN)	(ID)	667143344A	

2. PATIENT'S NAME (Last Name, First Name, Middle Initial)
NICHOLS, REBECCA

3. PATIENT'S BIRTH DATE MM DD YY **SEX**
10 12 1925 M [ ] F [X]

4. INSURED'S NAME (Last Name, First Name, Middle Initial)
SAME

5. PATIENT'S ADDRESS (No., Street)
384 DEAN STREET

6. PATIENT'S RELATIONSHIP TO INSURED
Self [X] Spouse [ ] Child [ ] Other [ ]

7. INSURED'S ADDRESS (No.. Street)
SAME

CITY ANYWHERE **STATE** US

8. PATIENT STATUS
Single [X] Married [ ] Other [ ]

Employed [ ] Full-Time Student [ ] Part-Time Student [ ]

CITY **STATE**

ZIP CODE 12345 **TELEPHONE (Include Area Code)** (101) 3335555

ZIP CODE **TELEPHONE (Include Area Code)** ( )

9. OTHER INSURED'S NAME (Last Name, First Name, Middle Initial)

11. INSURED'S POLICY GROUP OR FECA NUMBER
NONE

a. OTHER INSURED'S POLICY OR GROUP NUMBER
667143344

10. IS PATIENT'S CONDITION RELATED TO:

a. EMPLOYMENT? (Current or Previous)
YES [ ] NO [X]

a. INSURED'S DATE OF BIRTH MM DD YY **SEX**
M [ ] F [ ]

b. OTHER INSURED'S DATE OF BIRTH MM DD YY **SEX**
10 12 1925 M [ ] F [X]

b. AUTO ACCIDENT? **PLACE (State)**
YES [ ] NO [X]

b. EMPLOYER'S NAME OR SCHOOL NAME

c. EMPLOYER'S NAME OR SCHOOL NAME

c. OTHER ACCIDENT?
YES [ ] NO [X]

c. INSURANCE PLAN NAME OR PROGRAM NAME
BCBS

d. INSURANCE PLAN NAME OR PROGRAM NAME

10d. RESERVED FOR LOCAL USE

d. IS THERE ANOTHER HEALTH BENEFIT PLAN?
[X] YES [ ] NO *If yes, return to and complete item 9 a-d.*

READ BACK OF FORM BEFORE COMPLETING & SIGNING THIS FORM.

12. PATIENT'S OR AUTHORIZED PERSON'S SIGNATURE I authorize the release of any medical or other information necessary to process this claim. I also request payment of government benefits either to myself or to the party who accepts assignment below.

SIGNED SIGNATURE ON FILE DATE

13. INSURED'S OR AUTHORIZED PERSON'S SIGNATURE I authorize payment of medical benefits to the undersigned physcian or supplier for services described below.

SIGNED

14. DATE OF CURRENT: MM DD YY
08 06 YYYY ◄ ILLNESS (First symptom) OR INJURY (Accident) OR PREGNANCY (LMP)

15. IF PATIENT HAS HAD SAME OR SIMILAR ILLNESS, GIVE FIRST DATE MM DD YY

16. DATES PATIENT UNABLE TO WORK IN CURRENT OCCUPATION
MM DD YY MM DD YY
FROM TO

17. NAME OF REFERRING PROVIDER OR OTHER SOURCE

17a.
17b. NPI

18. HOSPITALIZATION DATES RELATED TO CURRENT SERVICES
MM DD YY MM DD YY
FROM TO

19. RESERVED FOR LOCAL USE

20. OUTSIDE LAB? **$ CHARGES**
YES [ ] NO [X]

21. DIAGNOSIS OR NATURE OF ILLNESS OR INJURY (Relate Items 1, 2, 3 or 4 to Item 24E by Line)

1. 569 3
2. 787 1
3. 783 21
4.

22. MEDICAID RESUBMISSION CODE ORIGINAL REF. NO.

23. PRIOR AUTHORIZATION NUMBER

24. A DATE(S) OF SERVICE From To MM DD YY MM DD YY	B. PLACE OF SERVICE	C. EMG	D. PROCEDURES, SERVICES, OR SUPPLIES (Explain Unusual Circumstances) CPT/HCPCS MODIFER	E. DIAGNOSIS POINTER	F. $ CHARGES	G. DAYS OR UNITS	H. EPSDT Family Plan	I. ID. QUAL.	J. RENDERING PROVIDER ID. #
1	08 06 YYYY	21		99223	123	175 00	1		NPI	
2	08 07 YYYY	21		99233	123	170 00	2		NPI	
3	08 09 YYYY	21		99232	123	75 00	1		NPI	
4	08 10 YYYY	21		99238	1	75 00	1		NPI	
5									NPI	
6									NPI	

25. FEDERAL TAX I.D. NUMBER SSN EIN
111234562 [X]

26. PATIENT'S ACCOUNT NO.
14-C

27. ACCEPT ASSIGNMENT? (For govt. claims, see back)
[X] YES [ ] NO

28. TOTAL CHARGE
$ 495 00

29. AMOUNT PAID
$

30. BALANCE DUE
$

31. SIGNATURE OF PHYSICIAN OR SUPPLIER INCLUDING DEGREES OR CREDENTIALS (I certify that the statements on the reverse apply to this bill and are made a part thereof.)

DONALD L GIVINGS MD

SIGNED DATE MMDDYYYY

32. SERVICE FACILITY LOCATION INFORMATION
MERCY HOSPITAL
ANYWHERE STREET
ANYWHERE US 12345

a. 987XYZ6543 b.

33. BILLING PROVIDER INFO & PH # (101)1115555
DONALD L GIVINGS MD
11350 MEDICAL DRIVE
ANYWHERE US 12345

a. 1234567890 b.

NUCC Instruction Manual available at: www.nucc.org

APPROVED OMB-0938-0999 FORM CMS-1500 (08/05)

Case Study 14-d

1500

HEALTH INSURANCE CLAIM FORM

APPROVED BY NATIONAL UNIFORM CLAIM COMMITTE 08/05

PICA		PICA

1. MEDICARE MEDICAID TRICARE CHAMPUS CHAMPVA GROUP HEALTH PLAN FECA BLK LUNG OTHER	1a. INSURED'S I.D. NUMBER (For Program in Item 1)
X (Medicare #) (Medicaid #) (Sponsor's SSN) (Member ID#) (SSN or ID) (SSN) (ID)	312785894A

2. PATIENT'S NAME (Last Name, First Name, Middle Initial)
MAHONEY JR, SAMUEL, T

3. PATIENT'S BIRTH DATE MM 09 DD 04 YY 1930 **SEX** M X F

4. INSURED'S NAME (Last Name, First Name, Middle Initial)
SAME

5. PATIENT'S ADDRESS (No., Street)
498 MEADOW LANE

6. PATIENT'S RELATIONSHIP TO INSURED
Self X Spouse Child Other

7. INSURED'S ADDRESS (No., Street)
SAME

CITY ANYWHERE **STATE** US

8. PATIENT STATUS
Single Married X Other

CITY **STATE**

ZIP CODE 12345 **TELEPHONE (Include Area Code)** (101) 3335555

Employed Full-Time Student Part-Time Student

ZIP CODE **TELEPHONE (Include Area Code)** ( )

9. OTHER INSURED'S NAME (Last Name, First Name, Middle Initial)
MAHONEY JR, SAMUEL, T

10. IS PATIENT'S CONDITION RELATED TO:

11. INSURED'S POLICY GROUP OR FECA NUMBER
NONE

a. OTHER INSURED'S POLICY OR GROUP NUMBER
312785894

a. EMPLOYMENT? (Current or Previous)
YES X NO

a. INSURED'S DATE OF BIRTH MM DD YY **SEX** M F

b. OTHER INSURED'S DATE OF BIRTH MM 09 DD 04 YY 1930 **SEX** M X F

b. AUTO ACCIDENT? PLACE (State)
YES X NO

b. EMPLOYER'S NAME OR SCHOOL NAME

c. EMPLOYER'S NAME OR SCHOOL NAME

c. OTHER ACCIDENT?
YES X NO

c. INSURANCE PLAN NAME OR PROGRAM NAME
AETNA

d. INSURANCE PLAN NAME OR PROGRAM NAME

10d. RESERVED FOR LOCAL USE

d. IS THERE ANOTHER HEALTH BENEFIT PLAN?
X YES NO *If yes,* return to and complete item 9 a-d.

READ BACK OF FORM BEFORE COMPLETING & SIGNING THIS FORM.
12. PATIENT'S OR AUTHORIZED PERSON'S SIGNATURE I authorize the release of any medical or other information necessary to process this claim. I also request payment of government benefits either to myself or to the party who accepts assignment below.

SIGNED **SIGNATURE ON FILE** DATE

13. INSURED'S OR AUTHORIZED PERSON'S SIGNATURE I authorize payment of medical benefits to the undersigned physcian or supplier for services described below.

SIGNED

14. DATE OF CURRENT: MM 01 DD 01 YY YYYY ILLNESS (First symptom) OR INJURY (Accident) OR PREGNANCY (LMP)

15. IF PATIENT HAS HAD SAME OR SIMILAR ILLNESS, GIVE FIRST DATE MM DD YY

16. DATES PATIENT UNABLE TO WORK IN CURRENT OCCUPATION FROM MM DD YY TO MM DD YY

17. NAME OF REFERRING PROVIDER OR OTHER SOURCE
17a.
17b. NPI

18. HOSPITALIZATION DATES RELATED TO CURRENT SERVICES FROM MM DD YY TO MM DD YY

19. RESERVED FOR LOCAL USE

20. OUTSIDE LAB? YES X NO **$ CHARGES**

21. DIAGNOSIS OR NATURE OF ILLNESS OR INJURY (Relate Items 1, 2, 3 or 4 to Item 24E by Line)
1. 493 90
2. 465 9
3.
4.

22. MEDICAID RESUBMISSION CODE ORIGINAL REF. NO.

23. PRIOR AUTHORIZATION NUMBER

24. A DATE(S) OF SERVICE From MM DD YY To MM DD YY	B. PLACE OF SERVICE	C. EMG	D. PROCEDURES, SERVICES, OR SUPPLIES (Explain Unusual Circumstances) CPT/HCPCS MODIFER	E. DIAGNOSIS POINTER	F. $ CHARGES	G. DAYS OR UNITS	H. EPSDT Family Plan	I. ID. QUAL.	J. RENDERING PROVIDER ID. #
1 10 03 YYYY	11		99212	12	25 16	1		NPI	
2								NPI	
3								NPI	
4								NPI	
5								NPI	
6								NPI	

25. FEDERAL TAX I.D. NUMBER SSN EIN
1149586792 X

26. PATIENT'S ACCOUNT NO.
14-D

27. ACCEPT ASSIGNMENT? (For govt. claims, see back)
YES X NO

28. TOTAL CHARGE $ 25 16

29. AMOUNT PAID $ 25 16

30. BALANCE DUE $

31. SIGNATURE OF PHYSICIAN OR SUPPLIER INCLUDING DEGREES OR CREDENTIALS (I certify that the statements on the reverse apply to this bill and are made a part thereof.)

LISA M MASON MD
SIGNED DATE MMDDYYYY

32. SERVICE FACILITY LOCATION INFORMATION
LISA M MASON MD
547 ANTIGUA ROAD
ANYWHERE US 12345
a. 456ABC7890 b.

33. BILLING PROVIDER INFO & PH # (101)1115555
LISA M MASON MD
547 ANTIGUA ROAD
ANYWHERE US 12345
a. 456ABC7890 b.

NUCC Instruction Manual available at: www.nucc.org

APPROVED OMB-0938-0999 FORM CMS-1500 (08/05)

PICA / CARRIER / PATIENT AND INSURED INFORMATION / PHYSICIAN OR SUPPLIER INFORMATION

ASSIGNMENT 14.3 Medicare/Medigap CMS-1500 Claims Completion

Case Study 14-e Primary

<table>
<tr><td colspan="3">

[1500]

HEALTH INSURANCE CLAIM FORM
APPROVED BY NATIONAL UNIFORM CLAIM COMMITTEE 08/05

</td></tr>
</table>

□□ PICA		PICA □□

1. MEDICARE ☐ (Medicare #) MEDICAID ☐ (Medicaid #) TRICARE CHAMPUS ☐ (Sponsor's SSN) CHAMPVA ☐ (Member ID#) GROUP HEALTH PLAN ☐ (SSN or ID) FECA BLK LUNG ☐ (SSN) OTHER ☐ (ID) **1a. INSURED'S I.D. NUMBER** (For Program in Item 1) **645454545A**

2. PATIENT'S NAME (Last Name, First Name, Middle Initial)
FREED, ABRAHAM, N

3. PATIENT'S BIRTH DATE MM 10 DD 03 YY 1922 SEX M [X] F ☐

4. INSURED'S NAME (Last Name, First Name, Middle Initial)

5. PATIENT'S ADDRESS (No., Street)
12 NOTTINGHAM CIRCLE

6. PATIENT'S RELATIONSHIP TO INSURED
Self ☐ Spouse ☐ Child ☐ Other ☐

7. INSURED'S ADDRESS (No., Street)

CITY
ANYWHERE   STATE US

8. PATIENT STATUS
Single ☐ Married [X] Other ☐
Employed ☐ Full-Time Student ☐ Part-Time Student ☐

CITY   STATE

ZIP CODE 12345   TELEPHONE (Include Area Code) (101) 3335555

ZIP CODE   TELEPHONE (Include Area Code) ( )

9. OTHER INSURED'S NAME (Last Name, First Name, Middle Initial)
SAME

10. IS PATIENT'S CONDITION RELATED TO:

11. INSURED'S POLICY GROUP OR FECA NUMBER
NONE

a. OTHER INSURED'S POLICY OR GROUP NUMBER
NXY645454545987

a. EMPLOYMENT? (Current or Previous)
YES ☐ [X] NO

a. INSURED'S DATE OF BIRTH MM DD YY SEX M ☐ F ☐

b. OTHER INSURED'S DATE OF BIRTH MM 10 DD 03 YY 1922 SEX M [X] F ☐

b. AUTO ACCIDENT? PLACE (State)
YES ☐ [X] NO

b. EMPLOYER'S NAME OR SCHOOL NAME

c. EMPLOYER'S NAME OR SCHOOL NAME

c. OTHER ACCIDENT?
YES ☐ [X] NO

c. INSURANCE PLAN NAME OR PROGRAM NAME

d. INSURANCE PLAN NAME OR PROGRAM NAME
BCBS MEDIGAP

10d. RESERVED FOR LOCAL USE

d. IS THERE ANOTHER HEALTH BENEFIT PLAN?
[X] YES ☐ NO *If yes,* return to and complete item 9 a-d.

READ BACK OF FORM BEFORE COMPLETING & SIGNING THIS FORM.
12. PATIENT'S OR AUTHORIZED PERSON'S SIGNATURE I authorize the release of any medical or other information necessary to process this claim. I also request payment of government benefits either to myself or to the party who accepts assignment below.
SIGNED SIGNATURE ON FILE DATE

13. INSURED'S OR AUTHORIZED PERSON'S SIGNATURE I authorize payment of medical benefits to the undersigned physican or supplier for services described below.
SIGNED

14. DATE OF CURRENT: MM 03 DD 07 YY YYYY ◄ ILLNESS (First symptom) OR INJURY (Accident) OR PREGNANCY (LMP)

15. IF PATIENT HAS HAD SAME OR SIMILAR ILLNESS, GIVE FIRST DATE MM DD YY

16. DATES PATIENT UNABLE TO WORK IN CURRENT OCCUPATION FROM MM DD YY TO MM DD YY

17. NAME OF REFERRING PROVIDER OR OTHER SOURCE
17a.
17b. NPI

18. HOSPITALIZATION DATES RELATED TO CURRENT SERVICES FROM MM DD YY TO MM DD YY

19. RESERVED FOR LOCAL USE

20. OUTSIDE LAB? YES ☐ [X] NO $ CHARGES

21. DIAGNOSIS OR NATURE OF ILLNESS OR INJURY (Relate Items 1, 2, 3 or 4 to Item 24E by Line)
1. 401 0
2. 780 2
3.
4.

22. MEDICAID RESUBMISSION CODE   ORIGINAL REF. NO.

23. PRIOR AUTHORIZATION NUMBER

24. A DATE(S) OF SERVICE From MM DD YY	To MM DD YY	B. PLACE OF SERVICE	C. EMG	D. PROCEDURES, SERVICES, OR SUPPLIES (Explain Unusual Circumstances) CPT/HCPCS | MODIFER	E. DIAGNOSIS POINTER	F. $ CHARGES	G. DAYS OR UNITS	H. EPSDT Family Plan	I. ID. QUAL.	J. RENDERING PROVIDER ID. #
1	03 07 YYYY		11		99204		12	100 00	1		NPI
2	03 07 YYYY		11		93000		12	50 00	1		NPI
3	03 07 YYYY		11		36415		2	8 00	1		NPI
4										NPI
5										NPI
6										NPI

25. FEDERAL TAX I.D. NUMBER SSN ☐ EIN [X]
111234562

26. PATIENT'S ACCOUNT NO.
14-E

27. ACCEPT ASSIGNMENT? (For govt. claims, see back) [X] YES ☐ NO

28. TOTAL CHARGE $ 158 00

29. AMOUNT PAID $

30. BALANCE DUE $

31. SIGNATURE OF PHYSICIAN OR SUPPLIER INCLUDING DEGREES OR CREDENTIALS (I certify that the statements on the reverse apply to this bill and are made a part thereof.)
DONALD L GIVINGS MD
SIGNED DATE MMDDYYYY

32. SERVICE FACILITY LOCATION INFORMATION
DONALD L GIVINGS MD
11350 MEDICAL DRIVE
ANYWHERE US 12345
1234567890   b.

33. BILLING PROVIDER INFO & PH # (101) 1115555
DONALD L GIVINGS MD
11350 MEDICAL DRIVE
ANYWHERE US 12345
a.1234567890   b.

NUCC Instruction Manual available at: www.nucc.org   APPROVED OMB-0938-0999 FORM CMS-1500 (08/05)

Case Study 14-e Secondary

[1500]

HEALTH INSURANCE CLAIM FORM

APPROVED BY NATIONAL UNIFORM CLAIM COMMITTE 08/05

| | PICA | | | | | | | | PICA | |

1. MEDICARE	MEDICAID	TRICARE CHAMPUS	CHAMPVA	GROUP HEALTH PLAN	FECA BLK LUNG	OTHER	1a. INSURED'S I.D. NUMBER (For Program in Item 1)
(Medicare #)	(Medicaid #)	(Sponsor's SSN)	(Member ID#)	(SSN or ID)	(SSN)	[X] (ID)	NXY6454545

2. PATIENT'S NAME (Last Name, First Name, Middle Initial)	3. PATIENT'S BIRTH DATE MM DD YY / SEX	4. INSURED'S NAME (Last Name, First Name, Middle Initial)
FREED, ABRAHAM, N	10 03 1922 M [X] F	SAME

5. PATIENT'S ADDRESS (No., Street)	6. PATIENT'S RELATIONSHIP TO INSURED	7. INSURED'S ADDRESS (No., Street)
12 NOTTINGHAM CIRCLE	Self [X] Spouse Child Other	SAME

CITY	STATE	8. PATIENT STATUS	CITY	STATE
ANYWHERE	US	Single Married [X] Other		

ZIP CODE	TELEPHONE (Include Area Code)		ZIP CODE	TELEPHONE (Include Area Code)
12345	(101) 3335555	Employed / Full-Time Student / Part-Time Student		( )

9. OTHER INSURED'S NAME (Last Name, First Name, Middle Initial)	10. IS PATIENT'S CONDITION RELATED TO:	11. INSURED'S POLICY GROUP OR FECA NUMBER
		987

a. OTHER INSURED'S POLICY OR GROUP NUMBER	a. EMPLOYMENT? (Current or Previous) YES [X] NO	a. INSURED'S DATE OF BIRTH MM DD YY / SEX
		10 03 1922 M [X] F

| b. OTHER INSURED'S DATE OF BIRTH MM DD YY SEX M F | b. AUTO ACCIDENT? PLACE (State) YES [X] NO | b. EMPLOYER'S NAME OR SCHOOL NAME |

| c. EMPLOYER'S NAME OR SCHOOL NAME | c. OTHER ACCIDENT? YES [X] NO | c. INSURANCE PLAN NAME OR PROGRAM NAME BCBS US |

| d. INSURANCE PLAN NAME OR PROGRAM NAME | 10d. RESERVED FOR LOCAL USE | d. IS THERE ANOTHER HEALTH BENEFIT PLAN? YES NO If yes, return to and complete item 9 a-d. |

READ BACK OF FORM BEFORE COMPLETING & SIGNING THIS FORM.

12. PATIENT'S OR AUTHORIZED PERSON'S SIGNATURE I authorize the release of any medical or other information necessary to process this claim. I also request payment of government benefits either to myself or to the party who accepts assignment below.

SIGNED **SIGNATURE ON FILE** DATE _____

13. INSURED'S OR AUTHORIZED PERSON'S SIGNATURE I authorize payment of medical benefits to the undersigned physcian or supplier for services described below.

SIGNED _____

14. DATE OF CURRENT: MM DD YY / ILLNESS (First symptom) OR INJURY (Accident) OR PREGNANCY (LMP) 03 07 YYYY	15. IF PATIENT HAS HAD SAME OR SIMILAR ILLNESS, GIVE FIRST DATE MM DD YY	16. DATES PATIENT UNABLE TO WORK IN CURRENT OCCUPATION MM DD YY MM DD YY FROM TO

| 17. NAME OF REFERRING PROVIDER OR OTHER SOURCE | 17a. / 17b. NPI | 18. HOSPITALIZATION DATES RELATED TO CURRENT SERVICES MM DD YY MM DD YY FROM TO |

| 19. RESERVED FOR LOCAL USE | | 20. OUTSIDE LAB? $ CHARGES YES [X] NO |

21. DIAGNOSIS OR NATURE OF ILLNESS OR INJURY (Relate Items 1, 2, 3 or 4 to Item 24E by Line)

1. 401 0
2. 780 2
3. _____
4. _____

22. MEDICAID RESUBMISSION CODE ORIGINAL REF. NO.

23. PRIOR AUTHORIZATION NUMBER

24. A DATE(S) OF SERVICE From MM DD YY To MM DD YY	B. PLACE OF SERVICE	C. EMG	D. PROCEDURES, SERVICES, OR SUPPLIES (Explain Unusual Circumstances) CPT/HCPCS MODIFER	E. DIAGNOSIS POINTER	F. $ CHARGES	G. DAYS OR UNITS	H. EPSDT Family Plan	I. ID. QUAL.	J. RENDERING PROVIDER ID. #
1 03 07 YYYY	11		99204	12	100 00	1		NPI	
2 03 07 YYYY	11		93000	12	50 00	1		NPI	
3 03 07 YYYY	11		36415	12	8 00	1		NPI	
4								NPI	
5								NPI	
6								NPI	

25. FEDERAL TAX I.D. NUMBER SSN EIN	26. PATIENT'S ACCOUNT NO.	27. ACCEPT ASSIGNMENT? (For govt. claims, see back)	28. TOTAL CHARGE	29. AMOUNT PAID	30. BALANCE DUE
111234562 [X]	14-E	[X] YES NO	$ 158 00	$	$

| 31. SIGNATURE OF PHYSICIAN OR SUPPLIER INCLUDING DEGREES OR CREDENTIALS (I certify that the statements on the reverse apply to this bill and are made a part thereof.) DONALD L GIVINGS MD SIGNED DATE MMDDYYYY | 32. SERVICE FACILITY LOCATION INFORMATION DONALD L GIVINGS MD 11350 MEDICAL DRIVE ANYWHERE US 12345 1234567890 b. | 33. BILLING PROVIDER INFO & PH # (101)1115555 DONALD L GIVINGS MD 11350 MEDICAL DRIVE ANYWHERE US 12345 a 1234567890 b. |

NUCC Instruction Manual available at: www.nucc.org

APPROVED OMB-0938-0999 FORM CMS-1500 (08/05)

ASSIGNMENT 14.4 Medicare/Medicaid CMS-1500 Claims Completion

Case Study 14-f

Case Study 14-g

1500

HEALTH INSURANCE CLAIM FORM

APPROVED BY NATIONAL UNIFORM CLAIM COMMITTE 08/05

| | PICA | | | | | | | PICA | |

1. MEDICARE	MEDICAID	TRICARE CHAMPUS	CHAMPVA	GROUP HEALTH PLAN	FECA BLK LUNG	OTHER	1a. INSURED'S I.D. NUMBER (For Program in Item 1)
X (Medicare #)	X (Medicaid #)	(Sponsor's SSN)	(Member ID#)	(SSN or ID)	(SSN)	(ID)	485375869A

2. PATIENT'S NAME (Last Name, First Name, Middle Initial)
DELANEY, PATRICIA, S

3. PATIENT'S BIRTH DATE   SEX
MM DD YY
04 12 1931   M☐ F☒

4. INSURED'S NAME (Last Name, First Name, Middle Initial)

5. PATIENT'S ADDRESS (No., Street)
485 GARDEN LANE

6. PATIENT'S RELATIONSHIP TO INSURED
Self☐ Spouse☐ Child☐ Other☐

7. INSURED'S ADDRESS (No., Street)

CITY
ANYWHERE

STATE
US

8. PATIENT STATUS
Single ☒ Married☐ Other☐

CITY

STATE

ZIP CODE
12345

TELEPHONE (Include Area Code)
(101) 3335555

Employed☐ Full-Time Student☐ Part-Time Student☐

ZIP CODE

TELEPHONE (Include Area Code)
( )

9. OTHER INSURED'S NAME (Last Name, First Name, Middle Initial)

10. IS PATIENT'S CONDITION RELATED TO:

11. INSURED'S POLICY GROUP OR FECA NUMBER
NONE

a. OTHER INSURED'S POLICY OR GROUP NUMBER

a. EMPLOYMENT? (Current or Previous)
YES☐ X NO☒

a. INSURED'S DATE OF BIRTH   SEX
MM DD YY
M☐ F☐

b. OTHER INSURED'S DATE OF BIRTH   SEX
MM DD YY
M☐ F☐

b. AUTO ACCIDENT?   PLACE (State)
YES☐ X NO☒

b. EMPLOYER'S NAME OR SCHOOL NAME

c. EMPLOYER'S NAME OR SCHOOL NAME

c. OTHER ACCIDENT?
YES☐ X NO☒

c. INSURANCE PLAN NAME OR PROGRAM NAME

d. INSURANCE PLAN NAME OR PROGRAM NAME

10d. RESERVED FOR LOCAL USE
MCD22886644XT

d. IS THERE ANOTHER HEALTH BENEFIT PLAN?
YES☐ NO☐ If yes, return to and complete item 9 a-d.

READ BACK OF FORM BEFORE COMPLETING & SIGNING THIS FORM.
12. PATIENT'S OR AUTHORIZED PERSON'S SIGNATURE I authorize the release of any medical or other information necessary to process this claim. I also request payment of government benefits either to myself or to the party who accepts assignment below.

SIGNED SIGNATURE ON FILE   DATE

13. INSURED'S OR AUTHORIZED PERSON'S SIGNATURE I authorize payment of medical benefits to the undersigned physcian or supplier for services described below.

SIGNED

14. DATE OF CURRENT: ILLNESS (First symptom) OR
MM DD YY   INJURY (Accident) OR
12 15 YYYY   PREGNANCY (LMP)

15. IF PATIENT HAS HAD SAME OR SIMILAR ILLNESS, GIVE FIRST DATE MM DD YY

16. DATES PATIENT UNABLE TO WORK IN CURRENT OCCUPATION
MM DD YY   MM DD YY
FROM   TO

17. NAME OF REFERRING PROVIDER OR OTHER SOURCE

17a.
17b. NPI 1234567890

18. HOSPITALIZATION DATES RELATED TO CURRENT SERVICES
MM DD YY   MM DD YY
FROM   TO

19. RESERVED FOR LOCAL USE

20. OUTSIDE LAB? $ CHARGES
YES☐ X NO☒

21. DIAGNOSIS OR NATURE OF ILLNESS OR INJURY (Relate Items 1, 2, 3 or 4 to Item 24E by Line)
1. 695 . 3
2.
3.
4.

22. MEDICAID RESUBMISSION
CODE   ORIGINAL REF. NO.

23. PRIOR AUTHORIZATION NUMBER

24. A DATE(S) OF SERVICE From / To MM DD YY MM DD YY	B. PLACE OF SERVICE	C. EMG	D. PROCEDURES, SERVICES, OR SUPPLIES (Explain Unusual Circumstances) CPT/HCPCS / MODIFER	E. DIAGNOSIS POINTER	F. $ CHARGES	G. DAYS OR UNITS	H. EPSDT Family Plan	I. ID. QUAL.	J. RENDERING PROVIDER ID. #
1	12 18 YYYY	11		99243	1	85 00	1		NPI
2									NPI
3									NPI
4									NPI
5									NPI
6									NPI

25. FEDERAL TAX I.D. NUMBER   SSN EIN
115555552   ☒

26. PATIENT'S ACCOUNT NO.
14-G

27. ACCEPT ASSIGNMENT? (For govt. claims, see back)
X YES☒ NO☐

28. TOTAL CHARGE
$ 85 00

29. AMOUNT PAID
$

30. BALANCE DUE
$

31. SIGNATURE OF PHYSICIAN OR SUPPLIER INCLUDING DEGREES OR CREDENTIALS (I certify that the statements on the reverse apply to this bill and are made a part thereof.)
CLAIRE M SKINNER MD
SIGNED   DATE MMDDYYYY

32. SERVICE FACILITY LOCATION INFORMATION
CLAIRE M SKINNER MD
50 CLEAR VIEW DRIVE
ANYWHERE US 12345
a. 567ABC8901   b.

33. BILLING PROVIDER INFO & PH # (101)1115555
CLAIRE M SKINNER MD
50 CLEAR VIEW DRIVE
ANYWHERE US 12345
a. 567ABC8901   b.

NUCC Instruction Manual available at: www.nucc.org

APPROVED OMB-0938-0999 FORM CMS-1500 (08/05)

ASSIGNMENT 14.5 Roster Billing

Case Study 14-h Roster Billing-Flu Vaccine

| 1500 |
| HEALTH INSURANCE CLAIM FORM |

APPROVED BY NATIONAL UNIFORM CLAIM COMMITTE 08/05

| | PICA | | | | | | | | PICA | |

1. MEDICARE (Medicare #)	MEDICAID (Medicaid #)	TRICARE CHAMPUS (Sponsor's SSN)	CHAMPVA (Member ID#)	GROUP HEALTH PLAN (SSN or ID)	FECA BLK LUNG (SSN)	OTHER (ID)	1a. INSURED'S I.D. NUMBER (For Program in Item 1)
							SEE ATTACHED ROSTER

2. PATIENT'S NAME (Last Name, First Name, Middle Initial)

3. PATIENT'S BIRTH DATE MM DD YY   SEX M   F

4. INSURED'S NAME (Last Name, First Name, Middle Initial)

5. PATIENT'S ADDRESS (No., Street)

6. PATIENT'S RELATIONSHIP TO INSURED   Self   Spouse   Child   Other

7. INSURED'S ADDRESS (No., Street)

CITY   STATE

8. PATIENT STATUS   Single   Married   Other

CITY   STATE

ZIP CODE   TELEPHONE (Include Area Code) ( )

Employed   Full-Time Student   Part-Time Student

ZIP CODE   TELEPHONE (Include Area Code) ( )

9. OTHER INSURED'S NAME (Last Name, First Name, Middle Initial)

10. IS PATIENT'S CONDITION RELATED TO:

11. INSURED'S POLICY GROUP OR FECA NUMBER

a. OTHER INSURED'S POLICY OR GROUP NUMBER

a. EMPLOYMENT? (Current or Previous)   YES   NO

a. INSURED'S DATE OF BIRTH MM DD YY   SEX M   F

b. OTHER INSURED'S DATE OF BIRTH MM DD YY   SEX M   F

b. AUTO ACCIDENT?   PLACE (State)   YES   NO

b. EMPLOYER'S NAME OR SCHOOL NAME

c. EMPLOYER'S NAME OR SCHOOL NAME

c. OTHER ACCIDENT?   YES   NO

c. INSURANCE PLAN NAME OR PROGRAM NAME

d. INSURANCE PLAN NAME OR PROGRAM NAME

10d. RESERVED FOR LOCAL USE

d. IS THERE ANOTHER HEALTH BENEFIT PLAN?   YES   NO   **If yes,** return to and complete item 9 a-d.

READ BACK OF FORM BEFORE COMPLETING & SIGNING THIS FORM.
12. PATIENT'S OR AUTHORIZED PERSON'S SIGNATURE I authorize the release of any medical or other information necessary to process this claim. I also request payment of government benefits either to myself or to the party who accepts assignment below.

SIGNED _____ DATE _____

13. INSURED'S OR AUTHORIZED PERSON'S SIGNATURE I authorize payment of medical benefits to the undersigned physcian or supplier for services described below.

SIGNED _____

14. DATE OF CURRENT: MM DD YY   ILLNESS (First symptom) OR INJURY (Accident) OR PREGNANCY (LMP)

15. IF PATIENT HAS HAD SAME OR SIMILAR ILLNESS, GIVE FIRST DATE MM DD YY

16. DATES PATIENT UNABLE TO WORK IN CURRENT OCCUPATION MM DD YY   FROM   TO MM DD YY

17. NAME OF REFERRING PROVIDER OR OTHER SOURCE

17a.
17b. NPI

18. HOSPITALIZATION DATES RELATED TO CURRENT SERVICES MM DD YY   FROM   TO MM DD YY

19. RESERVED FOR LOCAL USE

20. OUTSIDE LAB?   YES   NO $ CHARGES

21. DIAGNOSIS OR NATURE OF ILLNESS OR INJURY (Relate Items 1, 2, 3 or 4 to Item 24E by Line)

1. V04 81
2.
3.
4.

22. MEDICAID RESUBMISSION CODE   ORIGINAL REF. NO.

23. PRIOR AUTHORIZATION NUMBER

24. A. DATE(S) OF SERVICE From MM DD YY To MM DD YY	B. PLACE OF SERVICE	C. EMG	D. PROCEDURES, SERVICES, OR SUPPLIES (Explain Unusual Circumstances) CPT/HCPCS MODIFER	E. DIAGNOSIS POINTER	F. $ CHARGES	G. DAYS OR UNITS	H. EPSDT Family Plan	I. ID. QUAL.	J. RENDERING PROVIDER ID. #
1	03 12 YYYY	60		90658	1	25 00	1		NPI	
2	03 12 YYYY	60		G0008	1	0 00	1		NPI	
3									NPI	
4									NPI	
5									NPI	
6									NPI	

25. FEDERAL TAX I.D. NUMBER   SSN EIN   346121151   X

26. PATIENT'S ACCOUNT NO.   14-H

27. ACCEPT ASSIGNMENT? (For govt. claims, see back)   X YES   NO

28. TOTAL CHARGE $ 0 00

29. AMOUNT PAID $

30. BALANCE DUE $

31. SIGNATURE OF PHYSICIAN OR SUPPLIER INCLUDING DEGREES OR CREDENTIALS (I certify that the statements on the reverse apply to this bill and are made a part thereof.)

SIGNATURE STAMP

SIGNED   DATE MMDDYYYY

32. SERVICE FACILITY LOCATION INFORMATION
MINGO RIVER CLINIC
103 PARK RD
ANYWHERE US 12345
a. 7375433213 b.

33. BILLING PROVIDER INFO & PH # (101)5551111
MINGO RIVER CLINIC
103 PARK RD
ANYWHERE US 12345
a. 7375433213 b.

NUCC Instruction Manual available at: www.nucc.org

APPROVED OMB-0938-0999 FORM CMS-1500 (08/05)

Case Study 14-i Roster Billing-Pneumonia Vaccine

1500

HEALTH INSURANCE CLAIM FORM

APPROVED BY NATIONAL UNIFORM CLAIM COMMITTE 08/05

| | PICA | | | | | | | | PICA | |

1.	MEDICARE	MEDICAID	TRICARE CHAMPUS	CHAMPVA	GROUP HEALTH PLAN	FECA BLK LUNG	OTHER	1a. INSURED'S I.D. NUMBER (For Program in Item 1)
	(Medicare #)	(Medicaid #)	(Sponsor's SSN)	(Member ID#)	(SSN or ID)	(SSN)	(ID)	SEE ATTACHED ROSTER

2. PATIENT'S NAME (Last Name, First Name, Middle Initial)

3. PATIENT'S BIRTH DATE MM DD YY   SEX M   F

4. INSURED'S NAME (Last Name, First Name, Middle Initial)

5. PATIENT'S ADDRESS (No., Street)

6. PATIENT'S RELATIONSHIP TO INSURED   Self Spouse Child Other

7. INSURED'S ADDRESS (No., Street)

CITY   STATE

8. PATIENT STATUS   Single Married Other

CITY   STATE

ZIP CODE   TELEPHONE (Include Area Code) ( )

Employed Full-Time Student Part-Time Student

ZIP CODE   TELEPHONE (Include Area Code) ( )

9. OTHER INSURED'S NAME (Last Name, First Name, Middle Initial)

10. IS PATIENT'S CONDITION RELATED TO:

11. INSURED'S POLICY GROUP OR FECA NUMBER

a. OTHER INSURED'S POLICY OR GROUP NUMBER

a. EMPLOYMENT? (Current or Previous) YES NO

a. INSURED'S DATE OF BIRTH MM DD YY   SEX M F

b. OTHER INSURED'S DATE OF BIRTH MM DD YY SEX M F

b. AUTO ACCIDENT?   PLACE (State) YES NO

b. EMPLOYER'S NAME OR SCHOOL NAME

c. EMPLOYER'S NAME OR SCHOOL NAME

c. OTHER ACCIDENT? YES NO

c. INSURANCE PLAN NAME OR PROGRAM NAME

d. INSURANCE PLAN NAME OR PROGRAM NAME

10d. RESERVED FOR LOCAL USE

d. IS THERE ANOTHER HEALTH BENEFIT PLAN? YES NO If yes, return to and complete item 9 a-d.

READ BACK OF FORM BEFORE COMPLETING & SIGNING THIS FORM.
12. PATIENT'S OR AUTHORIZED PERSON'S SIGNATURE I authorize the release of any medical or other information necessary to process this claim. I also request payment of government benefits either to myself or to the party who accepts assignment below.

SIGNED_____ DATE_____

13. INSURED'S OR AUTHORIZED PERSON'S SIGNATURE I authorize payment of medical benefits to the undersigned physcian or supplier for services described below.

SIGNED_____

14. DATE OF CURRENT: MM DD YY   ILLNESS (First symptom) OR INJURY (Accident) OR PREGNANCY (LMP)

15. IF PATIENT HAS HAD SAME OR SIMILAR ILLNESS, GIVE FIRST DATE MM DD YY

16. DATES PATIENT UNABLE TO WORK IN CURRENT OCCUPATION MM DD YY   FROM   TO MM DD YY

17. NAME OF REFERRING PROVIDER OR OTHER SOURCE

17a.
17b. NPI

18. HOSPITALIZATION DATES RELATED TO CURRENT SERVICES MM DD YY   FROM   TO MM DD YY

19. RESERVED FOR LOCAL USE

20. OUTSIDE LAB? YES NO $ CHARGES

21. DIAGNOSIS OR NATURE OF ILLNESS OR INJURY (Relate Items 1, 2, 3 or 4 to Item 24E by Line)

1. V03.82
2.
3.
4.

22. MEDICAID RESUBMISSION CODE   ORIGINAL REF. NO.

23. PRIOR AUTHORIZATION NUMBER

24. A DATE(S) OF SERVICE From MM DD YY To MM DD YY	B. PLACE OF SERVICE	C. EMG	D. PROCEDURES, SERVICES, OR SUPPLIES (Explain Unusual Circumstances) CPT/HCPCS MODIFER	E. DIAGNOSIS POINTER	F. $ CHARGES	G. DAYS OR UNITS	H. EPSDT Family Plan	I. ID. QUAL.	J. RENDERING PROVIDER ID. #
1	05 03 YYYY			90732	1	45 00	1		NPI	
2	05 03 YYYY			G0009	1	0 00	1		NPI	
3									NPI	
4									NPI	
5									NPI	
6									NPI	

25. FEDERAL TAX I.D. NUMBER   SSN EIN
346121151   X

26. PATIENT'S ACCOUNT NO.
14-I

27. ACCEPT ASSIGNMENT? (For govt. claims, see back) X YES NO

28. TOTAL CHARGE
$ 45 00

29. AMOUNT PAID
$ 00 00

30. BALANCE DUE
$

31. SIGNATURE OF PHYSICIAN OR SUPPLIER INCLUDING DEGREES OR CREDENTIALS (I certify that the statements on the reverse apply to this bill and are made a part thereof.)

SIGNATURE STAMP

SIGNED   DATE MMDDYYYY

32. SERVICE FACILITY LOCATION INFORMATION
MINGO RIVER CLINIC
103 PARK RD
ANYWHERE US 12345
a. 7375433213   b.

33. BILLING PROVIDER INFO & PH # (101)5551111
MINGO RIVER CLINIC
103 PARK RD
ANYWHERE US 12345
a. 7375433213   b.

NUCC Instruction Manual available at: www.nucc.org

APPROVED OMB-0938-0999 FORM CMS-1500 (08/05)

ASSIGNMENT 14.5 Multiple Choice Review

1.	a	**11.**	d
2.	a	**12.**	c
3.	c	**13.**	a
4.	a	**14.**	b
5.	d	**15.**	a
6.	c	**16.**	c
7.	d	**17.**	b
8.	b	**18.**	b
9.	c	**19.**	a
10.	a	**20.**	d

CHAPTER 15 Medicaid

ASSIGNMENT 15.1 Medicaid Primary CMS-1500 Claims Completion

Case Study 15-a

CPT copyright 2007 American Medical Association. All rights reserved.

Case Study 15-b

| 1500 |

HEALTH INSURANCE CLAIM FORM

APPROVED BY NATIONAL UNIFORM CLAIM COMMITTEE 08/05

| | PICA | | | | | | | | | PICA | | |

1. MEDICARE	MEDICAID	TRICARE CHAMPUS	CHAMPVA	GROUP HEALTH PLAN	FECA BLK LUNG	OTHER	1a. INSURED'S I.D. NUMBER (For Program in Item 1)
(Medicare #)	X (Medicaid #)	(Sponsor's SSN)	(Member ID#)	(SSN or ID)	(SSN)	(ID)	22334455

2. PATIENT'S NAME (Last Name, First Name, Middle Initial)
CASEY, SHARON,W

3. PATIENT'S BIRTH DATE MM DD YY: 10 06 1970 SEX M ☐ F X

4. INSURED'S NAME (Last Name, First Name, Middle Initial)

5. PATIENT'S ADDRESS (No., Street)
483 OAKDALE AVENUE

6. PATIENT'S RELATIONSHIP TO INSURED
Self X Spouse ☐ Child ☐ Other ☐

7. INSURED'S ADDRESS (No., Street)

CITY
ANYWHERE   STATE US

8. PATIENT STATUS
Single X Married ☐ Other ☐

CITY   STATE

ZIP CODE 12345   TELEPHONE (Include Area Code) (101) 3335555

Employed ☐ Full-Time Student ☐ Part-Time Student ☐

ZIP CODE   TELEPHONE (Include Area Code) ( )

9. OTHER INSURED'S NAME (Last Name, First Name, Middle Initial)

10. IS PATIENT'S CONDITION RELATED TO:

11. INSURED'S POLICY GROUP OR FECA NUMBER

a. OTHER INSURED'S POLICY OR GROUP NUMBER

a. EMPLOYMENT? (Current or Previous) ☐ YES X NO

a. INSURED'S DATE OF BIRTH MM DD YY   SEX M ☐ F ☐

b. OTHER INSURED'S DATE OF BIRTH MM DD YY   SEX M ☐ F ☐

b. AUTO ACCIDENT?   PLACE (State) ☐ YES X NO

b. EMPLOYER'S NAME OR SCHOOL NAME

c. EMPLOYER'S NAME OR SCHOOL NAME

c. OTHER ACCIDENT? ☐ YES X NO

c. INSURANCE PLAN NAME OR PROGRAM NAME

d. INSURANCE PLAN NAME OR PROGRAM NAME

10d. RESERVED FOR LOCAL USE

d. IS THERE ANOTHER HEALTH BENEFIT PLAN?
☐ YES ☐ NO If yes, return to and complete item 9 a-d.

READ BACK OF FORM BEFORE COMPLETING & SIGNING THIS FORM.
12. PATIENT'S OR AUTHORIZED PERSON'S SIGNATURE I authorize the release of any medical or other information necessary to process this claim. I also request payment of government benefits either to myself or to the party who accepts assignment below.

SIGNED_____ DATE_____

13. INSURED'S OR AUTHORIZED PERSON'S SIGNATURE I authorize payment of medical benefits to the undersigned physcian or supplier for services described below.

SIGNED_____

14. DATE OF CURRENT: MM DD YY ◄ ILLNESS (First symptom) OR INJURY (Accident) OR PREGNANCY (LMP)

15. IF PATIENT HAS HAD SAME OR SIMILAR ILLNESS, GIVE FIRST DATE MM DD YY

16. DATES PATIENT UNABLE TO WORK IN CURRENT OCCUPATION
FROM MM DD YY   TO MM DD YY

17. NAME OF REFERRING PROVIDER OR OTHER SOURCE
DONALD L GIVINGS MD

17a.
17b. NPI 1234567890

18. HOSPITALIZATION DATES RELATED TO CURRENT SERVICES
FROM MM DD YY   TO MM DD YY

19. RESERVED FOR LOCAL USE

20. OUTSIDE LAB? ☐ YES X NO $ CHARGES

21. DIAGNOSIS OR NATURE OF ILLNESS OR INJURY (Relate Items 1, 2, 3 or 4 to Item 24E by Line)
1. 626.2
2. 626.4
3. _____
4. _____

22. MEDICAID RESUBMISSION CODE   ORIGINAL REF. NO.

23. PRIOR AUTHORIZATION NUMBER

24. A	DATE(S) OF SERVICE		B.	C.	D. PROCEDURES, SERVICES, OR SUPPLIES		E.	F.	G.	H.	I.	J.
	From	To	PLACE OF	EMG	(Explain Unusual Circumstances)		DIAGNOSIS		DAYS	EPSDT	ID.	RENDERING
	MM DD YY	MM DD YY	SERVICE		CPT/HCPCS	MODIFER	POINTER	$ CHARGES	OR UNITS	Family Plan	QUAL.	PROVIDER ID. #
1	1120YYYY		11		99243		1	85 00	1		NPI	
2											NPI	
3											NPI	
4											NPI	
5											NPI	
6											NPI	

25. FEDERAL TAX I.D. NUMBER   SSN EIN
116699772   X

26. PATIENT'S ACCOUNT NO.
15-B

27. ACCEPT ASSIGNMENT? (For govt. claims, see back)
X YES ☐ NO

28. TOTAL CHARGE
$ 85 00

29. AMOUNT PAID
$

30. BALANCE DUE
$

31. SIGNATURE OF PHYSICIAN OR SUPPLIER INCLUDING DEGREES OR CREDENTIALS (I certify that the statements on the reverse apply to this bill and are made a part thereof.)
MARIA C SECTION MD
SIGNED   DATE MMDDYYYY

32. SERVICE FACILITY LOCATION INFORMATION

a. NPI   b.

33. BILLING PROVIDER INFO & PH # (101)1115555
MARIA C SECTION MD
11 NADEN LANE
ANYWHERE US 12345

a. 678ABC9012   b.

NUCC Instruction Manual available at: www.nucc.org

APPROVED OMB-0938-0999 FORM CMS-1500 (08/05)

ASSIGNMENT 15.2 Medicaid as Secondary Payer CMS-1500 Claims Completion

Case Study 15-c Medicaid Aetna-Primary

```
1500
```

HEALTH INSURANCE CLAIM FORM

APPROVED BY NATIONAL UNIFORM CLAIM COMMITTEE 08/05

| | PICA | | | | | | | PICA | |

1. MEDICARE	MEDICAID	TRICARE CHAMPUS	CHAMPVA	GROUP HEALTH PLAN	FECA BLK LUNG	OTHER	1a. INSURED'S I.D. NUMBER (For Program in Item 1)
(Medicare #)	(Medicaid #)	(Sponsor's SSN)	(Member ID#)	(SSN or ID)	(SSN) X	(ID)	55771122

2. PATIENT'S NAME (Last Name, First Name, Middle Initial)
JONES, FRED, R

3. PATIENT'S BIRTH DATE MM 01 DD 05 YY 1949 SEX M X F

4. INSURED'S NAME (Last Name, First Name, Middle Initial)
JONES, FRED, R

5. PATIENT'S ADDRESS (No., Street)
444 TAYLOR AVENUE

6. PATIENT'S RELATIONSHIP TO INSURED
Self X Spouse Child Other

7. INSURED'S ADDRESS (No.. Street)
444 TAYLOR AVENUE

CITY ANYWHERE STATE US

8. PATIENT STATUS
Single Married Other X

CITY ANYWHERE STATE US

ZIP CODE 12345 TELEPHONE (Include Area Code) (101) 3335555

Employed Full-Time Student Part-Time Student

ZIP CODE 12345 TELEPHONE (Include Area Code) ( )3335555

9. OTHER INSURED'S NAME (Last Name, First Name, Middle Initial)
JONES, FRED, R

10. IS PATIENT'S CONDITION RELATED TO:

11. INSURED'S POLICY GROUP OR FECA NUMBER
55771122

a. OTHER INSURED'S POLICY OR GROUP NUMBER
55771122

a. EMPLOYMENT? (Current or Previous)
YES X NO

a. INSURED'S DATE OF BIRTH MM 01 DD 05 YY 1949 SEX M X F

b. OTHER INSURED'S DATE OF BIRTH MM 01 DD 05 YY 1949 SEX M X F

b. AUTO ACCIDENT? PLACE (State)
YES X NO

b. EMPLOYER'S NAME OR SCHOOL NAME

c. EMPLOYER'S NAME OR SCHOOL NAME

c. OTHER ACCIDENT?
YES X NO

c. INSURANCE PLAN NAME OR PROGRAM NAME

d. INSURANCE PLAN NAME OR PROGRAM NAME
MEDICAID

10d. RESERVED FOR LOCAL USE

d. IS THERE ANOTHER HEALTH BENEFIT PLAN?
X YES NO *If yes,* return to and complete item 9 a-d.

READ BACK OF FORM BEFORE COMPLETING & SIGNING THIS FORM.
12. PATIENT'S OR AUTHORIZED PERSON'S SIGNATURE I authorize the release of any medical or other information necessary to process this claim. I also request payment of government benefits either to myself or to the party who accepts assignment below.

SIGNED SIGNATURE ON FILE DATE

13. INSURED'S OR AUTHORIZED PERSON'S SIGNATURE I authorize payment of medical benefits to the undersigned physcian or supplier for services described below.

SIGNED

14. DATE OF CURRENT: MM DD YY ILLNESS (First symptom) OR INJURY (Accident) OR PREGNANCY (LMP)

15. IF PATIENT HAS HAD SAME OR SIMILAR ILLNESS, GIVE FIRST DATE MM DD YY

16. DATES PATIENT UNABLE TO WORK IN CURRENT OCCUPATION
FROM MM DD YY TO MM DD YY

17. NAME OF REFERRING PROVIDER OR OTHER SOURCE

17a.
17b. NPI

18. HOSPITALIZATION DATES RELATED TO CURRENT SERVICES
FROM MM DD YY TO MM DD YY

19. RESERVED FOR LOCAL USE

20. OUTSIDE LAB? YES X NO $ CHARGES

21. DIAGNOSIS OR NATURE OF ILLNESS OR INJURY (Relate Items 1, 2, 3 or 4 to Item 24E by Line)
1. 719 07
2.
3.
4.

22. MEDICAID RESUBMISSION CODE ORIGINAL REF. NO.

23. PRIOR AUTHORIZATION NUMBER

24. A. DATE(S) OF SERVICE From MM DD YY To MM DD YY	B. PLACE OF SERVICE	C. EMG	D. PROCEDURES, SERVICES, OR SUPPLIES (Explain Unusual Circumstances) CPT/HCPCS MODIFER	E. DIAGNOSIS POINTER	F. $ CHARGES	G. DAYS OR UNITS	H. EPSDT Family Plan	I. ID. QUAL.	J. RENDERING PROVIDER ID. #
1	0619YYYY	11	99213	1	75 00	1		NPI	
2								NPI	
3								NPI	
4								NPI	
5								NPI	
6								NPI	

25. FEDERAL TAX I.D. NUMBER SSN EIN
111234562 X

26. PATIENT'S ACCOUNT NO.
15-C

27. ACCEPT ASSIGNMENT? (For govt. claims, see back)
X YES NO

28. TOTAL CHARGE
$ 75 00

29. AMOUNT PAID
$

30. BALANCE DUE
$

31. SIGNATURE OF PHYSICIAN OR SUPPLIER INCLUDING DEGREES OR CREDENTIALS (I certify that the statements on the reverse apply to this bill and are made a part thereof.)
DONALD L GIVINGS MD
SIGNED DATE MMDDYYYY

32. SERVICE FACILITY LOCATION INFORMATION

NPI
1234567890

33. BILLING PROVIDER INFO & PH # (101)1115555
DONALD L GIVINGS MD
11350 MEDICAL DRIVE
ANYWHERE US 12345
a1234567890 b

NUCC Instruction Manual available at: www.nucc.org

APPROVED OMB-0938-0999 FORM CMS-1500 (08/05)

Case Study 15-d Aetna-Primary

1500

HEALTH INSURANCE CLAIM FORM

APPROVED BY NATIONAL UNIFORM CLAIM COMMITTE 08/05

| | PICA | | | | | | PICA | |

1. MEDICARE	MEDICAID	TRICARE CHAMPUS	CHAMPVA	GROUP HEALTH PLAN	FECA BLK LUNG	OTHER	1a. INSURED'S I.D. NUMBER (For Program in Item 1)
(Medicare #)	(Medicaid #)	(Sponsor's SSN)	(Member ID#)	(SSN or ID)	(SSN)	[X] (ID)	55771122

2. PATIENT'S NAME (Last Name, First Name, Middle Initial)	3. PATIENT'S BIRTH DATE / SEX	4. INSURED'S NAME (Last Name, First Name, Middle Initial)
JONES, FRED, R	MM 01 DD 05 YY 1949 M [X] F [ ]	JONES, FRED, R

5. PATIENT'S ADDRESS (No., Street)	6. PATIENT'S RELATIONSHIP TO INSURED	7. INSURED'S ADDRESS (No., Street)
444 TAYLOR AVENUE	Self [X] Spouse [ ] Child [ ] Other [ ]	444 TAYLOR AVENUE

CITY	STATE	8. PATIENT STATUS	CITY	STATE
ANYWHERE	US	Single [ ] Married [ ] Other [X]	ANYWHERE	US

ZIP CODE	TELEPHONE (Include Area Code)		ZIP CODE	TELEPHONE (Include Area Code)
12345	(101) 3335555	Employed [ ] Full-Time Student [ ] Part-Time Student [ ]	12345	(101)3335555

9. OTHER INSURED'S NAME (Last Name, First Name, Middle Initial)	10. IS PATIENT'S CONDITION RELATED TO:	11. INSURED'S POLICY GROUP OR FECA NUMBER
JONES, FRED, R		55771122

a. OTHER INSURED'S POLICY OR GROUP NUMBER	a. EMPLOYMENT? (Current or Previous)	a. INSURED'S DATE OF BIRTH / SEX
55771122	YES [ ] [X] NO	MM 01 DD 05 YY 1949 M [X] F [ ]

b. OTHER INSURED'S DATE OF BIRTH / SEX	b. AUTO ACCIDENT? PLACE (State)	b. EMPLOYER'S NAME OR SCHOOL NAME
MM 01 DD 05 YY 1949 M [X] F [ ]	YES [ ] [X] NO	

c. EMPLOYER'S NAME OR SCHOOL NAME	c. OTHER ACCIDENT?	c. INSURANCE PLAN NAME OR PROGRAM NAME
	YES [ ] [X] NO	

d. INSURANCE PLAN NAME OR PROGRAM NAME	10d. RESERVED FOR LOCAL USE	d. IS THERE ANOTHER HEALTH BENEFIT PLAN?
MEDICAID		[X] YES [ ] NO If yes, return to and complete item 9 a-d.

READ BACK OF FORM BEFORE COMPLETING & SIGNING THIS FORM.

12. PATIENT'S OR AUTHORIZED PERSON'S SIGNATURE I authorize the release of any medical or other information necessary to process this claim. I also request payment of government benefits either to myself or to the party who accepts assignment below.

SIGNED **SIGNATURE ON FILE**   DATE

13. INSURED'S OR AUTHORIZED PERSON'S SIGNATURE I authorize payment of medical benefits to the undersigned physcian or supplier for services described below.

SIGNED

14. DATE OF CURRENT: ILLNESS (First symptom) OR INJURY (Accident) OR PREGNANCY (LMP)	15. IF PATIENT HAS HAD SAME OR SIMILAR ILLNESS. GIVE FIRST DATE MM DD YY	16. DATES PATIENT UNABLE TO WORK IN CURRENT OCCUPATION FROM MM DD YY TO MM DD YY

17. NAME OF REFERRING PROVIDER OR OTHER SOURCE	17a.	18. HOSPITALIZATION DATES RELATED TO CURRENT SERVICES
DONALD L GIVINGS MD	17b. NPI 1234567890	FROM MM DD YY TO MM DD YY

19. RESERVED FOR LOCAL USE	20. OUTSIDE LAB? $ CHARGES
	YES [ ] [X] NO

21. DIAGNOSIS OR NATURE OF ILLNESS OR INJURY (Relate Items 1, 2, 3 or 4 to Item 24E by Line)	22. MEDICAID RESUBMISSION CODE ORIGINAL REF. NO.
1. 826 0 3.	
2. 4.	23. PRIOR AUTHORIZATION NUMBER

24. A DATE(S) OF SERVICE From MM DD YY To MM DD YY	B. PLACE OF SERVICE	C. EMG	D. PROCEDURES, SERVICES, OR SUPPLIES (Explain Unusual Circumstances) CPT/HCPCS	MODIFER	E. DIAGNOSIS POINTER	F. $ CHARGES	G. DAYS OR UNITS	H. EPSDT Family Plan	I. ID. QUAL	J. RENDERING PROVIDER ID. #
1	06 23 YYYY	11		99242		1	75 00	1		NPI	
2	06 23 YYYY	11		73660		1	50 00	1		NPI	
3	06 23 YYYY	11		28490		1	65 00	1		NPI	
4										NPI	
5										NPI	
6										NPI	

25. FEDERAL TAX I.D. NUMBER SSN EIN	26. PATIENT'S ACCOUNT NO.	27. ACCEPT ASSIGNMENT? (For govt. claims, see back)	28. TOTAL CHARGE	29. AMOUNT PAID	30. BALANCE DUE
119933772 [X]	15-D	[X] YES [ ] NO	$ 190 00	$	$

31. SIGNATURE OF PHYSICIAN OR SUPPLIER INCLUDING DEGREES OR CREDENTIALS (I certify that the statements on the reverse apply to this bill and are made a part thereof.)	32. SERVICE FACILITY LOCATION INFORMATION	33. BILLING PROVIDER INFO & PH # (101)1115555
JOHN F WALKER DPM		JOHN F WALKER DPM 546 FOOTHILL PLACE ANYWHERE US 12345
SIGNED DATE MMDDYYYY	a. NPI b.	a. 890ABC1234 b.

APPROVED OMB-0938-0999 FORM CMS-1500 (08/05)

ASSIGNMENT 15.3 Medicaid Mother/Baby CMS-1500 Claims Completion

Case Study 15-e

```
┌─────────┐
│  1500   │
└─────────┘
```

HEALTH INSURANCE CLAIM FORM

APPROVED BY NATIONAL UNIFORM CLAIM COMMITTE 08/05

| | PICA | | | | | | | PICA | |

1. MEDICARE	MEDICAID	TRICARE CHAMPUS	CHAMPVA	GROUP HEALTH PLAN	FECA BLK LUNG	OTHER	1a. INSURED'S I.D. NUMBER	(For Program in Item 1)
(Medicare #)	[X] (Medicaid #)	(Sponsor's SSN)	(Member ID#)	(SSN or ID)	(SSN)	(ID)	77557755	

2. PATIENT'S NAME (Last Name, First Name, Middle Initial)
JACKSON, NEWBORN

3. PATIENT'S BIRTH DATE   SEX
MM 03 DD 10 YY 2006 M [X] F [ ]

4. INSURED'S NAME (Last Name, First Name, Middle Initial)
JACKSON, SANDY (MOM)

5. PATIENT'S ADDRESS (No., Street)
3764 RAVENWOOD AVENUE

6. PATIENT'S RELATIONSHIP TO INSURED
Self [ ] Spouse [ ] Child [X] Other [ ]

7. INSURED'S ADDRESS (No., Street)

CITY
ANYWHERE   STATE **US**

8. PATIENT STATUS
Single [ ] Married [ ] Other [ ]

CITY   STATE

ZIP CODE **12345**   TELEPHONE (Include Area Code) **(101) 3335555**

Employed [ ] Full-Time Student [ ] Part-Time Student [ ]

ZIP CODE   TELEPHONE (Include Area Code) ( )

9. OTHER INSURED'S NAME (Last Name, First Name, Middle Initial)

10. IS PATIENT'S CONDITION RELATED TO:

11. INSURED'S POLICY GROUP OR FECA NUMBER

a. OTHER INSURED'S POLICY OR GROUP NUMBER

a. EMPLOYMENT? (Current or Previous)
YES [ ] [X] NO

a. INSURED'S DATE OF BIRTH
MM DD YY   SEX
M [ ] F [ ]

b. OTHER INSURED'S DATE OF BIRTH
MM DD YY   SEX
M [ ] F [ ]

b. AUTO ACCIDENT?   PLACE (State)
YES [ ] [X] NO

b. EMPLOYER'S NAME OR SCHOOL NAME

c. EMPLOYER'S NAME OR SCHOOL NAME

c. OTHER ACCIDENT?
YES [ ] [X] NO

c. INSURANCE PLAN NAME OR PROGRAM NAME

d. INSURANCE PLAN NAME OR PROGRAM NAME

10d. RESERVED FOR LOCAL USE

d. IS THERE ANOTHER HEALTH BENEFIT PLAN?
YES [ ] NO [ ] *If yes,* return to and complete item 9 a-d.

READ BACK OF FORM BEFORE COMPLETING & SIGNING THIS FORM.
12. PATIENT'S OR AUTHORIZED PERSON'S SIGNATURE I authorize the release of any medical or other information necessary to process this claim. I also request payment of government benefits either to myself or to the party who accepts assignment below.

SIGNED _____   DATE _____

13. INSURED'S OR AUTHORIZED PERSON'S SIGNATURE I authorize payment of medical benefits to the undersigned physcian or supplier for services described below.

SIGNED _____

14. DATE OF CURRENT: ILLNESS (First symptom) OR
MM DD YY   INJURY (Accident) OR
PREGNANCY (LMP)

15. IF PATIENT HAS HAD SAME OR SIMILAR ILLNESS,
GIVE FIRST DATE MM DD YY

16. DATES PATIENT UNABLE TO WORK IN CURRENT OCCUPATION
FROM MM DD YY TO MM DD YY

17. NAME OF REFERRING PROVIDER OR OTHER SOURCE
17a.
17b. NPI

18. HOSPITALIZATION DATES RELATED TO CURRENT SERVICES
FROM MM DD YY TO MM DD YY

19. RESERVED FOR LOCAL USE

20. OUTSIDE LAB? $ CHARGES
YES [ ] [X] NO

21. DIAGNOSIS OR NATURE OF ILLNESS OR INJURY (Relate Items 1, 2, 3 or 4 to Item 24E by Line)
1. |V30 00
2. |_____
3. |_____
4. |_____

22. MEDICAID RESUBMISSION CODE   ORIGINAL REF. NO.

23. PRIOR AUTHORIZATION NUMBER

24. A. DATE(S) OF SERVICE		B. PLACE OF SERVICE	C. EMG	D. PROCEDURES, SERVICES, OR SUPPLIES (Explain Unusual Circumstances)		E. DIAGNOSIS POINTER	F. $ CHARGES	G. DAYS OR UNITS	H. EPSDT Family Plan	I. ID. QUAL.	J. RENDERING PROVIDER ID. #
From MM DD YY	To MM DD YY			CPT/HCPCS	MODIFER						
1	03 10 YYYY		21		99431		1	150 00	1		NPI	
2	03 10 YYYY		21		99436		1	400 00	1		NPI	
3	03 10 YYYY		21		99432		1	100 00	1		NPI	
4											NPI	
5											NPI	
6											NPI	

25. FEDERAL TAX I.D. NUMBER   SSN EIN
11234562   [X]

26. PATIENT'S ACCOUNT NO.
15-E

27. ACCEPT ASSIGNMENT?
(For govt. claims, see back)
[X] YES NO [ ]

28. TOTAL CHARGE
$ **650 00**

29. AMOUNT PAID
$

30. BALANCE DUE
$

31. SIGNATURE OF PHYSICIAN OR SUPPLIER INCLUDING DEGREES OR CREDENTIALS
(I certify that the statements on the reverse apply to this bill and are made a part thereof.)
DONALD L GIVINGS MD
SIGNED   DATE **MMDDYYYY**

32. SERVICE FACILITY LOCATION INFORMATION
GOODMEDICINE HOSPITAL
ANYWHERE ST
ANYWHERE US 12345
a. **112ABC3456** b.

33. BILLING PROVIDER INFO & PH # **(101) 1115555**
DONALD L GIVINGS MD
11350 MEDICAL DRIVE
ANYWHERE US 12345
a. **1234567890** b.

NUCC Instruction Manual available at: www.nucc.org

APPROVED OMB-0938-0999 FORM CMS-1500 (08/05)

ASSIGNMENT 15.3 Multiple Choice Review

1.	b	**11.**	c
2.	a	**12.**	d
3.	d	**13.**	c
4.	d	**14.**	b
5.	a	**15.**	d
6.	b	**16.**	a
7.	d	**17.**	a
8.	c	**18.**	b
9.	a	**19.**	a
10.	b	**20.**	b

CHAPTER 16 TRICARE

ASSIGNMENT 16.1 TRICARE Primary CMS-1500 Claims Completion

Case Study 16-a

```
1500
```

HEALTH INSURANCE CLAIM FORM
APPROVED BY NATIONAL UNIFORM CLAIM COMMITTE 08/05

PICA		PICA

1. MEDICARE (Medicare #) ☐ MEDICAID (Medicaid #) ☐ TRICARE CHAMPUS (Sponsor's SSN) ☒ CHAMPVA (Member ID#) ☐ GROUP HEALTH PLAN (SSN or ID) ☐ FECA BLK LUNG (SSN) ☐ OTHER (ID) ☐
1a. INSURED'S I.D. NUMBER (For Program in Item 1) **234556789**

2. PATIENT'S NAME (Last Name, First Name, Middle Initial) **HEEM, JEFFREY, D**

3. PATIENT'S BIRTH DATE MM **05** DD **05** YY **1964** SEX M ☒ F ☐

4. INSURED'S NAME (Last Name, First Name, Middle Initial) **SAME**

5. PATIENT'S ADDRESS (No., Street) **333 HEAVENLY PLACE**

6. PATIENT'S RELATIONSHIP TO INSURED Self ☒ Spouse ☐ Child ☐ Other ☐

7. INSURED'S ADDRESS (No., Street) **SAME**

CITY **ANYWHERE** STATE **US**

8. PATIENT STATUS Single ☐ Married ☒ Other ☐
Employed ☐ Full-Time Student ☐ Part-Time Student ☐

CITY STATE

ZIP CODE **12345** TELEPHONE (Include Area Code) **(101) 3335555**

ZIP CODE TELEPHONE (Include Area Code) (   )

9. OTHER INSURED'S NAME (Last Name, First Name, Middle Initial)

10. IS PATIENT'S CONDITION RELATED TO:

11. INSURED'S POLICY GROUP OR FECA NUMBER

a. OTHER INSURED'S POLICY OR GROUP NUMBER

a. EMPLOYMENT? (Current or Previous) YES ☐ NO ☒

a. INSURED'S DATE OF BIRTH MM DD YY SEX M ☐ F ☐

b. OTHER INSURED'S DATE OF BIRTH MM DD YY SEX M ☐ F ☐

b. AUTO ACCIDENT? PLACE (State) YES ☐ NO ☒

b. EMPLOYER'S NAME OR SCHOOL NAME

c. EMPLOYER'S NAME OR SCHOOL NAME

c. OTHER ACCIDENT? YES ☐ NO ☒

c. INSURANCE PLAN NAME OR PROGRAM NAME

d. INSURANCE PLAN NAME OR PROGRAM NAME

10d. RESERVED FOR LOCAL USE

d. IS THERE ANOTHER HEALTH BENEFIT PLAN? YES ☐ NO ☒ If yes, return to and complete item 9 a-d.

READ BACK OF FORM BEFORE COMPLETING & SIGNING THIS FORM.
12. PATIENT'S OR AUTHORIZED PERSON'S SIGNATURE I authorize the release of any medical or other information necessary to process this claim. I also request payment of government benefits either to myself or to the party who accepts assignment below.

SIGNED **SIGNATURE ON FILE** DATE

13. INSURED'S OR AUTHORIZED PERSON'S SIGNATURE I authorize payment of medical benefits to the undersigned physician or supplier for services described below.

SIGNED **SIGNATURE ON FILE**

14. DATE OF CURRENT: MM **11** DD **05** YY **YYYY** ILLNESS (First symptom) OR INJURY (Accident) OR PREGNANCY (LMP)

15. IF PATIENT HAS HAD SAME OR SIMILAR ILLNESS, GIVE FIRST DATE MM DD YY

16. DATES PATIENT UNABLE TO WORK IN CURRENT OCCUPATION FROM MM DD YY TO MM DD YY

17. NAME OF REFERRING PROVIDER OR OTHER SOURCE

17a.
17b. NPI

18. HOSPITALIZATION DATES RELATED TO CURRENT SERVICES FROM MM DD YY TO MM DD YY

19. RESERVED FOR LOCAL USE

20. OUTSIDE LAB? YES ☐ NO ☒ $ CHARGES

21. DIAGNOSIS OR NATURE OF ILLNESS OR INJURY (Relate Items 1, 2, 3 or 4 to Item 24E by Line)
1. **461 1**
2. **784 1**
3.
4.

22. MEDICAID RESUBMISSION CODE ORIGINAL REF. NO.

23. PRIOR AUTHORIZATION NUMBER

24. A. DATE(S) OF SERVICE From MM DD YY	To MM DD YY	B. PLACE OF SERVICE	C. EMG	D. PROCEDURES, SERVICES, OR SUPPLIES (Explain Unusual Circumstances) CPT/HCPCS	MODIFER	E. DIAGNOSIS POINTER	F. $ CHARGES	G. DAYS OR UNITS	H. EPSDT Family Plan	I. ID QUAL.	J. RENDERING PROVIDER ID. #
1	**1105YYYY**		**11**		**99202**		**1**	**70 00**	**1**		NPI
2											NPI
3											NPI
4											NPI
5											NPI
6											NPI

25. FEDERAL TAX I.D. NUMBER **11234562** SSN ☐ EIN ☒

26. PATIENT'S ACCOUNT NO. **16-A**

27. ACCEPT ASSIGNMENT? (For govt. claims, see back) YES ☒ NO ☐

28. TOTAL CHARGE $ **70 00**

29. AMOUNT PAID $

30. BALANCE DUE $ **70 00**

31. SIGNATURE OF PHYSICIAN OR SUPPLIER INCLUDING DEGREES OR CREDENTIALS (I certify that the statements on the reverse apply to this bill and are made a part thereof.)
DONALD L GIVINGS MD
SIGNED DATE **MMDDYYYY**

32. SERVICE FACILITY LOCATION INFORMATION
a. NPI b.

33. BILLING PROVIDER INFO & PH # **(101) 1115555**
DONALD L GIVINGS MD
11350 MEDICAL DRIVE
ANYWHERE US 12345
a. **1234567890** NPI

NUCC Instruction Manual available at: www.nucc.org

APPROVED OMB-0938-0999 FORM CMS-1500 (08/05)

Case Study 16-b

1500

HEALTH INSURANCE CLAIM FORM

APPROVED BY NATIONAL UNIFORM CLAIM COMMITTE 08/05

| | PICA | | | | | | | PICA | | |

1. MEDICARE	MEDICAID	TRICARE CHAMPUS	CHAMPVA	GROUP HEALTH PLAN	FECA BLK LUNG	OTHER	1a. INSURED'S I.D. NUMBER	(For Program in Item 1)
(Medicare #)	(Medicaid #) X	(Sponsor's SSN)	(Member ID#)	(SSN or ID)	(SSN)	(ID)	567565757	

2. PATIENT'S NAME (Last Name, First Name, Middle Initial)
BRIGHT, DANA, S

3. PATIENT'S BIRTH DATE: 07 05 1971 SEX M / F X

4. INSURED'S NAME (Last Name, First Name, Middle Initial)
BRIGHT, RON, L

5. PATIENT'S ADDRESS (No., Street)
28 UPTON CIRCLE

6. PATIENT'S RELATIONSHIP TO INSURED: Self / Spouse X / Child / Other

7. INSURED'S ADDRESS (No., Street)
21 NAVAL STATION

CITY ANYWHERE STATE US

8. PATIENT STATUS: Single / Married X / Other; Employed / Full-Time Student / Part-Time Student

CITY ANYWHERE STATE US

ZIP CODE 12345 TELEPHONE (101) 3335555

ZIP CODE 12345 TELEPHONE ( )

9. OTHER INSURED'S NAME

10. IS PATIENT'S CONDITION RELATED TO:

11. INSURED'S POLICY GROUP OR FECA NUMBER

a. EMPLOYMENT? YES / NO X

a. INSURED'S DATE OF BIRTH — SEX M / F

b. AUTO ACCIDENT? YES / NO X PLACE (State)

b. EMPLOYER'S NAME OR SCHOOL NAME

c. OTHER ACCIDENT? YES / NO X

c. INSURANCE PLAN NAME OR PROGRAM NAME

d. INSURANCE PLAN NAME OR PROGRAM NAME

10d. RESERVED FOR LOCAL USE

d. IS THERE ANOTHER HEALTH BENEFIT PLAN? YES / NO X

12. SIGNED SIGNATURE ON FILE DATE

13. SIGNED SIGNATURE ON FILE

14. DATE OF CURRENT: 06 22 YYYY

16. DATES PATIENT UNABLE TO WORK: FROM TO

17. NAME OF REFERRING PROVIDER; 17a; 17b NPI

18. HOSPITALIZATION DATES: FROM TO

19. RESERVED FOR LOCAL USE

20. OUTSIDE LAB? YES / NO X $ CHARGES

21. DIAGNOSIS: 1. 575.11 3. 2. 4.

22. MEDICAID RESUBMISSION CODE / ORIGINAL REF. NO.

23. PRIOR AUTHORIZATION NUMBER

24.A DATE(S) OF SERVICE	B. PLACE	C. EMG	D. CPT/HCPCS MODIFER	E. POINTER	F. $ CHARGES	G. UNITS	H.	I. QUAL	J. RENDERING PROVIDER ID#
0622YYYY	11		99214	1	85 00	1		NPI	
								NPI	
								NPI	
								NPI	
								NPI	
								NPI	

25. FEDERAL TAX I.D. NUMBER 11234562 SSN EIN X

26. PATIENT'S ACCOUNT NO. 16-B

27. ACCEPT ASSIGNMENT? X YES / NO

28. TOTAL CHARGE $ 85 00

29. AMOUNT PAID $

30. BALANCE DUE $ 85 00

31. SIGNATURE OF PHYSICIAN OR SUPPLIER
DONALD L GIVINGS MD SIGNED DATE MMDDYYYY

32. SERVICE FACILITY LOCATION INFORMATION a. NPI b.

33. BILLING PROVIDER INFO & PH # (101)1115555
DONALD L GIVINGS MD
11350 MEDICAL DRIVE
ANYWHERE US 12345
a. 1234567890

Case Study 16-c AmeriHealth/Supplemental

1500

HEALTH INSURANCE CLAIM FORM

APPROVED BY NATIONAL UNIFORM CLAIM COMMITTE 08/05

| | PICA | | | | | | PICA | |

| 1. MEDICARE (Medicare #) | MEDICAID (Medicaid #) | TRICARE CHAMPUS (Sponsor's SSN) | CHAMPVA (Member ID#) | GROUP HEALTH PLAN (SSN or ID) | FECA BLK LUNG (SSN) | OTHER [X] (ID) | 1a. INSURED'S I.D. NUMBER (For Program in Item 1) 415X678C |

| 2. PATIENT'S NAME (Last Name, First Name, Middle Initial) BRIGHT, DANA, S | 3. PATIENT'S BIRTH DATE MM 07 DD 05 YY 1971 SEX M [ ] F [X] | 4. INSURED'S NAME (Last Name, First Name, Middle Initial) BRIGHT, DANA, S |

| 5. PATIENT'S ADDRESS (No., Street) 28 UPTON CIRCLE | 6. PATIENT'S RELATIONSHIP TO INSURED Self [X] Spouse [ ] Child [ ] Other [ ] | 7. INSURED'S ADDRESS (No., Street) 28 UPTON CIRCLE |

| CITY ANYWHERE | STATE US | 8. PATIENT STATUS Single [ ] Married [X] Other [ ] | CITY ANYWHERE | STATE US |

| ZIP CODE 12345 | TELEPHONE (Include Area Code) (101) 3335555 | Employed [ ] Full-Time Student [ ] Part-Time Student [ ] | ZIP CODE 12345 | TELEPHONE (Include Area Code) (101) 3335555 |

| 9. OTHER INSURED'S NAME (Last Name, First Name, Middle Initial) BRIGHT, RON, L | 10. IS PATIENT'S CONDITION RELATED TO: | 11. INSURED'S POLICY GROUP OR FECA NUMBER |

| a. OTHER INSURED'S POLICY OR GROUP NUMBER 567566757 | a. EMPLOYMENT? (Current or Previous) YES [ ] NO [X] | a. INSURED'S DATE OF BIRTH MM DD YY SEX M [ ] F [ ] |

| b. OTHER INSURED'S DATE OF BIRTH MM 08 DD 12 YY 1970 SEX M [X] F [ ] | b. AUTO ACCIDENT? PLACE (State) YES [ ] NO [X] | b. EMPLOYER'S NAME OR SCHOOL NAME |

| c. EMPLOYER'S NAME OR SCHOOL NAME US NAVY | c. OTHER ACCIDENT? YES [ ] NO [X] | c. INSURANCE PLAN NAME OR PROGRAM NAME |

| d. INSURANCE PLAN NAME OR PROGRAM NAME TRICARE EXTRA | 10d. RESERVED FOR LOCAL USE | d. IS THERE ANOTHER HEALTH BENEFIT PLAN? [X] YES [ ] NO If yes, return to and complete item 9 a-d. |

READ BACK OF FORM BEFORE COMPLETING & SIGNING THIS FORM.

12. PATIENT'S OR AUTHORIZED PERSON'S SIGNATURE I authorize the release of any medical or other information necessary to process this claim. I also request payment of government benefits either to myself or to the party who accepts assignment below.

SIGNED **SIGNATURE ON FILE** DATE _____

13. INSURED'S OR AUTHORIZED PERSON'S SIGNATURE I authorize payment of medical benefits to the undersigned physician or supplier for services described below.

SIGNED **SIGNATURE ON FILE**

| 14. DATE OF CURRENT: ILLNESS (First symptom) OR INJURY (Accident) OR PREGNANCY (LMP) MM 06 DD 22 YY YYYY | 15. IF PATIENT HAS HAD SAME OR SIMILAR ILLNESS, GIVE FIRST DATE MM DD YY | 16. DATES PATIENT UNABLE TO WORK IN CURRENT OCCUPATION FROM MM DD YY TO MM DD YY |

| 17. NAME OF REFERRING PROVIDER OR OTHER SOURCE DONALD L GIVINGS MD | 17a. 17b. NPI 1234567890 | 18. HOSPITALIZATION DATES RELATED TO CURRENT SERVICES FROM MM 06 DD 29 YY YYYY TO MM 06 DD 30 YY YYYY |

| 19. RESERVED FOR LOCAL USE | | 20. OUTSIDE LAB? YES [ ] NO [X] $ CHARGES |

21. DIAGNOSIS OR NATURE OF ILLNESS OR INJURY (Relate Items 1, 2, 3 or 4 to Item 24E by Line)

1. 575 11   3.
2.   4.

| 22. MEDICAID RESUBMISSION CODE ORIGINAL REF. NO. |
| 23. PRIOR AUTHORIZATION NUMBER |

24. A. DATE(S) OF SERVICE From MM DD YY	To MM DD YY	B. PLACE OF SERVICE	C. EMG	D. PROCEDURES, SERVICES, OR SUPPLIES (Explain Unusual Circumstances) CPT/HCPCS	MODIFER	E. DIAGNOSIS POINTER	F. $ CHARGES	G. DAYS OR UNITS	H. EPSDT Family Plan	I. ID. QUAL.	J. RENDERING PROVIDER ID. #
1	06 29 YYYY		22		47562		1	2300 00	1		NPI	
2											NPI	
3											NPI	
4											NPI	
5											NPI	
6											NPI	

| 25. FEDERAL TAX I.D. NUMBER SSN EIN 115566772 [X] | 26. PATIENT'S ACCOUNT NO. 16-C | 27. ACCEPT ASSIGNMENT? (For govt. claims, see back) [X] YES [ ] NO | 28. TOTAL CHARGE $ 2300 00 | 29. AMOUNT PAID $ | 30. BALANCE DUE $ 2300 00 |

| 31. SIGNATURE OF PHYSICIAN OR SUPPLIER INCLUDING DEGREES OR CREDENTIALS (I certify that the statements on the reverse apply to this bill and are made a part thereof.) JONATHAN B KUTTER MD SIGNED DATE MMDDYYYY | 32. SERVICE FACILITY LOCATION INFORMATION MERCY HOSPITAL ANYWHERE STREET ANYWHERE US 12345 a. NPI b. | 33. BILLING PROVIDER INFO & PH # (101)1115555 JONATHAN B KUTTER MD 339 WOODLAND PLACE ANYWHERE US 12345 a.4567891132 |

NUCC Instruction Manual available at: www.nucc.org

APPROVED OMB-0938-0999 FORM CMS-1500 (08/05)

Case Study 16-d TRICARE AARP/Supplemental

(1500)		

HEALTH INSURANCE CLAIM FORM

APPROVED BY NATIONAL UNIFORM CLAIM COMMITTEE 08/05

PICA / PICA

1. MEDICARE (Medicare #)	MEDICAID (Medicaid #)	TRICARE CHAMPUS (Sponsor's SSN)	CHAMPVA (Member ID#)	GROUP HEALTH PLAN (SSN or ID)	FECA BLK LUNG (SSN)	OTHER [X] (ID)	1a. INSURED'S I.D. NUMBER (For Program in Item 1) 46444646B

2. PATIENT'S NAME (Last Name, First Name, Middle Initial)
RYER JR, ODEL, M

3. PATIENT'S BIRTH DATE 04 28 1949 SEX M [X] F

4. INSURED'S NAME (Last Name, First Name, Middle Initial)
SAME

5. PATIENT'S ADDRESS (No., Street)
484 PINEWOOD AVENUE

6. PATIENT'S RELATIONSHIP TO INSURED
Self [X] Spouse Child Other

7. INSURED'S ADDRESS (No., Street)
SAME

CITY ANYWHERE   STATE US

8. PATIENT STATUS
Single   Married [X]   Other
Employed   Full-Time Student   Part-Time Student

CITY   STATE

ZIP CODE 12345   TELEPHONE (Include Area Code) (101) 3335555

ZIP CODE   TELEPHONE (Include Area Code) ( )

9. OTHER INSURED'S NAME (Last Name, First Name, Middle Initial)
RYER JR, ODEL, M

10. IS PATIENT'S CONDITION RELATED TO:

11. INSURED'S POLICY GROUP OR FECA NUMBER

a. OTHER INSURED'S POLICY OR GROUP NUMBER
464444646

a. EMPLOYMENT? (Current or Previous) YES [X] NO

a. INSURED'S DATE OF BIRTH MM DD YY   SEX M F

b. OTHER INSURED'S DATE OF BIRTH 04 28 1949 SEX M [X] F

b. AUTO ACCIDENT? PLACE (State) YES [X] NO

b. EMPLOYER'S NAME OR SCHOOL NAME

c. EMPLOYER'S NAME OR SCHOOL NAME
US AIRFORCE RETIRED

c. OTHER ACCIDENT? YES [X] NO

c. INSURANCE PLAN NAME OR PROGRAM NAME

d. INSURANCE PLAN NAME OR PROGRAM NAME
TRICARE STANDARD

10d. RESERVED FOR LOCAL USE

d. IS THERE ANOTHER HEALTH BENEFIT PLAN?
[X] YES NO If yes, return to and complete item 9 a-d.

READ BACK OF FORM BEFORE COMPLETING & SIGNING THIS FORM.
12. PATIENT'S OR AUTHORIZED PERSON'S SIGNATURE I authorize the release of any medical or other information necessary to process this claim. I also request payment of government benefits either to myself or to the party who accepts assignment below.

SIGNED SIGNATURE ON FILE   DATE

13. INSURED'S OR AUTHORIZED PERSON'S SIGNATURE I authorize payment of medical benefits to the undersigned physcian or supplier for services described below.

SIGNED SIGNATURE ON FILE

14. DATE OF CURRENT: 04 12 YYYY ILLNESS (First symptom) OR INJURY (Accident) OR PREGNANCY (LMP)

15. IF PATIENT HAS HAD SAME OR SIMILAR ILLNESS. GIVE FIRST DATE MM DD YY

16. DATES PATIENT UNABLE TO WORK IN CURRENT OCCUPATION
FROM   TO

17. NAME OF REFERRING PROVIDER OR OTHER SOURCE

17a.
17b. NPI

18. HOSPITALIZATION DATES RELATED TO CURRENT SERVICES
FROM   TO

19. RESERVED FOR LOCAL USE

20. OUTSIDE LAB? YES [X] NO $ CHARGES

21. DIAGNOSIS OR NATURE OF ILLNESS OR INJURY (Relate Items 1, 2, 3 or 4 to Item 24E by Line)
1. 787 1
2.
3.
4.

22. MEDICAID RESUBMISSION CODE ORIGINAL REF. NO.

23. PRIOR AUTHORIZATION NUMBER

24. A DATE(S) OF SERVICE From To MM DD YY MM DD YY	B. PLACE OF SERVICE	C. EMG	D. PROCEDURES, SERVICES, OR SUPPLIES (Explain Unusual Circumstances) CPT/HCPCS MODIFER	E. DIAGNOSIS POINTER	F. $ CHARGES	G. DAYS OR UNITS	H. EPSDT Family Plan	I. ID. QUAL.	J. RENDERING PROVIDER ID. #
1 04 12 YYYY	11		99211	1	55 00	1		NPI	
2								NPI	
3								NPI	
4								NPI	
5								NPI	
6								NPI	

25. FEDERAL TAX I.D. NUMBER 11234562 SSN EIN [X]

26. PATIENT'S ACCOUNT NO. 16-D

27. ACCEPT ASSIGNMENT? (For govt. claims, see back) [X] YES NO

28. TOTAL CHARGE $ 55 00

29. AMOUNT PAID $

30. BALANCE DUE $

31. SIGNATURE OF PHYSICIAN OR SUPPLIER INCLUDING DEGREES OR CREDENTIALS (I certify that the statements on the reverse apply to this bill and are made a part thereof.)
DONALD L GIVINGS MD
SIGNED DATE MMDDYYYY

32. SERVICE FACILITY LOCATION INFORMATION
a. NPI b.

33. BILLING PROVIDER INFO & PH # (101)1115555
DONALD L GIVINGS MD
11350 MEDICAL DRIVE
ANYWHERE US 12345
a.1234567890 b.

NUCC Instruction Manual available at: www.nucc.org

APPROVED OMB-0938-0999 FORM CMS-1500 (08/05)

Case Study 16-e Highmark/Secondary

1500

HEALTH INSURANCE CLAIM FORM

APPROVED BY NATIONAL UNIFORM CLAIM COMMITTEE 08/05

| | PICA | | | | | | PICA | |

| 1. MEDICARE (Medicare #) | MEDICAID (Medicaid #) | TRICARE CHAMPUS (Sponsor's SSN) | CHAMPVA (Member ID#) | GROUP HEALTH PLAN (SSN or ID) | FECA BLK LUNG (SSN) | OTHER [X] (ID) | 1a. INSURED'S I.D. NUMBER (For Program in Item 1) 621334444 |

| 2. PATIENT'S NAME (Last Name, First Name, Middle Initial) FARIS, ANNALISA, M | 3. PATIENT'S BIRTH DATE MM 04 DD 04 YY 1999 SEX M [ ] F [X] | 4. INSURED'S NAME (Last Name, First Name, Middle Initial) FARIS, MARI, L |

| 5. PATIENT'S ADDRESS (No., Street) 394 MYRIAM COURT | 6. PATIENT'S RELATIONSHIP TO INSURED Self [ ] Spouse [ ] Child [X] Other [ ] | 7. INSURED'S ADDRESS (No., Street) 394 MYRIAM COURT |

| CITY ANYWHERE | STATE US | 8. PATIENT STATUS Single [X] Married [ ] Other [ ] | CITY ANYWHERE | STATE US |

| ZIP CODE 12345 | TELEPHONE (Include Area Code) (101) 3335555 | Employed [ ] Full-Time Student [X] Part-Time Student [ ] | ZIP CODE 12345 | TELEPHONE (Include Area Code) (101) 3335555 |

| 9. OTHER INSURED'S NAME (Last Name, First Name, Middle Initial) FARIS, NACIR, R | 10. IS PATIENT'S CONDITION RELATED TO: | 11. INSURED'S POLICY GROUP OR FECA NUMBER 621334444 |

| a. OTHER INSURED'S POLICY OR GROUP NUMBER 323233333 | a. EMPLOYMENT? (Current or Previous) YES [ ] NO [X] | a. INSURED'S DATE OF BIRTH MM 10 DD 12 YY 1976 SEX M [ ] F [X] |

| b. OTHER INSURED'S DATE OF BIRTH MM 06 DD 21 YY 1975 SEX M [X] F [ ] | b. AUTO ACCIDENT? YES [ ] NO [X] PLACE (State) | b. EMPLOYER'S NAME OR SCHOOL NAME PETCO |

| c. EMPLOYER'S NAME OR SCHOOL NAME US MARINES | c. OTHER ACCIDENT? YES [ ] NO [X] | c. INSURANCE PLAN NAME OR PROGRAM NAME HIGHMARK PLUS |

| d. INSURANCE PLAN NAME OR PROGRAM NAME TRICARE PRIME | 10d. RESERVED FOR LOCAL USE | d. IS THERE ANOTHER HEALTH BENEFIT PLAN? [X] YES [ ] NO If yes, return to and complete item 9 a-d. |

READ BACK OF FORM BEFORE COMPLETING & SIGNING THIS FORM.

12. PATIENT'S OR AUTHORIZED PERSON'S SIGNATURE I authorize the release of any medical or other information necessary to process this claim. I also request payment of government benefits either to myself or to the party who accepts assignment below.

SIGNED **SIGNATURE ON FILE** DATE

13. INSURED'S OR AUTHORIZED PERSON'S SIGNATURE I authorize payment of medical benefits to the undersigned physician or supplier for services described below.

SIGNED **SIGNATURE ON FILE**

| 14. DATE OF CURRENT: ILLNESS (First symptom) OR INJURY (Accident) OR PREGNANCY (LMP) MM DD YY | 15. IF PATIENT HAS HAD SAME OR SIMILAR ILLNESS, GIVE FIRST DATE MM DD YY | 16. DATES PATIENT UNABLE TO WORK IN CURRENT OCCUPATION FROM MM DD YY TO MM DD YY |

| 17. NAME OF REFERRING PROVIDER OR OTHER SOURCE | 17a. | 18. HOSPITALIZATION DATES RELATED TO CURRENT SERVICES FROM 06 02 YY TO 06 11 YY |
| | 17b. NPI | |

| 19. RESERVED FOR LOCAL USE | 20. OUTSIDE LAB? YES [ ] NO [X] $ CHARGES |

21. DIAGNOSIS OR NATURE OF ILLNESS OR INJURY (Relate Items 1, 2, 3 or 4 to Item 24E by Line)

1. 780 6
2. 780 7
3. 783 0
4. 783 21

| 22. MEDICAID RESUBMISSION CODE | ORIGINAL REF. NO. |
| 23. PRIOR AUTHORIZATION NUMBER | |

24. A DATE(S) OF SERVICE From MM DD YY To MM DD YY	B. PLACE OF SERVICE	C. EMG	D. PROCEDURES, SERVICES, OR SUPPLIES (Explain Unusual Circumstances) CPT/HCPCS MODIFIER	E. DIAGNOSIS POINTER	F. $ CHARGES	G. DAYS OR UNITS	H. EPSDT Family Plan	I. ID. QUAL.	J. RENDERING PROVIDER ID. #
1	06 02 YYYY	21		99223	1234	200 00	1		NPI	
2	06 03 YYYY 06 04 YYYY	21		99223	1234	170 00	2		NPI	
3	06 06 YYYY	21		00233	12	85 00	1		NPI	
4	06 07 YYYY	21		99232	234	75 00	1		NPI	
5	06 09 YYYY 06 10 YYYY	21		99232	1	150 00	2		NPI	
6									NPI	

| 25. FEDERAL TAX I.D. NUMBER SSN [ ] EIN [X] 11234562 | 26. PATIENT'S ACCOUNT NO. 16-E | 27. ACCEPT ASSIGNMENT? (For govt. claims, see back) YES [X] NO [ ] | 28. TOTAL CHARGE $ 680 00 | 29. AMOUNT PAID $ | 30. BALANCE DUE $ 680 00 |

| 31. SIGNATURE OF PHYSICIAN OR SUPPLIER INCLUDING DEGREES OR CREDENTIALS (I certify that the statements on the reverse apply to this bill and are made a part thereof.) DONALD L GIVINGS MD SIGNED DATE MMDDYYYY | 32. SERVICE FACILITY LOCATION INFORMATION MERCY HOSPITAL ANYWHERE STREET ANYWHERE US 12345 a. NPI b. | 33. BILLING PROVIDER INFO & PH # (101)1115555 DONALD L GIVINGS MD 11350 MEDICAL DRIVE ANYWHERE US 12345 a. 1234567890 b. |

NUCC Instruction Manual available at: www.nucc.org

APPROVED OMB-0938-0999 FORM CMS-1500 (08/05)

ASSIGNMENT 16.2 Multiple Choice Review

1. d
2. b
3. c
4. b
5. a
6. c
7. c
8. d
9. b
10. d

11. c
12. b
13. b
14. d
15. b
16. a
17. b
18. b
19. b
20. b

CHAPTER 17 Workers' Compensation

ASSIGNMENT 17.1 Workers' Compensation Primary CMS-1500 Claims Completion

Case Study 17-a

1500

HEALTH INSURANCE CLAIM FORM

APPROVED BY NATIONAL UNIFORM CLAIM COMMITTE 08/05

	PICA								PICA	

1. MEDICARE	MEDICAID	TRICARE CHAMPUS	CHAMPVA	GROUP HEALTH PLAN	FECA BLK LUNG	OTHER	1a. INSURED'S I.D. NUMBER (For Program in Item 1)
(Medicare #)	(Medicaid #)	(Sponsor's SSN)	(Member ID#)	(SSN or ID) [X]	(SSN)	(ID)	CLR5457

2. PATIENT'S NAME (Last Name, First Name, Middle Initial)
GRAND, SANDY, S

3. PATIENT'S BIRTH DATE MM 12 DD 03 YY 1972 **SEX** M [ ] F [X]

4. INSURED'S NAME (Last Name, First Name, Middle Initial)
STARPORT FITNESS CENTER

5. PATIENT'S ADDRESS (No., Street)
109 DARLING ROAD

6. PATIENT'S RELATIONSHIP TO INSURED
Self [ ] Spouse [ ] Child [ ] Other [X]

7. INSURED'S ADDRESS (No., Street)

CITY ANYWHERE **STATE** US

8. PATIENT STATUS
Single [ ] Married [ ] Other [ ]

CITY | **STATE**

ZIP CODE 12345 **TELEPHONE (Include Area Code)** (101) 3335555

Employed [X] Full-Time Student [ ] Part-Time Student [ ]

ZIP CODE | **TELEPHONE (Include Area Code)** ( )

9. OTHER INSURED'S NAME (Last Name, First Name, Middle Initial)

10. IS PATIENT'S CONDITION RELATED TO:

11. INSURED'S POLICY GROUP OR FECA NUMBER
CLR5457

a. OTHER INSURED'S POLICY OR GROUP NUMBER

a. EMPLOYMENT? (Current or Previous)
[X] YES [ ] NO

a. INSURED'S DATE OF BIRTH MM DD YY **SEX** M [ ] F [ ]

b. OTHER INSURED'S DATE OF BIRTH MM DD YY **SEX** M [ ] F [ ]

b. AUTO ACCIDENT? PLACE (State)
[ ] YES [X] NO

b. EMPLOYER'S NAME OR SCHOOL NAME
STARPORT FITNESS CENTER

c. EMPLOYER'S NAME OR SCHOOL NAME

c. OTHER ACCIDENT?
[ ] YES [X] NO

c. INSURANCE PLAN NAME OR PROGRAM NAME
WORKERS TRUST

d. INSURANCE PLAN NAME OR PROGRAM NAME

10d. RESERVED FOR LOCAL USE

d. IS THERE ANOTHER HEALTH BENEFIT PLAN?
[ ] YES [ ] NO **If yes,** return to and complete item 9 a-d.

READ BACK OF FORM BEFORE COMPLETING & SIGNING THIS FORM.
12. PATIENT'S OR AUTHORIZED PERSON'S SIGNATURE I authorize the release of any medical or other information necessary to process this claim. I also request payment of government benefits either to myself or to the party who accepts assignment below.

SIGNED _____ DATE _____

13. INSURED'S OR AUTHORIZED PERSON'S SIGNATURE I authorize payment of medical benefits to the undersigned physcian or supplier for services described below.

SIGNED _____

14. DATE OF CURRENT: MM 02 DD 03 YY YYYY ILLNESS (First symptom) OR INJURY (Accident) OR PREGNANCY (LMP)

15. IF PATIENT HAS HAD SAME OR SIMILAR ILLNESS. GIVE FIRST DATE MM DD YY

16. DATES PATIENT UNABLE TO WORK IN CURRENT OCCUPATION FROM MM DD YY TO MM DD YY

17. NAME OF REFERRING PROVIDER OR OTHER SOURCE

17a. | 17b. NPI

18. HOSPITALIZATION DATES RELATED TO CURRENT SERVICES FROM MM DD YY TO MM DD YY

19. RESERVED FOR LOCAL USE

20. OUTSIDE LAB? $ CHARGES
[ ] YES [X] NO

21. DIAGNOSIS OR NATURE OF ILLNESS OR INJURY (Relate Items 1, 2, 3 or 4 to Item 24E by Line)
1. 814 00
2. E884 2
3.
4.

22. MEDICAID RESUBMISSION CODE ORIGINAL REF. NO.

23. PRIOR AUTHORIZATION NUMBER

24. A. DATE(S) OF SERVICE From MM DD YY To MM DD YY	B. PLACE OF SERVICE	C. EMG	D. PROCEDURES, SERVICES, OR SUPPLIES (Explain Unusual Circumstances) CPT/HCPCS MODIFER	E. DIAGNOSIS POINTER	F. $ CHARGES	G. DAYS OR UNITS	H. EPSDT Family Plan	I. ID. QUAL.	J. RENDERING PROVIDER ID. #
1	02 03 YYYY	11		99204	1	100 00	1		NPI	
2									NPI	
3									NPI	
4									NPI	
5									NPI	
6									NPI	

25. FEDERAL TAX I.D. NUMBER SSN EIN
11234562 [X]

26. PATIENT'S ACCOUNT NO.
17-A

27. ACCEPT ASSIGNMENT? (For govt. claims, see back)
[X] YES [ ] NO

28. TOTAL CHARGE $

29. AMOUNT PAID $

30. BALANCE DUE $

31. SIGNATURE OF PHYSICIAN OR SUPPLIER INCLUDING DEGREES OR CREDENTIALS (I certify that the statements on the reverse apply to this bill and are made a part thereof.)

DONALD L GIVINGS MD

SIGNED _____ DATE MMDDYYYY

32. SERVICE FACILITY LOCATION INFORMATION

a. NPI b.

33. BILLING PROVIDER INFO & PH # (101)1115555
DONALD L GIVINGS MD
11350 MEDICAL DRIVE
ANYWHERE US 12345

a. 1234567890 b.

NUCC Instruction Manual available at: www.nucc.org

APPROVED OMB-0938-0999 FORM CMS-1500 (08/05)

Case Study 17-b

1500

HEALTH INSURANCE CLAIM FORM

APPROVED BY NATIONAL UNIFORM CLAIM COMMITTEE 08/05

| | PICA | | PICA | |

1. MEDICARE (Medicare #)	MEDICAID (Medicaid #)	TRICARE CHAMPUS (Sponsor's SSN)	CHAMPVA (Member ID#)	GROUP HEALTH PLAN (SSN or ID) [X]	FECA BLK LUNG (SSN)	OTHER (ID)	1a. INSURED'S I.D. NUMBER (For Program in Item 1)
							BA6788

2. PATIENT'S NAME (Last Name, First Name, Middle Initial)	3. PATIENT'S BIRTH DATE MM DD YY / SEX	4. INSURED'S NAME (Last Name, First Name, Middle Initial)
HOLLAND, MARIANNA, D	11 05 1977 M [ ] F [X]	HAIR ETC

5. PATIENT'S ADDRESS (No., Street)	6. PATIENT RELATIONSHIP TO INSURED	7. INSURED'S ADDRESS (No., Street)
509 DUTCH STREET	Self [ ] Spouse [ ] Child [ ] Other [X]	
CITY ANYWHERE	STATE US	8. PATIENT STATUS Single [ ] Married [ ] Other [ ]	CITY	STATE
ZIP CODE 12345	TELEPHONE (Include Area Code) (101) 4445555	Employed [X] Full-Time Student [ ] Part-Time Student [ ]	ZIP CODE	TELEPHONE (Include Area Code) ( )

9. OTHER INSURED'S NAME (Last Name, First Name, Middle Initial)	10. IS PATIENT'S CONDITION RELATED TO:	11. INSURED'S POLICY GROUP OR FECA NUMBER
		BA6788
a. OTHER INSURED'S POLICY OR GROUP NUMBER	a. EMPLOYMENT? (Current or Previous) [X] YES [ ] NO	a. INSURED'S DATE OF BIRTH MM DD YY / SEX M [ ] F [ ]
b. OTHER INSURED'S DATE OF BIRTH MM DD YY / SEX M [ ] F [ ]	b. AUTO ACCIDENT? PLACE (State) [ ] YES [X] NO	b. EMPLOYER'S NAME OR SCHOOL NAME HAIR ETC
c. EMPLOYER'S NAME OR SCHOOL NAME	c. OTHER ACCIDENT? [ ] YES [X] NO	c. INSURANCE PLAN NAME OR PROGRAM NAME WORKERS SHIELD
d. INSURANCE PLAN NAME OR PROGRAM NAME	10d. RESERVED FOR LOCAL USE	d. IS THERE ANOTHER HEALTH BENEFIT PLAN? [ ] YES [ ] NO If yes, return to and complete item 9 a-d.

READ BACK OF FORM BEFORE COMPLETING & SIGNING THIS FORM.

12. PATIENT'S OR AUTHORIZED PERSON'S SIGNATURE I authorize the release of any medical or other information necessary to process this claim. I also request payment of government benefits either to myself or to the party who accepts assignment below.

SIGNED _____ DATE _____

13. INSURED'S OR AUTHORIZED PERSON'S SIGNATURE I authorize payment of medical benefits to the undersigned physcian or supplier for services described below.

SIGNED _____

14. DATE OF CURRENT: MM DD YY / ILLNESS (First symptom) OR INJURY (Accident) OR PREGNANCY (LMP) 05 12 YYYY	15. IF PATIENT HAS HAD SAME OR SIMILAR ILLNESS. GIVE FIRST DATE MM DD YY	16. DATES PATIENT UNABLE TO WORK IN CURRENT OCCUPATION MM DD YY MM DD YY FROM 05 12 YYYY TO 05 15 YYYY
17. NAME OF REFERRING PROVIDER OR OTHER SOURCE	17a. / 17b. NPI	18. HOSPITALIZATION DATES RELATED TO CURRENT SERVICES MM DD YY MM DD YY FROM TO
19. RESERVED FOR LOCAL USE		20. OUTSIDE LAB? [ ] YES [X] NO $ CHARGES

21. DIAGNOSIS OR NATURE OF ILLNESS OR INJURY (Relate Items 1, 2, 3 or 4 to Item 24E by Line)	22. MEDICAID RESUBMISSION CODE ORIGINAL REF. NO.
1. 802 . 0 3. ___ . ___	
2. ___ . ___ 4. ___ . ___	23. PRIOR AUTHORIZATION NUMBER

24. A. DATE(S) OF SERVICE From MM DD YY To MM DD YY	B. PLACE OF SERVICE	C. EMG	D. PROCEDURES, SERVICES, OR SUPPLIES (Explain Unusual Circumstances) CPT/HCPCS / MODIFER	E. DIAGNOSIS POINTER	F. $ CHARGES	G. DAYS OR UNITS	H. EPSDT Family Plan	I. ID. QUAL.	J. RENDERING PROVIDER ID. #
1	05 12 YYYY		11		99203	1	80 00	1		NPI
2										NPI
3										NPI
4										NPI
5										NPI
6										NPI

25. FEDERAL TAX I.D. NUMBER SSN EIN 11234562 [X]	26. PATIENT'S ACCOUNT NO. 17-B	27. ACCEPT ASSIGNMENT? (For govt. claims, see back) [X] YES [ ] NO	28. TOTAL CHARGE $ 80 00	29. AMOUNT PAID $	30. BALANCE DUE $

31. SIGNATURE OF PHYSICIAN OR SUPPLIER INCLUDING DEGREES OR CREDENTIALS (I certify that the statements on the reverse apply to this bill and are made a part thereof.) DONALD L GIVINGS MD SIGNED DATE MMDDYYYY	32. SERVICE FACILITY LOCATION INFORMATION a. NPI b.	33. BILLING PROVIDER INFO & PH # (101)1115555 DONALD L GIVINGS MD 11350 MEDICAL DRIVE ANYWHERE US 12345 a.1234567890 b.

NUCC Instruction Manual available at: www.nucc.org

APPROVED OMB-0938-0999 FORM CMS-1500 (08/05)

ASSIGNMENT 17.2 Multiple Choice Review

1.	a	**11.**	c
2.	c	**12.**	c
3.	a	**13.**	b
4.	d	**14.**	a
5.	a	**15.**	a
6.	b	**16.**	a
7.	d	**17.**	c
8.	d	**18.**	a
9.	c	**19.**	b
10.	b	**20.**	d

SECTION VII Answer Key to WORKBOOK
Appendix A: Mock CMRS Exam

Medical Terminology

1. c
2. a
3. b
4. d
5. b
6. d
7. b
8. c
9. b
10. c

Anatomy and Physiology

11. c
12. d
13. c
14. a
15. a
16. a
17. c
18. c
19. b
20. c

Information Technology

21. b
22. a
23. d
24. b
25. d
26. c
27. b
28. b
29. d
30. b

Web and Information Technology

31. b
32. c
33. a
34. d
35. b
36. d
37. c
38. a
39. a
40. c

ICD-9-CM Coding

41. c
42. b
43. d
44. b
45. d
46. c
47. b
48. c
49. c
50. d

CPT Coding

51. b
52. a
53. b
54. b
55. d
56. c
57. c
58. c
59. d
60. a

Clearinghouses

61. b
62. d
63. c
64. d
65. b
66. c
67. a
68. d
69. d
70. a

CMS (HCFA) 1500 Form

71. b
72. d
73. b
74. c
75. b
76. d
77. a
78. c
79. d
80. d

Insurance

81.	c
82.	d
83.	c
84.	a
85.	d
86.	b
87.	c
88.	c
89.	b
90.	b

Fraud and Abuse

121.	b
122.	c
123.	d
124.	b
125.	a
126.	b
127.	a
128.	c
129.	c
130.	d

Insurance Carriers

91.	b
92.	d
93.	c
94.	b
95.	c
96.	a
97.	b
98.	d
99.	c
100.	c

Managed Care

131.	a
132.	b
133.	c
134.	a
135.	c
136.	c
137.	d
138.	b
139.	c
140.	d

Acronyms

101.	EGHP	Employer Group Health Plan
102.	ABN	Advance Beneficiary Notice
103.	OCE	Outpatient Code Editor
104.	LCD	Local Coverage Determination
105.	APC	Ambulatory Payment Classifications
106.	FCA	False Claims Act
107.	HIPAA	Health Insurance Portability and Accountability Act
108.	MCO	Managed Care Organization
109.	HMO	Health Maintenance Organization
110.	CPT	Current Procedural Terminology

General

141.	a
142.	d
143.	c
144.	c
145.	d
146.	b
147.	d
148.	a
149.	a
150.	d

Compliance

111.	c
112.	d
113.	b
114.	b
115.	a
116.	c
117.	d
118.	b
119.	d
120.	b

Medical Terminology

1.	b
2.	c
3.	d
4.	a
5.	b
6.	b
7.	a
8.	c
9.	c
10.	d
11.	c
12.	a
13.	b
14.	b
15.	c
16.	c
17.	d
18.	b
19.	d
20.	c

Anatomy

21.	c
22.	b
23.	b
24.	d
25.	a
26.	a
27.	b
28.	c
29.	d
30.	b
31.	c
32.	c
33.	b
34.	c
35.	a
36.	d
37.	b
38.	d
39.	b
40.	a

General Insurance

41.	a
42.	c
43.	b
44.	a
45.	c
46.	d

Payment Systems

47.	b
48.	c
49.	c
50.	b
51.	a

HIPAA

52.	d
53.	d
54.	c

Payment Impacts

55.	d
56.	c
57.	b
58.	a
59.	c

Inpatient

60.	c
61.	b
62.	d
63.	a
64.	b
65.	b
66.	d
67.	b
68.	c

ICD-9-CM Coding Rules

69.	d
70.	a
71.	c
72.	b
73.	a
74.	d
75.	b
76.	d
77.	a
78.	c
79.	b
80.	b

HCPCS

81.	d
82.	b
83.	d
84.	c

CPT Rules

85.	c
86.	b
87.	a
88.	d
89.	c
90.	c
91.	a
92.	c
93.	c
94.	a
95.	c
96.	b

CPT Sections/Applied Coding

97.	b
98.	a
99.	c
100.	b
101.	a
102.	b
103.	b
104.	a
105.	d
106.	a
107.	c
108.	b
109.	c

Hospital Coding/Applied Coding

110.	c
111.	b
112.	b
113.	d
114.	d
115.	c
116.	d

ICD-9-CM Sections

117.	b
118.	d
119.	c
120.	b
121.	a
122.	a
123.	c
124.	b
125.	b
126.	c
127.	b
128.	b
129.	b
130.	d
131.	a
132.	c
133.	d
134.	c
135.	a
136.	d
137.	c
138.	c

HCPCS Level II

139.	b
140.	c
141.	c
142.	a
143.	a
144.	c
145.	b

Modifiers

146.	b
147.	b
148.	c
149.	a
150.	c